W9-DHH-315

THE WORKS OF PLATO

THE WORKS
OF PLATO

Selected and Edited
By Irwin Edman

THE MODERN LIBRARY
NEW YORK

THE MODERN LIBRARY
is published by Random House, Inc.
New York, New York
Manufactured in the United States of America

Grateful acknowledgment is hereby made to the Trustees of the Jowett Copyright Fund, to the Delegates of the OXFORD UNIVERSITY PRESS and to Messrs. Simon and Schuster whose cooperation has made it possible to present this one volume edition of *The Works of Plato,* with the authoritative translation of Benjamin Jowett in final form.

THE MODERN LIBRARY, INC.

This is the standard, authorized text of the third edition of the Jowett translation.

PREFACE

It is difficult to select dialogues of Plato that shall adequately represent the range and diversity of his human and intellectual interests. The ten presented here are thought by the Editor to be fairly typical and to provide the student and the general reader an opportunity for an acquaintance with the best and most characteristic of Plato's writings. Considerations of space and the interests and equipment of the lay reader and the beginning student, made it seem wise to exclude some of the more purely metaphysical rather than the more clearly humanistic dialogues. But it is hoped the selection will give the reader a chance to follow Plato's characteristic methods and detect his essential gifts. The Theatetus and the selection from the Republic will provide a hint and approach to the central and difficult metaphysical insight and presumptions of Plato.

The Introduction aims to give, so far as can be done briefly, a conspectus of the leading themes in Plato's writings, and to facilitate, insofar as appreciative analysis can, the understanding and enjoyment of the dialogues. Each critic must locate differently the essence of a great writer. But critics do not violently diverge when they are actually talking about a great writer's work rather than about a critical tradition that has grown up to obscure it. The Editor has tried to speak out of an immediate love of and companionship with the dialogues themselves and not out of any special *a priori* canons concerning Plato's philosophy or his own. He has been helped particularly in his own understanding and pleasure in the dialogues by A. E. Taylor's Plato, a work important at once for its superb scholarship and its eschewing almost throughout of anything but a consideration of the text.

vii

The Editor wishes to thank the Oxford University Press for permission to use the Jowett translation, third edition. He wishes also to thank his friends and colleagues, Dr. Richard P. McKeon and Mr. James Gutmann for generous and helpful criticism and suggestion concerning the Introductory essay.

IRWIN EDMAN.

Columbia University,
September, 1927.

TABLE OF CONTENTS

INTRODUCTION

A reader of Plato, fresh to the dialogues, will be perplexed by the very quality of his delight. For in these
writings, unique at once in the history of literature and
the history of philosophy, he meets thought whose medium
is not dogma but drama, drama among whose chief excite-
ments are the subtle suspenses of thought. The reader is
at first puzzled. The "philosophy" of Plato is clearly not
the philosophy of the schools; his drama is profounder in
theme and more comprehensive in range than the constricted
little toys of the stage. For those who have not learned with
Plato that philosophy is the love of wisdom rather than the
pronouncement of truth, there is considerable mystification
in a thinker whose thoughts are all suggestions, whose suggestions are often playful, and who will not, despite the
attempt of more than one serious critic, be crammed into
a neat and lifeless system. The reader is haunted, too, by
the perturbed sense that, though these dialogues are full
of endless charm as poetic and ironic drama, they are
clearly something more than the by-play of a gifted writer.
The further one reads the more deeply does one come into
the presence of the profoundest and most serious issues of
human existence. What on its winning surface is the spirited
conversation between Socrates and a group of attractive
young Athenian aristocrats, closely read, stirs one profoundly to a consideration of the nature of good and evil,
of reality, of the paramount mystery of the human soul.
Plato never reveals nor seeks to reveal the secret of the
universe, yet in his pages, one seems constantly to hear it
whispered. Nothing is settled in the dialogues, but every-

thing is somehow clarified and enhanced. Especially on the moving and central themes of human experience, the excitement of beauty, the power of goodness, the tantalizing desire of knowledge, the insistent urgency of truth, on all these themes Plato can give more than the beginning of wisdom. Plato was deeply conscious that a philosopher can not hope to give much more than that. Indeed, in one of his own letters, now generally accepted as genuine, he expresses some doubt as to the validity or importance of any written exposition of a philosophy: "There does not exist, and there never shall, any treatise by myself on these matters. The subject does not admit, as the sciences in general do, of exposition. It is only after long association in the great business itself and a shared life that a light breaks out in the soul, kindled, so to say, by a leaping flame, and thereafter feeds itself" (Epistle VII).

THE DIALOGUES AS A PORTRAIT OF SOCRATES

The dialogues, then, are meant not to expound a "Platonic" system, but rather to be renditions of that conjoint co-operative thinking of younger spirits awakened by a great teacher to a spirit of independent personal thinking and search. The archetype of such a teacher (indeed, we almost owe the term "archetype" to him) is Socrates, and in no small measure the dialogues may be conceived to be intended as a memento to the memory of that philosophical conversationalist whom Plato had known and associated with as a quite young man, and whose life—and death—may be said to have converted Plato to philosophy. Indeed, the most definitive aspect of the Platonic dialogues may be said to be the portrait of Socrates that emerges, at once the picture of a great saint of thought and a symbol of the examined or philosophic life.

Grote in the title of his book, *Plato and the Other Companions of Socrates,* gives a telling suggestion as to how to approach the dialogues as well as the life of Plato. For the Platonic writings are largely an inspired tribute by a gifted pupil to the older man who was the source of his inspiration. Of the few facts which are unquestionably known about Plato's life one is that from about the age of eighteen to twenty-two he was one of the group who discussed with Socrates the various ethical issues which are the themes of the so-called Socratic dialogues. There is evidence, too, that Plato as a child knew Socrates, who was a close acquaintance of his uncle Charmides and his great-uncle Critias. Clearly Plato loved Socrates personally as a young man loves a revered older friend. It is clear, too, that he thought of him as a martyr. And the death of Socrates at the hands of the restored democracy in Athens seemed definitely to have turned Plato to philosophy from the social and legislative career to which his distinguished family's long-standing association with public affairs had early turned him. Political success in Athens seemed to depend on having a party, and there seemed now to be no party with whom an honorable man could connect himself.

THE LIFE OF PLATO

Apart from these fragmentary and inferential facts about Plato's relations to Socrates, the first sixty years of Plato's life are only in the most general sense known to us. We know he was born in 431 B. C.; died in 351 B. C. We know that he came from a distinguished family; one of the most distinguished of the Periclean age. On his father's side his ancestry is supposed to have gone back to the old kings of Athens. On his mother's side his ancestry went back to kinship with Solon. His uncle was Charmides, a powerful figure in the brief anarchic régime that followed on the collapse of Athens at the close of the Peloponnesian War. There is an allusion in Aristotle which makes it possible that Plato was a friend and a kind of pupil of Cratylus, a devotee of the Heraclitean philosophy of flux. Certainly in his youth Plato was by some one or somehow deeply impressed by the Heraclitean notion that the world revealed to us by the senses is one of endless and incalculable flow. Not in that incalculable chaos could science arise or did truth or reality reside.

After the execution of Socrates, at which Plato was apparently absent because of illness, Plato withdrew from Athens to the city of Megara, and after a short time travelled for a number of years in Italy, Cyrene, Sicily, and Egypt. On his return he founded the Academy. The Academy was in effect the first European university and institute of pure research. Isocrates, a somewhat older contemporary of Socrates, had a school in which he prepared young men for public life. But at the Academy, which was held in a suburb of Athens, the emphasis was on pure-genuine-science as the source of all wise political action instead of (as with Isocrates), on the arts of rhetoric and persuasion, which were designed to teach young men, not the way to political wisdom, but the avenue to public favor. The next twenty years of Plato's life seem to have been chiefly occupied in directing his school, lecturing (one important item of the Platonic tradition is Plato's unpublished lecture on the "Good" to which Aristotle seems to have particular reference in his discussion of Plato's "Ideas") and discussing philosophical and mathematical questions with the members of the school.

At the age of sixty Plato took advantage of an extraordinary opportunity to test some of his ideas as to the education of a philosopher-king on an actual reigning statesman, Dionysius II of Syracuse, a youth of thirty years who had just become the reigning "tyrant" of Syracuse. Plato was particularly interested in this young ruler because on his successful administration depended the checking of the Carthaginians, whose imperialistic advances were imperilling the whole Greek hegemony in Sicily. Plato, true to his

belief in the importance of scientific training for the making of a wise ruler, tried to interest and educate the young
ruler in the current mathematical science of the Academy.
But Dionysius tired of the exactions of his studies and
became jealous of his brother-in-law through whose inter-
cession Plato had come to Sicily. The scheme for the en-
lightening of Dionysius failed, and a subsequent visit a
year later failed also.

On his return from his unsuccessful intervention in the
political re-education of the Syracusan ruler, Plato returned
to the Academy and spent there the remaining twenty years
of his life. He died at the age of eighty-one.

This bare outline is all we know, and not all of that
with certainty, about Plato's life. There are numerous leg-
endary, gossipy anecdotes about the kind of life led by the
associates of the Academy, said to be modelled in its common life after the Pythagorean brotherhood, and about
Plato himself. It is traditionally said that Plato was a nick-
name, given him because of his broad brow or broad shoul-
ders. It is said that as a young man he wrote poetry, which
in his early twenties he destroyed. There is a tradition,
poetically just, that he was born on Apollo's birthday.
Legends speak of his being very handsome, as history speaks
of Socrates being very ugly. The details of his life are as
dubious as and scarcer than those of Shakespeare's, and
from his dialogues, since he had the reticence of a great
dramatist, we can judge as little as we can judge of Shakespeare's life from his plays.

THE WORLD IN WHICH PLATO LIVED

Fortunately, we know a great deal more about the setting of the world in which Plato grew up. There are certain
characteristic elements of his thinking that have no birthday and no native land, distinctively Platonic elements that
are true to all ages and might have occurred in any. But

the particular accents and illustrations of his philosophy are what they are because Plato was a Greek living at the close of the fifth and the first half of the fourth century B. C. in the Greek city of Athens. His birth came at the close of the great flowering period of Athenian democracy under Pericles; his death came only ten years before Philip of Macedon secured the hegemony of the whole Greek world. He saw the beginning of the end of the great city-state civilizations of Greece. The Athens in which he lived was alive with change and the spirit of change, in philosophy, in religion, and in government.

It was an age of discussion, under a government by discussion. And the young freemen of Athens were being trained by artful foreign teachers known as Sophists by the artifices of rhetoric to "make the worse appear the better cause." They learnt from current philosophical speculations to bring the corrections of physics to bear upon the traditional mythology, and the scepticisms of such relativists in morals as Protagoras to bear upon traditional moral standards. The man in the street, at least the freeman in the street, was being affected by a thousand little winds of doctrine. The interest of Greek speculation had veered from a concern with those physical speculations which had brought the old religious traditions into question. In an age of great political change and excitement, the interest had shifted to human and moral questions, and to the political and human arts of argument, intellectual adroitness, and effective and persuasive rhetoric, instruments for getting on in the political world.

THE PERSONALITY OF SOCRATES

It was into this bright, sly, worldly atmosphere that Socrates appeared, moving questioningly about the streets of Athens. About him collected an extraordinary group of young men, playing, like Alcibiades, destined to play, like

Charmides, important, sometimes disastrous, rôles in the political history of Athens. A whole group of the so-called Platonic dialogues, culminating in the *Apology,* the *Crito,* and the *Phaedo,* constitute a portrait of Socrates, a representation of his interests, his method, and his mission. They exhibit him in his characteristic scepticism of conventional epithets, in his cautious but pertinacious search for invulnerable definitions, and indubitable moral standards. They reveal him in his irony, his humanity, his scepticism, in his unwavering fidelity to the philosophic life at the ultimate cost of his own. They show him the insistently rational, unaccountably mystical, tender, and unyielding lover of the good.

The portrait that emerges is fiction, in the sense of being a dramatic creation. The Socrates that we know from Plato is a poet's legend, something larger, nobler, completer than even the real Socrates could have been. Socrates appears, in Plato's own phrase, "rejuvenated and beautified." Yet there is no good reason for doubting that Plato was giving us in essence his actual master, and sometimes, as in the *Apology,* something very like his exact words. There are presumably in the later dialogues views put into the mouth of Socrates that could scarcely have been the views of the actual historical figure. Nevertheless, it was the Socratic method and Socratic mission that determined the direction of Plato's own thinking. It is with a rendition of that mission and method that the earlier highly dramatic dialogues are concerned.

What Socrates' mission was, he himself is made to tell us with characteristic irony in the *Apology* (Jowett, 23). "And so I go about the world obedient to the god, and search and make inquiry into the wisdom of anyone, whether citizen or stranger, who appears to be wise, and if he is not wise, then in vindication of the oracle [who had told Socrates that he was the wisest man in Athens] I show him that he is not wise; and my own action quite absorbs me, and I have not time to give either to any matter of public interest or to any concern of my own." But Socrates' own concern was the love and pursuit of wisdom, and that seemed to him, too, the chief and fundamental concern of the state. For, again in his own words (*Apology,* Jowett), when on trial by a panel of fellow Athenians for corrupting youth, inventing new gods and denying the established gods of the city, Socrates thus addresses his judges: "For if you kill me, you will not easily find a successor to me, who am, if I may use a ludicrous figure of speech, a sort of gadfly, given to the state by god; and the state is a great and noble steed, who is tardy in his motions owing to his very size, and requires to be stirred to life. I am that gadfly which God has attached to the state, and all day long and in all places, am always fastening upon you, arousing and persuading and reproaching you."

Socrates conceived his mission, then, in a sense, to be essentially that of a stinging critic of the current conventional mores and conventional confusions which passed for wisdom in the market-place. But that was the negative half of his mission. Himself professing no knowledge at all, he yet was profoundly convinced that knowledge was possible, a knowledge at least of one's own soul, one's own mind, and genuine good and evil.

Like the Sophists, Socrates ascribed little value and displayed little interest in the physical sciences *per se* (Aristophanes in his burlesque of Socrates in *The Clouds* confused him with the earlier physical philosophers). But in a profound sense he believed in science, the science of dialectic, the clear, independent, and ultimate thinking out of the meaning of one's own thoughts. "Know thyself" was an old Greek maxim to which Socrates alludes. Know thine own mind and meaning was Socrates' interpretation of it. To the promotion of that logical clarity and intellectual honesty Socrates devoted his life in the conviction that on these depended moral health and political salvation. In the so-called Socratic dialogues, especially the *Lysis*, the *Charmides*, the *Euthydemus* (a burlesque of the "faked" logical method of the Sophists), and in the final dramatic sequence describing his trial and death, Socrates is portrayed in typical exhibitions of his method.

THE SOCRATIC METHOD

That method is partly one of irony. Pretending to complete ignorance, Socrates queries all and sundry concerning those traditional virtues about which for one reason or another they might be expected to know and which, indeed, they prided themselves on knowing. Thus in the *Euthyphro*, Socrates, meeting Euthyphro on the verge of prosecuting his father for killing a slave, is confident that Euthyphro must be perfectly certain of the nature of piety before undertaking such a prosecution so lightly. He first gives an instance of piety, "Doing as I am doing," but Socrates persists in asking for a general definition. Euthyphro replies that piety is what is dear to the gods and Socrates points out that there may be disagreement among the gods. Euthyphro hazards two further definitions and each is wrecked on the reefs of Socrates' unyielding dialectic. Socrates treats similarly the definitions offered of friendship in the *Lysis* and of courage in the *Laches*. His aim is not to win a debater's victory over an opponent, but to clear the atmosphere of false or irrelevant definitions, to arrive at the essential character or *essence* of a virtue or idea. If in these early dialogues the discussion is left unsettled, it is not that Socrates feels that some conclusive definition is impossible. The implication is rather that it is precisely the function of reason to work toward a definition. The failure of a reasoner is not to Socrates' mind the failure of reason.

Throughout the dialogues, the true mark of a philosopher for Socrates is ability in dialectics. That involves, among other things, for him, a talent for tracing any idea back to a postulate which it involves or upon which it is based, for detecting "the one in the many," the common element in an apparent diversity of ideas, and for following the implied consequences of the assertion or denial of a proposition.

But if logic was the method, ethics was the central interest of Socrates, and it is this dominant concern with the good and the good life that seems most forcibly to have impressed Plato and permanently to have given a stamp to his philosophy. For into whatever dialectical subtleties the dialogues may soar, as they do in the *Parmenides*, the *Theatetus*, and the *Sophist*, the dominant tone of Plato's thinking is that of a thinker profoundly concerned with the clarification and harmonizing of life by reason.

THE ETHICS OF SOCRATES

One cannot derive a dogmatic ethical system from the statements of Socrates in the dialogues, but one can detect a characteristic theme and direction which may be stated briefly as follows:

Men aim at the good. No man voluntarily chooses evil. To do evil or to choose evil is a matter of lack of insight; the central virtue turns out, therefore, to be knowledge. Health, wealth, beauty, all these are good insofar as they are well used. And a good use of the goods of life demands knowledge of their appropriate employment. "If we knew how to convert stones into gold, they would be of no use to us unless we also knew how to use the gold" (Euthydemus). Knowledge of good and evil, knowledge of that part of one's self, the soul, which alone can measure, estimate, choose, is the central wisdom, and wisdom is the essential virtue of which all the virtues turn out to be simply special instances or parts. For courage is courage when it is courage before appropriate dangers, fearlessness

before objects justly not to be feared; temperance is tem‑
perance when it is appropriate restraint of bodily passions;
justice is justice when it is equity of action in the character‑
istic situations of life; and appropriateness in all these in‑
stances it is the part of knowledge or wisdom to decide.
"Speaking generally," as A. E. Taylor puts it, "there is
for Socrates just one good thing, wisdom, and just one bad
thing, dullness or stupidity." In the *Protagoras* the appar‑
ent cases where knowledge is overcome by passion, as the
popular view has it, are shown by Socrates to be in essence
a miscalculation of expected pleasures and pains resulting
from a given action.

The Socratic dialogues exhibit at once Socrates' logical
method and his ethical intent. Both of these affect the whole
Platonic philosophy; that is, they both remain dominant
themes, recurrent in Plato's thinking. It is these themes
which constitute Plato's philosophy rather than a body of
dogmatic and systematic doctrine. The logical interest of
Socrates in pressing experience toward the universals which
experience implies, becomes the cue to Plato's metaphysical
concern with essences, forms, ideas. The moral interest of
Socrates in basing virtue on knowledge becomes the start‑
ing point for Plato's conviction that any sound politic is
based on sound science, that an adequate statesmanship and
an adequate philosophical vision are inseparable. The theme
which troubles the boyish Meno as to whether virtue can
be taught is ultimately answered by the educational pro‑
gram of the *Republic*. The tentative dialectical march
toward definitions of the virtues in the early dialogues be‑
comes in the *Parmenides,* the *Theatetus,* and the *States‑
man* the metaphysical plumbings of the relations of es‑
sences to existence, of ideas to things, of the one to the
many, of time to eternity. The definitions which for the
Socrates of the early dialogues have a purely logical and
moral and rational import, in the *Phaedrus* and *Symposium*

are the shining eternities of esthetic contemplation and mystical adoration; they are forms of beauty as well as essences of truth.

One could, under duress, make a table of Plato's comments on various phases of experience and knowledge pieced together from the various dialogues. In doing so one would miss the point of the Platonic dialogue form. The dialogue in Plato has a philosophical as well as a literary significance. Both demand attention.

THE DIALOGUE AS A LITERARY FORM

Plato was not unique in the use of the dialogue form. Several of the pupils of Plato wrote dialogues, and the fashion was in vogue until the time of Aristotle. Plato was part, too, of a general literary tradition in which drama was the humanistic vehicle of ideas. It was not for nothing that Plato had witnessed the comedies of Aristophanes and the tragedies of Euripides at Athens or read the comic dialogues of Epicharmis, the Sicilian. The Platonic dialogues are, in their lighter moments and moods, comedies of ideas; in the *Euthydemus* the dialogue becomes almost burlesque. In the more momentous dialogues they represent the dramatic crises of the soul and its inquiries. Plato takes actual personages, some contemporary, some belonging to the last generation, some of them public men, others friends or kinsmen of his own, and makes them the exponents of the philosophical ideas he wishes to set before us. These persons are not simply names given to the voices of philosophical notions as they are in the dialogues of Berkeley; they are live and picturesque characters, they have perceptible fidelity to the historical characters represented, though they are handled freely as a poet or a dramatist might handle them.

One might forget all the philosophical concerns and ideas

touched upon in the dialogues and still remember them as galleries of unforgettable personalities. Socrates stands out above all, almost, one might say, the Hamlet of Plato, and like Hamlet, too, torn, though not so sombrely, by the insoluble antinomies and irresolutions to which we are led by passion and by thought. But the Platonic picture gallery is crowded with a host of minor personalities. There are those beautiful youths whom some of his friends jestingly accuse Socrates of forever pursuing. (Socrates himself in the *Charmides* confesses that "almost all young persons appear to be beautiful in my eyes.") And on returning from the army to Athens, almost his first question is, "What about the present state of philosophy, and about the youth? Are any of them remarkable for wisdom or beauty or both?" These charming early dialogues on the amiable themes of friendship and courage and virtue have as their chief interlocutors, next to Socrates, almost the fairest group of youths in the history of literature. They are the literary counterpart of the Parthenaic frieze, Greek sculpture become blushing and conversational and alive. There is Lysis, on the beautiful edge of adolescence; the young Charmides, before his fiery entrance into politics, the incarnation of natural temperance; Thrasymachus, the Sophist, "leaping like a wild beast upon the argument"; and young Hippocrates blushing in the dawn as he comes to waken Socrates, begs him to take him to Protagoras, and confesses to him his own forensic ambitions. One recalls Phaedo, the beloved disciple whose head Socrates strokes as he talks with grave serenity, in the face of his doom, about immortality; the elegant and rhetorical Phaedrus, the reckless, beautiful, ill-starred Alcibiades, with his worldliness and his strange, unworldly devotion to Socrates.

There are young men, too, less glamorous in body, "but fair and good within," when we see their souls "naked and undisguised." Theatetus endures in the memory, ugly

—like Socrates—but with a look of attractive intelligence in his homely face, and a gift for philosophy; Cebes and Simias, timid about voicing their doubts of Socrates' arguments for immortality in the face of his own imminent death; Adeimantus, Plato's half-brother, solid and grave, and Ariston, who gave up philosophy for horses.

The picture gallery of Plato's dialogues is not composed, however, exclusively of young men. There are memorable portraits of notable Athenians Plato had known or known of. Chief among these, perhaps, is Protagoras (of Abdera) as rendered in the dialogue of that name, the grave, somewhat pontifical Sophist sincerely engaged in teaching wealthy young Athenians "prudence in affairs both public and private." Then there is Callias, the wealthy entertainer of Sophists, and Cephalus, in the serenity of wealthy old age speaking with grateful amenity of the pleasure of being wealthy enough to be just and old enough to be at peace.

But the dialogues are more than a picture gallery; they are genuine drama, save that written in Plato's old age which is, as in the case of the *Laws*, more austerely expository in character. The "ladder of love" in the *Symposium*, "the passage from the love of one fair form to all fair forms and to the love finally of absolute form and beauty itself," is a Platonic notion that has been of immense influence in the history of thought and letters and touches something deeply responsive in any reader who has ever known love or thought. But one need not love philosophy or philosophize about love to remember the magnificent dramatic comedy and beauty of the *Symposium*. The gathering of the wits and beauties of Athens, the decision to drink no more and instead to talk of love, the speeches of Eirxymachus the physician, of Aristophanes the jester, of Phaedrus the rhetorician, all in character, the hushed exaltation following the great mystical eloquence of Socrates; then comes the sudden breaking in of Alcibiades drunk,

with the vine leaves about his head, followed by a troupe
of revellers and flute girls, in his inebriate spontaneity
speaking startling words of insight about himself and
Socrates. And before dawn, with everyone asleep but Agathon and Aristophanes, Socrates explains or tries to explain
to the sleepy minds of this tragedian and comedian that
the essence of tragedy and comedy are essentially the same.
Leaving them, too, asleep Socrates departs in the dawn to
have his bath and go about the business of the day as
usual.

The *Protagoras,* in its raising of the question whether
virtue can be taught and its clear but subtle identification
of virtue and knowledge, is a key dialogue to the understanding of Plato's philosophical ideas, but it stays in the
memory, too, as a stage picture and stage play. The rhetorical gravity of Protagoras, his cluster of admirers, his
irritation at Socrates' shrewd thrusts and interruptions, the
"peripety" or reversal of rôles with Socrates finally defending the position he had originally attacked, that virtue
could be taught; the play of personalities, the crises of
emotional involvements, Protagoras' wounded pride and the
eagerness of the onlookers to have the argument continued,
—no stage artificer has handled these matters better than
this philosopher using the dialogue form. And in the tragic
crescendi of the Socratic panel, the *Apology* and the *Phaedo,*
no dramatist could better have conceived the representation
of a great and loyal spirit facing the world and its worldliness with equanimity. It is hard to say which is the more
dramatic portrait, Socrates in the *Apology* facing his accusers and his judges without compromise, with depths of
irony and humor all at once, or Socrates in the *Phaedo* facing the unknown, and comforting his young friends who
feel and fear for him in the shadow of his death, urging
them to be of good cheer, and persuading them by argument
and poetical fable to the "sweet hope" of immortality.

THE PHILOSOPHICAL SIGNIFICANCE OF THE DIALOGUE FORM

But the dialogue form has more than literary charm and dramatic effectiveness; it has genuine philosophical importance and typifies something fundamental in the whole Platonic attitude toward philosophy. We have grown so accustomed to thinking of philosophy as something written down in formal books and expounded by professors that it is difficult to realize that for Plato it was a living process, the uncertain movement of the mind toward a certainty which was in essence the possession of the gods, and became only with difficulty the possession of men.

The whole character of thought as Plato conceives it is the dialogue of a mind with itself. "A person who really thinks, elicits ideas from himself by questioning himself, and tests those ideas by questioning; he does, in fact, the same sort of things with himself that Socrates did with other people." [1] The mind, so to put it, asks itself a question to which it submits tentative replies. The process of thinking is refinement upon, reflection upon, those tentative replies, suggestions, or ideas. They appear vaguely and at random; they demand clarification, rectification, organization. They need to be separated from other notions, which seem but are not similar. They need to be reduced to prior notions from which, upon examination, they flow. Then they need to be followed out to further notions which they involve or imply.

This tentative clarifying quality of thought is admirably adapted to, and beautifully illustrated by, conversation. The Platonic dialogues are, indeed, refinements upon the actual method which Socrates employed in discussion with others. They remain, for all their freight of moral and cosmic insights, home-spun conversations, loiterings of the mind like the loiterings of Socrates, in the confused marketplaces of human uncertainty. But the dialogue, instead of

[1] P. L. Nettleship: Lectures on the *Republic* of Plato.

being as the unuttered self-dialectic of an individual, silent
and half-articulate, are the articulated thoughts of two or
three individuals playing upon the same theme. Those various elements and parties to an internal controversy are kept
marching forward by the movement of Socrates' own
thought. It is as if the various elements of thinking, the
various "parties" to a debate we carry on with ourselves,
had become suddenly objectified and personalized, transferred from the invisible hermitage of the individual mind
to the theatre of many minds. The closet drama of an inner
argument among the conflicting voices of one intelligence
becomes the objective drama of audible discussion of the
diverse characters in a Platonic dialogue.

It is a question among psychologists whether thought is
not simply mute speech, words without the music of the
voice. The Platonic dialogues, at any rate, are the silences
of thought finding speech, the phases of an argument or
an issue put into the mouths of various living interlocutors.
For the minor characters in Plato are not mere yes-sayers
as Faguet in his adroit parody makes them out. They are
the intelligent articulators of intelligible and plausible positions. Protagoras is more or less vanquished in the dialogue
by that name, but it is no fool who falls at Socrates' hands.
When Simias and Cebes raise objections to Socrates' arguments for immortality in the *Phaedo,* their objections have
point and weight. They are like the other side of an argument that one thinks of when one is thinking to one's self.
Theatetus' first suggestion in the dialogue called after him,
that knowledge is perception, is like the first tentative idea
that arises in the reverie that is the beginning of thought
or the first tentative solution for the problem that incites
it. Socrates' criticisms of Theatetus' various suggestions in
the dialogue are, in his own phrase, like the art of the midwife, helping to bring the spiritual first-born of men to
birth, and then trying to see whether the first-born of
thought is a genuine thought or merely a changeling.

The conversation that carries forward and clarifies
thought is not a rigid process, for all the discipline of dialectical criticism that Plato counsels and exhibits. Private
thought, like the conversation of a group, originates from
unpredictable incitements and is unpredictable in its diva-
gations. Thus the business of cobblers and flute-players
may lead Socrates and his associates to a consideration or
vision of absolute justice; the remark of a friend that
Theatetus resembles Socrates may lead to a consideration
of the nature of knowledge. Thought, too, in this dramatic
externalization of it that Plato gives, must not be confined
too tightly if it is to be living, creative thinking, rather
than the beaded formulas of past thinking. "After the manner of philosophers," Socrates says in the *Theatetus*, "we
are digressing. . . . A philosopher is a gentleman; he can
have his talk out and wander from one subject to another."
One of the lessons as well as one of the charms of the
Platonic dialogue is the ease and flexibility with which it
wanders on, allowing all sorts of little streams of suggestion to flow into the river of the argument, whether it be
a brief excursion into the criticism of poetry, a paean to
philosophy, a myth, a homely metaphor like "the leaky
pot," or a jest, like Socrates' saying in the Phaedo that he
cannot be accused in discussing death on the eve of his
own, to be discussing a subject that does not concern him.

But while a conversation, unlike a lecture, has no fixed
a priori structure, in good conversation on a serious theme,
there is established a pervasive atmosphere which fixes the
character even of the anecdotes that suggest themselves.
So it is in the long discussion about justice in the *Republic*.
One seems to have touched a thousand subjects, from Homer
and Hesiod to cooks and hairdressers, one has met a score
of striking metaphors, the cave wherein human intelligence
is refracted upon the shadows of knowledge, the false philosopher as the bald-headed thinker marrying his master's
daughter, the argument of the *Republic* as the three waves

which threaten to overwhelm us, the gold, silver, and bronze men, the myth of Er at the end. Yet the whole has a march, a movement, and an integration. The sense of casualness is a subtle achievement of art; as a matter of actual fact the argument of the *Republic* can without distortion be diagramed. And justice, which has been sought for, if it has not, precisely speaking, been found, has been vividly suggested and exemplified.

But not much more than that. Most conversations do not end in any definite conclusions and the Platonic dialogues almost never do. For though Plato was convinced deeply of the immitigable difference between "certainty" and mere "opinion," he was aware that opinion was as much as most human conversation—or thought—could arrive at. So in the *Lysis*, though it be two good friends, and Socrates the friend to both, who are discussing friendship, they cannot tell at the close what friendship is. Socrates challenges Euthyphro with not knowing what he is talking about when he talks of piety, but he offers no definition of piety himself. Charmides is the very soul of temperance; yet temperance, even under Socrates' skillful guidance, remains undefined. Even the *Theatetus*, where some partial validity is assigned to the successive definitions of knowledge, the latter are ultimately all rejected.

There is a certain type of negative criticism current in all ages, which takes a sadistic delight in destroying the "first-born" of anyone else's thought. It was not that perverse pleasure that Plato shared. The inconclusiveness of the Platonic dialogue is not the scepticism of the cynic. It is rather the scrupulousness of the philosopher and the tolerance, the sympathetic memory of all that may be said on all sides, which are the signs of the humanistic and, in the best sense, of the academic temper, in all ages. For it is clear to Plato and from Plato that, let thinking be as disciplined and comprehensive as may be, yet doubtless some aspect of a problem will have been untouched. One must be wary of assertion in a world where we are tempted to clutch at shadows as if they were realities. "Perhaps it may be" is one of Socrates' favorite phrases.

This tentativeness of thought has its own sober and aseptic felicity. At the end of the *Theatetus* where Socrates has shown Theatetus' spiritual offspring, the definitions of knowledge, to be not worth bringing up, he says:

"But, Theatetus, if you should ever conceive afresh, you will be all the better for the present investigation, and if not, you will be soberer and gentler and humbler to other men, and will be too modest to fancy that you know what you do not know."

But these apparently inconclusive dialogues do more than conduct us at the hands of a master through the very process of the soul talking to itself. We have learnt more than intellectual fastidiousness and the modesty of negation: we have learned the *arrière pensée*, that is the mark of a critical mind. One may not at the end of *Lysis* be able to say exactly what friendship is, but in that beautiful and grave, ironic and tender conversation between Socrates and the two boys, we have come into something very like its atmosphere and presence. The long search for justice in the *Republic* has not revealed it in a formula, but we have had an unfolding vision or exemplification of what the just man and the good life are like. We have felt, not defined, inspiration in the *Phaedrus*, and even if we have not demonstrated immortality in the *Phaedo*, we close it with a near sense of the immortal. The dialogues, like sensitive conversations, move tactfully in the moods which befit the themes of the discourses. A passion for beauty, a homesickness for Heaven, brood upon the talk of recollection of divinity in the *Phaedrus*. In the *Gorgias*, which Socrates so carefully distinguishes between the flattery that is rhetoric and the validity that is justice, the whole is pervaded by a solemn sense of the paramount gravity of the moral issue involved. Throughout these little dramas of thought, there is always the suggestion of an unspoken obbligato, philosophy itself being, as Socrates says in the *Phaedo*, a finer kind of music. One hears a depth that is never said; one learns more than is ever actually concluded.

Likewise, just as good talk by wise men bursts every so often beyond the bounds of measured logic into little uncharted, unpremeditated flights of imagination or eloquence, so, too, do in these philosophic conversations of Plato's. Plato knew these moments of "enthusiasm," in the old Greek sense of "being filled with a god." And his hero, Socrates, every so often ceases to be merely the adroit argumentative critic and becomes a vessel of pure and rapturous eloquence. There is, as Socrates himself is made to explain, a "divine" madness, by which incidentally at the high water marks of the dialogues, Socrates himself is overtaken. "He who having no touch of the Muses' madness in his soul, comes to the door and thinks that he will get into the temple with the help of art—he, I say, and his poetry are not admitted." "And there is the madness, too, of love, the greatest of Heaven's blessing." Socrates, as represented by Plato, shared both madnesses, and Plato must be read in certain pages as, in his own phrase, "an inspired madman." It may be said of him what he had Socrates say in the *Ion* of poets, "god himself is the speaker and through him he is conversing with us."

THE MYTH IN PLATO

There are moments, Plato seems to say, when speech has gone as far as thought can reach, when the point by point demonstrations of logic must be abandoned, since, after all, all human intelligence is for the most part playing sketchily over the probable. It is at such points when Plato is touching issues, hopes, and ideals very dear and very uncertain,

that he passes from argument to myth. These myths are
not allegories; they are not symbolic paraphrases of demonstration. They are poetic creations which give in the
immediacy of an imaginative picture a sense of the atmosphere, the beauty, the validity of some human aspiration,
some human faith, some human vision which the senses
cannot touch nor the methods of dialectic prove. It is, again,
as if in conversation after long and weary argument, one
of the speakers felt deeply the reality, the emotional compulsion of some object of hope or love which he could not
prove, and yet without which he could not live. The "sweet
hope" of immortality, the faith that in the next world as
well as this, it is important to present the soul whole and
undefiled, that in the next world as well as this, justice is
better than injustice, these are the characteristic subjects
of the Platonic myths. The three great myths about the
future life occur in the *Gorgias,* the *Phaedo,* and the *Republic.* In no case does Plato offer them as literal truths;
they are given rather as renderings of a mood which moral
hope, human aspiration demand; they are visions by which
it were well to live, "as if" they were. "Perhaps," says
Socrates at the end of the myth in the *Gorgias,* "this may
appear to you to be only an old wife's tale, which you
will contemn. And there might be reason in contemning
such tales, if by searching we could find anything better
or truer." Or again, in the *Phaedo,* "a man of sense ought
not to say, nor will I be very confident that the description
which I have given of the soul and her mansions is exactly
true. But I do say that, inasmuch as the soul is shown to
be immortal, he may venture to think not improperly or
unworthily that something of the kind is true."

There is another kind of myth in Plato, with a different
subject-matter, the past history of the soul before birth, not
its history after death. The myth in the *Phaedrus* is frankly
imaginative, but it has, as all the myths in Plato, a poetic
truth. Plato is trying to account for the extraordinary pas-

sion of the soul for any fair or beautiful objects, to account
for the conflict in the soul between a pure spiritual contemplation of beauty and the lust for its physical enjoyment. Beauty seen on earth "reminds" the soul of those
absolute and unclouded essences in the circuit of the immortal Heavens which was the soul's life before earth
Wisdom, justice, temperance, have not their visible counterparts; absolute beauty alone has its visible image. The
soul in seeing beauty is stirred to nostalgic recollection of
that purer beauty, that more real beauty it had known in
Heaven. The love of beauty is a longing for the homeland
of the soul. This is pure myth, but it is myth with a rele-
vance. That excess and ecstasy which is the human response
to beauty must, to the poetic imagination, have a transcendent source. The experience of love is the recollection of
Heaven. Here, again, discourse touches something deeper
than reason. These myths are the inventions of the poet
to give body to the longings of the imagination passionately
determined to believe in the reality of the objects of its
aspiration.

THE "DOCTRINE" OF IDEAS

At the beginning of this Introduction it was insisted that
one could not derive a synthetic doctrine from Plato, and
it has just been pointed out that we are dealing in the case
of this philosopher with a thinker whose thoughts tend to
pass every so often quite beyond the limits of logic to the
realm of the freely poetic imagination. All that does not
contravene the fact that there are characteristic themes, and
dominant ideas in the Platonic writings, that Plato was
essentially a careful and disciplined exponent of intellectual method and discipline in philosophy. Plato was no
dogmatist, but he reveals certain dominant convictions and
interests. He was a poet, but his flights were the functions
of a responsible philosophical mind. Precisely because he
understood the poetic temper, he himself was a little ironic

and suspicious of it. There is irony in the *Ion* where it is pointed out that God had robbed poets of their minds that he might make them the expression of his own. There is austerity and deliberateness in censoring in the early part of the *Republic* the irresponsible inventions of the poets, and altogether excluding their tawdry third-hand "imitations" of reality at the end. For all the conversational charm and poetic eloquence of the dialogues, Plato is none the less a serious metaphysician, logician, and moralist. Though he had no fixed system of either morals or metaphysics, he had recurrent and characteristic points of view about both and about the relations between them. Though one can tabulate inconsistencies in his positions in the dialogues, there is in him, if not the unity of a system of thought, the unity of a certain spiritual temper.

That spiritual temper has in the literate popular imagination been associated with the so-called doctrine of ideas. It has time and again been pointed out that in any literal sense, there is no such doctrine to be elicited out of the many places in Plato where "ideas" are with varying interest and interpretation referred to. It would be better, perhaps, to refer to Plato's interest in ideas, an interest which in various dialogues has different though related accents.

It has been said by someone that Parmenides divided by Heraclitus gives Plato. The apothegm is at least suggestive. Plato had certainly learned from the Heracliteans to look at the world of sensible phenomena as in constant flux. "All is changing save the law of change," Heraclitus had said, "you cannot step in the same river twice." Nor, indeed, was he who stepped into the river the second time the same person. The outer world of phenomena, the inner world of sensation, the world and the individual, were all in constant change. In such a world stable knowledge was impossible, even seeing was not believing since it was but the appearance of a moment and the seeing and the object of vision were already as if they had never been. In a world conceived as in eternal flux, no stable knowledge was possible, certainly no stability of moral values was possible. "Man was the measure of all things" and himself the most inconstant of measures.

Plato had learnt from Parmenides and his followers, however, an escape from this phantasmagoria of the flux. "Being, alone remains unmoved, which is the name for all." "This is the language," says Socrates in the *Theatetus*, "of Parmenides, Mileissus, and his followers, who stoutly maintain that all being is one and self-contained, and has no place in which to move." Parmenides has found pure unity, an immutable reality, against which the whole world of phenomena became merely the world of illusion, the world of appearance, an invalid mirage of the senses. On the one hand was the absolute world of the One, unchanging, unified, and eternal, on the other hand the shifting world of appearances, ceaselessly changing, eternally unreal, the realm of non-being.

Plato had the poet's sense of the changing colors and appearances of the diurnal world. He had the poet's dejection at the vanishing and decay which was the doom and taint upon existence, the poet's thirst for a beauty and order that would not fade. Plato was, moreover, logician as well as poet, and recognized the impossibility of knowledge in a universe where both the objects perceived and the minds perceiving them were in constant change. Heraclitus' "flux" left the intelligence dizzy with its lack of grippable permanences. Parmenides' changeless One left the mind paralyzed by its remoteness from possible experience. In Socrates' suggestion of the permanence of moral values and logical definitions, Plato found a clue to his own more developed position.

For in their simplest statement, Plato's ideas are those logical definitions toward which Socrates was working. There are universals, Socrates had indicated, which all discourse involves. Cases of justice involve the concept of justice. Examples of piety involve the definition of piety. Those definitions might be difficult to arrive at, but without assuming their existence, all discourse, all knowledge was impossible.

The Socratic definitions or universals are Platonic ideas in one of their aspects. Socrates had said that discourse was shot through with concepts which all discourse involved. Plato saw experience shot through with universals, or essences, which the existence of all perceptible things involved. Beautiful things are doomed to decay, but the "idea" of beauty is immortal. There is a common quality in all things called by the same name. That common quality for Plato is the essence of the thing, and the essences of all things constitute the world of ideas. These essences or "forms" or "ideas" are Socratic definitions converted into eternal beings, having, or so it appears from at least some of the Platonic writings, their own existence, constituting their own order, the true world of authentic being, whose hierarchy and pattern revolves around and is determined by the Idea of the Good. Plato saw, and Aristotle did after him, the difficulties in such a notion, and there is good ground for believing that he never pressed his own metaphors about the relations between the world of ideas and the world of things into too rigid a metaphysics. But that he took the world of ideas seriously as metaphysics is apparent from the *Theatetus,* the *Philebus,* and the metaphysical sections of the *Republic.*

Plato was subtly alive to all the problems raised about such a doctrine and no one has stated the possible objections more cogently than he. This realm of eternal forms and ideas— How are the ideas in the world of ideas related to each other? How is a man related to the idea of a man, the idea of a chair to a chair? If the ideas are confined exclusively to the realm of absolute ideas, and we are conversant only with the things of sense or opinion, how are we ever to know ideas? Are there ideas only of such amiable matters as Truth and Justice and Wisdom, or also of mud, and hair, and dirt? If ideas are thought, do they think, or who thinks them?

There are essays toward explaining these difficulties; especially does Plato try to explain the relation of things in the changing world of sense to their archetypes in the changeless world of ideas. But the explanation is usually more metaphorical than metaphysical. The idea is like the sun whose light shines upon a thousand different objects; things "participate" in ideas. Things are the shadows of ideas thrown upon the screen of experience.

As one reads the dialogues, one notes half a dozen different ways in which the ideas are used. In the Socratic dialogues they are primarily logical concepts, in the *Parmenides* and the *Sophist* they are metaphysical essences, in the *Philebus* they become primarily logical categories constituting at the same time the structure of reality, in the *Phaedrus* and the *Symposium,* they are esthetic objects and moral objectives and ideals. They are eternal, they are absolute, they constitute a divine order of reality transcendent to human knowledge or earthly existence. Again they can be known through the dialectical operations of mind disciplined and purified of sensuous experience; they are immanent; it is their being which informs and constitutes empirical and understandable and livable reality. They are the forms in which the supreme Idea of the Good manifests itself in the order of the world. Again they are the forms which constitute the beauty of any beautiful object. They are the remembered eternities of beauty which the senses stir the soul to remember. They are the objects of all longing and aspiration, and what is really loved in anything beloved. They can be known, they can be thought; they can be remembered from the discarnate existence before birth when the mind lived among them; they can be loved in acts of ultimate and intuitive vision; they can be adored as the term toward which life and passion move. The business of education is to turn the eye of the soul from the seductions and illusions of sense to these divine eternal patterns bound together in the "empire of the gods" by the Idea of the Good, which transcends all thought and all being, and is the goal of both.

PLATONIC IDEAS AND MORAL VALUES

But the world of Platonic ideas, if it is one thing more than another, is a world of values. Shining in implacable eternal beauty, it constitutes a metaphysician's dream of order amid the harassing and perplexing confusions of the world of experience. For though Socrates in the *Parmenides* is made to admit that in strict logic there must be Ideas, also, of mud and hair and dust and dirt, as well as of Beauty, Goodness, and Truth, he makes the admission reluctantly. "What," as Professor Dewey suggests, "is the realm of ideas in Plato, but the realm of things with all their imperfections removed." It is a universe constituted out of the purified essences of the heart's desire. It is a realm of changelessness for a heart saddened by the spectacle of inevitable change. It is order for a mind perturbed by a nightmare of endless chaos. It is the cosmos of reason of which one may have a glimpse in any thing of beauty, in any item of clarity in the turbulent regions here below the moon. It is the pattern which the mind of man may come to know, and the life of man and of society within limits exemplify and follow.

For in addition to being a metaphysician and a poet, Plato was also, perhaps above all, a moralist. He was not a moralizer. He was a moralist in the grand architectonic sense of believing that it was possible to educate men, at least a small group of philosophic spirits, to a disciplined knowledge of reality, as contrasted with veering opinions about appearance; in the light and by the guidance of that steady vision of the truth, they could bring to being on earth something like a realization, at least a decent approximation of the divine pattern of the good. Plato's whole enterprise, taken in the total context of the dialogues, might be said to be that of indicating how the Good Life might be lived. The whole body of the Platonic writings aims to define the Good Life, to define it, not in a formula, but in a series of suggestions, converging around the ideas of unity, consistency and validity in the individual soul, and in that co-operation of souls which is Society or the State.

The early Socratic dialogues indicate the insistence of Plato, here closely following his master, on the identity of virtue and knowledge. In the *Republic* both knowledge and virtue become clarified in their meaning and broadened in their scope. To know is to know Reality, the eternal invariant nature of things. To have knowledge of the Real as contrasted with having opinions about the apparent, to know the real in nature, in society, in one's own soul, is for Plato the foundation of the Good Life. To know the real in the universe is to know the valid in the state and in one's own being, as a matter of course. To know the truth is inevitably to choose the good as Socrates had earlier contended. Truth itself is a manifestation of the supreme and encompassing Idea of the Good. A virtuous action is a true, valid, just action, the functioning of a soul according to its unswerving following of a clear vision of eternal order.

THE REPUBLIC

All these considerations find their focus in Plato's central work, the *Republic*. This long dialogue, which starts out ostensibly as an inquiry into the meaning of Justice, turns early into an examination of the life of the Just Man, which can be read "writ large" in the life of the "just" state. For Justice is Plato's name for that kind of individual life where every "part of the soul" "does its own business," that life of the state where each individual and each class performs its appropriate function. Justice in the individual and Justice in the state are a realm of order, an earthly anagram of that unearthly eternal order which is the world of ideas. "Time," says Plato in the *Timaeus*, "is a moving picture of eternity." The perfectly ordered soul, the perfectly ordered state, are temporal incarnations of eternal reason.

The *Republic* has generally been called the first Utopia. The construction of the Perfect City has been praised and dismissed as the poet's dream. It is rather the vision of the imaginative philosopher who says, as does Socrates, that the Perfect City exists in the sky, that in beholding it men may make their cities on earth more perfect.

If any city is to be perfect, it will have, Plato seems to insist, something very like this perfect pattern exhibited here. And first of all, if there is to be anything even remotely resembling this Perfect City, it will have to be one ruled by men who know perfection at close and certain range, philosophers with their eyes upon the fixed Idea of the Good. "Cities will not cease from evil until kings are philosophers or philosophers are kings." Only when the rule of men is the rule of reason, when the rulers of a state possess wisdom and govern in the light of it, can one hope for a just state where the individual may live a just life.

The *Republic* is often enough, and with a certain plausibility, treated as an item in the history of Greek political theory. There is no doubt that Plato, seeing the decay and corruption of Athens going on about him, was partly proposing some of his austere perfections with a reformer's ameliorative zeal. But in a profounder sense, the *Republic* is not a book in politics, but a book in morals. We seek "justice" writ large in the state, but it is the state as the adequate condition for moral integrity, for the health and integrity of the individual soul.

Since the pattern of the Perfect State is dependent on

the acquaintance with perfection of the ruling philosophers, a large part of the *Republic* is concerned with the education of the philosopher, the description of the philosopher and of true philosophy. There is also an exhibition of those declinations from divinity or perfection in states ruled, not by the love and possession of wisdom, but by the love of wealth, or of honor, or the confused compulsions of lust.

But a state is not composed of rulers only. There are the guardians or warriors, soldiers in time of war, the armed auxiliaries in times of peace, the loyal administrators. The peculiar virtue of the philosophers is wisdom; the peculiar virtue of the guardians is courage. The philosophers are to the state what mind is to the individual; the warriors or auxiliaries are to the state what enlightened passion, courage, and loyalty to the maintenance of right convictions are to the individual. The warriors are those once removed from originative wisdom, who have a passionate devotion to a wisdom they can appreciate and follow if they themselves cannot discover it or understand it completely. Finally there is the class of workers, whose virtues are those of temperance, a control of physical desires. Their function is the carrying on of the physical and industrial activities of the state, and their special virtue is that of a temperate control, whose form is fixed by the wisdom of the guardians and enforced by the loyal administrative zeal of the warriors. Mind and will and animal impulse constitute the triune soul of the individual. Mind, will, and animal impulse demarcate the classes in the state. Justice appears as a consequence of the functioning of the other three virtues. If the philosophers are truly wise, the warriors loyal and courageous, the workers temperate and disciplined, then the state will function perfectly; justice will appear.

It is beside the point to argue that this state of Plato's is aristocratic, or despotic, or austere. It may be all three.

But in a political world of chaos, what Plato above all desired was order. "There is a music in the affairs of men which one may take one's part in or which one may spoil." Indeed, after Socrates has described the life of renunciation which the philosopher guardians of the state are to lead, with no family or property of their own, for many years, indeed, no freedom to pursue without regard to the concerns of the state their own enjoyment of the beatific vision, the young men murmur. Socrates replies that the aim of the state is not to make the citizens, nor even the guardians, happy. It is to make the state, and by the same token the individual, just. However before the great myth at the end of the *Republic* is concluded, Plato leaves no uncertain implication that the just state is indeed the happiest, and thus, too, with the just man.

THE FIRST SCHEME OF EDUCATION IN THE REPUBLIC

But if it is a pattern of order that the state is to exemplify, it is above all the education of its two ruling classes that the state has to be concerned with, and ultimately the education of the philosopher on whose insight the architecture of the whole edifice depends. In the preliminary sketch of the education of the guardian class, here taken to include both warriors and philosophers, Plato displays at once the sensitiveness of the poet to the educative importance of the imagination, and the cautiousness of the moralist recognizing its dangers. Before children can be expected to understand the formulas of reason they may reasonably be expected to be charmed by the forms of the imagination. Myth and music may early be made the sweet insinuators of the principle of reasonable morality into the naïve poet's consciousness that is the soul of the young child.

But if the child is susceptible to the suasion of the lyre and the tale, he is susceptible to corruption by them. There is a relaxing quality about romantic art, about the erotic stories of the gods current in the traditional mythology. Plato would purify all that. Simplicity, austerity, truth must be the themes of our discourses and be in the sounds of our music. Plato turns censor in the interest of the Perfect State. The poets and musicians must be the persuasive but responsible spokesmen of reason, not the hypnotic corruptors of youth. Even the great tragedians were suspect, for where Aristotle thought that they wholesomely effected the discharge, Plato insisted that they disturbingly aroused the emotions of men. In the Perfect State only such emotion was to be stirred as was serviceable to the purposes of reason.

"Wrongness of form and the lack of rhythm, the lack of harmony, are," says Socrates, "fraternal to wrongness of mind and character, and the opposite qualities to the opposite condition,—the temperate and good character: fraternal, aye, and copies of them." The state was to be the political form of the perfect, and the arts were early to habituate the mind through the eye and ear to the rhythmical contours of perfection. The esthetically fair was brother to the morally just; the esthetically foul to the morally evil.

THE TRUE PHILOSOPHER

But it is the education of the philosopher upon whose insight into reality ("la vraie verité,") the health of the state depends. Before outlining the education of this small class of philosopher kings, Socrates divagates to outline the nature of true philosophy and of the true philosopher. For Plato is aware enough of the ridicule that will arise from the ranks of the Philistines at the thought that philosophy should be the source of political wisdom, that the philosopher should rule the state. In his day as in ours, there were the usual gibes about the elaborate day-dreams that were the baseless fabric of speculative vision, the distracted hair splittings that were the preoccupations of philosophers.

Some of the most eloquent and biting pages in Plato are devoted to distinguishing between the "pretenders" to philosophy and the authentic philosophers, between the quibbles of the eristics and the dialectical discipline, the informed vision of the true philosophers. The latter have "courage, magnificence, apprehension, memory, as their natural gifts." They are a group who in youth, displaying an imaginative quickness toward reason, in maturity, through the discipline of a sound education, may become, in Plato's magnificent language, "the spectators of all time and all existence." The true philosophers are "lovers of the vision of the truth." They are the ideal rulers of the ideal state (in another state would they be tolerated?) first because their minds are fixed upon the pattern of perfection, secondly because their absorption in those eternal values will raise them above the corruptions of wealth and honor.

"For he, Adeimantus, whose mind is fixed upon true being, has surely no time to look down upon the affairs of earth, or to be filled with malice and envy, contending against men; his eye is ever directed toward things fixed and immutable, which he sees neither injuring nor being injured by one another; but all in order moving according to reason; these he imitates, and to these he will as far as he can conform himself. Can a man help imitating that with which he holds reverential converse?"

The philosopher king will be, in the Platonic vision, at once a prophet, a statesman, and a saint, a seer whose vision is centered on the encompassing ideas of True Being, and ultimately on the Idea of the Good itself. He will be a saint whose object of adoration is that divinity, a statesman whose administration is governed always by that steady and absorbing vision.

THE EDUCATION OF THE PHILOSOPHER

Obviously only the choicest youths, gifted with a love of truth and beauty, quickness of mind and perdurance of memory, preferably themselves fair, will be chosen as candidates for that "education of the philosopher" which is to terminate in the vision of the Good, a vision to be used among the shadows among which men in the Cave of the world move, in the interest of the state as a whole.

Plato bestows a loving, detailed care upon the program for the education of the philosophers. "For wherewith shall it be salted if the salt have lost its savor?" It is chiefly important to point out that the whole aim and technique of that education revolves around the notion of passing gradually from temporal things to eternal essences, "turning the eye of the soul" from shifting shadows to changeless realities. That mathematics should be the initial step in that enterprise is not surprising in a philosopher who, as Aristotle points out, gave to his hearers, come to hear a lecture on the Good, a lecture on forms and numbers. For Plato had been immensely influenced by the Pythagorean conviction that number, mathematical order, was somehow at the heart of things. But dialectics is the coping stone, the final discipline; it leads the thinker directly into the presence of essences, to the eternal invariant characters which constitute the forms of the governing concept of good "which he must be able to abstract and define."

Having moved through this gradual training in abstraction until they can "define the good," the philosophic candidates for royal rule will have arrived at the age of thirty-five. For fifteen years they must interrupt their philosophic absorptions, return to the "cave" of the world, gain experience of life, and have an opportunity of trying whether, when they are drawn all manner of ways by temptation, they "will stand firm or flinch."

At the age of fifty, after they have distinguished themselves in every action of their lives and in every branch of knowledge, they "come at last to their consummation; the time has now come at which they must raise the eye of the soul to the universal light which lightens all things and is the absolute good; for that is the pattern according to which they are to order the state and their own lives also, making philosophy their chief pursuit, but when their time comes, toiling also at politics and ruling for the public good."

THE REPUBLIC AS THE KEYSTONE TO PLATO'S THINKING

This is the keystone of the whole arch of the *Republic*, the keystone, indeed, to the whole of Plato's thinking. There are a hundred minor themes in the *Republic*, a theory of literary criticism, of sex equality, of eugenics, of the origins of imperialism, of the decay of states and individuals, of natural *versus* conventional justice, of the lies and imitations of the poets, of the evils of a corrupt theology. But this is the heart of the matter, that a sound politic is dependent on the sound education of its rulers, that a sound education is an education toward the final vision of that absolute good whose radiance "sets in order," as Plato elsewhere says of the love of beauty, "the empire of the gods," that the philosophic vision, the perception of the metaphysically real is the basis of the valid in politics, in art, in the life of the individual soul.

For the mind of Plato saw shining through the transparencies and transiences of shifting things the imperishable order of truth and beauty, the radiation of the Good. As a political philosopher it is his aim to conceive, if possible to construct a city that shall be the incarnation in life and in stone of that beatific vision which is the ultimate term of the most disciplined dialectic thought. To have that ultimate vision will make a man a true statesman, and will raise him by its absolute absorption above the possibility of corruption and deflection, will keep the city he governs out of the danger of disintegration and decay. And the souls, too, of that city will be steady, will be temperate, will be loyal and, up to the measure of their capacities, wise. Justice will be eternal good become operative in their lives. The just man will be the happy incarnation of the divine order of reason.

If, as a moral and political thinker, Plato tries to conceive a state that shall be the human realization of perfection, as a poet he turns his eyes less unreservedly toward the vision of the absolute itself. The Philosopher educated by the state must run from the hill of vision back to the cave that he may help to communicate and realize that vision as Buddha turned from the Bo-Tree to bring others, too, to the enlightenment.

But the philosopher, could he be released, would turn to that communion, that ultimate intuition of the good, with the ardor which had taken him along the difficult path toward its attainment. In the *Symposium* Socrates himself, in that divine madness which in the *Phaedrus* he attributes to poets and lovers and prophets, defines the progress of the soul, this time not through the path of moral and mathematical discipline, but through the path of beauty to Beauty itself, the lover's name and synonym for the good. Incited to love by a fair human form, one passes thence to the love of all fair forms, to the love of Form or Beauty itself, that compassing order and beauty which is the summit of the mystic vision. What the dialectician sees coolly under the form of the Good, the lover sees passionately under the form of Beauty. Both love and logic for Plato, pressed to their ultimate terms, end in an apocalypse, a mystic vision. And as Socrates rehearses it in the myth in the *Phaedrus,* all experience in its passionate moments of absorption, is a reminder of that complete absorption in undimmed purity of immortal truth and goodness and beauty, an opportune retrieval of the soul's experience before it was corrupted by life in the world. And finally, as is clear through all the tangle of mythical physics in the *Timaeus*, the universe itself is the radiation of the pattern of the good which is the goal of thought, of art, of love, and, indeed, the sustaining constitution of all being.

One turns to Plato thus to find a philosopher with many facets: the thinker with a passion for passionless, disciplined thought, the poet with the mystic's sense of beauty transcending analysis and an absolute transcending being, the statesman with a vision of a state conceived and ordered by an adoring, disinterested comprehension of the good. Because one finds in this philosopher not a set of formulas, but the whole repertory of human idealism and aspiration, he remains, not the teacher of a system, but the dramatist of the soul, of the soul eternally asking itself questions about the mystery of itself and its world, eternally piercing beyond the mists of time to the clearer sunlight of eternity. It was Coleridge who marked that everyone was born into the world either a Platonist or an Aristotelian. Plato is peculiarly for those who feel the light that never was on sea or land, for those who are hungry that that light be realized somehow, even if a little clouded, amid the affairs of men.

LYSIS

LYSIS, OR FRIENDSHIP

PERSONS OF THE DIALOGUE

SOCRATES, *who is the narrator.*   MENEXENUS.
HIPPOTHALES.   LYSIS.
CTESIPPUS.

SCENE: A newly erected Palaestra outside the walls of Athens.

I was going from the Academy straight to the Lyceum, intending to take the outer road, which is close under the wall. When I came to the postern gate of the city, which is by the fountain of Panops, I fell in with Hippothales, the son of Hieronymus, and Ctesippus the Paeanian, and a company of young men who were standing with them. Hippothales, seeing me approach, asked whence I came and whither I was going.

I am going, I replied, from the Academy straight to the Lyceum.

Then come straight to us, he said, and put in here; you may as well.

Who are you, I said; and where am I to come?

He showed me an enclosed space and an open door over against the wall. And there, he said, is the building at which we all meet: and a goodly company we are.

And what is this building, I asked; and what sort of entertainment have you?

The building, he replied, is a newly erected Palaestra; and the entertainment is generally conversation, to which you are welcome.

Thank you, I said; and is there any teacher there?

Yes, he said, your old friend and admirer, Miccus.

Indeed, I replied; he is a very eminent professor.

Are you disposed, he said, to go with me and see them?

Yes, I said; but I should like to know first, what is expected of me, and who is the favourite among you?

Some persons have one favourite, Socrates, and some another, he said.

And who is yours? I asked: tell me that, Hippothales.

At this he blushed; and I said to him, O Hippothales, thou son of Hieronymus! I do not say that you are, or that you are not, in love; the confession is too late; for I see that you are not only in love, but are already far gone in your love. Simple and foolish as I am, the Gods have given me the power of understanding affections of this kind.

Whereupon he blushed more and more.

Ctesippus said: I like to see you blushing, Hippothales, and hesitating to tell Socrates the name; when, if he were with you but for a very short time, you would have plagued him to death by talking about nothing else. Indeed, Socrates, he has literally deafened us, and stopped our ears with the praises of Lysis; and, if he is a little intoxicated, there is every likelihood that we may have our sleep murdered with a cry of Lysis. His performances in prose are bad enough, but nothing at all in comparison with his verse; and when he drenches us with his poems and other compositions, it is really too bad; and worse still is his manner of singing them to his love; he has a voice which is truly appalling, and we cannot help hearing him: and now, having a question put to him by you, behold he is blushing.

Who is Lysis? I said: I suppose that he must be young; for the name does not recall any one to me.

Why, he said, his father being a very well-known man, he retains his patronymic, and is not as yet commonly called by his own name; but, although you do not know his name, I am sure that you must know his face, for that is quite enough to distinguish him.

But tell me whose son he is, I said.

He is the eldest son of Democrates, of the deme of Aexone.

Ah, Hippothales, I said; what a noble and really perfect love you have found! I wish that you would favour me with the exhibition which you have been making to the rest of the company, and then I shall be able to judge whether you know what a lover ought to say about his love, either to the youth himself, or to others.

Nay, Socrates, he said; you surely do not attach any importance to what he is saying.

Do you mean, I said, that you disown the love of the person whom he says that you love?

No; but I deny that I make verses or address compositions to him.

He is not in his right mind, said Ctesippus; he is talking nonsense, and is stark mad.

O Hippothales, I said, if you have ever made any verses or songs in honour of your favourite, I do not want to hear them; but I want to know the purport of them, that I may be able to judge of your mode of approaching your fair one.

Ctesippus will be able to tell you, he said; for if, as he avers, the sound of my words is always dinning in his ears, he must have a very accurate knowledge and recollection of them.

Yes, indeed, said Ctesippus; I know only too well; and very ridiculous the tale is: for although he is a lover, and very devotedly in love, he has nothing particular to talk about to his beloved which a child might not say. Now, is not that ridiculous? He can only speak of the wealth of Democrates, which the whole city celebrates, and grandfather Lysis, and the other ancestors of the youth, and their stud of horses, and their victory at the Pythian games, and at the Isthmus, and at Nemea with four horses and single horses—these are the tales which he composes and repeats. And there is greater twaddle still. Only the day before yesterday he made a poem in which he described the entertainment of Heracles, who was a connexion of the family, setting forth how in virtue of this relationship he was hospitably received by an ancestor of Lysis; this ancestor was himself begotten of Zeus by the daughter of the founder of the deme. And these are the sort of old wives' tales which he sings and recites to us, and we are obliged to listen to him.

When I heard this, I said: O ridiculous Hippothales! how can you be making and singing hymns in honour of yourself before you have won?

But my songs and verses, he said, are not in honour of myself, Socrates.

You think not? I said.

Nay, but what do you think? he replied.

Most assuredly, I said, these songs are all in your own honour; for if you win your beautiful love, your discourses and songs will be a glory to you, and may be truly regarded as hymns of praise composed in honour of you who have conquered and won such a love; but if he slips away from you, the more you have praised him, the more ridiculous you will look at having lost this fairest and best of blessings; and therefore the wise lover does not praise his beloved until he has won him, because he is afraid of accidents. There is also another danger: the fair, when any one praises or magnifies them, are filled with the spirit of pride and vainglory. Do you not agree with me?

Yes, he said.

And the more vainglorious they are, the more difficult is the capture of them?

I believe you.

What should you say of a hunter who frightened away his prey, and made the capture of the animals which he is hunting more difficult?

He would be a bad hunter, undoubtedly.

Yes; and if, instead of soothing them, he were to infuriate

them with words and songs, that would show a great want of wit: do you not agree?

Yes.

And now reflect, Hippothales, and see whether you are not guilty of all these errors in writing poetry. For I can hardly suppose that you will affirm a man to be a good poet who injures himself by his poetry.

Assuredly not, he said; such a poet would be a fool. And this is the reason why I take you into my counsels, Socrates, and I shall be glad of any further advice which you may have to offer. Will you tell me by what words or actions I may become endeared to my love?

That is not easy to determine, I said; but if you will bring your love to me, and will let me talk with him, I may perhaps be able to show you how to converse with him, instead of singing and reciting in the fashion of which you are accused.

There will be no difficulty in bringing him, he replied; if you will only go with Ctesippus into the Palaestra and sit down and talk, I believe that he will come of his own accord; for he is fond of listening, Socrates. And as this is the festival of the Hermaea, the young men and boys are all together, and there is no separation between them. He will be sure to come: but if he does not, Ctesippus, with whom he is familiar, and whose relation, Menexenus, is his great friend, shall call him.

That will be the way, I said. Thereupon I led Ctesippus into the Palaestra, and the rest followed.

Upon entering we found that the boys had just been sacrificing; and this part of the festival was nearly at an end. They were all in their white array, and games at dice were going on among them. Most of them were in the outer court amusing themselves; but some were in a corner of the Apodyterium playing at odd and even with a number of dice, which they took out of little wicker baskets. There was also a circle of lookers-on; among them was Lysis

He was standing with the other boys and youths, having a crown upon his head, like a fair vision, and not less worthy of praise for his goodness than for his beauty. We left them, and went over to the opposite side of the room, where, finding a quiet place, we sat down; and then we began to talk. This attracted Lysis, who was constantly turning round to look at us—he was evidently wanting to come to us. For a time he hesitated and had not the courage to come alone; but, first of all, his friend Menexenus, leaving his play, entered the Palaestra from the court, and when he saw Ctesippus and myself, was going to take a seat by us; and then Lysis, seeing him, followed, and sat down by his side; and the other boys joined. I should observe that Hippothales, when he saw the crowd, got behind them, where he thought that he would be out of sight of Lysis, lest he should anger him; and there he stood and listened.

I turned to Menexenus, and said: Son of Demophon, which of you two youths is the elder?

That is a matter of dispute between us, he said.

And which is the nobler? Is that also a matter of dispute?

Yes, certainly.

And another disputed point is, which is the fairer?

The two boys laughed.

I shall not ask which is the richer of the two, I said; for you are friends, are you not?

Certainly, they replied.

And friends have all things in common, so that one of you can be no richer than the other, if you say truly that you are friends.

They assented. I was about to ask which was the juster of the two, and which was the wiser of the two; but at this moment Menexenus was called away by some one who came and said that the gymnastic master wanted him. I suppose that he had to offer sacrifice. So he went away, and I asked Lysis some more questions. I dare say, Lysis,

I said, that your father and mother love you very much.

Certainly, he said.

And they would wish you to be perfectly happy.

Yes.

But do you think that any one is happy who is in the condition of a slave, and who cannot do what he likes?

I should think not indeed, he said.

And if your father and mother love you, and desire that you should be happy, no one can doubt that they are very ready to promote your happiness.

Certainly, he replied.

And do they then permit you to do what you like, and never rebuke you or hinder you from doing what you desire?

Yes, indeed, Socrates; there are a great many things which they hinder me from doing.

What do you mean? I said. Do they want you to be happy, and yet hinder you from doing what you like? for example, if you want to mount one of your father's chariots, and take the reins at a race, they will not allow you to do so—they will prevent you?

Certainly, he said, they will not allow me to do so.

Whom then will they allow?

There is a charioteer, whom my father pays for driving.

And do they trust a hireling more than you? and may he do what he likes with the horses? and do they pay him for this?

They do.

But I dare say that you may take the whip and guide the mule-cart if you like;—they will permit that?

Permit me! indeed they will not.

Then, I said, may no one use the whip to the mules?

Yes, he said, the muleteer.

And is he a slave or a free man?

A slave, he said.

And do they esteem a slave of more value than you who

are their son? And do they entrust their property to him rather than to you? and allow him to do what he likes, when they prohibit you? Answer me now: Are you your own master, or do they not even allow that?

Nay, he said; of course they do not allow it.

Then you have a master?

Yes, my tutor; there he is.

And is he a slave?

To be sure; he is our slave, he replied.

Surely, I said, this is a strange thing, that a free man should be governed by a slave. And what does he do with you?

He takes me to my teachers.

You do not mean to say that your teachers also rule over you?

Of course they do.

Then I must say that your father is pleased to inflict many lords and masters on you. But at any rate when you go home to your mother, she will let you have your own way, and will not interfere with your happiness; her wool, or the piece of cloth which she is weaving, are at your disposal: I am sure that there is nothing to hinder you from touching her wooden spathe, or her comb, or any other of her spinning implements.

Nay, Socrates, he replied, laughing; not only does she hinder me, but I should be beaten, if I were to touch one of them.

Well, I said, this is amazing. And did you ever behave ill to your father or your mother?

No, indeed, he replied.

But why then are they so terribly anxious to prevent you from being happy, and doing as you like?—keeping you all day long in subjection to another, and, in a word, doing nothing which you desire; so that you have no good, as would appear, out of their great possessions, which are under the control of anybody rather than of you, and have no use of your own fair person, which is tended and taken care of by another; while you, Lysis, are master of nobody, and can do nothing?

Why, he said, Socrates, the reason is that I am not of age.

I doubt whether that is the reason, I said; for I should imagine that your father Democrates, and your mother, do permit you to do many things already, and do not wait until you are of age: for example, if they want anything read or written, you, I presume, would be the first person in the house who is summoned by them.

Very true.

And you would be allowed to write or read the letters in any order which you please, or to take up the lyre and tune the notes, and play with the fingers, or strike with the plectrum, exactly as you please, and neither father nor mother would interfere with you.

That is true, he said.

Then what can be the reason, Lysis, I said, why they allow you to do the one and not the other?

I suppose, he said, because I understand the one, and not the other.

Yes, my dear youth, I said, the reason is not any deficiency of years, but a deficiency of knowledge; and whenever your father thinks that you are wiser than he is, he will instantly commit himself and his possessions to you.

I think so.

Aye, I said; and about your neighbour, too, does not the same rule hold as about your father? If he is satisfied that you know more of housekeeping than he does, will he continue to administer his affairs himself, or will he commit them to you?

I think that he will commit them to me.

Will not the Athenian people, too, entrust their affairs to you when they see that you have wisdom enough to manage them?

Yes.

And, oh! let me put another case, I said: There is the great king, and he has an eldest son, who is the Prince of Asia;—suppose that you and I go to him and establish to his satisfaction that we are better cooks than his son, will he not entrust to us the prerogative of making soup, and putting in anything that we like while the pot is boiling, rather than to the Prince of Asia, who is his son?

To us, clearly.

And we shall be allowed to throw in salt by handfuls, whereas the son will not be allowed to put in as much as he can take up between his fingers?

Of course.

Or suppose again that the son has bad eyes, will he allow him, or will he not allow him, to touch his own eyes if he thinks that he has no knowledge of medicine?

He will not allow him.

Whereas, if he supposes us to have a knowledge of medicine, he will allow us to do what we like with him— even to open the eyes wide and sprinkle ashes upon them, because he supposes that we know what is best?

That is true.

And everything in which we appear to him to be wiser than himself or his son he will commit to us?

That is very true, Socrates, he replied.

Then now, my dear Lysis, I said, you perceive that in things which we know every one will trust us,—Hellenes and barbarians, men and women,—and we may do as we please about them, and no one will like to interfere with us; we shall be free, and masters of others; and these things will be really ours, for we shall be benefited by them. But in things of which we have no understanding, no one will trust us to do as seems good to us—they will hinder us as far as they can; and not only strangers, but father and mother, and the friend, if there be one, who is dearer still, will also hinder us; and we shall be subject to others; and these things will not be ours, for we shall not be benefited by them. Do you agree?

He assented.

And shall we be friends to others, and will any others love us, in as far as we are useless to them?

Certainly not.

Neither can your father or mother love you, nor can anybody love anybody else, in so far as they are useless to them?

No.

And therefore, my boy, if you are wise, all men will be your friends and kindred, for you will be useful and good; but if you are not wise, neither father, nor mother, nor kindred, nor any one else, will be your friends. And in matters of which you have as yet no knowledge, can you have any conceit of knowledge?

That is impossible, he replied.

And you, Lysis, if you require a teacher, have not yet attained to wisdom.

True.

And therefore you are not conceited, having nothing of which to be conceited.

Indeed, Socrates, I think not.

When I heard him say this, I turned to Hippothales, and was very nearly making a blunder, for I was going to say to him: That is the way, Hippothales, in which you should talk to your beloved, humbling and lowering him, and not as you do, puffing him up and spoiling him. But I saw that he was in great excitement and confusion at what had been said, and I remembered that, although he was in the neighbourhood, he did not want to be seen by Lysis; so upon second thoughts I refrained.

In the mean time Menexenus came back and sat down in his place by Lysis; and Lysis, in a childish and affection-ate manner, whispered privately in my ear, so that Menexenus should not hear: Do, Socrates, tell Menexenus what you have been telling me.

Suppose that you tell him yourself, Lysis, I replied; for I am sure that you were attending.

Certainly, he replied.

Try, then, to remember the words, and be as exact as you can in repeating them to him, and if you have forgotten anything, ask me again the next time that you see me.

I will be sure to do so, Socrates; but go on telling him something new, and let me hear, as long as I am allowed to stay.

I certainly cannot refuse, I said, since you ask me; but then, as you know, Menexenus is very pugnacious, and therefore you must come to the rescue if he attempts to upset me.

Yes, indeed, he said; he is very pugnacious, and that is the reason why I want you to argue with him.

That I may make a fool of myself?

No, indeed, he said; but I want you to put him down.

That is no easy matter, I replied; for he is a terrible fellow—a pupil of Ctesippus. And there is Ctesippus himself: do you see him?

Never mind, Socrates, you shall argue with him.

Well, I suppose that I must, I replied.

Hereupon Ctesippus complained that we were talking in secret, and keeping the feast to ourselves.

I shall be happy, I said, to let you have a share. Here is Lysis, who does not understand something that I was saying, and wants me to ask Menexenus, who, as he thinks, is likely to know.

And why do you not ask him? he said.

Very well, I said, I will; and do you, Menexenus, answer. But first I must tell you that I am one who from my childhood upward have set my heart upon a certain thing. All people have their fancies; some desire horses, and others dogs; and some are fond of gold, and others of honour.

Now, I have no violent desire of any of these things; but I have a passion for friends; and I would rather have a good friend than the best cock or quail in the world: I would even go further, and say the best horse or dog. Yea, by the dog of Egypt, I should greatly prefer a real friend to all the gold of Darius, or even to Darius himself: I am such a lover of friends as that. And when I see you and Lysis, at your early age, so easily possessed of this treasure, and so soon, he of you, and you of him, I am amazed and delighted, seeing that I myself, although I am now advanced in years, am so far from having made a similar acquisition, that I do not even know in what way a friend is acquired. But I want to ask you a question about this, for you have experience: tell me, then, when one loves another, is the lover or the beloved the friend; or may either be the friend?

Either may, I should think, be the friend of either.

Do you mean, I said, that if only one of them loves the other, they are mutual friends?

Yes, he said; that is my meaning.

But what if the lover is not loved in return? which is a very possible case.

Yes.

Or is, perhaps, even hated? which is a fancy which sometimes is entertained by lovers respecting their beloved. Nothing can exceed their love; and yet they imagine either that they are not loved in return, or that they are hated. Is not that true?

Yes, he said, quite true.

In that case, the one loves, and the other is loved?

Yes.

Then which is the friend of which? Is the lover the friend of the one beloved, whether he be loved in return, or hated; or is the beloved the friend; or is there no friendship at all on either side, unless they both love one another?

There would seem to be none at all.

Then this notion is not in accordance with our previous one. We were saying that both were friends, if one only loved; but now, unless they both love, neither is a friend.

That appears to be true.

Then nothing which does not love in return is beloved by a lover?

I think not.

Then they are not lovers of horses, whom the horses do not love in return; nor lovers of quails, nor of dogs, nor of wine, nor of gymnastic exercises, who have no return of love; no, nor of wisdom, unless wisdom loves them in return. Or shall we say that they do love them, although they are not beloved by them; and that the poet was wrong who sings—

"Happy the man to whom his children are dear, and steeds having single hoofs, and dogs of chase, and the stranger of another land"?

I do not think that he was wrong.

You think that he is right?

Yes.

Then, Menexenus, the conclusion is, that what is beloved, whether loving or hating, may be dear to the lover of it: for example, very young children, too young to love, or even hating their father or mother when they are punished by them, are never dearer to them than at the time when they are being hated by them.

I think that what you say is true.

And, if so, not the lover, but the beloved, is the friend or dear one?

Yes.

And the hated one, and not the hater, is the enemy?

Clearly.

Then many men are loved by their enemies, and hated

by their friends, and are the friends of their enemies, and the enemies of their friends. Yet how absurd, my dear friend, or indeed impossible, is this paradox of a man being an enemy to his friend or a friend to his enemy.

I quite agree, Socrates, in what you say.

But if this cannot be, the lover will be the friend of that which is loved?

True.

And the hater will be the enemy of that which is hated?

Certainly.

Yet we must acknowledge in this, as in the preceding instance, that a man may be the friend of one who is not his friend, or who may be his enemy, when he loves that which does not love him or which even hates him. And he may be the enemy of one who is not his enemy, and is even his friend: for example, when he hates[1] that which does not hate him, or which even loves him.

That appears to be true.

But if the lover is not a friend, nor the beloved a friend, nor both together, what are we to say? Whom are we to call friends to one another? Do any remain?

Indeed, Socrates, I cannot find any.

But, O Menexenus! I said, may we not have been altogether wrong in our conclusions?

I am sure that we have been wrong, Socrates, said Lysis. And he blushed as he spoke, the words seeming to come from his lips involuntarily, because his whole mind was taken up with the argument; there was no mistaking his attentive look while he was listening.

I was pleased at the interest which was shown by Lysis, and I wanted to give Menexenus a rest, so I turned to him and said, I think, Lysis, that what you say is true, and that, if we had been right, we should never have gone so far wrong; let us proceed no further in this direction (for the road seems to be getting troublesome), but take the

---

[1] Omitting φιλῇ, or reading μισῇ instead.

other path into which we turned, and see what the poets
have to say; for they are to us in a manner the fathers
and authors of wisdom, and they speak of friends in no
light or trivial manner, but God himself, as they say, makes
them and draws them to one another; and this they express, if I am not mistaken, in the following words:—

"God is ever drawing like towards like, and making them
    acquainted."

I dare say that you have heard those words.

Yes, he said; I have.

And have you not also met with the treatises of philosophers who say that like must love like? they are the people
who argue and write about nature and the universe.

Very true, he replied.

And are they right in saying this?

They may be.

Perhaps, I said, about half, or possibly, altogether, right,
if their meaning were rightly apprehended by us. For the
more a bad man has to do with a bad man, and the more
nearly he is brought into contact with him, the more he
will be likely to hate him, for he injures him; and injurer
and injured cannot be friends. Is not that true?

Yes, he said.

Then one half of the saying is untrue, if the wicked are
like one another?

That is true.

But the real meaning of the saying, as I imagine, is,
that the good are like one another, and friends to one another; and that the bad, as is often said of them, are never
at unity with one another or with themselves; for they are
passionate and restless, and anything which is at variance
and enmity with itself is not likely to be in union or harmony with any other thing. Do you not agree?

Yes, I do.

Then, my friend, those who say that the like is friendly to the like mean to intimate, if I rightly apprehend them, that the good only is the friend of the good, and of him only; but that the evil never attains to any real friendship, either with good or evil. Do you agree?

He nodded assent.

Then now we know how to answer the question "Who are friends?" for the argument declares "That the good are friends."

Yes, he said, that is true.

Yes, I replied; and yet I am not quite satisfied with this answer. By heaven, and shall I tell you what I suspect? I will. Assuming that like, inasmuch as he is like, is the friend of like, and useful to him—or rather let me try another way of putting the matter: Can like do any good or harm to like which he could not do to himself, or suffer anything from his like which he would not suffer from himself? And if neither can be of any use to the other how can they be loved by one another? Can they now?

They cannot.

And can he who is not loved be a friend?

Certainly not.

But say that the like is not the friend of the like in so far as he is like; still the good may be the friend of the good in so far as he is good?

True.

But then again, will not the good, in so far as he is good, be sufficient for himself? Certainly he will. And he who is sufficient wants nothing—that is implied in the word sufficient.

Of course not.

And he who wants nothing will desire nothing?

He will not.

Neither can he love that which he does not desire?

He cannot.

And he who loves not is not a lover or friend?

Clearly not.

What place then is there for friendship, if, when absent, good men have no need of one another (for even when alone they are sufficient for themselves), and when present have no use of one another? How can such persons ever be induced to value one another?

They cannot.

And friends they cannot be, unless they value one another?

Very true.

But see now, Lysis, whether we are not being deceived in all this—are we not indeed entirely wrong?

How so? he replied.

Have I not heard some one say, as I just now recollect, that the like is the greatest enemy of the like, the good of the good? Yes, and he quoted the authority of Hesiod, who says:

"Potter quarrels with potter, bard with bard,
    Beggar with beggar";

and of all other things he affirmed, in like manner, "That of necessity the most like are most full of envy, strife, and hatred of one another, and the most unlike, of friendship. For the poor man is compelled to be the friend of the rich, and the weak requires the aid of the strong, and the sick man of the physician; and every one who is ignorant, has to love and court him who knows." And indeed he went on to say in grandiloquent language, that the idea of friendship existing between similars is not the truth, but the very reverse of the truth, and that the most opposed are the most friendly; for that everything desires not like but that which is most unlike: for example, the dry desires the moist, the cold the hot, the bitter the sweet, the sharp the blunt, the void the full, the full the void, and so of all other things; for the opposite is the food of the opposite, whereas like receives nothing from like. And I thought that he who said this was a charming man, and that he spoke well. What do the rest of you say?

I should say, at first hearing, that he is right, said Menexenus.

Then we are to say that the greatest friendship is of opposites?

Exactly.

Yes, Menexenus; but will not that be a monstrous answer? and will not the all-wise eristics be down upon us in triumph, and ask, fairly enough, whether love is not the very opposite of hate; and what answer shall we make to them—must we not admit that they speak the truth?

We must.

They will then proceed to ask whether the enemy is the friend of the friend, or the friend the friend of the enemy?

Neither, he replied.

Well, but is a just man the friend of the unjust, or the temperate of the intemperate, or the good of the bad?

I do not see how that is possible.

And yet, I said, if friendship goes by contraries, the contraries must be friends.

They must.

Then neither like and like, nor unlike and unlike are friends.

I suppose not.

And yet there is a further consideration; may not all these notions of friendship be erroneous? but may not that which is neither good nor evil still in some cases be the friend of the good?

How do you mean? he said.

Why, really, I said, the truth is that I do not know; but my head is dizzy with thinking of the argument, and therefore I hazard the conjecture, that "the beautiful is the friend," as the old proverb says. Beauty is certainly a soft, smooth, slippery thing, and therefore of a nature which easily slips in and permeates our souls. For I affirm that the good is the beautiful. You will agree to that?

Yes.

This I say from a sort of notion that what is neither good nor evil is the friend of the beautiful and the good, and I will tell you why I am inclined to think so: I assume that there are three principles—the good, the bad, and that which is neither good nor bad. You would agree —would you not?

I agree.

And neither is the good the friend of the good, nor the evil of the evil, nor the good of the evil; these alternatives are excluded by the previous argument; and therefore, if there be such a thing as friendship or love at all, we must infer that what is neither good nor evil must be the friend, either of the good, or of that which is neither good nor evil, for nothing can be the friend of the bad.

True.

But neither can like be the friend of like, as we were just now saying.

True.

And if so, that which is neither good nor evil can have no friend which is neither good nor evil.

Clearly not.

Then the good alone is the friend of that only which is neither good nor evil.

That may be assumed to be certain.

And does not this seem to put us in the right way? Just remark, that the body which is in health requires neither medical nor any other aid, but is well enough; and the healthy man has no love of the physician, because he is in health.

He has none.

But the sick loves him, because he is sick?

Certainly.

And sickness is an evil, and the art of medicine a good and useful thing?

Yes.

But the human body, regarded as a body, is neither good nor evil?

True.

And the body is compelled by reason of disease to court and make friends of the art of medicine?

Yes.

Then that which is neither good nor evil becomes the friend of good, by reason of the presence of evil?

So we may infer.

And clearly this must have happened before that which was neither good nor evil had become altogether corrupted with the element of evil—if itself had become evil it would not still desire and love the good; for, as we are saying, the evil cannot be the friend of the good.

Impossible.

Further, I must observe that some substances are assimilated when others are present with them; and there are some which are not assimilated: take, for example, the case of an ointment or colour which is put on another substance.

Very good.

In such a case, is the substance which is anointed the same as the colour or ointment?

What do you mean? he said.

This is what I mean: Suppose that I were to cover your auburn locks with white lead, would they be really white, or would they only appear to be white?

They would only appear to be white, he replied.

And yet whiteness would be present in them?

True.

But that would not make them at all the more white, notwithstanding the presence of white in them—they would not be white any more than black?

No.

But when old age infuses whiteness into them, then they become assimilated, and are white by the presence of white.

Certainly.

Now, I want to know whether in all cases a substance is assimilated by the presence of another substance; or must the presence be after a peculiar sort?

The latter, he said.

Then that which is neither good nor evil may be in the presence of evil, but not as yet evil, and that has happened before now?

Yes.

And when anything is in the presence of evil, not being as yet evil, the presence of good arouses the desire of good in that thing; but the presence of evil, which makes a thing evil, takes away the desire and friendship of the good; for that which was once both good and evil has now become evil only, and the good was supposed to have no friendship with evil?

None.

And therefore we say that those who are already wise, whether Gods or men, are no longer lovers of wisdom; nor can they be lovers of wisdom who are ignorant to the extent of being evil, for no evil or ignorant person is a lover of wisdom. There remain those who have the misfortune to be ignorant, but are not yet hardened in their ignorance, or void of understanding, and do not as yet fancy that they know what they do not know: and therefore those who are the lovers of wisdom are as yet neither good nor bad. But the bad do not love wisdom any more than the good; for, as we have already seen, neither is unlike the friend of unlike, nor like of like. You remember that?

Yes, they both said.

And so, Lysis and Menexenus, we have discovered the nature of friendship—there can be no doubt of it: Friendship is the love which by reason of the presence of evil the neither good nor evil has of the good, either in the soul, or in the body, or anywhere.

They both agreed and entirely assented, and for a moment I rejoiced and was satisfied like a huntsman just holding fast his prey. But then a most unaccountable suspicion came across me, and I felt that the conclusion was untrue. I was pained, and said, Alas! Lysis and Menexenus, I am afraid that we have been grasping at a shadow only.

Why do you say so? said Menexenus.

I am afraid, I said, that the argument about friendship is false: arguments, like men, are often pretenders.

How do you mean? he asked.

Well, I said; look at the matter in this way: a friend is the friend of some one; is he not?

Certainly he is.

And has he a motive and object in being a friend, or has he no motive and object?

He has a motive and object.

And is the object which makes him a friend, dear to him, or neither dear nor hateful to him?

I do not quite follow you, he said.

I do not wonder at that, I said. But perhaps, if I put the matter in another way, you will be able to follow me, and my own meaning will be clearer to myself. The sick man, as I was just now saying, is the friend of the physician—is he not?

Yes.

And he is the friend of the physician because of disease, and for the sake of health?

Yes.

And disease is an evil?

Certainly.

And what of health? I said. Is that good or evil, or neither?

Good, he replied.

And we were saying, I believe, that the body being neither good nor evil, because of disease, that is to say, because of evil, is the friend of medicine, and medicine is a good: and medicine has entered into his friendship for the sake of health, and health is a good.

True.

And is health a friend, or not a friend?

A friend.

And disease is an enemy?

Yes.

Then that which is neither good nor evil is the friend of the good because of the evil and hateful, and for the sake of the good and the friend?

Clearly.

Then the friend is a friend for the sake of the friend, and because of the enemy?

That is to be inferred.

Then, at this point, my boys, let us take heed, and be on our guard against deceptions. I will not again repeat that the friend is the friend of the friend, and the like of the like, which has been declared by us to be an impossibility; but, in order that this new statement may not delude us, let us attentively examine another point, which I will proceed to explain: Medicine, as we were saying, is a friend, or dear to us for the sake of health?

Yes.

And health is also dear?

Certainly.

And if dear, then dear for the sake of something?

Yes.

And surely this object must also be dear, as is implied in our previous admissions?

Yes.

And that something dear involves something else dear?

Yes.

But then, proceeding in this way, shall we not arrive at some first principle of friendship or dearness which is not capable of being referred to any other, for the sake of which, as we maintain, all other things are dear, and, having there arrived, we shall stop?

True.

My fear is that all those other things, which, as we say, are dear for the sake of another, are illusions and deceptions only, but where that first principle is, there is the true ideal of friendship. Let me put the matter thus: Suppose the case of a great treasure (this may be a son, who is more precious to his father than all his other treasures), would not the father, who values his son above all things, value other things also for the sake of his son? I mean, for instance, if he knew that his son had drunk hemlock, and the father thought that wine would save him, he would value the wine?

He would.

And also the vessel which contains the wine?

Certainly.

But does he therefore value the three measures of wine, or the earthen vessel which contains them, equally with his son? Is not this rather the true state of the case? All his anxiety has regard not to the means which are provided for the sake of an object, but to the object for the sake of which they are provided. And although we may often say that gold and silver are highly valued by us, that is not the truth; for there is a further object, whatever it may be, which we value most of all, and for the sake of which gold and all our other possessions are acquired by us. Am I not right?

Yes, certainly.

And may not the same be said of the friend? That which is only dear to us for the sake of something else is improperly said to be dear, but the truly dear is that in which all these so-called dear friendships terminate.

That, he said, appears to be true.

And the truly dear or ultimate principle of friendship is not for the sake of any other or further dear.

True.

Then we have done with the notion that friendship has any further object. May we then infer that the good is the friend?

I think so.

And the good is loved for the sake of the evil? Let me put the case in this way: Suppose that of the three principles, good, evil, and that which is neither good nor evil, there remained only the good and the neutral, and that evil went far away, and in no way affected soul or body, nor ever at all that class of things which, as we say, are neither good nor evil in themselves;—would the good be of any use, or other than useless to us? For if there were nothing to hurt us any longer, we should have no need of anything that would do us good. Then would be clearly seen that we did but love and desire the good because of the evil, and as the remedy of the evil, which was the disease; but if there had been no disease, there would have been no need of a remedy. Is not this the nature of the good—to be loved by us who are placed between the two, because of the evil? but there is no use in the good for its own sake.

I suppose not.

Then the final principle of friendship, in which all other friendships terminate, those, I mean, which are relatively dear and for the sake of something else, is of another and a different nature from them. For they are called dear because of another dear or friend. But with the true friend or dear, the case is quite the reverse; for that is proved to be dear because of the hated, and if the hated were away it would be no longer dear.

Very true, he replied; at any rate not if our present view holds good.

But, oh! will you tell me, I said, whether if evil were to perish, we should hunger any more, or thirst any more, or have any similar desire? Or may we suppose that hunger will remain while men and animals remain, but not so as to be hurtful? And the same of thirst and the other desires,— that they will remain, but will not be evil because evil has perished? Or rather shall I say, that to ask what either will be then or will not be is ridiculous, for who knows? This we do know, that in our present condition hunger may injure us, and may also benefit us:—Is not that true?

Yes.

And in like manner thirst or any similar desire may sometimes be a good and sometimes an evil to us, and sometimes neither one nor the other?

To be sure.

But is there any reason why, because evil perishes, that which is not evil should perish with it?

None.

Then, even if evil perishes, the desires which are neither good nor evil will remain?

Clearly they will.

And must not a man love that which he desires and affects?

He must.

Then, even if evil perishes, there may still remain some elements of love or friendship?

Yes.

But not if evil is the cause of friendship: for in that case nothing will be the friend of any other thing after the destruction of evil; for the effect cannot remain when the cause is destroyed.

True.

And have we not admitted already that the friend loves something for a reason? and at the time of making the admission we were of opinion that the neither good nor evil loves the good because of the evil?

Very true.

But now our view is changed, and we conceive that there must be some other cause of friendship?

I suppose so.

May not the truth be rather, as we were saying just now, that desire is the cause of friendship; for that which desires is dear to that which is desired at the time of desiring it? and may not the other theory have been only a long story about nothing?

Likely enough.

But surely, I said, he who desires, desires that of which he is in want?

Yes.

And that of which he is in want is dear to him?

True.

And he is in want of that of which he is deprived?

Certainly.

Then love, and desire, and friendship, would appear to be of the natural or congenial. Such, Lysis and Menexenus, is the inference.

They assented.

Then, if you are friends, you must have natures which are congenial to one another?

Certainly, they both said.

And I say, my boys, that no one who loves or desires another would ever have loved or desired or affected him if he had not been in some way congenial to him, either in his soul, or in his character, or in his manners, or in his form.

Yes, yes, said Menexenus. But Lysis was silent.

Then, I said, the conclusion is, that what is of a congenial nature must be loved.

It follows, he said.

Then the lover, who is true and no counterfeit, must of necessity be loved by his love.

Lysis and Menexenus gave a faint assent to this; and

Hippothales changed into all manner of colours with delight.

Here, intending to revise the argument, I said: Can we point out any difference between the congenial and the like? For if that is possible, then, I think, Lysis and Menexenus, there may be some sense in our argument about friendship. But if the congenial is only the like, how will you get rid of the other argument, of the uselessness of like to like in as far as they are like; for to say that what is useless is dear, would be absurd? Suppose, then, that we agree to distinguish between the congenial and the like— in the intoxication of argument, that may perhaps be allowed.

Very true.

And shall we further say that the good is congenial, and the evil uncongenial to every one? Or again that the evil is congenial to the evil, and the good to the good; and that which is neither good nor evil to that which is neither good nor evil?

They agreed to the latter alternative.

Then, my boys, we have again fallen into the old discarded error; for the unjust will be the friend of the unjust, and the bad of the bad, as well as the good of the good.

That appears to be the result.

But, again, if we say that the congenial is the same as the good, in that case the good and he only will be the friend of the good.

True.

But that too was a position of ours which, as you will remember, has been already refuted by ourselves.

We remember.

Then what is to be done? Or rather is there anything to be done? I can only, like the wise men who argue in courts, sum up the arguments:—If neither the beloved, nor the lover, nor the like, nor the unlike, nor the good, nor the congenial, nor any other of whom we spoke—for there were such a number of them that I cannot remember all—if none of these are friends, I know not what remains to be said.

Here I was going to invite the opinion of some older person, when suddenly we were interrupted by the tutors of Lysis and Menexenus, who came upon us like an evil apparition with their brothers, and bade them go home, as it was getting late. At first, we and the bystanders drove them off; but afterwards, as they would not mind, and only went on shouting in their barbarous dialect, and got angry, and kept calling the boys—they appeared to us to have been drinking rather too much at the Hermaea, which made them difficult to manage—we fairly gave way and broke up the company.

I said, however, a few words to the boys at parting: O Menexenus and Lysis, how ridiculous that you two boys, and I, an old boy, who would fain be one of you, should imagine ourselves to be friends—this is what the bystanders will go away and say—and as yet we have not been able to discover what is a friend!

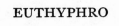

EUTHYPHRO

EUTHYPHRO

PERSONS OF THE DIALOGUE

SOCRATES.   EUTHYPHRO.

SCENE: The porch of the King Archon.

Euthyphro. Why have you left the lyceum, Socrates? and what are you doing in the porch of the King Archon? Surely you cannot be concerned in a suit before the king, like myself ?

Socrates. Not in a suit, Euthyphro; impeachment is the word which the Athenians use.

Euth. What! I suppose that some one has been prosecuting you, for I cannot believe that you are the prosecutor of another.

Soc. Certainly not.

Euth. Then some one else has been prosecuting you?

Soc. Yes.

Euth. And who is he?

Soc. A young man who is little known, Euthyphro; and I hardly know him: his name is Meletus, and he is one of the deme of Pitthis. Perhaps you may remember his appearance; he has a beak, and long straight hair, and a beard which is ill grown.

Euth. No, I do not remember him, Socrates. But what is the charge which he brings against you?

Soc. What is the charge? Well, a very serious charge, which shows a good deal of character in the young man, and for which he is certainly not to be despised. He says he knows how the youth are corrupted and who are their corrupters. I fancy that he must be a wise man, and seeing

35

that I am the reverse of a wise man, he has found me out, and is going to accuse me of corrupting his young friends. And of this our mother the State is to be the judge. Of all our political men he is the only one who seems to me to begin in the right way, with the cultivation of virtue in youth; like a good husbandman, he makes the young shoots his first care, and clears away us who are the destroyers of them. This is only the first step; he will afterwards attend to the elder branches; and if he goes on as he has begun, he will be a very great public benefactor.

Euth. I hope that he may; but I rather fear, Socrates, that the opposite will turn out to be the truth. My opinion is that in attacking you he is simply aiming a blow at the foundation of the State. But in what way does he say that you corrupt the young?

Soc. He brings a wonderful accusation against me, which at first hearing excites surprise: he says that I am a poet or maker of gods, and that I invent new gods and deny the existence of old ones; this is the ground of his indictment.

Euth. I understand, Socrates; he means to attack you about the familiar sign which occasionally, as you say, comes to you. He thinks that you are a neologian, and he is going to have you up before the court for this. He knows that such a charge is readily received by the world, as I myself know too well; for when I speak in the assembly about divine things, and foretell the future to them, they laugh at me and think me a madman. Yet every word that I say is true. But they are jealous of us all; and we must be brave and go at them.

Soc. Their laughter, friend Euthyphro, is not a matter of much consequence. For a man may be thought wise; but the Athenians, I suspect, do not much trouble themselves about him until he begins to impart his wisdom to others; and then for some reason or other, perhaps, as you say, from jealousy, they are angry.

Euth. I am never likely to try their temper in this way.

Soc. I dare say not, for you are reserved in your behaviour, and seldom impart your wisdom. But I have a benevolent habit of pouring out myself to everybody, and would even pay for a listener, and I am afraid that the Athenians may think me too talkative. Now if, as I was saying, they would only laugh at me, as you say that they laugh at you, the time might pass gaily enough in the court; but perhaps they may be in earnest, and then what the end will be you soothsayers only can predict.

Euth. I dare say that the affair will end in nothing, Socrates, and that you will win your cause; and I think that I shall win my own.

Soc. And what is your suit, Euthyphro? are you the pursuer or the defendant?

Euth. I am the pursuer.

Soc. Of whom?

Euth. You will think me mad when I tell you.

Soc. Why, has the fugitive wings?

Euth. Nay, he is not very volatile at his time of life.

Soc. Who is he?

Euth. My father.

Soc. Your father! my good man?

Euth. Yes.

Soc. And of what is he accused?

Euth. Of murder, Socrates.

Soc. By the powers, Euthyphro! how little does the common herd know of the nature of right and truth. A man must be an extraordinary man, and have made great strides in wisdom, before he could have seen his way to bring such an action.

Euth. Indeed, Socrates, he must.

Soc. I suppose that the man whom your father murdered was one of your relatives—clearly he was; for if he had been a stranger you would never have thought of prosecuting him.

Euth. I am amused, Socrates, at your making a distinction between one who is a relation and one who is not a relation; for surely the pollution is the same in either case, if you knowingly associate with the murderer when you ought to clear yourself and him by proceeding against him. The real question is whether the murdered man has been justly slain. If justly, then your duty is to let the matter alone; but if unjustly, then, even if the murderer lives under the same roof with you and eats at the same table, proceed against him. Now, the man who is dead was a poor dependent of mine who worked for us as a field labourer on our farm in Naxos, and one day in a fit of drunken passion he got into a quarrel with one of our domestic servants and slew him. My father bound him hand and foot and threw him into a ditch, and then sent to Athens to ask of a diviner what he should do with him. Meanwhile he never attended to him and took no care about him, for he regarded him as a murderer; and thought that no great harm would be done even if he did die. Now this was just what happened. For such was the effect of cold and hunger and chains upon him, that before the messenger returned from the diviner, he was dead. And my father and family are angry with me for taking the part of the murderer and prosecuting my father. They say that he did not kill him, and that if he did, the dead man was but a murderer, and I ought not to take any notice, for that a son is impious who prosecutes a father. Which shows, Socrates, how little they know what the gods think about piety and impiety.

Soc. Good heavens, Euthyphro! and is your knowledge of religion and of things pious and impious so very exact, that, supposing the circumstances to be as you state them, you are not afraid lest you too may be doing an impious thing in bringing an action against your father?

Euth. The best of Euthyphro, and that which distinguishes him, Socrates, from other men, is his exact knowledge of all such matters. What should I be good for without it?

Soc. Rare friend! I think that I cannot do better than be your disciple. Then before the trial with Meletus comes on I shall challenge him, and say that I have always had a great interest in religious questions, and now, as he charges me with rash imaginations and innovations in religion, I have become your disciple. You, Meletus, as I shall say to him, acknowledge Euthyphro to be a great theologian, and sound in his opinions; and if you approve of him you ought to approve of me, and not have me into court; but if you disapprove, you should begin by indicting him who is my teacher, and who will be the ruin, not of the young, but of the old; that is to say, of myself whom he instructs, and of his old father whom he admonishes and chastises. And if Meletus refuses to listen to me, but will go on, and will not shift the indictment from me to you, I cannot do better than repeat this challenge in the court.

Euth. Yes, indeed, Socrates; and if he attempts to indict me I am mistaken if I do not find a flaw in him; the court shall have a great deal more to say to him than to me.

Soc. And I, my dear friend, knowing this, am desirous of becoming your disciple. For I observe that no one appears to notice you—not even this Meletus; but his sharp eyes have found me out at once, and he has indicted me for impiety. And therefore I adjure you to tell me the nature of piety and impiety, which you said that you knew so well, and of murder, and of other offences against the gods. What are they? Is not piety in every action always the same? and impiety, again—is it not always the opposite of piety, and also the same with itself, having, as impiety, one notion which includes whatever is impious?

Euth. To be sure, Socrates.

Soc. And what is piety, and what is impiety?

Euth. Piety is doing as I am doing; that is to say, prose·

cuting any one who is guilty of murder, sacrilege, or of any
similar crime—whether he be your father or mother, or
whoever he may be—that makes no difference; and not to
prosecute them is impiety. And please to consider, Socrates,
what a notable proof I will give you of the truth of my
words, a proof which I have already given to others:—of
the principle, I mean, that the impious, whoever he may be,
ought not to go unpunished. For do not men regard Zeus
as the best and most righteous of the gods?—and yet they
admit that he bound his father (Cronos) because he wick-
edly devoured his sons, and that he too had punished his
own father (Uranus) for a similar reason, in a nameless
manner. And yet when I proceed against my father, they
are angry with me. So inconsistent are they in their way
of talking when the gods are concerned, and when I am
concerned.

Soc. May not this be the reason, Euthyphro, why I am
charged with impiety—that I cannot away with these stories
about the gods? and therefore I suppose that people think
me wrong. But, as you who are well informed about them
approve of them, I cannot do better than assent to your
superior wisdom. What else can I say, confessing as I do,
that I know nothing about them? Tell me, for the love of
Zeus, whether you really believe that they are true.

Euth. Yes, Socrates; and things more wonderful still, of
which the world is in ignorance.

Soc. And do you really believe that the gods fought with
one another, and had dire quarrels, battles, and the like, as
the poets say, and as you may see represented in the works
of great artists? The temples are full of them; and notably
the robe of Athene, which is carried up to the Acropolis
at the great Panathenaea, is embroidered with them. Are
all these tales of the gods true, Euthyphro?

Euth. Yes, Socrates; and, as I was saying, I can tell you,
if you would like to hear them, many other things about
the gods which would quite amaze you.

Soc. I dare say; and you shall tell me them at some other time when I have leisure. But just at present I would rather hear from you a more precise answer, which you have not as yet given, my friend, to the question, What is "piety"? When asked, you only replied, Doing as you do, charging your father with murder.

Euth. And what I said was true, Socrates.

Soc. No doubt, Euthyphro; but you would admit that there are many other pious acts?

Euth. There are.

Soc. Remember that I did not ask you to give me two or three examples of piety, but to explain the general idea which makes all pious things to be pious. Do you not recollect that there was one idea which made the impious impious, and the pious pious?

Euth. I remember.

Soc. Tell me what is the nature of this idea, and then I shall have a standard to which I may look, and by which I may measure actions, whether yours or those of any one else, and then I shall be able to say that such and such an action is pious, such another impious.

Euth. I will tell you, if you like.

Soc. I should very much like.

Euth. Piety, then, is that which is dear to the gods, and impiety is that which is not dear to them.

Soc. Very good, Euthyphro; you have now given me the sort of answer which I wanted. But whether what you say is true or not I cannot as yet tell, although I make no doubt that you will prove the truth of your words.

Euth. Of course.

Soc. Come, then, and let us examine what we are saying. That thing or person which is dear to the gods is pious, and that thing or person which is hateful to the gods is impious, these two being the extreme opposites of one another. Was not that said?

Euth. It was.

Soc. And well said?

Euth. Yes, Socrates, I thought so; it was certainly said.

Soc. And further, Euthyphro, the gods were admitted to have enmities and hatreds and differences?

Euth. Yes, that was also said.

Soc. And what sort of difference creates enmity and anger? Suppose, for example, that you and I, my good friend, differ about a number; do differences of this sort make us enemies and set us at variance with one another? Do we not go at once to arithmetic, and put an end to them by a sum?

Euth. True.

Soc. Or suppose that we differ about magnitudes, do we not quickly end the difference by measuring?

Euth. Very true.

Soc. And we end a controversy about heavy and light by resorting to a weighing machine?

Euth. To be sure.

Soc. But what differences are there which cannot be thus decided, and which therefore make us angry and set us at enmity with one another? I dare say the answer does not occur to you at the moment, and therefore I will suggest that these enmities arise when the matters of difference are the just and unjust, good and evil, honourable and dishonourable. Are not these the points about which men differ, and about which when we are unable satisfactorily to decide our differences, you and I and all of us quarrel, when we do quarrel?[1]

Euth. Yes, Socrates, the nature of the differences about which we quarrel is such as you describe.

Soc. And the quarrels of the gods, noble Euthyphro, when they occur, are of a like nature?

Euth. Certainly they are.

Soc. They have differences of opinion, as you say, about good and evil, just and unjust, honourable and dishonour-

[1] Cp. 1 Alcib. 111 foll.

able: there would have been no quarrels among them, if there had been no such differences—would there now?

Euth. You are quite right.

Soc. Does not every man love that which he deems noble and just and good, and hate the opposite of them?

Euth. Very true.

Soc. But, as you say, people regard the same things, some as just and others as unjust,—about these they dispute; and so there arise wars and fightings among them.

Euth. Very true.

Soc. Then the same things are hated by the gods and loved by the gods, and are both hateful and dear to them?

Euth. True.

Soc. And upon this view the same things, Euthyphro will be pious and also impious?

Euth. So I should suppose.

Soc. Then, my friend, I remark with surprise that you have not answered the question which I asked. For I certainly did not ask you to tell me what action is both pious and impious: but now it would seem that what is loved by the gods is also hated by them. And therefore, Euthyphro, in thus chastising your father you may very likely be doing what is agreeable to Zeus but disagreeable to Cronos or Uranus, and what is acceptable to Hephaestus but unacceptable to Here, and there may be other gods who have similar differences of opinion.

Euth. But I believe, Socrates, that all the gods would be agreed as to the propriety of punishing a murderer: there would be no difference of opinion about that.

Soc. Well, but speaking of men, Euthyphro, did you ever hear any one arguing that a murderer or any sort of evil-doer ought to be let off?

Euth. I should rather say that these are the questions which they are always arguing, especially in courts of law: they commit all sorts of crimes, and there is nothing which they will not do or say in their own defence.

Soc. But do they admit their guilt, Euthyphro, and yet say that they ought not to be punished?

Euth. No; they do not.

Soc. Then there are some things which they do not venture to say or do: for they do not venture to argue that the guilty are to be unpunished, but they deny their guilt, do they not?

Euth. Yes.

Soc. Then they do not argue that the evildoer should not be punished, but they argue about the fact of who the evildoer is, and what he did and when?

Euth. True.

Soc. And the gods are in the same case, if as you assert they quarrel about just and unjust, and some of them say while others deny that injustice is done among them. For surely neither God nor man will ever venture to say that the doer of injustice is not to be punished?

Euth. That is true, Socrates, in the main.

Soc. But they join issue about the particulars—gods and men alike; and, if they dispute at all, they dispute about some act which is called in question, and which by some is affirmed to be just, by others to be unjust. Is not that true?

Euth. Quite true.

Soc. Well, then, my dear friend Euthyphro, do tell me, for my better instruction and information, what proof have you that in the opinion of all the gods a servant who is guilty of murder, and is put in chains by the master of the dead man, and dies because he is put in chains before he who bound him can learn from the interpreters of the gods what he ought to do with him, dies unjustly; and that on behalf of such an one a son ought to proceed against his father and accuse him of murder? How would you show that all the gods absolutely agree in approving of his act? Prove to me that they do, and I will applaud your wisdom as long as I live.

Euth. It will be a difficult task; but I could make the matter very clear indeed to you.

Soc. I understand; you mean to say that I am not so quick of apprehension as the judges: for to them you will be sure to prove that the act is unjust, and hateful to the gods.

Euth. Yes, indeed, Socrates; at least if they will listen to me.

Soc. But they will be sure to listen if they find that you are a good speaker. There was a notion that came into my mind while you were speaking; I said to myself: "Well, and what if Euthyphro does prove to me that all the gods regarded the death of the serf as unjust, how do I know anything more of the nature of piety and impiety? for granting that this action may be hateful to the gods, still piety and impiety are not adequately defined by these distinctions, for that which is hateful to the gods has been shown to be also pleasing and dear to them." And therefore, Euthyphro, I do not ask you to prove this; I will suppose, if you like, that all the gods condemn and abominate such an action. But I will amend the definition so far as to say that what all the gods hate is impious, and what they love pious or holy; and what some of them love and others hate is both or neither. Shall this be our definition of piety and impiety?

Euth. Why not, Socrates?

Soc. Why not! certainly, as far as I am concerned, Euthyphro, there is no reason why not. But whether this admission will greatly assist you in the task of instructing me as you promised, is a matter for you to consider.

Euth. Yes, I should say that what all the gods love is pious and holy, and the opposite which they all hate, impious.

Soc. Ought we to enquire into the truth of this, Euthyphro, or simply to accept the mere statement on our own authority and that of others? What do you say?

Euth. We should enquire; and I believe that the statement will stand the test of enquiry.

Soc. We shall know better, my good friend, in a little while. The point which I should first wish to understand is whether the pious or holy is beloved by the gods because it is holy, or holy because it is beloved of the gods.

Euth. I do not understand your meaning, Socrates.

Soc. I will endeavour to explain: we speak of carrying and we speak of being carried, of leading and being led, seeing and being seen. You know that in all such cases there is a difference and you know also in what the difference lies?

Euth. I think that I understand.

Soc. And is not that which is beloved distinct from that which loves?

Euth. Certainly.

Soc. Well; and now tell me, is that which is carried in this state of carrying because it is carried, or for some other reason?

Euth. No; that is the reason.

Soc. And the same is true of what is led and of what is seen?

Euth. True.

Soc. And a thing is not seen because it is visible, but conversely, visible because it is seen; nor is a thing led because it is in the state of being led, or carried because it is in the state of being carried, but the converse of this. And now I think, Euthyphro, that my meaning will be intelligible; and my meaning is, that any state of action or passion implies previous action or passion. It does not become because it is becoming, but it is in a state of becoming because it becomes; neither does it suffer because it is in a state of suffering, but it is in a state of suffering because it suffers. Do you not agree?

Euth. Yes.

Soc. Is not that which is loved in some state either of becoming or suffering?

Euth. Yes.

Soc. And the same holds as in the previous instances; the state of being loved follows the act of being loved, and not the act the state.

Euth. Certainly.

Soc. And what do you say of piety, Euthyphro: is not piety, according to your definition, loved by all the gods?

Euth. Yes.

Soc. Because it is pious or holy, or for some other reason?

Euth. No, that is the reason.

Soc. It is loved because it is holy, not holy because it is loved?

Euth. Yes.

Soc. And that which is dear to the gods is loved by them, and is in a state to be loved of them because it is loved of them?

Euth. Certainly.

Soc. Then that which is dear to the gods, Euthyphro, is not holy, nor is that which is holy loved of God, as you affirm; but they are two different things.

Euth. How do you mean, Socrates?

Soc. I mean to say that the holy has been acknowledged by us to be loved of God because it is holy, not to be holy because it is loved.

Euth. Yes.

Soc. But that which is dear to the gods is dear to them because it is loved by them, not loved by them because it is dear to them.

Euth. True.

Soc. But, friend Euthyphro, if that which is holy is the same with that which is dear to God, and is loved because it is holy, then that which is dear to God would have been loved as being dear to God; but if that which is dear to

God is dear to him because loved by him, then that which is holy would have been holy because loved by him. But now you see that the reverse is the case, and that they are quite different from one another. For one (θεοφιλὲς) is of a kind to be loved because it is loved, and the other (ὅσιον) is loved because it is a kind to be loved. Thus you appear to me, Euthyphro, when I ask you what is the essence of holiness, to offer an attribute only, and not the essence— the attribute of being loved by all the gods. But you still refuse to explain to me the nature of holiness. And therefore, if you please, I will ask you not to hide your treasure, but to tell me once more what holiness or piety really is, whether dear to the gods or not (for that is a matter about which we will not quarrel); and what is impiety?

Euth. I really do not know, Socrates, how to express what I mean. For somehow or other our arguments, on whatever ground we rest them, seem to turn round and walk away from us.

Soc. Your words, Euthyphro, are like the handiwork of my ancestor Daedalus; and if I were the sayer or pro- pounder of them, you might say that my arguments walk away and will not remain fixed where they are placed be- cause I am a descendant of his. But now, since these no- tions are your own, you must find some other gibe, for they certainly, as you yourself allow, show an inclination to be on the move.

Euth. Nay, Socrates, I shall still say that you are the Daedalus who sets arguments in motion; not I, certainly, but you make them move or go round, for they would never have stirred, as far as I am concerned.

Soc. Then I must be a greater than Daedalus: for whereas he only made his own inventions to move, I move those of other people as well. And the beauty of it is, that I would rather not. For I would give the wisdom of Daedalus, and the wealth of Tantalus, to be able to detain them and keep them fixed. But enough of this. As I perceive that you are lazy, I will myself endeavour to show you how you might instruct me in the nature of piety; and I hope that you will not grudge your labour. Tell me, then,—Is not that which is pious necessarily just?

Euth. Yes.

Soc. And is, then, all which is just pious? or, is that which is pious all just, but that which is just, only in part and not all, pious?

Euth. I do not understand you, Socrates.

Soc. And yet I know that you are as much wiser than I am, as you are younger. But, as I was saying, revered friend, the abundance of your wisdom makes you lazy. Please do exert yourself, for there is no real difficulty in understanding me. What I mean I may explain by an illustration of what I do not mean. The poet (Stasinus) sings—

"Of Zeus, the author and creator of all these things,
  You will not tell: for where there is fear there is also
      reverence."

Now I disagree with this poet. Shall I tell you in what respect?

Euth. By all means.

Soc. I should not say that where there is fear there is also reverence; for I am sure that many persons fear poverty and disease, and the like evils, but I do not perceive that they reverence the objects of their fear.

Euth. Very true.

Soc. But where reverence is, there is fear; for he who has a feeling of reverence and shame about the commission of any action, fears and is afraid of an ill reputation.

Euth. No doubt.

Soc. Then we are wrong in saying that where there is fear there is also reverence; and we should say, where there is reverence there is also fear. But there is not always reverence where there is fear; for fear is a more extended notion, and reverence is a part of fear, just as the odd is a part of the number, and number is a more extended notion than the odd. I suppose that you follow me now?

Euth. Quite well.

Soc. That was the sort of question which I meant to raise when I asked whether the just is always the pious, or the pious always the just; and whether there may not be justice where there is not piety; for justice is the more extended notion of which piety is only a part. Do you dissent?

Euth. No, I think that you are quite right.

Soc. Then, if piety is a part of justice, I suppose that we should enquire what part? If you had pursued the enquiry in the previous cases; for instance, if you had asked me what is an even number, and what part of number the even is, I should have had no difficulty in replying, a number which represents a figure having two equal sides. Do you not agree?

Euth. Yes, I quite agree.

Soc. In like manner, I want you to tell me what part of justice is piety or holiness, that I may be able to tell Meletus not to do me injustice, or indict me for impiety, as I am now adequately instructed by you in the nature of piety or holiness, and their opposites.

Euth. Piety or holiness, Socrates, appears to me to be that part of justice which attends to the gods, as there is the other part of justice which attends to men.

Soc. That is good, Euthyphro; yet still there is a little point about which I should like to have further information, What is the meaning of "attention"? For attention can hardly be used in the same sense when applied to the gods as when applied to other things. For instance, horses are said to require attention, and not every person is able to attend to them, but only a person skilled in horsemanship. Is it not so?

Euth. Certainly.

Soc. I should suppose that the art of horsemanship is the art of attending to horses?

Euth. Yes.

Soc. Nor is every one qualified to attend to dogs, but only the huntsman?

Euth. True.

Soc. And I should also conceive that the art of the huntsman is the art of attending to dogs?

Euth. Yes.

Soc. As the art of the oxherd is the art of attending to oxen?

Euth. Very true.

Soc. In like manner holiness or piety is the art of attending to the gods?—that would be your meaning, Euthyphro?

Euth. Yes.

Soc. And is not attention always designed for the good or benefit of that to which the attention is given? As in the case of horses, you may observe that when attended to by the horseman's art they are benefited and improved, are they not?

Euth. True.

Soc. As the dogs are benefited by the huntsman's art, and the oxen by the art of the oxherd, and all other things are tended or attended for their good and not for their hurt?

Euth. Certainly, not for their hurt.

Soc. But for their good?

Euth. Of course.

Soc. And does piety or holiness, which has been defined to be the art of attending to the gods, benefit or improve them? Would you say that when you do a holy act you make any of the gods better?

Euth. No, no; that was certainly not what I meant.

Soc. And I, Euthyphro, never supposed that you did. I asked you the question about the nature of the attention, because I thought that you did not.

Euth. You do me justice, Socrates; that is not the sort of attention which I mean.

Soc. Good: but I must still ask what is this attention to the gods which is called piety?

Euth. It is such, Socrates, as servants show to their masters.

Soc. I understand—a sort of ministration to the gods.

Euth. Exactly.

Soc. Medicine is also a sort of ministration or service, having in view the attainment of some object—would you not say of health?

Euth. I should.

Soc. Again, there is an art which ministers to the ship-builder with a view to the attainment of some result?

Euth. Yes, Socrates, with a view to the building of a ship.

Soc. As there is an art which ministers to the house-builder with a view to the building of a house?

Euth. Yes.

Soc. And now tell me, my good friend, about the art which ministers to the gods: what work does that help to accomplish? For you must surely know if, as you say, you are of all men living the one who is best instructed in religion.

Euth. And I speak the truth, Socrates.

Soc. Tell me, then, oh, tell me—what is that fair work which the gods do by the help of our ministrations?

Euth. Many and fair, Socrates, are the works which they do.

Soc. Why, my friend, and so are those of a general. But the chief of them is easily told. Would you not say that victory in war is the chief of them?

Euth. Certainly.

Soc. Many and fair, too, are the works of the husband-man, if I am not mistaken; but his chief work is the production of food from the earth?

Euth. Exactly.

Soc. And of the many and fair things done by the gods, which is the chief or principal one?

Euth. I have told you already, Socrates, that to learn all these things accurately will be very tiresome. Let me simply say that piety or holiness is learning how to please the gods in word and deed, by prayers and sacrifices. Such piety is the salvation of families and States, just as the impious, which is unpleasing to the gods, is their ruin and destruction.

Soc. I think that you could have answered in much fewer words the chief question which I asked, Euthyphro, if you had chosen. But I see plainly that you are not disposed to instruct me—clearly not: else why, when we reached the point, did you turn aside? Had you only answered me, I should have truly learned of you by this time the nature of piety. Now, as the asker of a question is necessarily dependent on the answerer, whither he leads I must follow; and can only ask again, what is the pious, and what is piety? Do you mean that they are a sort of science of praying and sacrificing?

Euth. Yes, I do.

Soc. And sacrificing is giving to the gods, and prayer is asking of the gods?

Euth. Yes, Socrates.

Soc. Upon this view, then, piety is a science of asking and giving?

Euth. You understand me capitally, Socrates.

Soc. Yes, my friend; the reason is that I am a votary of your science, and give my mind to it, and therefore nothing which you say will be thrown away upon me. Please then to tell me, what is the nature of this service to the gods? Do you mean that we prefer requests and give gifts to them?

Euth. Yes, I do.

Soc. Is not the right way of asking to ask of them what we want?

Euth. Certainly.

Soc. And the right way of giving is to give to them in return what they want of us. There would be no meaning in an art which gives to any one that which he does not want.

Euth. Very true, Socrates.

Soc. Then piety, Euthyphro, is an art which gods and men have of doing business with one another?

Euth. That is an expression which you may use, if you like.

Soc. But I have no particular liking for anything but the truth. I wish, however, that you would tell me what benefit accrues to the gods from our gifts. There is no doubt about what they give to us; for there is no good thing which they do not give; but how we can give any good thing to them in return is far from being equally clear. If they give everything and we give nothing, that. must be an affair of business in which we have very greatly the advantage of them.

Euth. And do you imagine, Socrates, that any benefit accrues to the gods from our gifts?

Soc. But if not, Euthyphro, what is the meaning of gifts which are conferred by us upon the gods?

Euth. What else, but tributes of honour; and, as I was just now saying, what pleases them?

Soc. Piety, then, is pleasing to the gods, but not beneficial or dear to them?

Euth. I should say that nothing could be dearer.

Soc. Then once more the assertion is repeated that piety is dear to the gods?

Euth. Certainly.

Soc. And when you say this, can you wonder at your words not standing firm, but walking away? Will you accuse me of being the Daedalus who makes them walk away, not perceiving that there is another and far greater artist than Daedalus who makes them go round in a circle, and he is yourself; for the argument, as you will perceive, comes round to the same point. Were we not saying that the holy or pious was not the same with that which is loved of the gods? Have you forgotten?

Euth. I quite remember.

Soc. And are you not saying that what is loved of the gods is holy; and is not this the same as what is dear to them—do you see?

Euth. True.

Soc. Then either we were wrong in our former assertion; or, if we were right then, we are wrong now.

Euth. One of the two must be true.

Soc. Then we must begin again and ask, What is piety? That is an enquiry which I shall never be weary of pursuing as far as in me lies; and I entreat you not to scorn me, but to apply your mind to the utmost, and tell me the truth. For, if any man knows, you are he; and therefore I must detain you, like Proteus, until you tell. If you had not certainly known the nature of piety and impiety, I am confident that you would never, on behalf of a serf, have charged your aged father with murder. You would not have run such a risk of doing wrong in the sight of the gods, and you would have had too much respect for the opinions of men. I am sure, therefore, that you know the nature of piety and impiety. Speak out then, my dear Euthyphro, and do not hide your knowledge.

Euth. Another time, Socrates; for I am in a hurry, and must go now.

Soc. Alas! my companion, and will you leave me in despair? I was hoping that you would instruct me in the nature of piety and impiety; and then I might have cleared myself of Meletus and his indictment. I would have told him that I had been enlightened by Euthyphro, and had given up rash innovations and speculations, in which I indulged only through ignorance, and that now I am about to lead a better life.

APOLOGY

APOLOGY

How you, O Athenians, have been affected by my accusers, I cannot tell; but I know that they almost made me forget who I was—so persuasively did they speak; and yet they have hardly uttered a word of truth. But of the many falsehoods told by them, there was one which quite amazed me;—I mean when they said that you should be upon your guard and not allow yourselves to be deceived by the force of my eloquence. To say this, when they were certain to be detected as soon as I opened my lips and proved myself to be anything but a great speaker, did indeed appear to me most shameless—unless by the force of eloquence they mean the force of truth; for if such is their meaning, I admit that I am eloquent. But in how different a way from theirs! Well, as I was saying, they have scarcely spoken the truth at all; but from me you shall hear the whole truth: not, however, delivered after their manner in a set oration duly ornamented with words and phrases. No, by heaven! but I shall use the words and arguments which occur to me at the moment; for I am confident in the justice of my cause:[1] at my time of life I ought not to be appearing before you, O men of Athens, in the character of a juvenile orator—let no one expect it of me. And I must beg of you to grant me a favour:— If I defend myself in my accustomed manner, and you hear me using the words which I have been in the habit of using in the agora, at the tables of the money-changers, or anywhere else, I would ask you not to be surprised, and not to interrupt me on this account. For I am more than seventy years of age, and appearing now for the first time

[1] Or, I am certain that I am right in taking this course.

59

in a court of law, I am quite a stranger to the language of the place; and therefore I would have you regard me as if I were really a stranger, whom you would excuse if he spoke in his native tongue, and after the fashion of his country:—Am I making an unfair request of you? Never mind the manner, which may or may not be good; but think only of the truth of my words, and give heed to that: let the speaker speak truly and the judge decide justly.

And first, I have to reply to the older charges and to my first accusers, and then I will go on to the later ones. For of old I have had many accusers, who have accused me falsely to you during many years; and I am more afraid of them than of Anytus and his associates, who are dangerous, too, in their own way. But far more dangerous are the others, who began when you were children, and took possession of your minds with their falsehoods, telling of one Socrates, a wise man, who speculated about the heaven above, and searched into the earth beneath, and made the worse appear the better cause. The disseminators of this tale are the accusers whom I dread; for their hearers are apt to fancy that such enquirers do not believe in the existence of the gods. And they are many, and their charges against me are of ancient date, and they were made by them in the days when you were more impressible than you are now—in childhood, or it may have been in youth—and the cause when heard went by default, for there was none to answer. And hardest of all, I do not know and cannot tell the names of my accusers; unless in the chance case of a comic poet. All who from envy and malice have persuaded you—some of them having first convinced themselves—all this class of men are most difficult to deal with; for I cannot have them up here, and cross-examine them, and therefore I must simply fight with shadows in my own defence, and argue when there is no one who answers. I will ask you then to assume with me, as I was saying, that my opponents are of two kinds; one recent, the other ancient: and I hope that you will see the propriety of my answering the latter first, for these accusations you heard long before the others, and much oftener.

Well, then, I must make my defence, and endeavour to clear away in a short time, a slander which has lasted a long time. May I succeed, if to succeed be for my good and yours, or likely to avail me in my cause! The task is not an easy one; I quite understand the nature of it. And so leaving the event with God, in obedience to the law I will now make my defence.

I will begin at the beginning, and ask what is the accusation which has given rise to the slander of me, and in fact has encouraged Meletus to prefer this charge against me. Well, what do the slanderers say? They shall be my prosecutors, and I will sum up their words in an affidavit: "Socrates is an evildoer, and a curious person, who searches into things under the earth and in heaven, and he makes the worse appear the better cause; and he teaches the aforesaid doctrines to others." Such is the nature of the accusation: it is just what you have yourselves seen in the comedy of Aristophanes,[1] who has introduced a man whom he calls Socrates, going about and saying that he walks in air, and talking a deal of nonsense concerning matters of which I do not pretend to know either much or little—not that I mean to speak disparagingly of any one who is a student of natural philosophy. I should be very sorry if Meletus could bring so grave a charge against me. But the simple truth is, O Athenians, that I have nothing to do with physical speculations. Very many of those here present are witnesses to the truth of this, and to them I appeal. Speak then, you who have heard me, and tell your neighbours whether any of you have ever known me hold forth in few words or in many upon such matters. . . . You hear their answer. And from what they say of this part

---

[1] Aristoph., Clouds, 225 ff.

of the charge you will be able to judge of the truth of the rest.

As little foundation is there for the report that I am a teacher, and take money; this accusation has no more truth in it than the other. Although, if a man were really able to instruct mankind, to receive money for giving instruction would, in my opinion, be an honour to him. There is Gorgias of Leontium, and Prodicus of Ceos, and Hippias of Elis, who go the round of the cities, and are able to persuade the young men to leave their own citizens by whom they might be taught for nothing, and come to them whom they not only pay, but are thankful if they may be allowed to pay them. There is at this time a Parian philosopher residing in Athens, of whom I have heard; and I came to hear of him in this way:—I came across a man who has spent a world of money on the Sophists, Callias, the son of Hipponicus, and knowing that he had sons, I asked him: "Callias," I said, "if your two sons were foals or calves, there would be no difficulty in finding some one to put over them; we should hire a trainer of horses, or a farmer, probably, who would improve and perfect them in their own proper virtue and excellence; but as they are human beings, whom are you thinking of placing over them? Is there any one who understands human and political virtue? You must have thought about the matter, for you have sons; is there any one?" "There is," he said. "Who is he?" said I; "and of what country? and what does he charge?" "Evenus the Parian," he replied; "he is the man, and his charge is five minae." Happy is Evenus, I said to myself, if he really has this wisdom, and teaches at such a moderate charge. Had I the same, I should have been very proud and conceited; but the truth is that I have no knowledge of the kind.

I dare say, Athenians, that some one among you will reply, "Yes, Socrates, but what is the origin of these accusations which are brought against you; there must have been something strange which you have been doing? All these rumours and this talk about you would never have arisen if you had been like other men: tell us, then, what is the cause of them, for we should be sorry to judge hastily of you." Now, I regard this as a fair challenge, and I will endeavour to explain to you the reason why I am called wise and have such an evil fame. Please to attend then. And although some of you may think that I am joking, I declare that I will tell you the entire truth. Men of Athens, this reputation of mine has come of a certain sort of wisdom which I possess. If you ask me what kind of wisdom, I reply, wisdom such as may perhaps be attained by man, for to that extent I am inclined to believe that I am wise; whereas the persons of whom I was speaking have a superhuman wisdom, which I may fail to describe, because I have it not myself; and he who says that I have, speaks falsely, and is taking away my character. And here, O men of Athens, I must beg you not to interrupt me, even if I seem to say something extravagant. For the word which I will speak is not mine. I will refer you to a witness who is worthy of credit; that witness shall be the god of Delphi—he will tell you about my wisdom, if I have any, and of what sort it is. You must have known Chaerephon; he was early a friend of mine, and also a friend of yours, for he shared in the recent exile of the people, and returned with you. Well, Chaerephon, as you know, was very impetuous in all his doings, and he went to Delphi and boldly asked the oracle to tell him whether—as I was saying, I must beg you not to interrupt—he asked the oracle to tell him whether any one was wiser than I was, and the Pythian prophetess answered, that there was no man wiser. Chaerephon is dead himself; but his brother, who is in court, will confirm the truth of what I am saying.

Why do I mention this? Because I am going to explain to you why I have such an evil name. When I heard the answer, I said to myself, What can the god mean? and

what is the interpretation of his riddle? for I know that
I have no wisdom, small or great. What then can he mean
when he says that I am the wisest of men? And yet he is
a god, and cannot lie; that would be against his nature.
After long consideration, I thought of a method of trying
the question. I reflected that if I could only find a man
wiser than myself, then I might go to the god with a refutation in my hand. I should say to him, "Here is a man who
is wiser than I am; but you said that I was the wisest."
Accordingly I went to one who had the reputation of wisdom, and observed him—his name I need not mention; he
was a politician whom I selected for examination—and the
result was as follows: When I began to talk with him, I
could not help thinking that he was not really wise, although
he was thought wise by many, and still wiser by himself;
and thereupon I tried to explain to him that he thought
himself wise, but was not really wise; and the consequence
was that he hated me, and his enmity was shared by several
who were present and heard me. So I left him, saying to
myself, as I went away: Well, although I do not suppose
that either of us knows anything really beautiful and good,
I am better off than he is,—for he knows nothing, and thinks
that he knows; I neither know nor think that I know. In
this latter particular, then, I seem to have slightly the advantage of him. Then I went to another who had still higher
pretensions to wisdom, and my conclusion was exactly the
same. Whereupon I made another enemy of him, and of
many others besides him.

Then I went to one man after another, being not unconscious of the enmity which I provoked, and I lamented and
feared this: but necessity was laid upon me,—the word of
God, I thought, ought to be considered first. And I said to
myself, Go I must to all who appear to know, and find out
the meaning of the oracle. And I swear to you, Athenians,
by the dog I swear!—for I must tell you the truth—the

result of my mission was just this: I found that the men most in repute were all but the most foolish; and that others less esteemed were really wiser and better. I will tell you the tale of my wanderings and of the "Herculean" labours, as I may call them, which I endured only to find at last the oracle irrefutable. After the politicians, I went to the poets; tragic, dithyrambic, and all sorts. And there, I said to myself, you will be instantly detected; now you will find out that you are more ignorant than they are. Accordingly I took them some of the most elaborate passages in their own writings, and asked what was the meaning of them—thinking that they would teach me something. Will you believe me? I am almost ashamed to confess the truth, but I must say that there is hardly a person present who would not have talked better about their poetry than they did themselves. Then I knew that not by wisdom do poets write poetry, but by a sort of genius and inspiration; they are like diviners or soothsayers who also say many fine things, but do not understand the meaning of them. The poets appeared to me to be much in the same case; and I further observed that upon the strength of their poetry they believed themselves to be the wisest of men in other things in which they were not wise. So I departed, conceiving myself to be superior to them for the same reason that I was superior to the politicians.

At last I went to the artisans. I was conscious that I knew nothing at all, as I may say, and I was sure that they knew many fine things; and here I was not mistaken, for they did know many things of which I was ignorant, and in this they certainly were wiser than I was. But I observed that even the good artisans fell into the same error as the poets; —because they were good workmen they thought that they also knew all sorts of high matters, and this defect in them overshadowed their wisdom; and therefore I asked myself on behalf of the oracle, whether I would like to be as I was, neither having their knowledge nor their ignorance, or like them in both; and I made answer to myself and to the oracle that I was better off as I was.

This inquisition has led to my having many enemies of the worst and most dangerous kind, and has given occasion also to many calumnies. And I am called wise, for my hearers always imagine that I myself possess the wisdom which I find wanting in others: but the truth is, O men of Athens, that God only is wise; and by his answer he intends to show that the wisdom of men is worth little or nothing; he is not speaking of Socrates, he is only using my name by way of illustration, as if he said, He, O men, is the wisest, who, like Socrates, knows that his wisdom is in truth worth nothing. And so I go about the world obedient to the god, and search and make enquiry into the wisdom of any one, whether citizen or stranger, who appears to be wise; and if he is not wise, then in vindication of the oracle I show him that he is not wise; and my occupation quite absorbs me, and I have no time to give either to any public matter of interest or to any concern of my own, but I am in utter poverty by reason of my devotion to the god.

There is another thing:—young men of the richer classes, who have not much to do, come about me of their own accord; they like to hear the pretenders examined, and they often imitate me, and proceed to examine others; there are plenty of persons, as they quickly discover, who think that they know something, but really know little or nothing; and then those who are examined by them instead of being angry with themselves are angry with me: This confounded Socrates, they say; this villainous misleader of youth!—and then if somebody asks them, Why, what evil does he practise or teach? they do not know, and cannot tell; but in order that they may not appear to be at a loss, they repeat the ready-made charges which are used against all philosophers about teaching things up in the clouds and under the earth, and having no gods, and making the worse appear the better cause; for they do not like to confess that their pretence of knowledge has been detected—which is the truth; and as they are numerous and ambitious and energetic, and are drawn up in battle array and have persuasive tongues, they have filled your ears with their loud and inveterate calumnies. And this is the reason why my three accusers, Meletus and Anytus and Lycon, have set upon me; Meletus, who has a quarrel with me on behalf of the poets; Anytus, on behalf of the craftsmen and politicians; Lycon, on behalf of the rhetoricians: and, as I said at the beginning, I cannot expect to get rid of such a mass of calumny all in a moment. And this, O men of Athens, is the truth and the whole truth; I have concealed nothing, I have dissembled nothing. And yet, I know that my plainness of speech makes them hate me, and what is their hatred but a proof that I am speaking the truth? Hence has arisen the prejudice against me; and this is the reason of it, as you will find out either in this or in any future enquiry.

I have said enough in my defence against the first class of my accusers; I turn to the second class. They are headed by Meletus, that good man and true lover of his country, as he calls himself. Against these, too, I must try to make a defence:—Let their affidavit be read: it contains something of this kind: It says that Socrates is a doer of evil, who corrupts the youth; and who does not believe in the gods of the State, but has other new divinities of his own. Such is the charge; and now let us examine the particular counts. He says that I am a doer of evil, and corrupt the youth; but I say, O men of Athens, that Meletus is a doer of evil, in that he pretends to be in earnest when he is only in jest, and is so eager to bring men to trial from a pretended zeal and interest about matters in which he really never had the smallest interest. And the truth of this I will endeavour to prove to you.

Come hither, Meletus, and let me ask a question of you. You think a great deal about the improvement of youth?

Yes, I do.

Tell the judges, then, who is their improver; for you must know, as you have taken the pains to discover their corrupter, and are citing and accusing me before them. Speak, then, and tell the judges who their improver is.—Observe, Meletus, that you are silent, and have nothing to say. But is not this rather disgraceful, and a very considerable proof of what I was saying, that you have no interest in the matter? Speak up, friend, and tell us who their improver is.

The laws.

But that, my good sir, is not my meaning. I want to know who the person is, who, in the first place, knows the laws.

The judges, Socrates, who are present in court.

What, do you mean to say, Meletus, that they are able to instruct and improve youth?

Certainly they are.

What, all of them, or some only and not others?

All of them.

By the goddess Here, that is good news! There are plenty of improvers, then. And what do you say of the audience,—do they improve them?

Yes, they do.

And the senators?

Yes, the senators improve them.

But perhaps the members of the assembly corrupt them? —or do they improve them?

They improve them.

Then every Athenian improves and elevates them; all with the exception of myself; and I alone am their corrupter? Is that what you affirm?

That is what I stoutly affirm.

I am very unfortunate if you are right. But suppose I ask you a question: How about horses? Does one man do them harm and all the world good? Is not the exact opposite the truth? One man is able to do them good, or at least not many;—the trainer of horses, that is to say, does them

good, and others who have to do with them rather injure
them? Is not that true, Meletus, of horses, or of any other
animals? Most assuredly it is; whether you and Anytus say
yes or no. Happy indeed would be the condition of youth
if they had one corrupter only, and all the rest of the world
were their improvers. But you, Meletus, have sufficiently
shown that you never had a thought about the young: your
carelessness is seen in your not caring about the very things
which you bring against me.

And now, Meletus, I will ask you another question—by
Zeus I will: Which is better, to live among bad citizens, or
among good ones? Answer, friend, I say; the question is
one which may be easily answered. Do not the good do their
neighbours good, and the bad do them evil?

Certainly.

And is there any one who would rather be injured than
benefited by those who live with him? Answer, my good
friend, the law requires you to answer—does any one like
to be injured?

Certainly not.

And when you accuse me of corrupting and deteriorating
the youth, do you allege that I corrupt them intentionally
or unintentionally?

Intentionally, I say.

But you have just admitted that the good do their neighbours good, and the evil do them evil. Now, is that a truth
which your superior wisdom has recognized thus early in
life, and am I, at my age, in such darkness and ignorance
as not to know that if a man with whom I have to live is
corrupted by me, I am very likely to be harmed by him;
and yet I corrupt him, and intentionally, too—so you say,
although neither I nor any other human being is ever likely
to be convinced by you. But either I do not corrupt them,
or I corrupt them unintentionally; and on either view of the
case you lie. If my offence is unintentional, the law has no
cognizance of unintentional offences: you ought to have

taken me privately, and warned and admonished me; for if
I had been better advised, I should have left off doing what
I only did unintentionally—no doubt I should; but you
would have nothing to say to me and refused to teach me.
And now you bring me up in this court, which is a place
not of instruction, but of punishment.

It will be very clear to you, Athenians, as I was saying,
that Meletus has no care at all, great or small, about the
matter. But still I should like to know, Meletus, in what I
am affirmed to corrupt the young. I suppose you mean, as
I infer from your indictment, that I teach them not to
acknowledge the gods which the State acknowledges, but
some other new divinities or spiritual agencies in their stead.
These are the lessons by which I corrupt the youth, as you
say.

Yes, that I say emphatically.

Then, by the gods, Meletus, of whom we are speaking,
tell me and the court, in somewhat plainer terms, what you
mean! For I do not as yet understand whether you affirm
that I teach other men to acknowledge some gods, and
therefore that I do believe in gods, and am not an entire
atheist—this you do not lay to my charge,—but only you
say that they are not the same gods which the city recognizes—the charge is that they are different gods. Or, do you
mean that I am an atheist simply, and a teacher of atheism?

I mean the latter—that you are a complete atheist.

What an extraordinary statement! Why do you think so,
Meletus? Do you mean that I do not believe in the god-
head of the sun or moon, like other men?

I assure you, judges, that he does not: for he says that
the sun is stone, and the moon earth.

Friend Meletus, you think that you are accusing Anaxagoras: and you have but a bad opinion of the judges, if you
fancy them illiterate to such a degree as not to know that
these doctrines are found in the books of Anaxagoras the
Clazomenian, which are full of them. And so, forsooth, the

youth are said to be taught them by Socrates, when there are not infrequently exhibitions of them at the theatre[1] (price of admission one drachma at the most); and they might pay their money, and laugh at Socrates if he pretends to father these extraordinary views. And so, Meletus, you really think that I do not believe in any god?

I swear by Zeus that you believe absolutely in none at all.

Nobody will believe you, Meletus, and I am pretty sure that you do not believe yourself. I cannot help thinking, men of Athens, that Meletus is reckless and impudent, and that he has written this indictment in a spirit of mere wantonness and youthful bravado. Has he not compounded a riddle, thinking to try me? He said to himself:—I shall see whether the wise Socrates will discover my facetious contradiction, or whether I shall be able to deceive him and the rest of them. For he certainly does appear to me to con-tradict himself in the indictment as much as if he said that Socrates is guilty of not believing in the gods, and yet of believing in them—but this is not like a person who is in earnest.

I should like you, O men of Athens, to join me in exam-ing what I conceive to be his inconsistency; and do you, Meletus, answer. And I must remind the audience of my request that they would not make a disturbance if I speak in my accustomed manner:

Did ever man, Meletus, believe in the existence of human things, and not of human beings? . . . I wish, men of Athens, that he would answer, and not be always trying to get up an interruption. Did ever any man believe in horse-manship, and not in horses? or in flute-playing, and not in flute-players? No, my friend; I will answer to you and to the court, as you refuse to answer for yourself. There is no man who ever did. But now please to answer the next ques-

[1] Probably in allusion to Aristophanes who caricatured, and to Euripides who borrowed the notions of Anaxagoras, as well as to other dramatic poets.

tion: Can a man believe in spiritual and divine agencies, and not in spirits or demigods?

He cannot.

How lucky I am to have extracted that answer, by the assistance of the court! But then you swear in the indictment that I teach and believe in divine or spiritual agencies (new or old, no matter for that); at any rate, I believe in spiritual agencies,—so you say and swear in the affidavit; and yet if I believe in divine beings, how can I help believing in spirits or demigods;—must I not? To be sure I must; and therefore I may assume that your silence gives consent. Now what are spirits or demigods? are they not either gods or the sons of gods?

Certainly they are.

But this is what I call the facetious riddle invented by you: the demigods or spirits are gods, and you say first that I do not believe in gods, and then again that I do believe in gods; that is, if I believe in demigods. For if the demigods are the illegitimate sons of gods, whether by the nymphs or by any other mothers, of whom they are said to be the sons—what human being will ever believe that there are no gods if they are the sons of gods? You might as well affirm the existence of mules, and deny that of horses and asses. Such nonsense, Meletus, could only have been intended by you to make trial of me. You have put this into the indictment because you had nothing real of which to accuse me. But no one who has a particle of understanding will ever be convinced by you that the same men can believe in divine and superhuman things, and yet not believe that there are gods and demigods and heroes.

I have said enough in answer to the charge of Meletus: any elaborate defence is unnecessary; but I know only too well how many are the enmities which I have incurred, and this is what will be my destruction if I am destroyed;—not Meletus, nor yet Anytus, but the envy and detraction of the world, which has been the death of many good men, and will probably be the death of many more; there is no danger of my being the last of them.

Some one will say: And are you not ashamed, Socrates, of a course of life which is likely to bring you to an untimely end? To him I may fairly answer: There you are mistaken: a man who is good for anything ought not to calculate the chance of living or dying; he ought only to consider whether in doing anything he is doing right or wrong—acting the part of a good man or of a bad. Whereas, upon your view, the heroes who fell at Troy were not good for much, and the son of Thetis above all, who altogether despised danger in comparison with disgrace; and when he was so eager to slay Hector, his goddess mother said to him, that if he avenged his companion Patroclus, and slew Hector, he would die himself—"Fate," she said, in these or the like words, "waits for you next after Hector"; he, receiving this warning, utterly despised danger and death, and instead of fearing them, feared rather to live in dishonour, and not to avenge his friend. "Let me die forthwith," he replies, "and be avenged of my enemy, rather than abide here by the beaked ships, a laughing stock and a burden of the earth." Had Achilles any thought of death and danger? For wherever a man's place is, whether the place which he has chosen or that in which he has been placed by a commander, there he ought to remain in the hour of danger; he should not think of death or of anything but of disgrace. And this, O men of Athens, is a true saying.

Strange, indeed, would be my conduct, O men of Athens, if I, who, when I was ordered by the generals whom you chose to command me at Potidaea and Amphipolis and Delium, remained where they placed me, like any other man, facing death—if now, when, as I conceive and imagine, God orders me to fulfil the philosopher's mission of searching into myself and other men, I were to desert my post through fear of death, or any other fear; that would indeed by strange, and I might justly be arraigned in court for denying the existence of the gods, if I disobeyed the oracle because I was afraid of death, fancying that I was wise when I was not wise. For the fear of death is indeed the pretence of wisdom, and not real wisdom, being a pretence of knowing the unknown; and no one knows whether death, which men in their fear apprehend to be the greatest evil, may not be the greatest good. Is not this ignorance of a disgraceful sort, the ignorance which is the conceit that a man knows what he does not know? And in this respect only I believe myself to differ from men in general, and may perhaps claim to be wiser than they are:—that whereas I know but little of the world below, I do not suppose that I know: but I do know that injustice and disobedience to a better, whether God or man, is evil and dishonourable, and I will never fear or avoid a possible good rather than a certain evil. And therefore if you let me go now, and are not convinced by Anytus, who said that since I had been prosecuted I must be put to death; (or if not that I ought never to have been prosecuted at all); and that if I escape now, your sons will all be utterly ruined by listening to my words—if you say to me, Socrates, this time we will not mind Anytus, and you shall be let off, but upon one condition, that you are not to enquire and speculate in this way any more, and that if you are caught doing so again you shall die;—if this was the condition on which you let me go, I should reply: Men of Athens, I honour and love you; but I shall obey God rather than you, and while I have life and strength I shall never cease from the practice and teaching of philosophy, exhorting any one whom I meet and saying to him after my manner: You, my friend,—a citizen of the great and mighty and wise city of Athens,—are you not ashamed of heaping up the greatest amount of money and honour and reputation, and caring so little about wisdom and truth and the greatest improvement of the soul, which you never regard or heed at all? And if the person with whom I am arguing, says: Yes, but I do care; then I do not leave him or let him go at once; but I proceed to interrogate and examine and cross-examine him, and if I think that he has no virtue in him, but only says that he has, I reproach him with undervaluing the greater, and overvaluing the less. And I shall repeat the same words to every one whom I meet, young and old, citizen and alien, but especially to the citizens, inasmuch as they are my brethren. For know that this is the command of God; and I believe that no greater good has ever happened in the State than my service to the God. For I do nothing but go about persuading you all, old and young alike, not to take thought for your persons or your properties, but first and chiefly to care about the greatest improvement of the soul. I tell you that virtue is not given by money, but that from virtue comes money and every other good of man, public as well as private. This is my teaching, and if this is the doctrine which corrupts the youth, I am a mischievous person. But if any one says that this is not my teaching, he is speaking an untruth. Wherefore, O men of Athens, I say to you, do as Anytus bids or not as Anytus bids, and either acquit me or not; but whichever you do, understand that I shall never alter my ways, not even if I have to die many times.

Men of Athens, do not interrupt, but hear me; there was an understanding between us that you should hear me to the end: I have something more to say, at which you may be inclined to cry out; but I believe that to hear me will be good for you, and therefore I beg that you will not cry out. I would have you know, that if you kill such an one as I am, you will injure yourselves more than you will injure me. Nothing will injure me, not Meletus nor yet Anytus— they cannot, for a bad man is not permitted to injure a better than himself. I do not deny that Anytus may, per- haps, kill him, or drive him into exile, or deprive him of civil rights; and he may imagine, and others may imagine, that he is inflicting a great injury upon him: but there I do not

agree. For the evil of doing as he is doing—the evil of unjustly taking away the life of another—is greater far.

And now, Athenians, I am not going to argue for my own
sake, as you may think, but for yours, that you may not
sin against the God by condemning me, who am his gift to
you. For if you kill me you will not easily find a successor
to me, who, if I may use such a ludicrous figure of speech,
am a sort of gadfly, given to the State by God; and the
State is a great and noble steed who is tardy in his motions
owing to his very size, and requires to be stirred into life.
I am that gadfly which God has attached to the State, and
all day long and in all places am always fastening upon you,
arousing and persuading and reproaching you. You will not
easily find another like me, and therefore I would advise
you to spare me. I dare say that you may feel out of temper
(like a person who is suddenly awakened from sleep), and
you think that you might easily strike me dead as Anytus
advises, and then you would sleep on for the remainder of
your lives, unless God in his care of you sent you another
gadfly. When I say that I am given to you by God, the
proof of my mission is this:—if I had been like other men,
I should not have neglected all my own concerns or patiently seen the neglect of them during all these years, and
have been doing yours, coming to you individually like a
father or elder brother, exhorting you to regard virtue; such
conduct, I say, would be unlike human nature. If I had
gained anything, or if my exhortations had been paid, there
would have been some sense in my doing so; but now, as
you will perceive, not even the impudence of my accusers
dares to say that I have ever exacted or sought pay of any
one; of that they have no witness. And I have a sufficient
witness to the truth of what I say—my poverty.

Some one may wonder why I go about in private giving
advice and busying myself with the concerns of others, but
do not venture to come forward in public and advise the
State. I will tell you why. You have heard me speak at

sundry times and in divers places of an oracle or sign which comes to me, and is the divinity which Meletus ridicules in the indictment. This sign, which is a kind of voice, first began to come to me when I was a child; it always forbids but never commands me to do anything which I am going to do. This is what deters me from being a politician. And rightly, as I think. For I am certain, O men of Athens, that if I had engaged in politics, I should have perished long ago, and done no good either to you or to myself. And do not be offended at my telling you the truth: for the truth is, that no man who goes to war with you or any other multitude, honestly striving against the many lawless and unrighteous deeds which are done in a State, will save his life; he who will fight for the right, if he would live even for a brief space, must have a private station and not a public one.

I can give you convincing evidence of what I say, not words only, but what you value far more—actions. Let me relate to you a passage of my own life which will prove to you that I should never have yielded to injustice from any fear of death and that "as I should have refused to yield" I must have died at once. I will tell you a tale of the courts, not very interesting perhaps, but nevertheless true. The only office of State which I ever held, O men of Athens, was that of senator: the tribe Antiochis, which is my tribe, had the presidency at the trial of the generals who had not taken up the bodies of the slain after the battle of Arginusae; and you proposed to try them in a body, contrary to law, as you all thought afterwards; but at the time I was the only one of the Prytanes who was opposed to the illegality, and I gave my vote against you; and when the orators threatened to impeach and arrest me, and you called and shouted, I made up my mind that I would run the risk, having law and justice with me, rather than take part in your injustice because I feared imprisonment and death. This happened in the days of the democracy. But when the ɔligarchy of the Thirty was in power, they sent for me and four others into the rotunda, and bade us bring Leon the Salaminian from Salamis, as they wanted to put him to death. This was a specimen of the sort of commands which they were always giving with the view of implicating as many as possible in their crimes; and then I showed, not in word only but in deed, that, if I may be allowed to use such an expression, I cared not a straw for death, and that my great and only care was lest I should do an unrighteous or unholy thing. For the strong arm of that oppressive power did not frighten me into doing wrong; and when we came out of the rotunda the other four went to Salamis and fetched Leon, but I went quietly home. For which I might have lost my life, had not the power of the Thirty shortly afterwards come to an end. And many will witness to my words.

Now, do you really imagine that I could have survived all these years, if I had led a public life, supposing that like a good man I had always maintained the right and had made justice, as I ought, the first thing? No, indeed, men of Athens, neither I nor any other man. But I have been always the same in all my actions, public as well as private, and never have I yielded any base compliance to those who are slanderously termed my disciples, or to any other. Not that I have any regular disciples. But if any one likes to come and hear me while I am pursuing my mission, whether he be young or old, he is not excluded. Nor do I converse only with those who pay; but any one, whether he be rich or poor, may ask and answer me and listen to my words; and whether he turns out to be a bad man or a good one, neither result can be justly imputed to me; for I never taught or professed to teach him anything. And if any one says that he has ever learned or heard anything from me in private which all the world has not heard, let me tell you that he is lying.

But I shall be asked, Why do people delight in continually conversing with you? I have told you already, Athenians, the whole truth about this matter: they like to hear the cross-examination of the pretenders to wisdom; there is amusement in it. Now, this duty of cross-examining other men has been imposed upon me by God; and has been signified to me by oracles, visions, and in every way in which the will of divine power was ever intimated to any one. This is true, O Athenians; or, if not true, would be soon refuted. If I am or have been corrupting the youth, those of them who are now grown up and have become sensible that I gave them bad advice in the days of their youth should come forward as accusers, and take their revenge; or if they do not like to come themselves, some of their relatives, fathers, brothers, or other kinsmen, should say what evil their families have suffered at my hands Now is their time. Many of them I see in the court. There is Crito, who is of the same age and of the same deme with myself, and there is Critobulus his son, whom I also see. Then again there is Lysanias of Sphettus, who is the father of Aeschines—he is present; and also there is Antiphon of Cephisus, who is the father of Epigenes; and there are the brothers of several who have associated with me. There is Nicostratus the son of Theosdotides, and the brother of Theodotus (now Theodotus himself is dead, and therefore he, at any rate, will not seek to stop him); and there is Paralus the son of Demodocus, who had a brother Theages; and Adeimantus the son of Ariston, whose brother Plato is present; and Aeantodorus, who is the brother of Apollodorus, whom I also see. I might mention a great many others, some of whom Meletus should have produced as witnesses in the course of his speech; and let him still produce them, if he has forgotten—I will make way for him. And let him say, if he has any testimony of the sort which he can produce. Nay, Athenians, the very opposite is the truth. For all these are ready to witness on behalf of the corrupter, of the injurer of their kindred, as Meletus and

Anytus call me; not the corrupted youth only—there might have been a motive for that—but their uncorrupted elder relatives. Why should they too support me with their testimony? Why, indeed, except for the sake of truth and justice, and because they know that I am speaking the truth, and that Meletus is a liar.

Well, Athenians, this and the like of this is all the defence which I have to offer. Yet a word more. Perhaps there may be some one who is offended at me, when he calls to mind how he himself on a similar, or even a less serious occasion, prayed and entreated the judges with many tears, and how he produced his children in court, which was a moving spectacle, together with a host of relations and friends; whereas I, who am probably in danger of my life, will do none of these things. The contrast may occur to his mind, and he may be set against me, and vote in anger because he is displeased at me on this account. Now, if there be such a person among you,—mind, I do not say that there is,—to him I may fairly reply: My friend, I am a man, and like other men, a creature of flesh and blood, and not "of wood or stone," as Homer says; and I have a family, yes, and sons, O Athenians, three in number, one almost a man, and two others who are still young; and yet I will not bring any of them hither in order to petition you for an acquittal. And why not? Not from any self-assertion or want of respect for you. Whether I am or am not afraid of death is another question, of which I will not now speak. But, having regard to public opinion, I feel that such conduct would be discreditable to myself, and to you, and to the whole State. One who has reached my years, and who has a name for wisdom, ought not to demean himself. Whether this opinion of me be deserved or not, at any rate the world has decided that Socrates is in some way superior to other men. And if those among you who are said to be superior in wisdom and courage, and any other virtue, demean themselves in this way, how shameful is their conduct! I have seen men of reputation, when they have been condemned, behaving in the strangest manner: they seemed to fancy that they were going to suffer something dreadful if they died, and that they could be immortal if you only allowed them to live; and I think that such are a dishonour to the State, and that any stranger coming in would have said of them that the most eminent men of Athens, to whom the Athenians themselves give honour and command, are no better than women. And I say that these things ought not to be done by those of us who have a reputation; and if they are done, you ought not to permit them; you ought rather to show that you are far more disposed to condemn the man who gets up a doleful scene and makes the city ridiculous, than him who holds his peace.

But, setting aside the question of public opinion, there seems to be something wrong in asking a favour of a judge, and thus procuring an acquittal, instead of informing and convincing him. For his duty is, not to make a present of justice, but to give judgment; and he has sworn that he will judge according to the laws, and not according to his own good pleasure; and we ought not to encourage you, nor should you allow yourselves to be encouraged, in this habit of perjury—there can be no piety in that. Do not then require me to do what I consider dishonourable and impious and wrong, especially now, when I am being tried for impiety on the indictment of Meletus. For if, O men of Athens, by force of persuasion and entreaty I could over-power your oaths, then I should be teaching you to believe that there are no gods, and in defending should simply convict myself of the charge of not believing in them. But that is not so—far otherwise. For I do believe that there are gods, and in a sense higher than that in which any of my accusers believe in them. And to you and to God I commit my cause, to be determined by you as is best for you and me.

There are many reasons why I am not grieved, O men of Athens, at the vote of condemnation. I expected it, and am only surprised that the votes are so nearly equal; for I had thought that the majority against me would have been far larger; but now, had thirty votes gone over to the other side, I should have been acquitted. And I may say, I think, that I have escaped Meletus. I may say more; for without the assistance of Anytus and Lycon, any one may see that he would not have had a fifth part of the votes, as the law requires, in which case he would have incurred a fine of a thousand drachmae.

And so he proposes death as the penalty. And what shall I propose on my part, O men of Athens? Clearly that which is my due. And what is my due? What returns shall be made to the man who has never had the wit to be idle during his whole life; but has been careless of what the many care for—wealth, and family interests, and military offices, and speaking in the assembly, and magistracies, and plots, and parties. Reflecting that I was really too honest a man to be a politician and live, I did not go where I could do no good to you or to myself; but where I could do the greatest good privately to every one of you, thither I went, and sought to persuade every man among you that he must look to himself, and seek virtue and wisdom before he looks to his private interests, and look to the State before he looks to the interests of the State; and that this should be the order which he observes in all his actions. What shall be done to such an one? Doubtless some good thing, O men of Athens, if he has his reward; and the good should be of a kind suitable to him. What would be a reward suitable to a poor man who is your benefactor, and who desires leisure that he may instruct you? There can be no reward so fitting as maintenance in the Prytaneum, O men of Athens, a reward which he deserves far more than the citizen who has won the prize at Olympia in the horse or chariot race, whether the chariots were drawn by two horses or by many. For I am in want, and he has enough; and he only gives you the appearance of happiness, and I give you the reality. And if I am to estimate the penalty fairly, I should say that maintenance in the Prytaneum is the just return.

Perhaps you think that I am braving you in what I am saying now, as in what I said before about the tears and prayers. But this is not so. I speak rather because I am convinced that I never intentionally wronged any one, although I cannot convince you—the time has been too short; if there were a law at Athens, as there is in other cities, that a capital cause should not be decided in one day, then I believe that I should have convinced you. But I cannot in a moment refute great slanders; and, as I am convinced that I never wronged another, I will assuredly not wrong myself. I will not say of myself that I deserve any evil, or propose any penalty. Why should I? Because I am afraid of the penalty of death which Meletus proposes? When I do not know whether death is a good or an evil, why should I propose a penalty which would certainly be an evil? Shall I say imprisonment? And why should I live in prison, and be the slave of the magistrate of the year—of the Eleven? Or shall the penalty be a fine, and imprisonment until the fine is paid? There is the same objection. I should have to lie in prison, for money I have none, and cannot pay. And if I say exile (and this may possibly be the penalty which you will affix), I must indeed be blinded by the love of life, if I am so irrational as to expect that when you, who are my own citizens, cannot endure my discourses and words, and have found them so grievous and odious that you will have no more of them, others are likely to endure me. No, indeed, men of Athens, that is not very likely. And what a life should I lead, at my age, wandering from city to city, ever changing my place of exile, and always being driven out! For I am quite sure that wherever I go, there, as here, the young men will flock to me; and if I drive them away, their elders will drive me out at their request; and if I let them come, their fathers and friends will drive me out for their sakes.

Some one will say: Yes, Socrates, but cannot you hold your tongue, and then you may go into a foreign city, and no one will interfere with you? Now, I have great difficulty in making you understand my answer to this. For if I tell you that to do as you say would be a disobedience to the God, and therefore that I cannot hold my tongue, you will not believe that I am serious; and if I say again that daily to discourse about virtue, and of those other things about which you hear me examining myself and others, is the greatest good of man, and that the unexamined life is not worth living, you are still less likely to believe me. Yet I say what is true, although a thing of which it is hard for me to persuade you. Also, I have never been accustomed to think that I deserve to suffer any harm. Had I money I might have estimated the offence at what I was able to pay, and not have been much the worse. But I have none, and therefore I must ask you to proportion the fine to my means. Well, perhaps I could afford a mina, and therefore I propose that penalty: Plato, Crito, Critobulus, and Apollodorus, my friends here, bid me say thirty minae, and they will be the sureties. Let thirty minae be the penalty; for which sum they will be ample security to you.

Not much time will be gained, O Athenians, in return for the evil name which you will get from the detractors of the city, who will say that you killed Socrates, a wise man; for they will call me wise, even although I am not wise, when they want to reproach you. If you had waited a little while, your desire would have been fulfilled in the course of nature. For I am far advanced in years, as you may perceive, and not far from death. I am speaking now not to all of you, but only to those who have condemned

me to death. And I have another thing to say to them:
You think that I was convicted because I had no words
of the sort which would have procured my acquittal—I
mean, if I had thought fit to leave nothing undone or un-
said. Not so; the deficiency which led to my conviction
was not of words—certainly not. But I had not the boldness
or impudence or inclination to address you as you would
have liked me to do, weeping and wailing and lamenting,
and saying and doing many things which you have been
accustomed to hear from others, and which, as I maintain,
are unworthy of me. I thought at the time that I ought not
to do anything common or mean when in danger: nor do
I now repent of the style of my defence; I would rather
die having spoken after my manner, than speak in your
manner and live. For neither in war nor yet at law ought
I or any man to use every way of escaping death. Often
in battle there can be no doubt that if a man will throw
away his arms, and fall on his knees before his pursuers,
he may escape death; and in other dangers there are other
ways of escaping death, if a man is willing to say and do
anything. The difficulty, my friends, is not to avoid death,
but to avoid unrighteousness; for that runs faster than
death. I am old and move slowly, and the slower runner
has overtaken me, and my accusers are keen and quick,
and the faster runner, who is unrighteousness, has overtaken them. And now I depart hence condemned by you
to suffer the penalty of death,—they too go their ways condemned by the truth to suffer the penalty of villainy and
wrong; and I must abide by my award—let them abide by
theirs. I suppose that these things may be regarded as fated,
—and I think that they are well.

And now, O men who have condemned me, I would fain
prophesy to you; for I am about to die, and in the hour
of death men are gifted with prophetic power. And I prophesy to you who are my murderers, that immediately after
my departure punishment far heavier than you have in-

flicted on me will surely await you. Me you have killed because you wanted to escape the accuser, and not to give an account of your lives. But that will not be as you suppose: far otherwise. For I say that there will be more accusers of you than there are now; accusers whom hitherto I have restrained: and as they are younger they will be more inconsiderate with you, and you will be more offended at them. If you think that by killing men you can prevent some one from censuring your evil lives, you are mistaken; that is not a way of escape which is either possible or honourable; the easiest and the noblest way is not to be disabling others, but to be improving yourselves. This is the prophecy which I utter before my departure to the judges who have condemned me.

Friends, who would have acquitted me, I would like also to talk with you about the thing which has come to pass, while the magistrates are busy, and before I go to the place at which I must die. Stay then a little, for we may as well talk with one another while there is time. You are my friends, and I should like to show you the meaning of this event which has happened to me. O my judges—for you I may truly call judges—I should like to tell you of a wonderful circumstance. Hitherto the divine faculty of which the internal oracle is the source has constantly been in the habit of opposing me even about trifles, if I was going to make a slip or error in any matter; and now as you see there has come upon me that which may be thought, and is generally believed to be, the last and worst evil. But the oracle made no sign of opposition, either when I was leaving my house in the morning, or when I was on my way to the court, or while I was speaking, at anything which I was going to say; and yet I have often been stopped in the middle of a speech, but now in nothing I either said or did touching the matter in hand has the oracle opposed me. What do I take to be the explanation of this silence? I will tell you. It is an intimation that what has happened to me is a good, and that those of us who think that death is an evil are in error. For the customary sign would surely have opposed me had I been going to evil and not to good.

Let us reflect in another way, and we shall see that there is great reason to hope that death is a good; for one of two things—either death is a state of nothingness and utter unconsciousness, or, as men say, there is a change and migration of the soul from this world to another. Now, if you suppose that there is no consciousness, but a sleep like the sleep of him who is undisturbed even by dreams, death will be an unspeakable gain. For if a person were to select the night in which his sleep was undisturbed even by dreams, and were to compare with this the other days and nights of his life, and then were to tell us how many days and nights he had passed in the course of his life better and more pleasantly than this one, I think that any man, I will not say a private man, but even the great king will not find many such days or nights, when compared with the others. Now, if death be of such a nature, I say that to die is gain; for eternity is then only a single night. But if death is the journey to another place, and there, as men say, all the dead abide, what good, O my friends and judges, can be greater than this? If, indeed, when the pilgrim arrives in the world below, he is delivered from the professors of justice in this world, and finds the true judges who are said to give judgment there, Minos and Rhadamanthus and Aeacus and Triptolemus, and other sons of God who were righteous in their own life, that pilgrimage will be worth making. What would not a man give if he might converse with Orpheus and Musaeus and Hesiod and Homer? Nay, if this be true, let me die again and again. I myself, too, shall have a wonderful interest in there meeting and conversing with Palamedes, and Ajax the son of Telamon, and any other ancient hero who has suffered death through an unjust judgment; and there will be no small pleasure, as I think, in comparing my own sufferings with theirs. Above all, I shall then be able to continue my search into true and false knowledge; as in this world, so also in the next; and I shall find out who is wise, and who pretends to be wise, and is not. What would not a man give, O judges, to be able to examine the leader of the great Trojan expedition; or Odysseus or Sisyphus, or numberless others, men and women too! What infinite delight would there be in conversing with them and asking them questions! In another world they do not put a man to death for asking questions: assuredly not. For besides being happier than we are, they will be immortal, if what is said is true.

Wherefore, O judges, be of good cheer about death, and know of a certainty, that no evil can happen to a good man, either in life or after death. He and his are not neglected by the gods; nor has my own approaching end happened by mere chance. But I see clearly that the time had arrived when it was better for me to die and be released from trouble; wherefore the oracle gave no sign. For which reason, also, I am not angry with my condemners, or with my accusers; they have done me no harm, although they did not mean to do me any good; and for this I may gently blame them.

Still, I have a favour to ask of them. When my sons are grown up, I would ask you, O my friends, to punish them; and I would have you trouble them, as I have troubled you, if they seem to care about riches, or anything, more than about virtue; or if they pretend to be something when they are really nothing,—then reprove them, as I have reproved you, for not caring about that for which they ought to care, and thinking that they are something when they are really nothing. And if you do this, both I and my sons will have received justice at your hands.

The hour of departure has arrived, and we go our ways —I to die, and you to live. Which is better God only knows.

CRITO

CRITO

PERSONS OF THE DIALOGUE

SOCRATES.   CRITO.

SCENE: The Prison of Socrates.

Socrates. Why have you come at this hour, Crito? it must be quite early?

Crito. Yes, certainly.

Soc. What is the exact time?

Cr. The dawn is breaking.

Soc. I wonder that the keeper of the prisoner would let you in.

Cr. He knows me, because I often come, Socrates; moreover, I have done him a kindness.

Soc. And are you only just arrived?

Cr. No, I came some time ago.

Soc. Then why did you sit and say nothing, instead of at once awakening me?

Cr. I should not have liked myself, Socrates, to be in such great trouble and unrest as you are—indeed I should not: I have been watching with amazement your peaceful slumbers; and for that reason I did not awake you, because I wished to minimize the pain. I have always thought you to be of a happy disposition; but never did I see anything like the easy, tranquil manner in which you bear this calamity.

Soc. Why, Crito, when a man has reached my age he ought not to be repining at the approach of death.

Cr. And yet other old men find themselves in similar misfortunes, and age does not prevent them from repining.

Soc. That is true. But you have not told me why you come at this early hour.

Cr. I come to bring you a message which is sad and painful; not, as I believe, to yourself, but to all of us who are your friends, and saddest of all to me.

Soc. What? Has the ship come from Delos, on the arrival of which I am to die?

Cr. No, the ship has not actually arrived, but she will probably be here to-day, as persons who have come from Sunium tell me that they left her there; and therefore to-morrow, Socrates, will be the last day of your life.

Soc. Very well, Crito; if such is the will of God, I am willing; but my belief is that there will be a delay of a day.

Cr. Why do you think so?

Soc. I will tell you. I am to die on the day after the arrival of the ship.

Cr. Yes; that is what the authorities say.

Soc. But I do not think that the ship will be here until to-morrow; this I infer from a vision which I had last night, or rather only just now, when you fortunately allowed me to sleep.

Cr. And what was the nature of the vision?

Soc. There appeared to me the likeness of a woman, fair and comely, clothed in bright raiment, who called to me and said: O Socrates,

"The third day hence to fertile Phthia shalt thou go."[1]

Cr. What a singular dream, Socrates!

Soc. There can be no doubt about the meaning, Crito, I think.

Cr. Yes; the meaning is only too clear. But, oh! my beloved Socrates, let me entreat you once more to take my advice and escape. For if you die I shall not only lose a friend who can never be replaced, but there is another evil: people who do not know you and me will believe that I

[1] Homer, Il. ix. 363.

might have saved you if I had been willing to give money, but that I did not care. Now, can there be a worse disgrace than this—that I should be thought to value money more than the life of friend? For the many will not be persuaded that I wanted you to escape, and that you refused.

Soc. But why, my dear Crito, should we care about the opinion of the many? Good men, and they are the only persons who are worth considering, will think of these things truly as they occurred.

Cr. But you see, Socrates, that the opinion of the many must be regarded, for what is now happening shows that they can do the greatest evil to any one who has lost their good opinion.

Soc. I only wish it were so, Crito; and that the many could do the greatest evil; for then they would also be able to do the greatest good—and what a fine thing this would be! But in reality they can do neither; for they cannot make a man either wise or foolish; and whatever they do is the result of chance.

Cr. Well, I will not dispute with you; but please to tell me, Socrates, whether you are not acting out of regard to me and your other friends: are you not afraid that if you escape from prison we may get into trouble with the informers for having stolen you away, and lose either the whole or a great part of our property; or that even a worse evil may happen to us? Now, if you fear on our account, be at ease; for in order to save you, we ought surely to run this, or even a greater risk; be persuaded, then, and do as I say.

Soc. Yes, Crito, that is one fear which you mention, but by no means the only one.

Cr. Fear not—there are persons who are willing to get you out of prison at no great cost; and as for the informers, they are far from being exorbitant in their demands—a little money will satisfy them. My means, which are certainly ample, are at your service, and if you have a scruple about spending all mine, here are strangers who will give you the use of theirs; and one of them, Simmias the Theban, has brought a large sum of money for this very purpose; and Cebes and many others are prepared to spend their money in helping you to escape. I say, therefore, do not hesitate on our account, and do not say, as you did in the court, [1] that you will have a difficulty in knowing what to do with yourself anywhere else. For men will love you in other places to which you may go, and not in Athens only; there are friends of mine in Thessaly, if you like to go to them, who will value and protect you, and no Thessalian will give you any trouble. Nor can I think that you are at all justified, Socrates, in betraying your own life when you might be saved; in acting thus you are playing into the hands of your enemies, who are hurrying on your destruction. And further I should say that you are deserting your own children; for you might bring them up and educate them; instead of which you go away and leave them, and they will have to take their chance; and if they do not meet with the usual fate of orphans, there will be small thanks to you. No man should bring children into the world who is unwilling to persevere to the end in their nurture and education. But you appear to be choosing the easier part, not the better and manlier, which would have been more becoming in one who professes to care for virtue in all his actions, like yourself. And, indeed, I am ashamed not only of you, but of us who are your friends, when I reflect that the whole business will be attributed entirely to our want of courage. The trial need never have come on, or might have been managed differently; and this last act, or crowning folly, will seem to have occurred through our negligence and cowardice, who might have saved you, if we had been good for anything; and you might have saved yourself, for there was no difficulty at all. See now, Socra

[1] Cp. Apol. 37 C, D.

tes, how sad and discreditable are the consequences, both
to us and you. Make up your mind, then, or rather have
your mind already made up, for the time of deliberation is
over, and there is only one thing to be done, which must
be done this very night, and if we delay at all will be no
longer practicable or possible; I beseech you therefore, Socrates, be persuaded by me, and do as I say.

Soc. Dear Crito, your zeal is invaluable, if a right one;
but if wrong, the greater the zeal the greater the danger;
and therefore we ought to consider whether I shall or shall
not do as you say. For I am and always have been one
of those natures who must be guided by reason, whatever
the reason may be which upon reflection appears to me to
be the best; and now that this chance has befallen me, I
cannot repudiate my own words: the principles which I
have hitherto honoured and revered I still honour, and
unless we can at once find other and better principles, I
am certain not to agree with you; no, not even if the power
of the multitude could inflict many more imprisonments,
confiscations, deaths, frightening us like children with hobgoblin terrors.[1] What will be the fairest way of considering
the question? Shall I return to your old argument about
the opinions of men?—we were saying that some of them
are to be regarded, and others not. Now, were we right in
maintaining this before I was condemned? And has the
argument which was once good now proved to be talk for
the sake of talking—mere childish nonsense? That is what
I want to consider with your help, Crito:—whether, under
my present circumstances, the argument appears to be in
any way different or not; and is to be allowed by me or
disallowed. That argument, which, as I believe, is maintained by many persons of authority, was to the effect, as
I was saying, that the opinions of some men are to be regarded, and of other men not to be regarded. Now you,
Crito, are not going to die to-morrow—at least, there is no

[1] Cp. Apol. 30 C.

human probability of this—and therefore you are disinterested and not liable to be deceived by the circumstances in which you are placed. Tell me, then, whether I am right in saying that some opinions, and the opinions of some men only, are to be valued, and that other opinions, and the opinions of other men, are not to be valued. I ask you whether I was right in maintaining this?

Cr. Certainly.

Soc. The good are to be regarded, and not the bad?

Cr. Yes.

Soc. And the opinions of the wise are good, and the opinions of the unwise are evil?

Cr. Certainly.

Soc. And what was said about another matter? Is the pupil who devotes himself to the practice of gymnastics supposed to attend to the praise and blame and opinion of every man, or of one man only—his physician or trainer, whoever he may be?

Cr. Of one man only.

Soc. And he ought to fear the censure and welcome the praise of that one only, and not of the many?

Cr. Clearly so.

Soc. And he ought to act and train, and eat and drink in the way which seems good to his single master who has understanding, rather than according to the opinion of all other men put together?

Cr. True.

Soc. And if he disobeys and disregards the opinion and approval of the one, and regards the opinion of the many who have no understanding, will he not suffer?

Cr. Certainly he will.

Soc. And what will the evil be, whither tending and what affecting, in the disobedient person?

Cr. Clearly, affecting the body; that is what is destroyed by the evil.

Soc. Very good; and is not this true, Crito, of other

things which we need not separately enumerate? In questions of just and unjust, fair and foul, good and evil, which are the subjects of our present consultation, ought we to follow the opinion of the many and to fear them; or the opinion of the one man who has understanding? ought we not to fear and reverence him more than all the rest of the world: and if we desert him shall we not destroy and injure that principle in us which may be assumed to be improved by justice and deteriorated by injustice;—there is such a principle?

Cr. Certainly there is, Socrates.

Soc. Take a parallel instance:—if, acting under the advice of those who have no understanding, we destroy that which is improved by health and is deteriorated by disease, would life be worth having? And that which has been destroyed is—the body?

Cr. Yes.

Soc. Could we live, having an evil and corrupted body?

Cr. Certainly not.

Soc. And will life be worth having, if that higher part of man be destroyed, which is improved by justice and depraved by injustice? Do we suppose that principle, whatever it may be in man, which has to do with justice and injustice, to be inferior to the body?

Cr. Certainly not.

Soc. More honourable than the body?

Cr. Far more.

Soc. Then, my friend, we must not regard what the many say of us: but what he, the one man who has understanding of just and unjust, will say, and what the truth will say. And therefore you begin in error when you advise that we should regard the opinion of the many about just and unjust, good and evil, honourable and dishonourable —"Well," some one will say, "but the many can kill us."

Cr. Yes, Socrates; that will clearly be the answer.

Soc. And it is true: but still I find with surprise that the old argument is unshaken as ever. And I should like to know whether I may say the same of another proposition —that not life, but a good life, is to be chiefly valued?

Cr. Yes, that also remains unshaken.

Soc. And a good life is equivalent to a just and honourable one—that holds also?

Cr. Yes, it does.

Soc. From these premises I proceed to argue the question whether I ought or ought not to try to escape without the consent of the Athenians: and if I am clearly right in escaping, then I will make the attempt; but if not, I will abstain. The other considerations which you mention, of money and loss of character and the duty of educating one's children, are, I fear, only the doctrines of the multitude, who would be as ready to restore people to life, if they were able, as they are to put them to death—and with as little reason. But now, since the argument has thus far prevailed, the only question which remains to be considered is, whether we shall do rightly either in escaping or in suffering others to aid in our escape and paying them in money and thanks, or whether in reality we shall not do rightly; and if the latter, then death or any other calamity which may ensue on my remaining here must not be allowed to enter into the calculation.

Cr. I think that you are right, Socrates; how then shall we proceed?

Soc. Let us consider the matter together, and do you either refute me if you can, and I will be convinced; or else cease, my dear friend, from repeating to me that I ought to escape against the wishes of the Athenians: for I highly value your attempts to persuade me to do so, but I may not be persuaded against my own better judgment. And now please to consider my first position, and try how you can best answer me.

Cr. I will.

Soc. Are we to say that we are never intentionally to do

wrong, or that in one way we ought and in another way we ought not to do wrong, or is doing wrong always evil and dishonourable, as I was just now saying, and as has been already acknowledged by us? Are all our former admissions which were made within a few days to be thrown away? And have we, at our age, been earnestly discoursing with one another all our life long only to discover that we are no better than children? Or, in spite of the opinion of the many, and in spite of consequences whether better or worse, shall we insist on the truth of what was then said, that injustice is always an evil and dishonour to him who acts unjustly? Shall we say so or not?

Cr. Yes.

Soc. Then we must do no wrong?

Cr. Certainly not.

Soc. Nor when injured injure in return, as the many imagine; for we must injure no one at all? [1]

Cr. Clearly not.

Soc. Again, Crito, may we do evil?

Cr. Surely not, Socrates.

Soc. And what of doing evil in return for evil, which is the morality of the many—is that just or not?

Cr. Not just.

Soc. For doing evil to another is the same as injuring him?

Cr. Very true.

Soc. Then we ought not to retaliate or render evil for evil to any one, whatever evil we may have suffered from him. But I would have you consider, Crito, whether you really mean what you are saying. For this opinion has never been held, and never will be held, by any considerable number of persons; and those who are agreed and those who are not agreed upon this point have no common ground, and can only despise one another when they see how widely they differ. Tell me, then, whether you agree with and

[1] Cp. Rep. i. 355 E.

assent to my first principle, that neither injury nor retaliation nor warding off evil by evil is ever right. And shall
that be the premiss of our argument? Or do you decline
and dissent from this? For so I have ever thought, and
continue to think; but, if you are of another opinion, let
me hear what you have to say. If, however, you remain of
the same mind as formerly, I will proceed to the next step.

Cr. You may proceed, for I have not changed my mind.

Soc. Then I will go on to the next point, which may be
put in the form of a question:—Ought a man to do what
he admits to be right, or ought he to betray the right?

Cr. He ought to do what he thinks right.

Soc. But if this is true, what is the application? In leaving the prison against the will of the Athenians, do I wrong
any? or rather do I not wrong those whom I ought least to
wrong? Do I not desert the principles which were acknowledged by us to be just—what do you say?

Cr. I cannot tell, Socrates; for I do not know.

Soc. Then consider the matter in this way:—Imagine
that I am about to play truant (you may call the proceeding by any name which you like), and the laws and the
government come and interrogate me: "Tell us, Socrates,"
they say; "what are you about? are you not going by an
act of yours to overturn us—the laws, and the whole State,
as far as in you lies? Do you imagine that a State can sub-
sist and not be overthrown, in which the decisions of law
have no power, but are set aside and trampled upon by
individuals?" What will be our answer, Crito, to these and
the like words? Any one, and especially a rhetorician, will
have a good deal to say on behalf of the law which requires a sentence to be carried out. He will argue that this
law should not be set aside; and shall we reply, "Yes; but
the State has injured us and given an unjust sentence."
Suppose I say that?

Cr. Very good, Socrates.

Soc. "And was that our agreement with you?" the law

would answer; "or were you to abide by the sentence of
the State?" And if I were to express my astonishment at
their words, the law would probably add: "Answer, Socra,
tes, instead of opening your eyes—you are in the habit of
asking and answering questions. Tell us,—What complaint
have you to make against us which justifies you in at,
tempting to destroy us and the State? In the first place
did we not bring you into existence? Your father married
your mother by our aid and begat you. Say whether you
have any objection to urge against those of us who regulate
marriage?" None, I should reply. "Or against those of us
who after birth regulate the nurture and education of children, in which you also were trained? Were not the laws,
which have the charge of education, right in commanding
your father to train you in music and gymnastic?" Right,
I should reply. "Well, then, since you were brought into
the world and nurtured and educated by us, can you deny
in the first place that you are our child and slave, as your
fathers were before you? And if this is true, you are not
on equal terms with us; nor can you think that you have
a right to do to us what we are doing to you. Would you
have any right to strike or revile or do any other evil to
your father or your master, if you had one, because you
have been struck or reviled by him, or received some other
evil at his hands?—you would not say this? And because
we think right to destroy you, do you think that you have
any right to destroy us in return, and your country as far
as in you lies? Will you, O professor of true virtue, pretend
that you are justified in this? Has a philosopher like you
failed to discover that our country is more to be valued and
higher and holier far than mother or father or any ancestor,
and more to be regarded in the eyes of the gods and of
men of understanding? also to be soothed, and gently and
reverently entreated when angry, even more than a father,
and either to be persuaded, or if not persuaded, to be
obeyed? And when we are punished by her, whether with

imprisonment or stripes, the punishment is to be endured in silence; and if she lead us to wounds or death in battle, thither we follow as is right; neither may any one yield or retreat or leave his rank, but whether in battle or in a court of law, or in any other place, he must do what his city and his country order him; or he must change their view of what is just: and if he may do no violence to his father or mother, much less may he do violence to his country." What answer shall we make to this, Crito? Do the laws speak truly, or do they not?

Cr. I think that they do.

Soc. Then the laws will say: "Consider, Socrates, if we are speaking truly that in your present attempt you are going to do us an injury. For, having brought you into the world, and nurtured and educated you, and given you and every other citizen a share in every good which we had to give, we further proclaim to any Athenian by the liberty which we allow him, that if he does not like us when he has become of age and has seen the ways of the city, and made our acquaintance, he may go where he pleases and take his goods with him. None of us laws will forbid him or interfere with him. Any one who does not like us and the city, and who wants to emigrate to a colony or to any other city, may go where he likes, retaining his property. But he who has experience of the manner in which we order justice and administer the State, and still remains, has entered into an implied contract that he will do as we command him. And he who disobeys us is, as we maintain, thrice wrong; first, because in disobeying us he is disobeying his parents; secondly, because we are the authors of his education; thirdly, because he has made an agreement with us that he will duly obey our commands; and he neither obeys them nor convinces us that our commands are unjust; and we do not rudely impose them, but give him the alternative of obeying or convincing us;—that is what we offer, and he does neither.

"These are the sort of accusations to which, as we were saying, you, Socrates, will be exposed if you accomplish your intentions; you, above all other Athenians." Suppose now I ask, why I rather than anybody else? they will justly retort upon me that I above all other men have acknowl-edged the agreement. "There is clear proof," they will say, "Socrates, that we and the city were not displeasing to you. Of all Athenians you have been the most constant resident in the city, which, as you never leave, you may be supposed to love.[1] For you never went out of the city either to see the games, except once when you went to the Isthmus, or to any other place unless when you were on military serv-ice; nor did you travel as other men do. Nor had you any curiosity to know other States or their laws: your affec-tions did not go beyond us and our State; we were your special favourites, and you acquiesced in our government of you; and here in this city you begat your children, which is a proof of your satisfaction. Moreover, you might in the course of the trial, if you had liked, have fixed the penalty at banishment; the State which refuses to let you go now would have let you go then. But you pretended that you preferred death to exile,[2] and that you were not unwilling to die. And now you have forgotten these fine sentiments, and pay no respect to us, the laws, of whom you are the destroyer; and are doing what only a miserable slave would do, running away and turning your back upon the com-pacts and agreements which you made as a citizen. And, first of all, answer this very question: Are we right in say-ing that you agreed to be governed according to us in deed, and not in word only? Is that true or not?" How shall we answer, Crito? Must we not assent?

Cr. We cannot help it, Socrates.

Soc. Then will they not say: "You, Socrates, are break-ing the covenants and agreements which you made with

[1] Cp. Phaedr. 230 C.
[2] Cp. Apol. 37 D.

us at your leisure, not in any haste or under any compulsion or deception, but after you have had seventy years to think of them, during which time you were at liberty to leave the city, if we were not to your mind, or if our covenants appeared to you to be unfair. You had your choice, and might have gone either to Lacedaemon or Crete, both which States are often praised by you for their good government, or to some other Hellenic or foreign State. Whereas you, above all other Athenians, seemed to be so fond of the State, or, in other words, of us, her laws (and who would care about a State which has no laws?), that you never stirred out of her; the halt, the blind, the maimed were not more stationary in her than you were. And now you run away and forsake your agreements. Not so, Socrates, if you will take our advice; do not make yourself ridiculous by escaping out of the city.

"For just consider, if you transgress and err in this sort of way, what good will you do either to yourself or to your friends? That your friends will be driven into exile and deprived of citizenship, or will lose their property, is tolerably certain; and you yourself, if you fly to one of the neighbouring cities, as, for example, Thebes or Megara, both of which are well governed, will come to them as an enemy, Socrates, and their government will be against you, and all patriotic citizens will cast an evil eye upon you as a subverter of the laws, and you will confirm in the minds of the judges the justice of their own condemnation of you. For he who is a corrupter of the laws is more than likely to be a corrupter of the young and foolish portion of mankind. Will you then flee from well-ordered cities and virtuous men? and is existence worth having on these terms? Or will you go to them without shame, and talk to them, Socrates? And what will you say to them? What you say here about virtue and justice and institutions and laws being the best things among men? Would that be decent of you? Surely not. But if you go away from well-governed States to Crito's

friends in Thessaly, where there is great disorder and li-
cence, they will be charmed to hear the tale of your escape
from prison, set off with ludicrous particulars of the manner in which you were wrapped in a goatskin or some other
disguise, and metamorphosed as the manner is of runaways;
but will there be no one to remind you that in your old
age you were not ashamed to violate the most sacred laws
from a miserable desire of a little more life? Perhaps not,
if you keep them in a good temper; but if they are out of
temper you will hear many degrading things; you will live,
but how?—as the flatterer of all men, and the servant of
all men; and doing what?—eating and drinking in Thessaly,
having gone abroad in order that you may get a dinner.
And where will be your fine sentiments about justice and
virtue? Say that you wish to live for the sake of your children—you want to bring them up and educate them—will
you take them into Thessaly and deprive them of Athenian
citizenship? Is this the benefit which you will confer upon
them? Or are you under the impression that they will be
better cared for and educated here if you are still alive,
although absent from them; for your friends will take
care of them? Do you fancy that if you are an inhabitant
of Thessaly they will take care of them, and if you are an
inhabitant of the other world that they will not take care
of them? Nay; but if they who call themselves friends are
good for anything, they will—to be sure they will.

"Listen, then, Socrates, to us who have brought you up.
Think not of life and children first, and of justice afterwards, but of justice first, that you may be justified before
the princes of the world below. For neither will you nor
any that belong to you be happier or holier or juster in
this life, or happier in another, if you do as Crito bids. Now
you depart in innocence, a sufferer and not a doer of evil;
a victim, not of the laws but of men. But if you go forth,
returning evil for evil, and injury for injury, breaking the
covenants and agreements which you have made with us,

and wronging those whom you ought least of all to wrong, that is to say, yourself, your friends, your country, and us, we shall be angry with you while you live, and our brethren, the laws in the world below, will receive you as an enemy; for they will know that you have done your best to destroy us. Listen, then, to us and not to Crito."

This, dear Crito, is the voice which I seem to hear murmuring in my ears, like the sound of the flute in the ears of the mystic; that voice, I say, is humming in my ears, and prevents me from hearing any other. And I know that anything more which you may say will be vain. Yet speak, if you have anything to say.

Cr. I have nothing to say, Socrates.

Soc. Leave me then, Crito, to fulfil the will of God, and to follow whither he leads.

PHAEDO

PHAEDO

PERSONS OF THE DIALOGUE

PHAEDO, *who is the narrator*
of the Dialogue to
ECHECRATES *of Phlius.*
SOCRATES.
ATTENDANT OF THE PRISON.

APOLLODORUS
SIMMIAS.
CEBES.
CRITO.

SCENE: The prison of Socrates.

PLACE OF THE NARRATION:—Phlius.

Echecrates. Were you yourself, Phaedo, in the prison with
Socrates on the day when he drank the poison?

Phaedo. Yes, Echecrates, I was.

Ech. I should so like to hear about his death. What did
he say in his last hours? We were informed that he died by
taking poison, but no one knew anything more; for no
Phliasian ever goes to Athens now, and it is a long time since
any stranger from Athens has found his way hither; so that
we had no clear account.

Phaed. Did you not hear of the proceedings at the trial?

Ech. Yes; some one told us about the trial, and we could
not understand why, having been condemned, he should
have been put to death, not at the time, but long afterwards.
What was the reason of this?

Phaed. An accident, Echecrates: the stern of the ship
which the Athenians sent to Delos happened to have been
crowned on the day before he was tried.

Ech. What is this ship?

Phaed. It is the ship in which, according to Athenian
tradition, Theseus went to Crete when he took with him
the fourteen youths, and was the saviour of them and of

himself. And they are said to have vowed to Apollo at the time, that if they were saved they would send a yearly mission to Delos. Now this custom still continues, and the whole period of the voyage to and from Delos, beginning when the priest of Apollo crowns the stern of the ship, is a holy season, during which the city is not allowed to be polluted by public executions; and when the vessel is detained by contrary winds, the time spent in going and returning is very considerable. As I was saying, the ship was crowned on the day before the trial, and this was the reason why Socrates lay in prison and was not put to death until long after he was condemned.

Ech. What was the manner of his death, Phaedo? What was said or done? And which of his friends were with him? Or did the authorities forbid them to be present—so that he had no friends near him when he died?

Phaed. No; there were several of them with him.

Ech. If you have nothing to do, I wish that you would tell me what passed, as exactly as you can.

Phaed. I have nothing at all to do, and will try to gratify your wish. To be reminded of Socrates is always the greatest delight to me, whether I speak myself or hear another speak of him.

Ech. You will have listeners who are of the same mind with you, and I hope that you will be as exact as you can.

Phaed. I had a singular feeling at being in his company. For I could hardly believe that I was present at the death of a friend, and therefore I did not pity him, Echecrates; he died so fearlessly, and his words and bearing were so noble and gracious, that to me he appeared blessed. I thought that in going to the other world he could not be without a divine call, and that he would be happy, if any man ever was, when he arrived there; and therefore I did not pity him as might have seemed natural at such an hour. But I had not the pleasure which I usually feel in philosophical discourse (for philosophy was the theme of which we spoke). I was pleased, but in the pleasure there was also a strange admixture of pain; for I reflected that he was soon to die, and this double feeling was shared by us all; we were laughing and weeping by turns, especially the excitable Apollodorus—you know the sort of man?

Ech. Yes.

Phaed. He was quite beside himself; and I and all of us were greatly moved.

Ech. Who were present?

Phaed. Of native Athenians there were, besides Apollodorus, Critobulus and his father Crito, Hermogenes, Epigenes, Aeschines, Antisthenes; likewise Ctesippus of the deme of Paeania, Menexenus, and some others; Plato, if I am not mistaken, was ill.

Ech. Were there any strangers?

Phaed. Yes, there were; Simmias the Theban, and Cebes, and Phaedondes; Euclid and Terpsion, who came from Megara.

Ech. And was Aristippus there, and Cleombrotus?

Phaed. No, they were said to be in Aegina.

Ech. Any one else?

Phaed. I think that these were nearly all.

Ech. Well, and what did you talk about?

Phaed. I will begin at the beginning, and endeavour to repeat the entire conversation. On the previous days we had been in the habit of assembling early in the morning at the court in which the trial took place, and which is not far from the prison. There we used to wait talking with one another until the opening of the doors (for they were not opened very early); then we went in and generally passed the day with Socrates. On the last morning we assembled sooner than usual, having heard on the day before when we quitted the prison in the evening that the sacred ship had come from Delos; and so we arranged to meet very early at the accustomed place. On our arrival the jailer who answered the door, instead of admitting us, came out

and told us to stay until he called us. "For the Eleven,"
he said, "are now with Socrates; they are taking off his
chains, and giving orders that he is to die to-day." He soon
returned and said that we might come in. On entering we
found Socrates just released from chains, and Xanthippe,
whom you know, sitting by him, and holding his child in
her arms. When she saw us she uttered a cry and said, as
women will: "O Socrates, this is the last time that either
you will converse with your friends, or they with you."
Socrates turned to Crito and said: "Crito, let some one
take her home." Some of Crito's people accordingly led her
away, crying out and beating herself. And when she was
gone, Socrates, sitting up on the couch, bent and rubbed
his leg, saying, as he was rubbing: How singular is the
thing called pleasure, and how curiously related to pain,
which might be thought to be the opposite of it; for they
are never present to a man at the same instant, and yet he
who pursues either is generally compelled to take the other;
their bodies are two, but they are joined by a single head.
And I cannot help thinking that if Aesop had remembered
them, he would have made a fable about God trying to
reconcile their strife, and how, when he could not, he
fastened their heads together; and this is the reason why
when one comes the other follows: as I know by my own
experience now, when after the pain in my leg which was
caused by the chain pleasure appears to succeed.

Upon this Cebes said: I am glad, Socrates, that you have
mentioned the name of Aesop. For it reminds me of a
question which has been asked by many, and was asked
of me only the day before yesterday by Evenus the poet—
he will be sure to ask it again, and therefore if you would
like me to have an answer ready for him, you may as well
tell me what I should say to him:—he wanted to know
why you, who never before wrote a line of poetry, now
that you are in prison are turning Aesop's fables into verse,
and also composing that hymn in honour of Apollo.

Tell him, Cebes, he replied, what is the truth—that I had no idea of rivalling him or his poems; to do so, as I knew, would be no easy task. But I wanted to see whether I could purge away a scruple which I felt about the meaning of certain dreams. In the course of my life I have often had intimations in dreams "that I should compose music." The same dream came to me sometimes in one form, and sometimes in another, but always saying the same or nearly the same words: "Cultivate and make music," said the dream. And hitherto I had imagined that this was only intended to exhort and encourage me in the study of philosophy, which has been the pursuit of my life, and is the noblest and best of music. The dream was bidding me do what I was already doing, in the same way that the competitor in a race is bidden by the spectators to run when he is already running. But I was not certain of this; for the dream might have meant music in the popular sense of the word, and being under sentence of death, and the festival giving me a respite, I thought that it would be safer for me to satisfy the scruple, and, in obedience to the dream, to compose a few verses before I departed. And first I made a hymn in honour of the god of the festival, and then considering that a poet, if he is really to be a poet, should not only put together words, but should invent stories, and that I have no invention, I took some fables of Aesop, which I had ready at hand and which I knew—they were the first I came upon—and turned them into verse. Tell this to Evenus, Cebes, and bid him be of good cheer; say that I would have him come after me if he be a wise man, and not tarry; and that to-day I am likely to be going, for the Athenians say that I must.

Simmias said: What a message for such a man! having been a frequent companion of his I should say that, as far as I know him, he will never take your advice unless he is obliged.

Why, said Socrates,—is not Evenus a philosopher?

I think that he is, said Simmias.

Then he, or any man who has the spirit of philosophy, will be willing to die; but he will not take his own life, for that is held to be unlawful.

Here he changed his position, and put his legs off the couch on to the ground, and during the rest of the conversation he remained sitting.

Why do you say, enquired Cebes, that a man ought not to take his own life, but that the philosopher will be ready to follow the dying?

Socrates replied: And have you, Cebes and Simmias, who are the disciples of Philolaus, never heard him speak of this?

Yes, but his language was obscure, Socrates.

My words, too, are only an echo; but there is no reason why I should not repeat what I have heard: and, indeed, as I am going to another place, it is very meet for me to be thinking and talking of the nature of the pilgrimage which I am about to make. What can I do better in the interval between this and the setting of the sun?

Then tell me, Socrates, why is suicide held to be unlawful? as I have certainly heard Philolaus, about whom you were just now asking, affirm when he was staying with us at Thebes; and there are others who say the same, although I have never understood what was meant by any of them.

Do not lose heart, replied Socrates, and the day may come when you will understand. I suppose that you wonder why, when other things which are evil may be good at certain times and to certain persons, death is to be the only exception, and why, when a man is better dead, he is not permitted to be his own benefactor, but must wait for the hand of another.

Very true, said Cebes, laughing gently and speaking in his native Boeotian.

I admit the appearance of inconsistency in what I am saying; but there may not be any real inconsistency after all. There is a doctrine whispered in secret that man is a prisoner who has no right to open the door and run away; this is a great mystery which I do not quite understand. Yet I too believe that the gods are our guardians, and that we men are a possession of theirs. Do you not agree?

Yes, I quite agree, said Cebes.

And if one of your own possessions, an ox or an ass, for example, took the liberty of putting himself out of the way when you had given no intimation of your wish that he should die, would you not be angry with him, and would you not punish him if you could?

Certainly, replied Cebes.

Then, if we look at the matter thus, there may be reason in saying that a man should wait, and not take his own life until God summons him, as he is now summoning me.

Yes, Socrates, said Cebes, there seems to be truth in what you say. And yet how can you reconcile this seemingly true belief that God is our guardian and we his possessions, with the willingness to die which you were just now attributing to the philosopher? That the wisest of men should be willing to leave a service in which they are ruled by the gods, who are the best of rulers, is not reasonable; for surely no wise man thinks that when set at liberty he can take better care of himself than the gods take of him. A fool may perhaps think so—he may argue that he had better run away from his master, not considering that his duty is to remain to the end, and not to run away from the good, and that there would be no sense in his running away. The wise man will want to be ever with him who is better than himself. Now this, Socrates, is the reverse of what was just now said; for upon this view the wise man should sorrow and the fool rejoice at passing out of life.

The earnestness of Cebes seemed to please Socrates. Here, said he, turning to us, is a man who is always enquiring, and is not so easily convinced by the first thing which he hears.

And certainly, added Simmias, the objection which he is

now making does appear to me to have some force. For what can be the meaning of a truly wise man wanting to fly away and lightly leave a master who is better than himself? And I rather imagine that Cebes is referring to you; he thinks that you are too ready to leave us, and too ready to leave the gods whom you acknowledge to be our good masters.

Yes, replied Socrates; there is reason in what you say. And so you think that I ought to answer your indictment as if I were in a court?

We should like you to do so, said Simmias.

Then I must try to make a more successful defence before you than I did before the judges. For I am quite ready to admit, Simmias and Cebes, that I ought to be grieved at death, if I were not persuaded in the first place that I am going to other gods who are wise and good (of which I am as certain as I can be of any such matters), and secondly (though I am not so sure of this last) to men departed, better than those whom I leave behind; and therefore I do not grieve as I might have done, for I have good hope that there is yet something remaining for the dead, and as has been said of old, some far better thing for the good than for the evil.

But do you mean to take away your thoughts with you, Socrates? said Simmias. Will you not impart them to us?—for they are a benefit in which we too are entitled to share. Moreover, if you succeed in convincing us, that will be an answer to the charge against yourself.

I will do my best, replied Socrates. But you must first let me hear what Crito wants; he has long been wishing to say something to me.

Only this, Socrates, replied Crito:—the attendant who is to give you the poison has been telling me, and he wants me to tell you, that you are not to talk much; talking, he says, increases heat, and this is apt to interfere with the action of the poison; persons who excite themselves are sometimes obliged to take a second or even a third dose.

Then, said Socrates, let him mind his business and be prepared to give the poison twice or even thrice if necessary; that is all.

I knew quite well what you would say, replied Crito; but I was obliged to satisfy him.

Never mind him, he said.

And now, O my judges, I desire to prove to you that the real philosopher has reason to be of good cheer when he is about to die, and that after death he may hope to obtain the greatest good in the other world. And how this may be, Simmias and Cebes, I will endeavour to explain. For I deem that the true votary of philosophy is likely to be misunderstood by other men; they do not perceive that he is always pursuing death and dying; and if this be so, and he has had the desire of death all his life long, why when his time comes should he repine at that which he had been always pursuing and desiring?

Simmias said laughingly: Though not in a laughing humour, you have made me laugh, Socrates; for I cannot help thinking that the many when they hear your words will say how truly you have described philosophers, and our people at home will likewise say that the life which philosophers desire is in reality death, and that they have found them out to be deserving of the death which they desire.

And they are right, Simmias, in thinking so, with the exception of the words "they have found them out"; for they have not found out either what is the nature of that death which the true philosopher deserves, or how he deserves or desires death. But enough of them:—let us discuss the matter among ourselves. Do we believe that there is such a thing as death?

To be sure, replied Simmias.

Is it not the separation of soul and body? And to be

dead is the completion of this; when the soul exists in
herself, and is released from the body and the body is released from the soul, what is this but death?

Just so, he replied.

There is another question, which will probably throw
light on our present enquiry if you and I can agree about
it:—Ought the philosopher to care about the pleasures—
if they are to be called pleasures—of eating and drinking?

Certainly not, answered Simmias.

And what about the pleasures of love—should he care
for them?

By no means.

And will he think much of the other ways of indulging
the body, for example, the acquisition of costly raiment,
or sandals, or other adornments of the body? Instead of
caring about them, does he not rather despise anything
more than nature needs? What do you say?

I should say that the true philosopher would despise them.

Would you not say that he is entirely concerned with
the soul and not with the body? He would like, as far
as he can, to get away from the body and to turn to the
soul.

Quite true.

In matters of this sort philosophers, above all other men,
may be observed in every sort of way to dissever the soul
from the communion of the body.

Very true.

Whereas, Simmias, the rest of the world are of opinion
that to him who has no sense of pleasure and no part in
bodily pleasure, life is not worth having; and that he who
is indifferent about them is as good as dead.

That is also true.

What again shall we say of the actual acquirement of
knowledge?—is the body, if invited to share in the enquiry,
a hinderer or a helper? I mean to say, have sight and
hearing any truth in them? Are they not, as the poets are

always telling us, inaccurate witnesses? and yet, if even they are inaccurate and indistinct, what is to be said of the other senses?—for you will allow that they are the best of them?

Certainly, he replied.

Then when does the soul attain truth?—for in attempting to consider anything in company with the body she is obviously deceived.

True.

Then must not true existence be revealed to her in thought, if at all?

Yes.

And thought is best when the mind is gathered into herself and none of these things trouble her—neither sounds nor sights nor pain nor any pleasure,—when she takes leave of the body, and has as little as possible to do with it, when she has no bodily sense or desire, but is aspiring after true being?

Certainly.

And in this the philosopher dishonours the body; his soul runs away from his body and desires to be alone and by herself?

That is true.

Well, but there is another thing, Simmias: Is there or is there not an absolute justice?

Assuredly there is.

And an absolute beauty and absolute good?

Of course.

But did you ever behold any of them with your eyes?

Certainly not.

Or did you ever reach them with any other bodily sense? —and I speak not of these alone, but of absolute greatness, and health, and strength, and of the essence or true nature of everything. Has the reality of them ever been perceived by you through the bodily organs? or rather, is not the nearest approach to the knowledge of their several natures

made by him who so orders his intellectual vision as to
have the most exact conception of the essence of each thing
which he considers?

Certainly.

And he attains to the purest knowledge of them who
goes to each with the mind alone, not introducing or in-
truding in the act of thought sight or any other sense
together with reason, but with the very light of the mind
in her own clearness searches into the very truth of each;
he who has got rid, as far as he can, of eyes and ears and,
so to speak, of the whole body, these being in his opinion
distracting elements which when they infect the soul hinder
her from acquiring truth and knowledge—who, if not he,
is likely to attain to the knowledge of true being?

What you say has a wonderful truth in it, Socrates,
replied Simmias.

And when real philosophers consider all these things, will
they not be led to make a reflection which they will express
in words something like the following? "Have we not found,"
they will say, "a path of thought which seems to bring us
and our argument to the conclusion, that while we are in
the body, and while the soul is infected with the evils of
the body, our desire will not be satisfied, and our desire
is of the truth? For the body is a source of endless trouble
to us by reason of the mere requirement of food; and is
liable also to diseases which overtake and impede us in the
search after true being: it fills us full of loves, and lusts,
and fears, and fancies of all kinds, and endless foolery,
and, in fact, as men say, takes away from us the power of
thinking at all. Whence come wars, and fightings, and fac-
tions? whence but from the body and the lusts of the body?
Wars are occasioned by the love of money, and money has
to be acquired for the sake and service of the body; and
by reason of all these impediments we have no time to
give to philosophy; and, last and worst of all, even if we
are at leisure and betake ourselves to some speculation, the

body is always breaking in upon us, causing turmoil and confusion in our enquiries, and so amazing us that we are prevented from seeing the truth. It has been proved to us by experience that if we would have pure knowledge of anything we must be quit of the body—the soul in herself must behold things in themselves: and then we shall attain the wisdom which we desire, and of which we say that we are lovers; not while we live, but after death; for if while in company with the body, the soul cannot have pure knowledge, one of two things follows—either knowledge is not to be attained at all, or, if at all, after death. For then, and not till then, the soul will be parted from the body and exist in herself alone. In this present life, I reckon that we make the nearest approach to knowledge when we have the least possible intercourse or communion with the body, and are not surfeited with the bodily nature, but keep ourselves pure until the hour when God himself is pleased to release us. And thus having got rid of the foolishness of the body we shall be pure and hold converse with the pure, and know of ourselves the clear light everywhere, which is no other than the light of truth." For the impure are not permitted to approach the pure. These are the sort of words, Simmias, which the true lovers of knowledge cannot help saying to one another, and thinking. You would agree; would you not?

Undoubtedly, Socrates.

But, O my friend, if this be true, there is great reason to hope that, going whither I go, when I have come to the end of my journey, I shall attain that which has been the pursuit of my life. And therefore I go on my way rejoicing, and not I only, but every other man who believes that his mind has been made ready and that he is in a manner purified.

Certainly, replied Simmias.

And what is purification but the separation of the soul from the body, as I was saying before; the habit of the soul gathering and collecting herself into herself from all sides out of the body; the dwelling in her own place alone, as in another life, so also in this, as far as she can;—the release of the soul from the chains of the body?

Very true, he said.

And this separation and release of the soul from the body is termed death?

To be sure, he said.

And the true philosophers, and they only, are ever seeking to release the soul. Is not the separation and release of the soul from the body their especial study?

That is true.

And, as I was saying at first, there would be a ridiculous contradiction in men studying to live as nearly as they can in a state of death, and yet repining when it comes upon them.

Clearly.

And the true philosophers, Simmias, are always occupied in the practice of dying, wherefore also to them least of all men is death terrible. Look at the matter thus:—if they have been in every way the enemies of the body, and are wanting to be alone with the soul, when this desire of theirs is granted, how inconsistent would they be if they trembled and repined, instead of rejoicing at their departure to that place where, when they arrive, they hope to gain that which in life they desired—and this was wisdom—and at the same time to be rid of the company of their enemy. Many a man has been willing to go to the world below animated by the hope of seeing there an earthly love, or wife, or son, and conversing with them. And will he who is a true lover of wisdom, and is strongly persuaded in like manner that only in the world below he can worthily enjoy her, still repine at death? Will he not depart with joy? Surely he will, O my friend, if he be a true philosopher. For he will have a firm conviction that there, and there only, he can find wisdom in her purity. And if this be true, he would be very absurd, as I was saying, if he were afraid of death.

He would indeed, replied Simmias.

And when you see a man who is repining at the approach of death, is not his reluctance a sufficient proof that he is not a lover of wisdom, but a lover of the body, and probably at the same time a lover of either money or power, or both?

Quite so, he replied.

And is not courage, Simmias, a quality which is specially characteristic of the philosopher?

Certainly.

There is temperance again, which even by the vulgar is supposed to consist in the control and regulation of the passions, and in the sense of superiority to them—is not temperance a virtue belonging to those only who despise the body, and who pass their lives in philosophy?

Most assuredly.

For the courage and temperance of other men, if you will consider them, are really a contradiction.

How so?

Well, he said, you are aware that death is regarded by men in general as a great evil.

Very true, he said.

And do not courageous men face death because they are afraid of yet greater evils?

That is quite true.

Then all but the philosophers are courageous only from fear, and because they are afraid; and yet that a man should be courageous from fear, and because he is a coward, is surely a strange thing.

Very true.

And are not the temperate exactly in the same case? They are temperate because they are intemperate—which might seem to be a contradiction, but is nevertheless the sort of thing which happens with this foolish temperance.

For there are pleasures which they are afraid of losing; and in their desire to keep them, they abstain from some pleasures, because they are overcome by others; and although to be conquered by pleasure is called by men intemperance, to them the conquest of pleasure consists in being conquered by pleasure. And that is what I mean by saying that, in a sense, they are made temperate through intemperance.

Such appears to be the case.

Yet the exchange of one fear or pleasure or pain for another fear or pleasure or pain, and of the greater for the less, as if they were coins, is not the exchange of virtue. O my blessed Simmias, is there not one true coin for which all things ought to be exchanged?—and that is wisdom; and only in exchange for this, and in company with this, is anything truly bought or sold, whether courage or temperance or justice. And is not all true virtue the companion of wisdom, no matter what fears or pleasures or other similar goods or evils may or may not attend her? But the virtue which is made up of these goods, when they are severed from wisdom and exchanged with one another, is a shadow of virtue only, nor is there any freedom or health or truth in her; but in the true exchange there is a purging away of all these things, and temperance, and justice, and courage, and wisdom herself are the purgation of them. The founders of the mysteries would appear to have had a real meaning, and were not talking nonsense when they intimated in a figure long ago that he who passes unsanctified and uninitiated into the world below will lie in a slough, but that he who arrives there after initiation and purification will dwell with the gods. For "many," as they say in the mysteries, "are the thyrsus-bearers, but few are the mystics,"—meaning, as I interpret the words, "the true philosophers." In the number of whom, during my whole life, I have been seeking, according to my ability, to find a place;—whether I have sought in a right way or not, and whether I have succeeded or not, I shall truly know in a little while, if God will, when I myself arrive in the other world—such is my belief. And therefore I maintain that I am right, Simmias and Cebes, in not grieving or repining at parting from you and my masters in this world, for I believe that I shall equally find good masters and friends in another world. But most men do not believe this saying; if then I succeed in convincing you by my defence better than I did the Athenian judges, it will be well.

Cebes answered: I agree, Socrates, in the greater part of what you say. But in what concerns the soul, men are apt to be incredulous; they fear that when she has left the body her place may be nowhere, and that on the very day of death she may perish and come to an end—immediately on her release from the body, issuing forth dispersed like smoke or air and in her flight vanishing away into nothingness. If she could only be collected into herself after she has obtained release from the evils of which you were speaking, there would be good reason to hope, Socrates, that what you say is true. But surely it requires a great deal of argument and many proofs to show that when the man is dead his soul yet exists, and has any force or intelligence.

True, Cebes, said Socrates; and shall I suggest that we converse a little of the probabilities of these things?

I am sure, said Cebes, that I should greatly like to know your opinion about them.

I reckon, said Socrates, that no one who heard me now, not even if he were one of my old enemies, the comic poets, could accuse me of idle talking about matters in which I have no concern:—If you please, then, we will proceed with the enquiry.

Suppose we consider the question whether the souls of men after death are or are not in the world below. There comes into my mind an ancient doctrine which affirms that they go from hence into the other world, and returning hither, are born again from the dead. Now, if it be true that the living come from the dead, then our souls must exist in the other world, for if not, how could they have been born again? And this would be conclusive, if there were any real evidence that the living are only born from the dead; but if this is not so, then other arguments will have to be adduced.

Very true, replied Cebes.

Then let us consider the whole question, not in relation to man only, but in relation to animals generally, and to plants, and to everything of which there is generation, and the proof will be easier. Are not all things which have opposites generated out of their opposites? I mean such things as good and evil, just and unjust—and there are innumerable other opposites which are generated out of opposites. And I want to show that in all opposites there is of necessity a similar alternation; I mean to say, for example, that anything which becomes greater must become greater after being less.

True.

And that which becomes less must have been once greater and then have become less.

Yes.

And the weaker is generated from the stronger, and the swifter from the slower.

Very true.

And the worse is from the better, and the more just is from the more unjust.

Of course.

And is this true of all opposites? and are we convinced that all of them are generated out of opposites?

Yes.

And in this universal opposition of all things, are there not also two intermediate processes which are ever going on, from one to the other opposite, and back again; where there is a greater and a less there is also an intermediate process of increase and diminution, and that which grows is said to wax, and that which decays to wane?

Yes, he said.

And there are many other processes, such as division and composition, cooling and heating, which equally involve a passage into and out of one another. And this necessarily holds of all opposites, even though not always expressed in words—they are really generated out of one another, and there is a passing or process from one to the other of them?

Very true, he replied.

Well, and is there not an opposite of life, as sleep is the opposite of waking?

True, he said.

And what is it?

Death, he answered.

And these, if they are opposites, are generated the one from the other, and have their two intermediate processes also?

Of course.

Now, said Socrates, I will analyze one of the two pairs of opposites which I have mentioned to you, and also its intermediate processes, and you shall analyze the other to me. One of them I term sleep, the other waking. The state of sleep is opposed to the state of waking, and out of sleeping waking is generated, and out of waking, sleeping; and the process of generation is in the one case falling asleep, and in the other waking up. Do you agree?

I entirely agree.

Then suppose that you analyze life and death to me in the same manner. Is not death opposed to life?

Yes.

And they are generated one from the other?

Yes.

What is generated from the living?

The dead.

And what from the dead?

I can only say in answer—the living.

Then the living, whether things or persons, Cebes, are generated from the dead?

That is clear, he replied.

Then the inference is that our souls exist in the world below?

That is true.

And one of the two processes or generations is visible— for surely the act of dying is visible?

Surely, he said.

What then is to be the result? Shall we exclude the opposite process? and shall we suppose nature to walk on one leg only? Must we not rather assign to death some corresponding process of generation?

Certainly, he replied.

And what is that process?

Return to life.

And return to life, if there be such a thing, is the birth of the dead into the world of the living?

Quite true.

Then here is a new way by which we arrive at the conclusion that the living come from the dead, just as the dead come from the living; and this, if true, affords a most certain proof that the souls of the dead exist in some place out of which they come again.

Yes, Socrates, he said; the conclusion seems to flow necessarily out of our previous admissions.

And that these admissions were not unfair, Cebes, he said, may be shown, I think, as follows: If generation were in a straight line only, and there were no compensation or circle in nature, no turn or return of elements into their opposites, then you know that all things would at last have the same form and pass into the same state, and there would be no more generation of them.

What do you mean? he said.

A simple thing enough, which I will illustrate by the case of sleep, he replied. You know that if there were no alternation of sleeping and waking, the tale of the sleeping Endymion would in the end have no meaning, because all other things would be asleep too, and he would not be distinguishable from the rest. Or if there were composition only, and no division of substances, then the chaos of Anaxagoras would come again. And in like manner, my dear Cebes, if all things which partook of life were to die, and after they were dead remained in the form of death, and did not come to life again, all would at last die, and nothing would be alive—what other result could there be? For if the living spring from any other things, and they too die, must not all things at last be swallowed up in death?[1]

There is no escape, Socrates, said Cebes; and to me your argument seems to be absolutely true.

Yes, he said, Cebes, it is and must be so, in my opinion; and we have not been deluded in making these admissions; but I am confident that there truly is such a thing as living again, and that the living spring from the dead, and that the souls of the dead are in existence and that the good souls have a better portion than the evil.

Cebes added: Your favourite doctrine, Socrates, that knowledge is simply recollection, if true, also necessarily implies a previous time in which we have learned that which we now recollect. But this would be impossible unless our soul had been in some place before existing in the form of man; here then is another proof of the soul's immortality.

But tell me, Cebes, said Simmias, interposing, what arguments are urged in favour of this doctrine of recollection. I am not very sure at the moment that I remember them.

One excellent proof, said Cebes, is afforded by questions. If you put a question to a person in a right way, he will

[1] But cp. Rep. x 611 A.

give a true answer of himself, but how could he do this unless there were knowledge and right reason already in him? And this is most clearly shown when he is taken to a diagram or to anything of that sort.[1]

But if, said Socrates, you are still incredulous, Simmias, I would ask you whether you may not agree with me when you look at the matter in another way;—I mean, if you are still incredulous as to whether knowledge is recollection?

Incredulous I am not, said Simmias; but I want to have this doctrine of recollection brought to my own recollection, and, from what Cebes has said, I am beginning to recollect and be convinced: but I should still like to hear what you were going to say.

This is what I would say, he replied:—We should agree, if I am not mistaken, that what a man recollects he must have known at some previous time.

Very true.

And what is the nature of this knowledge or recollection? I mean to ask, Whether a person who, having seen or heard or in any way perceived anything, knows not only that, but has a conception of something else which is the subject, not of the same but of some other kind of knowledge, may not be fairly said to recollect that of which he has the conception?

What do you mean?

I mean what I may illustrate by the following instance:— The knowledge of a lyre is not the same as the knowledge of a man?

True.

And yet what is the feeling of lovers when they recognize a lyre, or a garment, or anything else which the beloved has been in the habit of using? Do not they, from knowing the lyre, form in the mind's eye an image of the youth to whom the lyre belongs? And this is recollection. In like manner any one who sees Simmias may remember

[1] Cp. Meno 83 ff.

Cebes; and there are endless examples of the same thing.

Endless, indeed, replied Simmias.

And recollection is most commonly a process of recovering that which has been already forgotten through time and inattention.

Very true, he said.

Well; and may you not also from seeing the picture of a horse or a lyre remember a man? and from the picture of Simmias, you may be led to remember Cebes?

True.

Or you may also be led to the recollection of Simmias himself?

Quite so.

And in all these cases, the recollection may be derived from things either like or unlike?

It may be.

And when the recollection is derived from like things, then another consideration is sure to arise, which is— whether the likeness in any degree falls short or not of that which is recollected?

Very true, he said.

And shall we proceed a step further, and affirm that there is such a thing as equality, not of one piece of wood or stone with another, but that, over and above this, there is absolute equality? Shall we say so?

Say so, yes, replied Simmias, and swear to it, with all the confidence in life.

And do we know the nature of this absolute essence?

To be sure, he said.

And whence did we obtain our knowledge? Did we not see equalities of material things, such as pieces of wood and stones, and gather from them the idea of an equality which is different from them? For you will acknowledge that there is a difference. Or look at the matter in another way:—Do not the same pieces of wood or stone appear at one time equal, and at another time unequal?

That is certain.

But are real equals ever unequal? or is the idea of equality the same as of inequality?

Impossible, Socrates.

Then these (so-called) equals are not the same with the idea of equality?

I should say, clearly not, Socrates.

And yet from these equals, although differing from the idea of equality, you conceived and attained that idea?

Very true, he said.

Which might be like, or might be unlike them?

Yes.

But that makes no difference: whenever from seeing one thing you conceived another, whether like or unlike, there must surely have been an act of recollection?

Very true.

But what would you say of equal portions of wood and stone, or other material equals? and what is the impression produced by them? Are they equals in the same sense in which absolute equality is equal? or do they fall short of this perfect equality in a measure?

Yes, he said, in a very great measure too.

And must we not allow, that when I or any one, looking at any object, observes that the thing which he sees aims at being some other thing, but falls short of, and cannot be, that other thing, but is inferior, he who makes this observation must have had a previous knowledge of that to which the other, although similar, was inferior?

Certainly.

And has not this been our own case in the matter of equals and of absolute equality?

Precisely.

Then we must have known equality previously to the time when we first saw the material equals, and reflected that all these apparent equals strive to attain absolute equality, but fall short of it?

Very true.

And we recognize also that this absolute equality has only been known, and can only be known, through the medium of sight or touch, or of some other of the senses, which are all alike in this respect?

Yes, Socrates, as far as the argument is concerned, one of them is the same as the other.

From the senses then is derived the knowledge that all sensible things aim at an absolute equality of which they fall short?

Yes.

Then before we began to see or hear or perceive in any way, we must have had a knowledge of absolute equality, or we could not have referred to that standard the equals which are derived from the senses?—for to that they all aspire, and of that they fall short.

No other inference can be drawn from the previous statements.

And did we not see and hear and have the use of our other senses as soon as we were born?

Certainly.

Then we must have acquired the knowledge of equality at some previous time?

Yes.

That is to say, before we were born, I suppose?

True.

And if we acquired this knowledge before we were born, and were born having the use of it, then we also knew before we were born and at the instant of birth not only the equal or the greater or the less, but all other ideas; for we are not speaking only of equality, but of beauty, goodness, justice, holiness, and of all which we stamp with the name of essence in the dialectical process, both when we ask and when we answer questions. Of all this we may certainly affirm that we acquired the knowledge before birth?

We may.

But if, after having acquired, we have not forgotten what in each case we acquired, then we must always have come into life having knowledge, and shall always continue to know as long as life lasts—for knowing is the acquiring and retaining knowledge and not forgetting. Is not forgetting, Simmias, just the losing of knowledge?

Quite true, Socrates.

But if the knowledge which we acquired before birth was lost by us at birth, and if afterwards by the use of the senses we recovered what we previously knew, will not the process which we call learning be a recovering of the knowledge which is natural to us, and may not this be rightly termed recollection?

Very true.

So much is clear—that when we perceive something, either by the help of sight, or hearing, or some other sense, from that perception we are able to obtain a notion of some other thing like or unlike which is associated with it but has been forgotten. Whence, as I was saying, one of two alternatives follows:—either we had this knowledge at birth, and continued to know through life; or, after birth, those who are said to learn only remember, and learning is simply recollection.

Yes, that is quite true, Socrates.

And which alternative, Simmias, do you prefer? Had we the knowledge at our birth, or did we recollect the things which we knew previously to our birth?

I cannot decide at the moment.

At any rate you can decide whether he who has knowledge will or will not be able to render an account of his knowledge? What do you say?

Certainly, he will.

But do you think that every man is able to give an account of these very matters about which we are speaking?

Would that they could, Socrates, but I rather fear that

to-morrow, at this time, there will no longer be any one alive who is able to give an account of them such as ought to be given.

Then you are not of opinion, Simmias, that all men know these things?

Certainly not.

They are in process of recollecting that which they learned before?

Certainly.

But when did our souls acquire this knowledge?—not since we were born as men?

Certainly not.

And therefore, previously?

Yes.

Then, Simmias, our souls must also have existed without bodies before they were in the form of man, and must have had intelligence.

Unless indeed you suppose, Socrates, that these notions are given us at the very moment of birth; for this is the only time which remains.

Yes, my friend, but if so, when do we lose them? for they are not in us when we are born—that is admitted. Do we lose them at the moment of receiving them, or, if not, at what other time?

No, Socrates, I perceive that I was unconsciously talking nonsense.

Then may we not say, Simmias, that if, as we are always repeating, there is an absolute beauty, and goodness, and an absolute essence of all things; and if to this, which is now discovered to have existed in our former state, we refer all our sensations, and with this compare them, finding these ideas to be pre-existent and our inborn possession —then our souls must have had a prior existence, but, if not, there would be no force in the argument? There is the same proof that these ideas must have existed before we were born, as that our souls existed before we were born; and if not the ideas, then not the souls.

Yes, Socrates; I am convinced that there is precisely the same necessity for the one as for the other; and the argument retreats successfully to the position that the existence of the soul before birth cannot be separated from the existence of the essence of which you speak. For there is nothing which to my mind is so patent as that beauty, goodness, and the other notions of which you were just now speaking, have a most real and absolute existence; and I am satisfied with the proof.

Well, but is Cebes equally satisfied? for I must convince him too.

I think, said Simmias, that Cebes is satisfied: although he is the most incredulous of mortals, yet I believe that he is sufficiently convinced of the existence of the soul before birth. But that after death the soul will continue to exist is not yet proven even to my own satisfaction. I cannot get rid of the feeling of the many to which Cebes was referring—the feeling that when the man dies the soul will be dispersed, and that this may be the extinction of her. For admitting that she may have been born elsewhere, and framed out of other elements, and was in existence before entering the human body, why after having entered in and gone out again may she not herself be destroyed and come to an end?

Very true, Simmias, said Cebes; about half of what was required has been proven; to wit, that our souls existed before we were born:—that the soul will exist after death as well as before birth is the other half of which the proof is still wanting, and has to be supplied; when that is given the demonstration will be complete.

But that proof, Simmias and Cebes, has been already given, said Socrates, if you put the two arguments together —I mean this and the former one, in which we admitted that everything living is born of the dead. For if the soul exists before birth, and in coming to life and being born can be born only from death and dying, must she not after death continue to exist, since she has to be born again?—Surely the proof which you desire has been already furnished. Still I suspect that you and Simmias would be glad to probe the argument further. Like children, you are haunted with a fear that when the soul leaves the body, the wind may really blow her away and scatter her; especially if a man should happen to die in a great storm and not when the sky is calm.

Cebes answered with a smile: Then, Socrates, you must argue us out of our fears—and yet, strictly speaking, they are not our fears, but there is a child within us to whom death is a sort of hobgoblin: him too we must persuade not to be afraid when he is alone in the dark.

Socrates said: Let the voice of the charmer be applied daily until you have charmed away the fear.

And where shall we find a good charmer of our fears, Socrates, when you are gone?

Hellas, he replied, is a large place, Cebes, and has many good men, and there are barbarous races not a few: seek for him among them all, far and wide, sparing neither pains nor money; for there is no better way of spending your money. And you must seek among yourselves too; for you will not find others better able to make the search.

The search, replied Cebes, shall certainly be made. And now, if you please, let us return to the point of the argument at which we digressed.

By all means, replied Socrates; what else should I please?

Very good.

Must we not, said Socrates, ask ourselves what that is which, as we imagine, is liable to be scattered, and about which we fear? and what again is that about which we have no fear? And then we may proceed further to enquire whether that which suffers dispersion is or is not of the nature of soul—our hopes and fears as to our own souls will turn upon the answers to these questions.

Very true, he said.

Now the compound or composite may be supposed to be naturally capable, as of being compounded, so also of being dissolved; but that which is uncompounded, and that only, must be, if anything is, indissoluble.

Yes; I should imagine so, said Cebes.

And the uncompounded may be assumed to be the same and unchanging, whereas the compound is always changing and never the same.

I agree, he said.

Then now let us return to the previous discussion. Is that idea or essence, which in the dialectical process we define as essence or true existence—whether essence of equality, beauty, or anything else—are these essences, I say, liable at times to some degree of change? or are they each of them always what they are, having the same simple self-existent and unchanging forms, not admitting of variation at all, or in any way, or at any time?

They must be always the same, Socrates, replied Cebes.

And what would you say of the many beautiful—whether men or horses or garments or any other things which are named by the same names and may be called equal or beautiful,—are they all unchanging and the same always, or quite the reverse? May they not rather be described as almost always changing and hardly ever the same, either with themselves or with one another?

The latter, replied Cebes; they are always in a state of change.

And these you can touch and see and perceive with the senses, but the unchanging things you can only perceive with the mind—they are invisible and are not seen?

That is very true, he said.

Well, then, added Socrates, let us suppose that there are two sorts of existences—one seen, the other unseen.

Let us suppose them.

The seen is the changing, and the unseen is the unchanging?

That may be also supposed.

And, further, is not one part of us body, another part soul?

To be sure.

And to which class is the body more alike and akin?

Clearly to the seen—no one can doubt that.

And is the soul seen or not seen?

Not by man, Socrates.

And what we mean by "seen" and "not seen" is that which is or is not visible to the eye of man?

Yes, to the eye of man.

And is the soul seen or not seen?

Not seen.

Unseen then?

Yes.

Then the soul is more like to the unseen, and the body to the seen?

That follows necessarily, Socrates.

And were we not saying long ago that the soul when using the body as an instrument of perception, that is to say, when using the sense of sight or hearing or some other sense (for the meaning of perceiving through the body is perceiving through the senses)—were we not saying that the soul too is then dragged by the body into the region of the changeable, and wanders and is confused; the world spins round her, and she is like a drunkard, when she touches change?

Very true.

But when returning into herself she reflects, then she passes into the other world, the region of purity, and eternity, and immortality, and unchangeableness, which are her kindred, and with them she ever lives, when she is by herself and is not let or hindered; then she ceases from her erring ways, and being in communion with the unchanging is unchanging. And this state of the soul is called wisdom?

That is well and truly said, Socrates, he replied.

And to which class is the soul more nearly alike and akin, as far as may be inferred from this argument, as well as from the preceding one?

I think, Socrates, that, in the opinion of every one who follows the argument, the soul will be infinitely more like the unchangeable—even the most stupid person will not deny that.

And the body is more like the changing?

Yes.

Yet once more consider the matter in another light: When the soul and the body are united, then nature orders the soul to rule and govern, and the body to obey and serve. Now, which of these two functions is akin to the divine? and which to the mortal? Does not the divine appear to you to be that which naturally orders and rules, and the mortal to be that which is subject and servant?

True.

And which does the soul resemble?

The soul resembles the divine, and the body the mortal—there can be no doubt of that, Socrates.

Then reflect, Cebes: of all which has been said is not this the conclusion?—that the soul is in the very likeness of the divine, and immortal, and intellectual, and uniform, and indissoluble, and unchangeable; and that the body is in the very likeness of the human, and mortal, and unintellectual, and multiform, and dissoluble, and changeable. Can this, my dear Cebes, be denied?

It cannot.

But if it be true, then is not the body liable to speedy dissolution? and is not the soul almost or altogether indissoluble?

Certainly.

And do you further observe, that after a man is dead, the body, or visible part of him, which is lying in the visible world, and is called a corpse, and would naturally be dissolved and decomposed and dissipated, is not dissolved or decomposed at once, but may remain for some time, nay, even for a long time, if the constitution be sound at the time of death, and the season of the year favourable? For the body when shrunk and embalmed, as the manner is in Egypt, may remain almost entire through infinite ages; and even in decay, there are still some portions, such as the bones and ligaments, which are practically indestructible:—Do you agree?

Yes.

And is it likely that the soul, which is invisible, in passing to the place of the true Hades, which like her is invisible, and pure, and noble, and on her way to the good and wise God, whither, if God will, my soul is also soon to go,— that the soul, I repeat, if this be her nature and origin, will be blown away and destroyed immediately on quitting the body, as the many say? That can never be, my dear Simmias and Cebes. The truth rather is, that the soul which is pure at departing and draws after her no bodily taint, having never voluntarily during life had connection with the body, which she is ever avoiding, herself gathered into herself;—and making such abstraction her perpetual study—which means that she has been a true disciple of philosophy; and therefore has in fact been always engaged in the practice of dying? For is not philosophy the study of death?—

Certainly—

That soul, I say, herself invisible, departs to the invisible world—to the divine and immortal and rational: thither arriving, she is secure of bliss and is released from the error and folly of men, their fears and wild passions and all other human ills, and forever dwells, as they say of the initiated, in company with the gods.[1] Is not this true, Cebes?

Yes, said Cebes, beyond a doubt.

[1] Cp. Apol. 40 E.

But the soul which has been polluted, and is impure at the time of her departure, and is the companion and servant of the body always, and is in love with and fascinated by the body and by the desires and pleasures of the body, until she is led to believe that the truth only exists in a bodily form, which a man may touch and see and taste, and use for the purposes of his lusts,—the soul, I mean, accustomed to hate and fear and avoid the intellectual principle, which to the bodily eye is dark and invisible, and can be attained only by philosophy;—do you suppose that such a soul will depart pure and unalloyed?

Impossible, he replied.

She is held fast by the corporeal, which the continual association and constant care of the body have wrought into her nature.

Very true.

And this corporeal element, my friend, is heavy and weighty and earthy, and is that element of sight by which a soul is depressed and dragged down again into the visible world, because she is afraid of the invisible and of the world below—prowling about tombs and sepulchres, near which, as they tell us, are seen certain ghostly apparitions of souls which have not departed pure, but are cloyed with sight and therefore visible.[1]

That is very likely, Socrates.

[1] Compare Milton, Comus, 463 foll.:—

> "But when lust,
> By unchaste looks, loose gestures, and foul talk,
> But most by lewd and lavish act of sin,
> Lets in defilement to the inward parts,
> The soul grows clotted by contagion,
> Imbodies, and imbrutes, till she quite lose,
> The divine property of her first being.
> Such are those thick and gloomy shadows damp
> Oft seen in charnel vaults and sepulchres,
> Lingering, and sitting by a new made grave,
> As loath to leave the body that it lov'd,
> And linked itself by carnal sensualty
> To a degenerate and degraded state."

Yes, that is very likely, Cebes; and these must be the souls, not of the good, but of the evil, which are compelled to wander about such places in payment of the penalty of their former evil way of life; and they continue to wander until through the craving after the corporeal which never leaves them they are imprisoned finally in another body. And they may be supposed to find their prisons in the same natures which they have had in their former lives.

What natures do you mean, Socrates?

What I mean is that men who have followed after glut· tony, and wantonness, and drunkenness, and have had no thought of avoiding them, would pass into asses and animals of that sort. What do you think?

I think such an opinion to be exceedingly probable.

And those who have chosen the portion of injustice, and tyranny, and violence, will pass into wolves, or into hawks and kites;—whither else can we suppose them to go?

Yes, said Cebes; with such natures, beyond question.

And there is no difficulty, he said, in assigning to all of them places answering to their several natures and pro-pensities?

There is not, he said.

Some are happier than others; and the happiest both in themselves and in the place to which they go are those who have practised the civil and social virtues which are called temperance and justice, and are acquired by habit and attention without philosophy of mind.[1]

Why are they the happiest?

Because they may be expected to pass into some gentle and social kind which is like their own, such as bees or wasps or ants, or back again into the form of man, and just and moderate men may be supposed to spring from them.

Very likely.

No one who has not studied philosophy and who is not

[1] Cp. Rep. x. 619 C.

entirely pure at the time of his departure is allowed to enter the company of the gods, but the lover of knowledge only. And this is the reason, Simmias and Cebes, why the true votaries of philosophy abstain from all fleshly lusts, and hold out against them and refuse to give themselves up to them,—not because they fear poverty or the ruin of their families, like the lovers of money, and the world in general; nor like the lovers of power and honour, because they dread the dishonour or disgrace of evil deeds.

No, Socrates, that would not become them, said Cebes.

No, indeed, he replied; and therefore they who have any care of their own souls, and do not merely live moulding and fashioning the body, say farewell to all this; they will not walk in the ways of the blind: and when philosophy offers them purification and release from evil, they feel that they ought not to resist her influence, and whither she leads they turn and follow.

What do you mean, Socrates?

I will tell you, he said. The lovers of knowledge are conscious that the soul was simply fastened and glued to the body—until philosophy received her, she could only view real existence through the bars of a prison, not in and through herself; she was wallowing in the mire of every sort of ignorance, and by reason of lust had become the principal accomplice in her own captivity. This was her original state; and then, as I was saying, and as the lovers of knowledge are well aware, philosophy, seeing how terrible was her confinement, of which she was herself the cause, received and gently comforted her and sought to release her, pointing out that the eye and the ear and the other senses are full of deception, and persuading her to retire from them, and abstain from all the necessary use of them, and be gathered up and collected into herself, bidding her trust in herself and her own pure apprehension of pure existence, and to mistrust whatever comes to her through other channels and is subject to variation; for such things are visible and tangible, but what she sees in her own nature is intelligible and invisible. And the soul of the true philosopher thinks that she ought not to resist this deliverance, and therefore abstains from pleasures and desires and pains and fears, as far as she is able; reflecting that when a man has great joys or sorrows or fears or desires, he suffers from them, not merely the sort of evil which might be anticipated—as, for example, the loss of his health or property which he has sacrificed to his lusts— but an evil greater far, which is the greatest and worst of all evils, and one of which he never thinks.

What is it, Socrates? said Cebes.

The evil is that when the feeling of pleasure or pain is most intense, every soul of man imagines the objects of this intense feeling to be then plainest and truest: but this is not so, they are really the things of sight.

Very true.

And is not this the state in which the soul is most en-thralled by the body?

How so?

Why, because each pleasure and pain is a sort of nail which nails and rivets the soul to the body, until she becomes like the body, and believes that to be true which the body affirms to be true; and from agreeing with the body and having the same delights she is obliged to have the same habits and haunts, and is not likely ever to be pure at her departure to the world below, but is always infected by the body; and so she sinks into another body and there germinates and grows, and has therefore no part in the communion of the divine and pure and simple.

Most true, Socrates, answered Cebes.

And this, Cebes, is the reason why the true lovers of knowledge are temperate and brave; and not for the reason which the world gives.

Certainly not.

Certainly not! The soul of a philosopher will reason in

quite another way; she will not ask philosophy to release her in order that when released she may deliver herself up again to the thraldom of pleasures and pains, doing a work only to be outdone again, weaving instead of unweaving her Penelope's web. But she will calm passion, and follow reason, and dwell in the contemplation of her, beholding the true and divine (which is not matter of opinion), and thence deriving nourishment. Thus she seeks to live while she lives, and after death she hopes to go to her own kindred and to that which is like her, and to be freed from human ills. Never fear, Simmias and Cebes, that a soul which has been thus nurtured and has had these pursuits, will at her departure from the body be scattered and blown away by the winds and be nowhere and nothing.

When Socrates had done speaking, for a considerable time there was silence; he himself appeared to be meditating, as most of us were, on what had been said; only Cebes and Simmias spoke a few words to one another. And Socrates observing them asked what they thought of the argument, and whether there was anything wanting? For, said he, there are many points still open to suspicion and attack, if any one were disposed to sift the matter thoroughly. Should you be considering some other matter I say no more, but if you are still in doubt do not hesitate to say exactly what you think, and let us have anything better which you can suggest; and if you think that I can be of any use, allow me to help you.

Simmias said: I must confess, Socrates, that doubts did arise in our minds, and each of us was urging and inciting the other to put the question which we wanted to have answered but which neither of us liked to ask, fearing that our importunity might be troublesome at such a time.

Socrates replied with a smile: O Simmias, what are you saying? I am not very likely to persuade other men that I do not regard my present situation as a misfortune, if I cannot even persuade you that I am no worse off now than

at any other time in my life. Will you not allow that I have
as much of the spirit of prophecy in me as the swans? For
they, when they perceive that they must die, having sung
all their life long, do then sing more lustily than ever, rejoicing in the thought that they are about to go away to
the god whose ministers they are. But men, because they
are themselves afraid of death, slanderously affirm of the
swans that they sing a lament at the last, not considering
that no bird sings when cold, or hungry, or in pain, not
even the nightingale, nor the swallow, nor yet the hoopoe;
which are said indeed to tune a lay of sorrow, although I
do not believe this to be true of them any more than of
the swans. But because they are sacred to Apollo, they
have the gift of prophecy, and anticipate the good things
of another world; wherefore they sing and rejoice in that
day more than ever they did before. And I, too, believing
myself to be the consecrated servant of the same God, and
the fellow-servant of the swans, and thinking that I have
received from my master gifts of prophecy which are not
inferior to theirs, would not go out of life less merrily
than the swans. Never mind then, if this be your only
objection, but speak and ask anything which you like, while
the eleven magistrates of Athens allow.

Very good, Socrates, said Simmias; then I will tell you
my difficulty, and Cebes will tell you his. I feel myself
(and I dare say that you have the same feeling) how hard
or rather impossible is the attainment of any certainty
about questions such as these in the present life. And yet
I should deem him a coward who did not prove what is
said about them to the uttermost, or whose heart failed
him before he had examined them on every side. For he
should persevere until he has achieved one of two things:
either he should discover, or be taught the truth about
them; or, if this be impossible, I would have him take the
best and most irrefragable of human theories, and let this
be the raft upon which he sails through life—not without

risk, as I admit, if he cannot find some word of God which
will more surely and safely carry him. And now, as you bid
me, I will venture to question you, and then I shall not
have to reproach myself hereafter with not having said at
the time what I think. For when I consider the matter,
either alone or with Cebes, the argument does certainly
appear to me, Socrates, to be not sufficient.

Socrates answered: I dare say, my friend, that you may
be right, but I should like to know in what respect the
argument is insufficient.

In this respect, replied Simmias:—Suppose a person to
use the same argument about harmony and the lyre—
might he not say that harmony is a thing invisible, in-
corporeal, perfect, divine, existing in the lyre which is
harmonized, but that the lyre and the strings are matter
and material, composite, earthy, and akin to mortality?
And when some one breaks the lyre, or cuts and rends the
strings, then he who takes this view would argue as you
do, and on the same analogy, that the harmony survives
and has not perished—you cannot imagine, he would say,
that the lyre without the strings, and the broken strings
themselves which are mortal remain, and yet that the
harmony, which is of heavenly and immortal nature and
kindred, has perished—perished before the mortal. The
harmony must still be somewhere, and the wood and strings
will decay before anything can happen to that. The thought,
Socrates, must have occurred to your own mind that such
is our conception of the soul; and that when the body is
in a manner strung and held together by the elements of
hot and cold, wet and dry, then the soul is the harmony
or due proportionate admixture of them. But if so, whenever the strings of the body are unduly loosened or over-
strained through disease or other injury, then the soul,
though most divine, like other harmonies of music or of
works of art, of course perishes at once; although the
material remains of the body may last for a considerable

time, until they are either decayed or burnt. And if any one maintains that the soul, being the harmony of the elements of the body, is first to perish in that which is called death, how shall we answer him?

Socrates looked fixedly at us as his manner was, and said with a smile: Simmias has reason on his side; and why does not some one of you who is better able than myself answer him? for there is force in his attack upon me. But perhaps, before we answer him, we had better also hear what Cebes has to say that we may gain time for reflection, and when they have both spoken, we may either assent to them, if there is truth in what they say, or if not, we will maintain our position. Please to tell me then, Cebes, he said, what was the difficulty which troubled you?

Cebes said: I will tell you. My feeling is that the argument is where it was, and open to the same objections which were urged before; for I am ready to admit that the existence of the soul before entering into the bodily form has been very ingeniously, and, if I may say so, quite sufficiently proven; but the existence of the soul after death is still, in my judgment, unproven. Now, my objection is not the same as that of Simmias; for I am not disposed to deny that the soul is stronger and more lasting than the body, being of opinion that in all such respects the soul very far excels the body. Well, then, says the argument to me, why do you remain unconvinced?—When you see that the weaker continues in existence after the man is dead, will you not admit that the more lasting must also survive during the same period of time? Now, I will ask you to consider whether the objection, which, like Simmias, I will express in a figure, is of any weight. The analogy which I will adduce is that of an old weaver, who dies, and after his death somebody says:—He is not dead, he must be alive;—see, there is the coat which he himself wove and wore, and which remains whole and undecayed. And then he proceeds to ask of some one who is incredulous, whether a man lasts longer, or the coat which is in use and wear; and when he is answered that a man lasts far longer, thinks that he has thus certainly demonstrated the survival of the man, who is the more lasting, because the less lasting remains. But that, Simmias, as I would beg you to remark, is a mistake; any one can see that he who talks thus is talking nonsense. For the truth is, that the weaver aforesaid, having woven and worn many such coats, outlived several of them; and was outlived by the last; but a man is not therefore proved to be slighter and weaker than a coat. Now the relation of the body to the soul may be expressed in a similar figure; and any one may very fairly say in like manner that the soul is lasting, and the body weak and shortlived in comparison. He may argue in like manner that every soul wears out many bodies, especially if a man live many years. While he is alive the body deliquesces and decays, and the soul always weaves another garment and repairs the waste. But of course, whenever the soul perishes, she must have on her last garment, and this will survive her; and then at length, when the soul is dead, the body will show its native weakness, and quickly decompose and pass away. I would therefore rather not rely on the argument from superior strength to prove the continued existence of the soul after death. For granting even more than you affirm to be possible, and acknowledging not only that the soul existed before birth, but also that the souls of some exist, and will continue to exist after death, and will be born and die again and again, and that there is a natural strength in the soul which will hold out and be born many times—nevertheless, we may be still inclined to think that she will weary in the labours of successive births, and may at last succumb in one of her deaths and utterly perish; and this death and dissolution of the body which brings destruction to the soul may be unknown to any of us, for no one of us can have had any experience of it: and if so, then I maintain that he who is confident about death has but a foolish confidence, unless he is able to prove that the soul is altogether immortal and imperishable. But if he cannot prove the soul's immortality, he who is about to die will always have reason to fear that when the body is disunited, the soul also may utterly perish.

All of us, as we afterwards remarked to one another, had an unpleasant feeling at hearing what they said. When we had been so firmly convinced before, now to have our faith shaken seemed to introduce a confusion and uncertainty, not only into the previous argument, but into any future one; either we were incapable of forming a judgment, or there were no grounds of belief.

Ech. There I feel with you—by heaven I do, Phaedo, and when you were speaking, I was beginning to ask myself the same question: What argument can I ever trust again? For what could be more convincing than the argument of Socrates, which has now fallen into discredit? That the soul is a harmony is a doctrine which has always had a wonderful attraction for me, and, when mentioned, came back to me at once, as my own original conviction. And now I must begin again and find another argument which will assure me that when the man is dead the soul survives. Tell me, I implore you, how did Socrates proceed? Did he appear to share the unpleasant feeling which you mention? or did he calmly meet the attack? And did he answer forcibly or feebly? Narrate what passed as exactly as you can.

Phaed. Often, Echecrates, I have wondered at Socrates, but never more than on that occasion. That he should be able to answer was nothing, but what astonished me was, first, the gentle and pleasant and approving manner in which he received the words of the young men, and then his quick sense of the wound which had been inflicted by the argument, and the readiness with which he healed it. He might be compared to a general rallying his defeated and broken army, urging them to accompany him and return to the field of argument.

Ech. What followed?

Phaed. You shall hear, for I was close to him on his right hand, seated on a sort of stool, and he on a couch which was a good deal higher. He stroked my hand, and pressed the hair upon my neck—he had a way of playing with my hair; and then he said: To-morrow, Phaedo, I suppose that these fair locks of yours will be severed.

Yes, Socrates, I suppose that they will, I replied.

Not so, if you will take my advice.

What shall I do with them? I said.

To-day, he replied, and not to-morrow, if this argument dies and we cannot bring it to life again, you and I will both shave our locks: and if I were you, and the argument got away from me, and I could not hold my ground against Simmias and Cebes, I would myself take an oath, like the Argives, not to wear hair any more until I had renewed the conflict and defeated them.

Yes, I said; but Heracles himself is said not to be a match for two.

Summon me, then, he said, and I will be your Iolaus until the sun goes down.

I summon you rather, I rejoined, not as Heracles summoning Iolaus, but as Iolaus might summon Heracles.

That will do as well, he said. But first let us take care that we avoid a danger.

Of what nature? I said.

Lest we become misologists, he replied: no worse thing can happen to a man than this. For as there are misanthropists, or haters of men, there are also misologists, or haters of ideas, and both spring from the same cause, which is ignorance of the world. Misanthropy arises out of the too great confidence of inexperience;—and trust a man and think him altogether true and sound and faithful, and then in a little while he turns out to be false and knavish; and then another and another, and when this has happened several times to a man, especially when it happens among those whom he deems to be his own most trusted and familiar friends, and he has often quarrelled with them, he at last hates all men, and believes that no one has any good in him at all. You must have observed this trait of character?

I have.

And is not the feeling discreditable? It is not obvious that such an one having to deal with other men, was clearly without any experience of human nature; for experience would have taught him the true state of the case, that few are the good and few the evil, and that the great majority are in the interval between them.

What do you mean? I said.

I mean, he replied, as you might say of the very large and very small—that nothing is more uncommon than a very large or very small man; and this applies generally to all extremes, whether of great and small, or swift and slow, or fair and foul, or black and white: and whether the instances you select be men or dogs or anything else, few are the extremes, but many are in the mean between them. Did you never observe this?

Yes, I said, I have.

And do you not imagine, he said, that if there were a competition in evil, the worst would be found to be very few?

Yes, that is very likely, I said.

Yes, that is very likely, he replied; although in this respect arguments are unlike men—there I was led on by you to say more than I had intended; but the point of comparison was, that when a simple man who has no skill in dialectics believes an argument to be true which he afterwards imagines to be false, whether really false or not, and then another and another, he has no longer any faith left, and great disputers, as you know, come to think at last that they have grown to be the wisest of mankind; for they alone perceive the utter unsoundness and instability of all arguments, or indeed, of all things, which, like the currents in the Euripus, are going up and down in never-ceasing ebb and flow.

That is quite true, I said.

Yes, Phaedo, he replied, and how melancholy, if there be such a thing as truth or certainty or possibility of knowledge —that a man should have lighted upon some argument or other which at first seemed true and then turned out to be false, and instead of blaming himself and his own want of wit, because he is annoyed, should at last be too glad to transfer the blame from himself to arguments in general: and for ever afterwards should hate and revile them, and lose truth and the knowledge of realities.

Yes, indeed, I said; that is very melancholy.

Let us, then, in the first place, he said, be careful of allowing or of admitting into our souls the notion that there is no health or soundness in any arguments at all. Rather say that we have not yet attained to soundness in ourselves, and that we must struggle manfully and do our best to gain health of mind—you and all other men having regard to the whole of your future life, and I myself in the prospect of death. For at this moment I am sensible that I have not the temper of a philosopher; like the vulgar, I am only a partisan. Now, the partisan, when he is engaged in a dispute, cares nothing about the rights of the question, but is anxious only to convince his hearers of his own assertions. And the difference between him and me at the present moment is merely this—that whereas he seeks to convince his hearers that what he says is true, I am rather seeking to convince myself; to convince my hearers is a secondary matter with me. And do but see how much I gain by the argument. For if what I say is true, then I do well to be persuaded of the truth; but if there is nothing after death, still, during the short time that remains, I shall not distress my friends with lamentations, and my ignorance will not last, but will die with me, and therefore no harm will be done. This is the state of mind, Simmias and Cebes, in which I approach the argument. And I would ask you to be thinking of the truth and not of Socrates: agree with me, if I seem to you to be speaking the truth; or if not, withstand me might and main, that I may not deceive you as well as myself in my enthusiasm, and like the bee, leave my sting in you before I die.

And now let us proceed, he said. And first of all let me be sure that I have in my mind what you were saying, Simmias, if I remember rightly, has fears and misgivings whether the soul, although a fairer and diviner thing than the body, being as she is in the form of harmony, may not perish first. On the other hand, Cebes appeared to grant that the soul was more lasting than the body, but he said that no one could know whether the soul, after having worn out many bodies, might not perish herself and leave her last body behind her; and that this is death, which is the destruction not of the body but of the soul, for in the body the work of destruction is ever going on. Are not these, Simmias and Cebes, the points which we have to consider?

They both agreed to this statement of them.

He proceeded: And did you deny the force of the whole preceding argument, or of a part only?

Of a part only, they replied.

And what did you think, he said, of that part of the argument in which we said that knowledge was recollection, and hence inferred that the soul must have previously existed somewhere else before she was enclosed in the body?

Cebes said that he had been wonderfully impressed by that part of the argument, and that his conviction remained absolutely unshaken. Simmias agreed, and added that he himself could hardly imagine the possibility of his ever thinking differently.

But, rejoined Socrates, you will have to think differently, my Theban friend, if you still maintain that harmony is a compound, and that the soul is a harmony which is made out of strings set in the frame of the body; for you will surely never allow yourself to say that a harmony is prior to the elements which compose it.

Never, Socrates.

But do you not see that this is what you imply when you say that the soul existed before she took the form and body of man, and was made up of elements which as yet had no existence? For harmony is not like the soul, as you suppose; but first the lyre, and the strings, and the sounds exist in a state of discord, and then harmony is made last of all, and perishes first. And how can such a notion of the soul as this agree with the other?

Not at all, replied Simmias.

And yet, he said, there surely ought to be harmony in a discourse of which harmony is the theme?

There ought, replied Simmias.

But there is no harmony, he said, in the two propositions that knowledge is recollection, and that the soul is a harmony. Which of them will you retain?

I think, he replied, that I have a much stronger faith, Socrates, in the first of the two, which has been fully demonstrated to me, than in the latter, which has not been demonstrated at all, but rests only on probable and plausible grounds; and is therefore believed by the many. I know too well that these arguments from probabilities are impostors, and unless great caution is observed in the use of them, they are apt to be deceptive—in geometry, and in other things too. But the doctrine of knowledge and recollection has been proven to me on trustworthy grounds: and the proof was that the soul must have existed before she came into the body, because to her belongs the essence of which the very name implies existence. Having, as I am convinced, rightly accepted this conclusion, and on sufficient grounds, I must, as I suppose, cease to argue or allow others to argue that the soul is a harmony.

Let me put the matter, Simmias, he said, in another point of view: Do you imagine that a harmony or any other

composition can be in a state other than that of the elements, out of which it is compounded?

Certainly not.

Or do or suffer anything other than they do or suffer?

He agreed.

Then a harmony does not, properly speaking, lead the
parts or elements which make up the harmony, but only
follows them.

He assented.

For harmony cannot possibly have any motion, or sound,
or other quality which is opposed to its parts.

That would be impossible, he replied.

And does not the nature of every harmony depend upon
the manner in which the elements are harmonized?

I do not understand you, he said.

I mean to say that a harmony admits of degrees, and is
more of a harmony, and more completely a harmony, when
more truly and fully harmonized, to any extent which is
possible; and less of a harmony, and less completely a
harmony, when less truly and fully harmonized.

True.

But does the soul admit of degrees? or is one soul in the
very least degree more or less, or more or less completely,
a soul than another?

Not in the least.

Yet surely of two souls, one is said to have intelligence
and virtue, and to be good, and the other to have folly and
vice, and to be an evil soul: and this is said truly?

Yes, truly.

But what will those who maintain the soul to be a harmony say of this presence of virtue and vice in the soul?—
will they say that here is another harmony, and another
discord, and that the virtuous soul is harmonized, and herself being a harmony has another harmony within her, and
that the vicious soul is inharmonical and has no harmony
within her?

I cannot tell, replied Simmias; but I suppose that something of the sort would be asserted by those who say that the soul is a harmony.

And we have already admitted that no soul is more a soul than another; which is equivalent to admitting that harmony is not more or less harmony, or more or less completely a harmony?

Quite true.

And that which is not more or less a harmony is not more or less harmonized?

True.

And that which is not more or less harmonized cannot have more or less of harmony, but only an equal harmony?

Yes, an equal harmony.

Then one soul not being more nor less absolutely a soul than another, is not more or less harmonized?

Exactly.

And therefore has neither more or less of discord, nor yet of harmony?

She has not.

And having neither more nor less of harmony or of discord, one soul has no more vice or virtue than another, if vice be discord and virtue harmony?

Not at all more.

Or speaking more correctly, Simmias, the soul, if she is a harmony, will never have any vice; because a harmony, being absolutely a harmony, has no part in the inharmonical.

No.

And therefore a soul which is absolutely a soul has no vice?

How can she have, if the previous argument holds?

Then, if all souls are equally by their nature souls, all souls of all living creatures will be equally good?

I agree with you, Socrates, he said.

And can all this be true, think you? he said; for these

are the consequences which seem to follow from the assumption that the soul is a harmony?

It cannot be true.

Once more, he said, what ruler is there of the elements of human nature other than the soul, and especially the wise soul? Do you know of any?

Indeed, I do not.

And is the soul in agreement with the affections of the body? or is she at variance with them? For example, when the body is hot and thirsty, does not the soul incline us against drinking? and when the body is hungry, against eating? And this is only one instance out of ten thousand of the opposition of the soul to the things of the body.

Very true.

But we have already acknowledged that the soul, being a harmony, can never utter a note at variance with the tensions and relaxations and vibrations and other affections of the strings out of which she is composed; she can only follow, she cannot lead them?

It must be so, he replied.

And yet do we not now discover the soul to be doing the exact opposite—leading the elements of which she is believed to be composed; almost always opposing and coercing them in all sorts of ways throughout life, sometimes more violently with the pains of medicine and gymnastic; then again more gently; now threatening, now admonishing the desires, passions, fears, as if talking to a thing which is not herself, as Homer in the Oyssey represents Odysseus doing in the words—

"He beat his breast, and thus reproached his heart:
Endure, my heart; far worse hast thou endured!"

Do you think that Homer wrote this under the idea that the soul is a harmony capable of being led by the affections of the body, and not rather of a nature which should lead and master them—herself a far diviner thing than any harmony?

Yes, Socrates, I quite think so.

Then, my friend, we can never be right in saying that the soul is a harmony, for we should contradict the divine Homer, and contradict ourselves.

True, he said.

Thus much, said Socrates, of Harmonia, your Theban goddess, who has graciously yielded to us; but what shall I say, Cebes, to her husband Cadmus, and how shall I make peace with him?

I think that you will discover a way of propitiating him, said Cebes; I am sure that you have put the argument with Harmonia in a manner that I could never have expected. For when Simmias was mentioning his difficulty, I quite imagined that no answer could be given to him, and therefore I was surprised at finding that his argument could not sustain the first onset of yours, and not impossibly the other, whom you call Cadmus, may share a similar fate.

Nay, my good friend, said Socrates, let us not boast, lest some evil eye should put to flight the word which I am about to speak. That, however, may be left in the hands of those above; while I draw near in Homeric fashion, and try the mettle of your words. Here lies the point:—You want to have it proven to you that the soul is imperishable and immortal, and the philosopher who is confident in death appears to you to have but a vain and foolish confidence, if he believes that he will fare better in the world below than one who has led another sort of life, unless he can prove this: and you say that the demonstration of the strength and divinity of the soul, and of her existence prior to our becoming men, does not necessarily imply her immortality. Admitting the soul to be longlived, and to have known and done much in a former state, still she is not on that account immortal; and her entrance into the human form may be a sort of disease which is the beginning of dissolution, and may at last, after the toils of life are over, end in that which is called death. And whether the soul enters into the body once only or many times, does not, as you say, make any difference in the fears of individuals. For any man, who is not devoid of sense, must fear, if he has no knowledge and can give no account of the soul's immortality. This, or something like this, I suspect to be your notion, Cebes; and I designedly recur to it in order that nothing may escape us, and that you may, if you wish, add or subtract anything.

But, said Cebes, as far as I see at present, I have nothing to add or subtract: I mean what you say that I mean.

Socrates paused awhile, and seemed to be absorbed in reflection. At length he said: You are raising a tremendous question, Cebes, involving the whole nature of generation and corruption, about which, if you like, I will give you my own experience; and if anything which I say is likely to avail towards the solution of your difficulty you may make use of it.

I should very much like, said Cebes, to hear what you have to say.

Then I will tell you, said Socrates. When I was young, Cebes, I had a prodigious desire to know that department of philosophy which is called the investigation of nature; to know the causes of things, and why a thing is and is created or destroyed appeared to me to be a lofty profession; and I was always agitating myself with the consideration of questions such as these:—Is the growth of animals the result of some decay which the hot and cold principle contracts, as some have said? Is the blood the element with which we think, or the air, or the fire? or perhaps nothing of the kind—but the brain may be the originating power of the perceptions of hearing and sight and smell, and memory and opinion may come from them, and science may be based on memory and opinion when they have attained fixity. And then I went on to examine the corruption of them, and then to the things of heaven and earth, and at last I concluded myself to be utterly and absolutely incapaable of these enquiries, as I will satisfactorily prove to you. For I was fascinated by them to such a degree that my eyes grew blind to things which I had seemed to myself, and also to others, to know quite well; I forgot what I had before thought self-evident truths; for example, such a fact as that the growth of man is the result of eating and drinking; for when by the digestion of food flesh is added to flesh and bone to bone, and whenever there is an aggregation of congenial elements, the lesser bulk becomes larger and the small man great. Was not that a reasonable notion?

Yes, said Cebes, I think so.

Well; but let me tell you something more. There was a time when I thought that I understood the meaning of greater and less pretty well; and when I saw a great man standing by a little one, I fancied that one was taller than the other by a head; or one horse would appear to be greater than another horse: and still more clearly did I seem to perceive that ten is two more than eight, and that two cubits are more than one, because two is the double of one.

And what is now your notion of such matters? said Cebes.

I should be far enough from imagining, he replied, that I knew the cause of any of them, by heaven I should; for I cannot satisfy myself that, when one is added to one, the one to which the addition is made becomes two, or that the two units added together make two by reason of the addition. I cannot understand how, when separated from the other, each of them was one and not two, and now, when they are brought together, the mere juxtaposition or meeting of them should be the cause of their becoming two: neither can I understand how the division of one is the way to make two; for then a different cause would produce the same effect,—as in the former instance the

addition and juxtaposition of one to one was the cause of
two, in this the separation and subtraction of one from
the other would be the cause. Nor am I any longer satisfied
that I understand the reason why one or anything else is
either generated or destroyed or is at all, but I have in
my mind some confused notion of a new method, and can
never admit the other.

Then I heard some one reading, as he said, from a book
of Anaxagoras, that mind was the disposer and cause of all,
and I was delighted at this notion, which appeared quite
admirable, and I said to myself: If mind is the disposer,
mind will dispose all for the best, and put each particular
in the best place; and I argued that if any one desired to
find out the cause of the generation or destruction or
existence of anything, he must find out what state of being
or doing or suffering was best for that thing, and therefore a
man had only to consider the best for himself and others,
and then he would also know the worse, since the same science comprehended both. And I rejoiced to think that I had
found in Anaxagoras a teacher of the causes of existence
such as I desired, and I imagined that he would tell me
first whether the earth is flat or round; and whichever
was true, he would proceed to explain the cause and the
necessity of this being so, and then he would teach me the
nature of the best and show that this was best; and if
he said that the earth was in the centre, he would further
explain that this position was the best, and I should be
satisfied with the explanation given, and not want any other
sort of cause. And I thought that I would then go on and
ask him about the sun and moon and stars, and that he
would explain to me their comparative swiftness, and their
returnings and various states, active and passive, and how
all of them were for the best. For I could not imagine that
when he spoke of mind as the disposer of them, he would
give any other account of their being as they are, except
that this was best; and I thought that when he had ex-

plained to me in detail the cause of each and the cause of all, he would go on to explain to me what was best for each and what was good for all. These hopes I would not have sold for a large sum of money, and I seized the books and read them as fast as I could in my eagerness to know the better and the worse.

What expectations I had formed, and how grievously was I disappointed! As I proceeded, I found my philosopher altogether forsaking mind or any other principle of order, but having recourse to air, and ether, and water, and other eccentricities. I might compare him to a person who began by maintaining generally that mind is the cause of the actions of Socrates, but who, when he endeavoured to explain the causes of my several actions in detail, went on to show that I sit here because my body is made up of bone and muscles; and the bones, as he would say, are hard and have joints which divide them, and the muscles are elastic, and they cover the bones, which have also a covering or environment of flesh and skin which contains them; and as the bones are lifted at their joints by the contraction or relaxation of the muscles, I am able to bend my limbs, and this is why I am sitting here in a curved posture —that is what he would say; and he would have a similar explanation of my talking to you, which he would attribute to sound, and air, and hearing, and he would assign ten thousand other causes of the same sort, forgetting to mention the true cause, which is, that the Athenians have thought fit to condemn me, and accordingly I have thought it better and more right to remain here and undergo my sentence; for I am inclined to think that these muscles and bones of mine would have gone off long ago to Megara or Boeotia—by the dog they would, if they had been moved only by their own idea of what was best, and if I had not chosen the better and nobler part, instead of playing truant and running away, of enduring any punishment which the State inflicts. There is surely a strange confusion of causes and conditions in all this. It may be said, indeed, that without bones and muscles and the other parts of the body I cannot execute my purposes. But to say that I do as I do because of them, and that this is the way in which mind acts, and not from the choice of the best, is a very careless and idle mode of speaking. I wonder that they cannot distinguish the cause from the condition, which the many, feeling about in the dark, are always mistaking and misnaming. And thus one man makes a vortex all round and steadies the earth by the heaven; another gives the air as a support to the earth, which is a sort of broad trough. Any power which in arranging them as they are arranges them for the best never enters into their minds; and instead of finding any superior strength in it, they rather expect to discover another Atlas of the world who is stronger and more everlasting and more containing than the good;— of the obligatory and containing power of the good they think nothing; and yet this is the principle which I would fain learn if any one would teach me. But as I have failed either to discover myself, or to learn of any one else, the nature of the best, I will exhibit to you, if you like, what I have found to be the second best mode of enquiring into the cause.

I should very much like to hear, he replied.

Socrates proceeded:—I thought that as I had failed in the contemplation of true existence, I ought to be careful that I did not lose the eye of my soul; as people may injure their bodily eye by observing and gazing on the sun during an eclipse, unless they take the precaution of only looking at the image reflected in the water, or in some similar medium. So in my own case, I was afraid that my soul might be blinded altogether if I looked at things with my eyes or tried to apprehend them by the help of the senses. And I thought that I had better have recourse to the world of mind and seek there the truth of existence. I dare say that the simile is not perfect—for I am very far from admitting that he who contemplates existences through the medium of thought, sees them only "through a glass darkly," any more than he who considers them in action and operation. However, this was the method which I adopted: I first assumed some principle which I judged to be the strongest, and then I affirmed as true whatever seemed to agree with this, whether relating to the cause or to anything else; and that which disagreed I regarded as untrue. But I should like to explain my meaning more clearly, as I do not think that you as yet understand me.

No indeed, replied Cebes, not very well.

There is nothing new, he said, in what I am about to tell you; but only what I have been always and everywhere repeating in the previous discussion and on other occasions: I want to show you the nature of that cause which has occupied my thoughts. I shall have to go back to those familiar words which are in the mouth of every one, and first of all assume that there is an absolute beauty and goodness and greatness, and the like; grant me this, and I hope to be able to show you the nature of the cause, and to prove the immortality of the soul.

Cebes said: You may proceed at once with the proof, for I grant you this.

Well, he said, then I should like to know whether you agree with me in the next step; for I cannot help thinking, if there be anything beautiful other than absolute beauty, should there be such, that it can be beautiful only in so far as it partakes of absolute beauty—and I should say the same of everything. Do you agree in this notion of the cause?

Yes, he said, I agree.

He proceeded: I know nothing and can understand nothing of any other of those wise causes which are alleged; and if a person says to me that the bloom of colour, or form, or any such thing is a source of beauty, I leave all that, which is only confusing to me, and simply and singly, and perhaps foolishly, hold and am assured in my own mind that nothing makes a thing beautiful but the presence and participation of beauty in whatever way or manner obtained; for as to the manner I am uncertain, but I stoutly contend that by beauty all beautiful things become beautiful. This appears to me to be the safest answer which I can give, either to myself or to another, and to this I cling, in the persuasion that this principle will never be overthrown, and that to myself or to any who asks the question, I may safely reply, That by beauty beautiful things become beautiful. Do you not agree with me?

I do.

And that by greatness only great things become great and greater greater, and by smallness the less become less?

True.

Then if a person were to remark that A is taller by a head than B, and B less by a head than A, you would refuse to admit his statement, and would stoutly contend that what you mean is only that the greater is greater by, and by reason of, greatness, and the less is less only by, and by reason of, smallness; and thus you would avoid the danger of saying that the greater is greater and the less less by the measure of the head, which is the same in both, and would also avoid the monstrous absurdity of supposing that the greater man is greater by reason of the head, which is small. You would be afraid to draw such an inference, would you not?

Indeed, I should, said Cebes, laughing.

In like manner you would be afraid to say that ten exceeded eight by, and by reason of, two; but would say by, and by reason of, number; or you would say that two cubits exceed one cubit not by a half, but by magnitude?—for there is the same liability to error in all these cases.

Very true, he said.

Again, would you not be cautious of affirming that the addition of one to one, or the division of one, is the cause of two? And you would loudly asseverate that you know of no way in which anything comes into existence except by participation in its own proper essence, and consequently, as far as you know, the only cause of two is the participation in duality—this is the way to make two, and the participation in one is the way to make one. You would say: I will let alone puzzles of division and addition—wiser heads than mine may answer them; inexperienced as I am, and ready to start, as the proverb says, at my own shadow, I cannot afford to give up the sure ground of a principle. And if any one assails you there, you would not mind him, or answer him, until you had seen whether the consequences which follow agree with one another or not, and when you are further required to give an explanation of this principle, you would go on to assume a higher principle, and a higher, until you found a resting-place in the best of the higher; but you would not confuse the principle and the consequences in your reasoning, like the Eristics— at least if you wanted to discover real existence. Not that this confusion signifies to them, who never care or think about the matter at all, for they have the wit to be well pleased with themselves however great may be the turmoil of their ideas. But you, if you are a philosopher, will certainly do as I say.

What you say is most true, said Simmias and Cebes, both speaking at once.

Ech. Yes, Phaedo; and I do not wonder at their assenting. Any one who has the least sense will acknowledge the wonderful clearness of Socrates' reasoning.

Phaed. Certainly, Echecrates; and such was the feeling of the whole company at the time.

Ech. Yes, and equally of ourselves, who were not of the company, and are now listening to your recital. But what followed?

Phaed. After all this had been admitted, and they had agreed that ideas exist, and that other things participate

in them and derive their names from them, Socrates, if
I remember rightly, said:—

This is your way of speaking; and yet when you say that
Simmias is greater than Socrates and less than Phaedo, do
you not predicate of Simmias both greatness and smallness?

Yes, I do.

But still you allow that Simmias does not really exceed
Socrates, as the words may seem to imply, because he is
Simmias, but by reason of the size which he has; just as
Simmias does not exceed Socrates because he is Simmias,
any more than because Socrates is Socrates, but because
he has smallness when compared with the greatness of
Simmias?

True.

And if Phaedo exceeds him in size, this is not because
Phaedo is Phaedo, but because Phaedo has greatness relatively to Simmias, who is comparatively smaller?

That is true.

And therefore Simmias is said to be great, and is also
said to be small, because he is in a mean between them,
exceeding the smallness of the one by his greatness, and
allowing the greatness of the other to exceed his smallness.
He added, laughing, I am speaking like a book, but I
believe that what I am saying is true.

Simmias assented.

I speak as I do because I want you to agree with me
in thinking, not only that absolute greatness will never be
great and also small, but that greatness in us or in the
concrete will never admit the small or admit of being exceeded: instead of this, one of two things will happen, either
the greater will fly or retire before the opposite, which is
the less, or at the approach of the less has already ceased
to exist; but will not, if allowing or admitting of smallness,
be changed by that; even as I, having received and admitted smallness when compared with Simmias, remain just
as I was, and am the same small person. And as the idea of

greatness cannot condescend ever to be or become small,
in like manner the smallness in us cannot be or become
great; nor can any other opposite which remains the same
ever be or become its own opposite, but either passes away
or perishes in the change.

That, replied Cebes, is quite my notion.

Hereupon one of the company, though I do not exactly
remember which of them, said: In heaven's name, is not
this the direct contrary of what was admitted before—that
out of the greater came the less and out of the less the
greater, and that opposites were simply generated from
opposites; but now this principle seems to be utterly denied.

Socrates inclined his head to the speaker and listened. I
like your courage, he said, in reminding us of this. But you
do not observe that there is a difference in the two cases.
For then we were speaking of opposites in the concrete,
and now of the essential opposite which, as is affirmed,
neither in us nor in nature can ever be at variance with
itself: then, my friend, we were speaking of things in which
opposites are inherent and which are called after them, but
now about the opposites which are inherent in them and
which give their name to them; and these essential opposites
will never, as we maintain, admit of generation into or out
of one another. At the same time, turning to Cebes, he said:
Are you at all disconcerted, Cebes, at our friend's objection?

No, I do not feel so, said Cebes; and yet I cannot deny
that I am often disturbed by objections.

Then we are agreed after all, said Socrates, that the
opposite will never in any case be opposed to itself?

To that we are quite agreed, he replied.

Yet once more let me ask you to consider the question
from another point of view, and see whether you agree
with me:—There is a thing which you term heat, and
another thing which you term cold?

Certainly.

But are they the same as fire and snow?

Most assuredly not.

Heat is a thing different from fire, and cold is not the same with snow?

Yes.

And yet you will surely admit, that when snow, as was before said, is under the influence of heat, they will not remain snow and heat; but at the advance of the heat, the snow will either retire or perish?

Very true, he replied.

And the fire too at the advance of the cold will either retire or perish; and when the fire is under the influence of the cold, they will not remain as before, fire and cold.

That is true, he said.

And in some cases the name of the idea is not only attached to the idea in an eternal connection, but anything else which, not being the idea, exists only in the form of the idea, may also lay claim to it. I will try to make this clearer by an example:—The odd number is always called by the name of odd?

Very true.

But is this the only thing which is called odd? Are there not other things which have their own name, and yet are called odd, because, although not the same as oddness, they are never without oddness?—that is what I mean to ask— whether numbers, such as the number three, are not of the class of odd. And there are many other examples: would you not say, for example, that three may be called by its proper name, and also be called odd, which is not the same with three? and this may be said not only of three but also of five, and of every alternate number—each of them without being oddness is odd; and in the same way two and four, and the other series of alternate numbers, has every number even, without being evenness. Do you agree?

Of course.

Then now mark the point at which I am aiming:—not only do essential opposites exclude one another, but also concrete things, which, although not in themselves opposed, contain opposites; these, I say, likewise reject the idea which is opposed to that which is contained in them, and when it approaches them they either perish or withdraw. For example: Will not the number three endure annihilation or anything sooner than be converted into an even number, while remaining three?

Very true, said Cebes.

And yet, he said, the number two is certainly not opposed to the number three?

It is not.

Then not only do opposite ideas repel the advance of one another, but also there are other natures which repel the approach of opposites.

Very true, he said.

Suppose, he said, that we endeavour, if possible, to determine what these are.

By all means.

Are they not, Cebes, such as compel the things of which they have possession, not only to take their own form, but also the form of some opposite?

What do you mean?

I mean, as I was just now saying, and as I am sure that you know, that those things which are possessed by the number three must not only be there in number, but must also be odd.

Quite true.

And on this oddness, of which the number three has the impress, the opposite idea will never intrude?

No.

And this impress was given by the odd principle?

Yes.

And to the odd is opposed the even?

True.

Then the idea of the even number will never arrive at three?

No.

Then three has no part in the even?

None.

Then the triad or number three is uneven?

Very true.

To return then to my distinction of natures which are not opposed, and yet do not admit opposites—as, in the instance given, three, although not opposed to the even, does not any the more admit of the even, but always brings the opposite into play on the other side; or as two does not receive the odd, or fire the cold—from these examples (and there are many more of them) perhaps you may be able to arrive at the general conclusion, that not only opposites will not receive opposites, but also that nothing which brings the opposite will admit the opposite of that which it brings, in that to which it is brought. And here let me recapitulate—for there is no harm in repetition. The number five will not admit the nature of the even, any more than ten, which is the double of five, will admit the nature of the odd. The double has another opposite, and is not strictly opposed to the odd, but nevertheless rejects the odd altogether. Nor again will parts in the ratio 3:2, nor any fraction in which there is a half, nor again in which there is a third, admit the notion of the whole, although they are not opposed to the whole: You will agree?

Yes, he said, I entirely agree and go along with you in that.

And now, he said, let us begin again; and do not you answer my questions in the words in which I ask it: let me have not the old safe answer of which I spoke at first, but another equally safe, of which the truth will be inferred by you from what has been just said. I mean that if any one asks you "what that is, of which the inherence makes the body hot," you will reply not heat (this is what I call the safe and stupid answer), but fire, a far superior answer, which we are now in a condition to give. Or if any one asks you "why a body is diseased," you will not say from disease, but from fever; and instead of saying that oddness is the cause of odd numbers, you will say that the monad is the cause of them: and so of things in general, as I dare say that you will understand sufficiently without my adducing any further examples.

Yes, he said, I quite understand you.

Tell me, then, what is that of which the inherence will render the body alive?

The soul, he replied.

And is this always the case?

Yes, he said, of course.

Then whatever the soul possesses, to that she comes bearing life?

Yes, certainly.

And is there any opposite to life?

There is, he said.

And what is that?

Death.

Then the soul, as has been acknowledged, will never receive the opposite of what she brings.

Impossible, replied Cebes.

And now, he said, what did we just now call that principle which repels the even?

The odd.

And that principle which repels the musical or the just?

The unmusical, he said, and the unjust.

And what do we call that principle which does not admit of death?

The immortal, he said.

And does the soul admit of death?

No.

Then the soul is immortal?

Yes, he said.

And may we say that this has been proven?

Yes, abundantly proven, Socrates, he replied.

Supposing that the odd were imperishable, must not three be imperishable?

Of course.

And if that which is cold were imperishable, when the warm principle came attacking the snow, must not the snow have retired whole and unmelted—for it could never have perished, nor could it have remained and admitted the heat?

True, he said.

Again, if the uncooling or warm principle were imperishable, the fire when assailed by cold would not have perished or have been extinguished, but would have gone away unaffected?

Certainly, he said.

And the same may be said of the immortal: if the immortal is also imperishable, the soul when attacked by death cannot perish; for the preceding argument shows that the soul will not admit of death, or ever be dead, any more than three or the odd number will admit of the even, or fire, or the heat in the fire, of the cold. Yet a person may say: "But although the odd will not become even at the approach of the even, why may not the odd perish and the even take the place of the odd?" Now to him who makes this objection, we cannot answer that the odd principle is imperishable; for this has not been acknowledged, but if this had been acknowledged, there would have been no difficulty in contending that at the approach of the even the odd principle and the number three took their departure; and the same argument would have held good of fire and heat and any other thing.

Very true.

And the same may be said of the immortal: if the immortal is also imperishable, then the soul will be imperishable as well as immortal; but if not, some other proof of her imperishableness will have to be given.

No other proof is needed, he said; for if the immortal,

being eternal, is liable to perish, then nothing is imperishable.

Yes, replied Socrates, and yet all men will agree that God, and the essential form of life, and the immortal in general, will never perish.

Yes, all men, he said—that is true; and what is more, gods, if I am not mistaken, as well as men.

Seeing then that the immortal is indestructible, must not the soul, if she is immortal, be also imperishable?

Most certainly.

Then when death attacks a man, the mortal portion of him may be supposed to die, but the immortal retires at the approach of death and is preserved safe and sound?

True.

Then, Cebes, beyond question, the soul is immortal and imperishable, and our souls will truly exist in another world!

I am convinced, Socrates, said Cebes, and have nothing more to object; but if my friend Simmias, or any one else, has any further objection to make, he had better speak out, and not keep silence, since I do not know to what other season he can defer the discussion, if there is anything which he wants to say or to have said.

But I have nothing more to say, replied Simmias; nor can I see any reason for doubt after what has been said. But I still feel and cannot help feeling uncertain in my own mind, when I think of the greatness of the subject and the feebleness of man.

Yes, Simmias, replied Socrates, that is well said: and I may add that first principles, even if they appear certain, should be carefully considered; and when they are satisfactorily ascertained, then, with a sort of hesitating confidence in human reason, you may, I think, follow the course of the argument; and if that be plain and clear, there will be no need for any further enquiry.

Very true.

But then, O my friends, he said, if the soul is really im-mortal, what care should be taken of her, not only in respect of the portion of time which is called life, but of eternity! And the danger of neglecting her from this point of view does indeed appear to be awful. If death had only been the end of all, the wicked would have had a good bargain in dying, for they would have been happily quit not only of their body, but of their own evil together with their souls. But now, inasmuch as the soul is manifestly immortal, there is no release or salvation from evil except the attainment of the highest virtue and wisdom. For the soul when on her progress to the world below takes nothing with her but nurture and education; and these are said greatly to bene-fit or greatly to injure the departed, at the very beginning of his journey thither.

For after death, as they say, the genius of each individ-ual, to whom he belonged in life, leads him to a certain place in which the dead are gathered together, whence after judgment has been given they pass into the world below, following the guide, who is appointed to conduct them from this world to the other: and when they have there received their due and remained their time, another guide brings them back again after many revolutions of ages. Now this way to the other world is not, as Aeschylus says in the Telephus, a single and straight path—if that were so no guide would be needed, for no one could miss it; but there are many partings of the road, and windings, as I infer from the rites and sacrifices which are offered to the gods below in places where three ways meet on earth. The wise and orderly soul follows in the straight path and is con-scious of her surroundings; but the soul which desires the body, and which, as I was relating before, has long been fluttering about the lifeless frame and the world of sight, is after many struggles and many sufferings hardly and with violence carried away by her attendant genius; and when she arrives at the place where the other souls are gathered, if she be impure and have done impure deeds, whether foul murders or other crimes which are the brothers of these, and the works of brothers in crime—from that soul every one flees and turns away; no one will be her companion, no one her guide, but alone she wanders in extremity of evil until certain times are fulfilled, and when they are fulfilled, she is borne irresistibly to her own fitting habitation; as every pure and just soul which has passed through life in the company and under the guidance of the gods has also her own proper home.

Now the earth has divers wonderful regions, and is indeed in nature and extent very unlike the notions of geographers, as I believe on the authority of one who shall be nameless.

What do you mean, Socrates? said Simmias. I have myself heard many descriptions of the earth, but I do not know, and I should very much like to know, in which of these you put faith.

And I, Simmias, replied Socrates, if I had the art of Glaucus would tell you; although I know not that the art of Glaucus could prove the truth of my tale, which I myself should never be able to prove, and even if I could, I fear, Simmias, that my life would come to an end before the argument was completed. I may describe to you, however, the form and regions of the earth according to my conception of them.

That, said Simmias, will be enough.

Well, then, he said, my conviction is that the earth is a round body in the centre of the heavens, and therefore has no need of air or any similar force to be a support, but is kept there and hindered from falling or inclining any way by the equability of the surrounding heaven and by her own equipoise. For that which, being in equipoise, is in the centre of that which is equably diffused, will not incline any way in any degree, but will always remain in the same state and not deviate. And this is my first notion.

Which is surely a correct one, said Simmias.

Also I believe that the earth is very vast, and that we who dwell in the region extending from the river Phasis to the Pillars of Heracles inhabit a small portion only about the sea, like ants or frogs about a marsh, and that there are other inhabitants of many other like places; for everywhere on the face of the earth there are hollows of various forms and sizes, into which the water and the mist and the lower air collect. But the true earth is pure and situated in the pure heaven—there are the stars also; and it is the heaven which is commonly spoken of by us as the ether, and of which our own earth is the sediment gathering in the hollows beneath. But we who live in these hollows are deceived into the notion that we are dwelling above on the surface of the earth; which is just as if a creature who was at the bottom of the sea were to fancy that he was on the surface of the water, and that the sea was the heaven through which he saw the sun and the other stars, he having never come to the surface by reason of his feebleness and sluggishness, and having never lifted up his head and seen, nor ever heard from one who had seen, how much purer and fairer the world above is than his own. And such is exactly our case: for we are dwelling in a hollow of the earth, and fancy that we are on the surface; and the air we call the heaven, in which we imagine that the stars move. But the fact is, that owing to our feebleness and sluggishness we are prevented from reaching the surface of the air: for if any man could arrive at the exterior limit, or take the wings of a bird and come to the top, then like a fish who puts his head out of the water and sees this world, he would see a world beyond; and, if the nature of man could sustain the sight, he would acknowledge that this other world was the place of the true heaven and the true light and the true earth. For our earth, and the stones, and the entire region which surrounds us, are spoilt and corroded, as in the sea all things are corroded by the brine, neither is there any noble or perfect growth, but caverns only, and sand, and an endless slough of mud; and even the shore is not to be compared to the fairer sights of this world. And still less is this our world to be compared with the other. Of that upper earth which is under the heaven, I can tell you a charming tale, Simmias, which is well worth hearing.

And we, Socrates, replied Simmias, shall be charmed to listen to you.

The tale, my friend, he said, is as follows:—In the first place, the earth, when looked at from above, is in appearance streaked like one of those balls which have leather coverings in twelve pieces, and is decked with various colours, of which the colours used by painters on earth are in a manner samples. But there the whole earth is made up of them, and they are brighter far and clearer than ours; there is a purple of wonderful lustre, also the radiance of gold, and the white which is in the earth is whiter than any chalk or snow. Of these and other colours the earth is made up, and they are more in number and fairer than the eye of man has ever seen; the very hollows (of which I was speaking) filled with air and water have a colour of their own, and are seen like light gleaming amid the diversity of the other colours, so that the whole presents a single and continuous appearance of variety in unity. And in this fair region everything that grows—trees, and flowers, and fruits—are in a like degree fairer than any here; and there are hills, having stones in them in a like degree smoother, and more transparent, and fairer in colour than our highly valued emeralds and sardonyxes and jaspers, and other gems, which are but minute fragments of them: for there all the stones are like our precious stones, and fairer still.[1]   The reason is, that they are pure, and not, like our precious stones, infected or corroded by the corrupt briny elements which coagulate among us, and which breed foulness and disease both in earth and stones, as well as in animals and plants. They are the jewels of the upper

[1] Cp. Rev., esp. c. xxi. v. 18 ff.

earth, which also shines with gold and silver and the like, and they are set in the light of day and are large and abundant and in all places, making the earth a sight to gladden the beholder's eye. And there are animals and men, some in a middle region, others dwelling about the air as we dwell about the sea; others in islands which the air flows round, near the continent; and, in a word, the air is used by them as the water and the sea are by us, and the ether is to them what the air is to us. Moreover, the temperament of their seasons is such that they have no disease, and live much longer than we do, and have sight and hearing and smell, and all the other senses, in far greater perfection, in the same proportion that air is purer than water or the ether than air. Also they have temples and sacred places in which the gods really dwell, and they hear their voices and receive their answers, and are conscious of them and hold converse with them; and they see the sun, moon, and stars as they truly are, and their other blessedness is of a piece with this.

Such is the nature of the whole earth, and of the things which are around the earth; and there are divers regions in the hollows on the faces of the globe everywhere, some of them deeper and more extended than that which we inhabit, others deeper but with a narrower opening than ours, and some are shallower and also wider. All have numerous perforations, and there are passages broad and narrow in the interior of the earth, connecting them with one another; and there flows out of and into them, as into basins, a vast tide of water, and huge subterranean streams of perennial rivers, and springs hot and cold, and a great fire, and great rivers of fire, and streams of liquid mud, thin or thick (like the rivers of mud in Sicily, and the lava streams which follow them), and the regions about which they happen to flow are filled up with them. And there is a swinging or seesaw in the interior of the earth which moves all this up and down, and is due to the following cause:—There is a chasm which is the vastest of them all, and pierces right through the whole earth; this is that chasm which Homer describes in the words,—

"Far off, where is the inmost depth beneath the earth";

and which he in other places, and many other poets, have called Tartarus. And the seesaw is caused by the streams flowing into and out of this chasm, and they each have the nature of the soil through which they flow. And the reason why the streams are always flowing in and out, is that the watery element has no bed or bottom, but is swinging and surging up and down, and the surrounding wind and air do the same; they follow the water up and down, hither and thither, over the earth—just as in the act of respiration the air is always in process of inhalation and exhalation,—and the wind swinging with the water in and out produces fearful and irresistible blasts: when the waters retire with a rush into the lower parts of the earth, as they are called, they flow through the earth in those regions, and fill them up like water raised by a pump, and then when they leave those regions and rush back hither, they again fill the hollows here, and when these are filled, flow through subterranean channels and find their way to their several places, forming seas, and lakes, and rivers, and springs. Thence they again enter the earth, some of them making a long circuit into many lands, others going to a few places and not so distant; and again fall into Tartarus, some at a point a good deal lower than that at which they rose, and others not much lower, but all in some degree lower than the point from which they came. And some burst forth again on the opposite side, and some on the same side, and some wind round the earth with one or many folds like the coils of a serpent, and descend as far as they can, but always return and fall into the chasm. The rivers flowing in either direction can descend only to the centre and no further, for opposite to the rivers is a precipice.

Now these rivers are many, and mighty, and diverse, and there are four principal ones, of which the greatest and outermost is that called Oceanus, which flows round the earth in a circle; and in the opposite direction flows Ache-ron, which passes under the earth through desert places into the Acherusian lake: this is the lake to the shores of which the souls of the many go when they are dead, and after waiting an appointed time, which is to some a longer and to some a shorter time, they are sent back to be born again as animals. The third river passes out between the two, and near the place of outlet pours into a vast region of fire, and forms a lake larger than the Mediterranean Sea, boiling with water and mud; and proceeding muddy and turbid, and winding about the earth, comes, among other places, to the extremities of the Acherusian lake, but mingles not with the waters of the lake, and after making many coils about the earth plunges into Tartarus at a deeper level. This is that Pyriphlegethon, as the stream is called, which throws up jets of fire in different parts of the earth. The fourth river goes out on the opposite side, and falls first of all into a wild and savage region, which is all of a dark blue colour, like lapis lazuli; and this is that river which is called the Stygian river, and falls into and forms the Lake Styx, and after falling into the lake and receiving strange powers in the waters, passes under the earth, winding round in the opposite direction, and comes near the Acherusian lake from the opposite side to Pyr-iphlegethon. And the water of this river too mingles with no other, but flows round in a circle and falls into Tartarus over against Pyriphlegethon; and the name of the river, as the poets say, is Cocytus.

Such is the nature of the other world; and when the dead arrive at the place to which the genius of each sever-ally guides them, first of all, they have sentence passed upon them, as they have lived well and piously or not. And those who appear to have lived neither well nor ill, go to the river Acheron, and embarking in any vessels which they may find, are carried in them to the lake, and there they dwell and are purified of their evil deeds, and having suffered the penalty of the wrongs which they have done to others, they are absolved, and receive the rewards of their good deeds, each of them according to his deserts. But those who appear to be incurable by reason of the greatness of their crimes—who have committed many and terrible deeds of sacrilege, murders foul and violent, or the like—such are hurled into Tartarus which is their suitable destiny, and they never come out. Those again who have committed crimes, which, although great, are not irremediable—who in a moment of anger, for example, have done some violence to a father or a mother, and have repented for the remainder of their lives, or, who have taken the life of another under the like extenuating circumstances —these are plunged into Tartarus, the pains of which they are compelled to undergo for a year, but at the end of the year the wave casts them forth—mere homicides by way of Cocytus, parricides and matricides by Pyriphlegethon— and they are borne to the Acherusian lake, and there they lift up their voices and call upon the victims whom they have slain or wronged, to have pity on them, and to be kind to them, and let them come out into the lake. And if they prevail, then they come forth and cease from their troubles; but if not, they are carried back again into Tartarus and from thence into the rivers unceasingly, until they obtain mercy from those whom they have wronged: for that is the sentence inflicted upon them by their judges. Those too who have been pre-eminent for holiness of life are released from this earthly prison, and go to their pure home which is above, and dwell in the purer earth; and of these, such as have duly purified themselves with philosophy live henceforth altogether without the body, in mansions fairer still which may not be described, and of which the time would fail me to tell.

Wherefore, Simmias, seeing all these things, what ought not we to do that we may obtain virtue and wisdom in this life? Fair is the prize, and the hope great!

A man of sense ought not to say, nor will I be very confident, that the description which I have given of the soul and her mansions is exactly true. But I do say that, inasmuch as the soul is shown to be immortal, he may venture to think, not improperly or unworthily, that something of the kind is true. The venture is a glorious one, and he ought to comfort himself with words like these, which is the reason why I lengthen out the tale. Wherefore, I say, let a man be of good cheer about his soul, who having cast away the pleasures and ornaments of the body as alien to him and working harm rather than good, has sought after the pleasures of knowledge; and has arrayed the soul, not in some foreign attire, but in her own proper jewels, temperance, and justice, and courage, and nobility, and truth —in these adorned she is ready to go on her journey to the world below, when her hour comes. You, Simmias and Cebes, and all other men, will depart at some time or other. Me already, as a tragic poet would say, the voice of fate calls. Soon I must drink the poison; and I think that I had better repair to the bath first, in order that the women may not have the trouble of washing my body after I am dead.

When he had done speaking, Crito said: And have you any commands for us, Socrates—anything to say about your children, or any other matter in which we can serve you?

Nothing particular, Crito, he replied: only, as I have always told you, take care of yourselves; that is a service which you may be ever rendering to me and mine and to all of us, whether you promise to do so or not. But if you have no thought for yourselves, and care not to walk according to the rule which I have prescribed for you, not now for the first time, however much you may profess or promise at the moment, it will be of no avail.

We will do our best, said Crito: And in what way shall we bury you?

In any way that you like; but you must get hold of me, and take care that I do not run away from you. Then he turned to us, and added with a smile:—I cannot make Crito believe that I am the same Socrates who have been talking and conducting the argument; he fancies that I am the other Socrates whom he will soon see, a dead body—and he asks, How shall he bury me? And though I have spoken many words in the endeavour to show that when I have drunk the poison I shall leave you and go to the joys of the blessed,—these words of mine, with which I was comforting you and myself, have had, as I perceive, no effect upon Crito. And therefore I want you to be surety for me to him now, as at the trial he was surety to the judges for me: but let the promise be of another sort; for he was surety for me to the judges that I would remain, and you must be my surety to him that I shall not remain, but go away and depart; and then he will suffer less at my death, and not be grieved when he sees my body being burned or buried. I would not have him sorrow at my hard lot, or say at the burial, Thus we lay out Socrates, or, Thus we follow him to the grave or bury him; for false words are not only evil in themselves, but they inflict the soul with evil. Be of good cheer then, my dear Crito, and say that you are burying my body only, and do with that whatever is usual, and what you think best.

When he had spoken these words, he arose and went into a chamber to bathe; Crito followed him and told us to wait. So we remained behind, talking and thinking of the subject of discourse, and also of the greatness of our sorrow; he was like a father of whom we were being bereaved, and we were about to pass the rest of our lives as orphans.

When he had taken the bath his children were brought to him (he had two young sons and an elder one); and the women of his family also came, and he talked to them and gave them a few directions in the presence of Crito; then he dismissed them and returned to us.

Now the hour of sunset was near, for a good deal of time had passed while he was within. When he came out, he sat down with us again after his bath, but not much was said. Soon the jailer, who was the servant of the Eleven, entered and stood by him, saying:—To you, Socrates, whom I know to be the noblest and gentlest and best of all who ever came to this place, I will not impute the angry feeling of other men, who rage and swear at me, when, in obedience to the authorities, I bid them drink the poison —indeed, I am sure that you will not be angry with me; for others, as you are aware, and not I, are to blame. And so fare you well, and try to bear lightly what must needs be—you know my errand. Then bursting into tears he turned away and went out.

Socrates looked at him and said: I return your good wishes, and will do as you bid. Then turning to us, he said, How charming the man is: since I have been in prison he has always been coming to see me, and at times he would talk to me, and was as good to me as could be, and now see how generously he sorrows on my account. We must do as he says, Crito; and therefore let the cup be brought, if the poison is prepared: if not, let the attendant prepare some.

Yet, said Crito, the sun is still upon the hill-tops, and I know that many a one has taken the draught late, and after the announcement has been made to him, he has eaten and drunk, and enjoyed the society of his beloved: do not hurry—there is time enough.

Socrates said: Yes, Crito, and they of whom you speak are right in so acting, for they think that they will be gainers by the delay; but I am right in not following their

example, for I do not think that I should gain anything
by drinking the poison a little later; I should only be ridiculous in my own eyes for sparing and saving a life which
is already forfeit. Please then to do as I say, and not to
refuse me.

Crito made a sign to the servant, who was standing by;
and he went out, and having been absent for some time,
returned with the jailer carrying the cup of poison. Socrates said: You, my good friend, who are experienced in these
matters, shall give me directions how I am to proceed. The
man answered: You have only to walk about until your
legs are heavy, and then to lie down, and the poison will
act. At the same time he handed the cup to Socrates, who
in the easiest and gentlest manner, without the least fear
or change of colour or feature, looking at the man with
all his eyes. Echecrates, as his manner was, took the cup
and said: What do you say about making a libation out
of this cup to any god? May I, or not? The man answered:
We only prepare, Socrates, just so much as we deem enough.
I understand, he said: but I may and must ask the gods
to prosper my journey from this to the other world—even
so—and so be it according to my prayer. Then raising the
cup to his lips, quite readily and cheerfully he drank off
the poison. And hitherto most of us had been able to control our sorrow; but now when we saw him drinking, and
saw too that he had finished the draught, we could no
longer forbear, and in spite of myself my own tears were
flowing fast; so that I covered my face and wept, not for
him, but at the thought of my own calamity in having to
part from such a friend. Nor was I the first; for Crito,
when he found himself unable to restrain his tears, had
got up, and I followed; and at that moment, Apollodorus,
who had been weeping all the time, broke out in a loud
and passionate cry which made cowards of us all. Socrates
alone retained his calmness: What is this strange outcry?
he said. I sent away the women mainly in order that they

might not misbehave in this way, for I have been told that a man should die in peace. Be quiet then, and have patience. When we heard his words we were ashamed, and refrained our tears; and he walked about until, as he said, his legs began to fail, and then he lay on his back, according to directions, and the man who gave him the poison now and then looked at his feet and legs; and after a while he pressed his foot hard, and asked him if he could feel; and he said, No; and then his leg, and so upwards and upwards, and showed us that he was cold and stiff. And he felt them himself, and said: When the poison reaches the heart, that will be the end. He was beginning to grow cold about the groin, when he uncovered his face, for he had covered himself up, and said—they were his last words —he said: Crito, I owe a cock to Asclepius; will you remember to pay the debt? The debt shall be paid, said Crito; is there anything else? There was no answer to this question; but in a minute or two a movement was heard, and the attendants uncovered him; his eyes were set, and Crito closed his eyes and mouth.

Such was the end, Echecrates, of our friend; concerning whom I may truly say, that of all men of his time whom I have known, he was the wisest and justest and best.

PROTAGORAS

PROTAGORAS

PERSONS OF THE DIALOGUE

SOCRATES, *who is the narrator of the Dialogue to his Companion.*
HIPPOCRATES.
ALCIBIADES.

CRITIAS.
PROTAGORAS,
HIPPIAS,   } *Sophists.*
PRODICUS,
CALLIAS, *a wealthy Athenian.*

SCENE: The House of Callias.

Companion. Where do you come from, Socrates? And yet I need hardly ask the question, for I know that you have been in chase of the fair Alcibiades. I saw him the day before yesterday; and he had got a beard like a man,— and he is a man, as I may tell you in your ear. But I thought that he was still very charming.

Soc. What of his beard? Are you not of Homer's opinion, who says,[1]

"Youth is most charming when the beard appears"?

And that is now the charm of Alcibiades.

Com. Well, and how do matters proceed? Have you been visiting him, and was he gracious to you?

Soc. Yes, I thought that he was very gracious; and especially to-day, for I have just come from him, and he has been helping me in an argument. But shall I tell you a strange thing? I paid no attention to him, and several times I quite forgot that he was present.

Com. What is the meaning of this? Has anything happened between you and him? For surely you cannot have discovered a fairer love than he is; certainly not in this city of Athens.

[1] Il. xxiv. 348.

Soc. Yes, much fairer.

Com. What do you mean—a citizen or a foreigner?

Soc. A foreigner.

Com. Of what country?

Soc. Of Abdera.

Com. And is this stranger really in your opinion a fairer love than the son of Cleinias?

Soc. And is not the wiser always the fairer, sweet friend?

Com. But have you really met, Socrates, with some wise one?

Soc. Say rather, with the wisest of all living men, if you are willing to accord that title to Protagoras.

Com. What! Is Protagoras in Athens?

Soc. Yes; he has been here two days.

Com. And do you just come from an interview with him?

Soc. Yes; and I have heard and said many things.

Com. Then, if you have no engagement, suppose that you sit down and tell me what passed, and my attendant here shall give up his place to you.

Soc. To be sure; and I shall be grateful to you for listening.

Com. Thank you, too, for telling us.

Soc. That is thank you twice over. Listen then:—

Last night, or rather very early this morning, Hippocrates, the son of Apollodorus and the brother of Phason, gave a tremendous thump with his staff at my door; some one opened to him, and he came rushing in and bawled out: Socrates, are you awake or asleep?

I knew his voice, and said: Hippocrates, is that you? and do you bring any news?

Good news, he said; nothing but good.

Delightful, I said; but what is the news? and why have you come hither at this unearthly hour?

He drew nearer to me and said: Protagoras is come.

Yes, I replied; he came two days ago: have you only just heard of his arrival?

Yes, by the gods, he said; but not until yesterday evening.

At the same time he felt for the truckle-bed, and sat down at my feet, and then he said: Yesterday, quite late in the evening, on my return from Oenoe, whither I had gone in pursuit of my runaway slave Satyrus, as I meant to have told you, if some other matter had not come in the way;—on my return, when we had done supper and were about to retire to rest, my brother said to me: Protagoras is come. I was going to you at once, and then I thought that the night was far spent. But the moment sleep left me after my fatigue, I got up and came hither direct.

I, who knew the very courageous madness of the man, said: What is the matter? Has Protagoras robbed you of anything?

He replied, laughing: Yes, indeed he has, Socrates, of the wisdom which he keeps from me.

But, surely, I said, if you give him money, and make friends with him, he will make you as wise as he is himself.

Would to heaven, he replied, that this were the case! He might take all that I have, and all that my friends have, if he pleased. But that is why I have come to you now, in order that you may speak to him on my behalf; for I am young and also I have never seen nor heard him (when he visited Athens before I was but a child); and all men praise him, Socrates; he is reputed to be the most accomplished of speakers. There is no reason why we should not go to him at once, and then we shall find him at home. He lodges, as I hear, with Callias the son of Hipponicus: let us start.

I replied: Not yet, my good friend; the hour is too early. But let us rise and take a turn in the court and wait about there until daybreak; when the day breaks, then we will go. For Protagoras is generally at home, and we shall be sure to find him; never fear.

Upon this we got up and walked about in the court, and I thought that I would make trial of the strength of his resolution. So I examined him and put questions to him. Tell me, Hippocrates, I said, as you are going to Protagoras, and will be paying your money to him, what is he to whom you are going? and what will he make of you? If, for example, you had thought of going to Hippocrates of Cos, the Asclepiad, and were about to give him your money, and some one had said to you: You are paying money to your namesake Hippocrates, O Hippocrates; tell me, what is he that you give him money? how would you have answered?

I should say, he replied, that I gave money to him as a physician.

And what will he make of you?

A physician, he said.

And if you were resolved to go to Polycleitus the Argive, or Pheidias the Athenian, and were intending to give them money, and some one had asked you: What are Polycleitus and Pheidias? and why do you give them this money?— how would you have answered?

I should have answered, that they were statuaries.

And what will they make of you?

A statuary, of course.

Well, now, I said, you and I are going to Protagoras, and we are ready to pay him money on your behalf. If our own means are sufficient, and we can gain him with these, we shall be only too glad; but if not, then we are to spend the money of your friends as well. Now suppose that while we are thus enthusiastically pursuing our object some one were to say to us: Tell me, Socrates, and you Hippocrates, what is Protagoras, and why are you going to pay him money?—how should we answer? I know that Pheidias is a sculptor, and that Homer is a poet; but what appellation is given to Protagoras? how is he designated?

They call him a Sophist, Socrates, he replied.

Then we are going to pay our money to him in the character of a Sophist?

Certainly.

But suppose a person were to ask this further question: And how about yourself? What will Protagoras make of you, if you go to see him?

He answered, with a blush upon his face (for the day was just beginning to dawn, so that I could see him): Unless this differs in some way from the former instances, I suppose that he will make a Sophist of me.

By the gods, I said, and are you not ashamed at having to appear before the Hellenes in the character of a Sophist?

Indeed, Socrates, to confess the truth, I am.

But you should not assume, Hippocrates, that the instruction of Protagoras is of this nature: may you not learn of him in the same way that you learned the arts of the grammarian, or musician, or trainer, not with the view of making any of them a profession, but only as a part of education, and because a private gentleman and freeman ought to know them?

Just so, he said; and that, in my opinion, is a far truer account of the teaching of Protagoras.

I said: I wonder whether you know what you are doing?

And what am I doing?

You are going to commit your soul to the care of a man whom you call a Sophist. And yet I hardly think that you know what a Sophist is; and if not, then you do not even know to whom you are committing your soul and whether the thing to which you commit yourself be good or evil.

I certainly think that I do know, he replied.

Then tell me, what do you imagine that he is?

I take him to be one who knows wise things, he replied, as his name implies.

And might you not, I said, affirm this of the painter and of the carpenter also: Do not they, too, know wise things?

But suppose a person were to ask us: In what are the painters wise? We should answer: In what relates to the making of likenesses, and similarly of other things. And if he were further to ask: What is the wisdom of the Sophist, and what is the manufacture over which he presides?—how should we answer him?

How should we answer him, Socrates? What other answer could there be but that he presides over the art which makes men eloquent?

Yes, I replied, that is very likely true, but not enough; for in the answer a further question is involved: Of what does the Sophist make a man talk eloquently? The player on the lyre may be supposed to make a man talk eloquently about that which he makes him understand, that is about playing the lyre. Is not that true?

Yes.

Then about what does the Sophist make him eloquent? Must not he make him eloquent in that which he understands?

Yes, that may be assumed.

And what is that which the Sophist knows and makes his disciples know?

Indeed, he said, I cannot tell.

Then I proceeded to say: Well, but are you aware of the danger which you are incurring? If you were going to commit your body to some one, who might do good or harm to it, would you not carefully consider and ask the opinion of your friends and kindred, and deliberate many days as to whether you should give him the care of your body? But when the soul is in question, which you hold to be of far more value than the body, and upon the good or evil of which depends the well-being of your all,—about this you never consulted either with your father or with your brother or with any one of us who are your companions. But no sooner does this foreigner appear, than you instantly commit your soul to his keeping. In the evening, as you say, you hear of him, and in the morning you go to him, never deliberating or taking the opinion of any one as to whether you ought to entrust yourself to him or not;—you have quite made up your mind that you will at all hazards be a pupil of Protagoras, and are prepared to expend all the property of yourself and of your friends in carrying out at any price this determination, although, as you admit, you do not know him, and have never spoken with him: and you call him a Sophist, but are manifestly ignorant of what a Sophist is; and yet you are going to commit yourself to his keeping.

When he heard me say this, he replied: No other inference, Socrates, can be drawn from your words.

I proceeded: Is not a Sophist, Hippocrates, one who deals wholesale or retail in the food of the soul? To me that appears to be his nature.

And what, Socrates, is the food of the soul?

Surely, I said, knowledge is the food of the soul; and we must take care, my friend, that the Sophist does not deceive us when he praises what he sells, like the dealers wholesale or retail who sell the food of the body; for they praise indiscriminately all their goods, without knowing what are really beneficial or hurtful: neither do their customers know, with the exception of any trainer or physician who may happen to buy of them. In like manner those who carry about the wares of knowledge, and make the round of the cities, and sell or retail them to any customer who is in want of them, praise them all alike; though I should not wonder, O my friend, if many of them were really ignorant of their effect upon the soul; and their customers equally ignorant, unless he who buys of them happens to be a physician of the soul. If, therefore, you have understanding of what is good and evil, you may safely buy knowledge of Protagoras or of any one; but if not, then, O my friend, pause, and do not hazard your dearest interests at a game of chance. For there is far greater peril in buying knowledge than in buying meat and drink: the one you purchase of the wholesale or retail dealer, and carry them away in other vessels, and before you receive them into the body as food, you may deposit them at home and call in any experienced friend who knows what is good to be eaten or drunken, and what not, and how much, and when; and then the danger of purchasing them is not so great. But you cannot buy the wares of knowledge and carry them away in another vessel; when you have paid for them you must receive them into the soul and go your way, either greatly harmed or greatly benefited; and therefore we should deliberate and take counsel with our elders; for we are still young—too young to determine such a matter. And now let us go, as we were intending, and hear Protagoras; and when we have heard what he has to say, we may take counsel of others; for not only is Protagoras at the house of Callias, but there is Hippias of Elis, and, if I am not mistaken, Prodicus of Ceos, and several other wise men.

To this we agreed, and proceeded on our way until we reached the vestibule of the house; and there we stopped in order to conclude a discussion which had arisen between us as we were going along; and we stood talking in the vestibule until we had finished and come to an understanding. And I think that the doorkeeper, who was a eunuch, and who was probably annoyed at the great inroad of the Sophists, must have heard us talking. At any rate, when we knocked at the door, and he opened and saw us, he grumbled: They are Sophists—he is not at home; and instantly gave the door a hearty bang with both his hands. Again we knocked, and he answered without opening: Did you not hear me say that he is not at home, fellows? But, my friend, I said, you need not be alarmed; for we are not Sophists, and we are not come to see Callias, but we want to see Protagoras; and I must request you to announce us.

At last, after a good deal of difficulty, the man was persuaded to open the door.

When we entered, we found Protagoras taking a walk
in the cloister; and next to him, on one side, were walking
Callias, the son of Hipponicus, and Paralus, the son of
Pericles, who, by the mother's side, is his half-brother, and
Charmides, the son of Glaucon. On the other side of him
were Xanthippus, the other son of Pericles, Philippides,
the son of Philomeus; also Antimoerus of Mende, who of
all the disciples of Protagoras is the most famous, and intends to make sophistry his profession. A train of listeners
followed him; the greater part of them appeared to be foreigners, whom Protagoras had brought with him out of
the various cities visited by him in his journeys, he, like
Orpheus, attracting them by his voice, and they following.[1]
I should mention also that there were some Athenians in
the company. Nothing delighted me more than the precision
of their movements: they never got into his way at all;
but when he and those who were with him turned back,
then the band of listeners parted regularly on either side;
he was always in front, and they wheeled round and took
their places behind him in perfect order.

After him, as Homer says, "I lifted my eyes and saw"
Hippias the Elean sitting in the opposite cloister on a
chair of state, and around him were seated on benches
Eryximachus, the son of Acumenus, and Phaedrus the Myrrhinusian, and Andron the son of Androtion, and there were
strangers whom he had brought with him from his native
city of Elis, and some others: they were putting to Hippias
certain physical and astronomical questions, and he, *ex
cathedra*, was determining their several questions to them,
and discoursing of them.

Also, "my eyes beheld Tantalus"; for Prodicus the Cean
was at Athens: he had been lodged in a room which, in

[1] Cp. Rep. x. 600 D.   [1] Od. xi. 601 foll.   [1] Od. xi. 582.

the days of Hipponicus, was a storehouse; but, as the house was full, Callias had cleared this out and made the room into a guest chamber. Now Prodicus was still in bed, wrapped up in sheepskins and bedclothes, of which there seemed to be a great heap; and there was sitting by him on the couches near, Pausanias of the deme of Cerameis, and with Pausanias was a youth quite young, who is certainly remarkable for his good looks, and, if I am not mistaken, is also of a fair and gentle nature. I thought that I heard him called Agathon, and my suspicion is that he is the beloved of Pausanias. There was this youth, and also there were the two Adeimantuses, one the son of Cepis, and the other of Leucolophides, and some others. I was very anxious to hear what Prodicus was saying, for he seems to me to be an all-wise and inspired man; but I was not able to get into the inner circle, and his fine deep voice made an echo in the room which rendered his words inaudible.

No sooner had we entered than there followed us Alcibiades the beautiful, as you say, and I believe you; and also Critias the son of Callaeschrus.

On entering we stopped a little, in order to look about us, and then walked up to Protagoras, and I said: Protagoras, my friend Hippocrates and I have come to see you.

Do you wish, he said, to speak with me alone, or in the presence of the company?

Whichever you please, I said; you shall determine when you have heard the purpose of our visit.

And what is your purpose? he said.

I must explain, I said, that my friend Hippocrates is a native Athenian; he is the son of Apollodorus, and of a great and prosperous house, and he is himself in natural ability quite a match for anybody of his own age. I believe that he aspires to political eminence; and this he thinks that conversation with you is most likely to procure for him. And now you can determine whether you would wish to speak to him of your teaching alone or in the presence of the company.

Thank you, Socrates, for your consideration of me. For certainly a stranger finding his way into great cities, and persuading the flower of the youth in them to leave the company of their kinsmen or any other acquaintances, old or young, and live with him, under the idea that they will be improved by his conversation, ought to be very cautious; great jealousies are aroused by his proceedings, and he is the subject of many enmities and conspiracies. Now the art of the Sophist is, as I believe, of great antiquity; but in ancient times those who practised it, fearing this odium, veiled and disguised themselves under various names, some under that of poets, as Homer, Hesiod, and Simonides, some, of hierophants and prophets, as Orpheus and Musaeus, and some, as I observe, even under the name of gymnastic masters, like Iccus of Tarentum, or the more recently cele- brated Herodicus, now of Selymbria and formerly of Megara, who is a first-rate Sophist. Your own Agathocles pretended to be a musician, but was really an eminent Sophist; also Pythocleides the Cean; and there were many others; and all of them, as I was saying, adopted these arts as veils or disguises because they were afraid of the odium which they would incur. But that is not my way, for I do not believe that they effected their purpose, which was to deceive the government, who were not blinded by them; and as to the people, they have no understanding, and only repeat what their rulers are pleased to tell them. Now to run away, and to be caught in running away, is the very height of folly, and also greatly increases the exasperation of mankind; for they regard him who runs away as a rogue, in addition to any other objections which they have to him; and therefore I take an entirely opposite course, and ac- knowledge myself to be a Sophist and instructor of man- kind; such an open acknowledgment appears to me to be a better sort of caution than concealment. Nor do I neglect

other precautions, and therefore I hope, as I may say, by
the favour of heaven that no harm will come of the acknowledgment that I am a Sophist. And I have been now
many years in the profession—for all my years when added
up are many: there is no one here present of whom I might
not be the father. Wherefore I should much prefer conversing with you, if you want to speak with me, in the
presence of the company.

As I suspected that he would like to have a little display
and glorification in the presence of Prodicus and Hippias,
and would gladly show us to them in the light of his admirers, I said: But why should we not summon Prodicus
and Hippias and their friends to hear us?

Very good, he said.

Suppose, said Callias, that we hold a council in which
you may sit and discuss.—This was agreed upon, and great
delight was felt at the prospect of hearing wise men talk;
we ourselves took the chairs and benches, and arranged
them by Hippias, where the other benches had been already placed. Meanwhile Callias and Alcibiades got Prodicus out of bed and brought in him and his companions.

When we were all seated, Protagoras said: Now that
the company are assembled, Socrates, tell me about the
young man of whom you were just now speaking.

I replied: I will begin again at the same point, Protagoras, and tell you once more the purport of my visit: this
is my friend Hippocrates, who is desirous of making your
acquaintance; he would like to know what will happen
to him if he associates with you. I have no more to say.

Protagoras answered: Young man, if you associate with
me, on the very first day you will return home a better
man than you came, and better on the second day than on
the first, and better every day than you were on the day
before.

When I heard this, I said: Protagoras, I do not at all
wonder at hearing you say this; even at your age, and

with all your wisdom, if any one were to teach you what
you did not know before, you would become better no
doubt: but please to answer in a different way—I will
explain how by an example. Let me suppose that Hippocrates, instead of desiring your acquaintance, wished to
become acquainted with the young man Zeuxippus of Hera-
clea, who has lately been in Athens, and he had come to
him as he has come to you, and had heard him say, as he
has heard you say, that every day he would grow and
become better if he associated with him: and then suppose
that he were to ask him, "In what shall I become better,
and in what shall I grow?" Zeuxippus would answer, "In
painting." And suppose that he went to Orthagoras the
Theban, and heard him say the same thing, and asked
him, "In what shall I become better day by day?" He
would reply, "In flute-playing." Now I want you to make
the same sort of answer to this young man and to me, who
am asking questions on his account. When you say that
on the first day on which he associates with you he will
return home a better man, and on every day will grow in
like manner,—in what, Protagoras, will he be better? and
about what?

When Protagoras heard me say this, he replied: You ask
questions fairly, and I like to answer a question which is
fairly put. If Hippocrates comes to me he will not experience the sort of drudgery with which other Sophists are
in the habit of insulting their pupils; who, when they have
just escaped from the arts, are taken and driven back into
them by these teachers, and made to learn calculation, and
astronomy, and geometry, and music (he gave a look at
Hippias as he said this); but if he comes to me, he will
learn that which he comes to learn. And this is prudence
in affairs private as well as public; he will learn to order
his own house in the best manner, and he will be able to
speak and act for the best in the affairs of the State.

Do I understand you, I said; and is your meaning that

you teach the art of politics, and that you promise to make men good citizens?

That, Socrates, is exactly the profession which I make.

Then, I said, you do indeed possess a noble art, if there is no mistake about this; for I will freely confess to you, Protagoras, that I have a doubt whether this art is capable of being taught, and yet I know not how to disbelieve your assertion. And I ought to tell you why I am of opinion that this art cannot be taught or communicated by man to man. I say that the Athenians are an understanding people, and indeed they are esteemed to be such by the other Hellenes. Now I observe that when we are met together in the assembly, and the matter in hand relates to building, the builders are summoned as advisers; when the question is one of shipbuilding, then the shipwrights; and the like of other arts which they think capable of being taught and learned. And if some person offers to give them advice who is not supposed by them to have any more skill in the art than they, but to be good-looking, and rich, and noble, they don't listen to him, but laugh at him, and hoot him, until either he is clamoured down and retires of himself; or he persists, but is dragged away or put out by the constables at the command of the prytanes. This is their way of behaving about professors of the arts. But when the question is an affair of state, then everybody is free to have a say —carpenter, tinker, cobbler, sailor, passenger; rich and poor, high and low—any one who likes gets up, and no one reproaches him, as in the former case, with not having learned, and having no teacher, and yet giving advice; evidently because they are under the impression that this sort of knowledge cannot be taught. And not only is this true of the State, but of individuals; the best and wisest of our citizens are unable to impart their political wisdom to others: as for example, Pericles, the father of these young men, who gave them excellent instruction in all that could be learned from masters, in his own department of politics neither taught them, nor gave them teachers; but they were allowed to wander at their own free will in a sort of hope that they would light upon virtue of their own accord. Or take another example: there was Cleinias the younger brother of our friend Alcibiades, of whom this very same Pericles was the guardian; and he being in fact under the apprehension that Cleinias would be corrupted by Alcibiades, took him away, and placed him in the house of Ariphron to be educated; but before six months had elapsed, Ariphron sent him back, not knowing what to do with him. And I could mention numberless other instances of persons who were good themselves, and never yet made any one else good, whether friend or stranger. Now I, Protagoras, having these examples before me, am inclined to think that virtue cannot be taught. But then again, when I listen to your words, I waver; and am disposed to think that there must be something in what you say, because I know that you have great experience, and learning, and invention. And I wish that you would, if possible, show me a little more clearly that virtue can be taught. Will you be so good?

That I will, Socrates, and gladly. But what would you like? Shall I, as an elder, speak to you as younger men in an apologue or myth, or shall I argue out the question?

To this several of the company answered that he should choose for himself.

Well, then, he said, I think that the myth will be more interesting.

Once upon a time there were gods only, and no mortal creatures. But when the time came that these also should be created, the gods fashioned them out of earth and fire and various mixtures of both elements in the interior of the earth; and when they were about to bring them into the light of day, they ordered Prometheus and Epimetheus to equip them, and to distribute to them severally their proper qualities. Epimetheus said to Prometheus: "Let me

distribute, and do you inspect." This was agreed, and
Epimetheus made the distribution. There were some to
whom he gave strength without swiftness, while he equipped
the weaker with swiftness; some he armed, and others he
left unarmed; and devised for the latter some other means
of preservation, making some large, and having their size
as a protection, and others small, whose nature was to fly
in the air or burrow in the ground; this was to be their
way of escape. Thus did he compensate them with the
view of preventing any race from becoming extinct. And
when he had provided against their destruction by one
another, he contrived also a means of protecting them
against the seasons of heaven; clothing them with close
hair and thick skins sufficient to defend them against the
winter cold and able to resist the summer heat, so that
they might have a natural bed of their own when they
wanted to rest; also he furnished them with hoofs and hair
and hard and callous skins under their feet. Then he gave
them varieties of food,—herb of the soil to some, to others
fruits of trees, and to others roots, and to some again he
gave other animals as food. And some he made to have few
young ones, while those who were their prey were very
prolific; and in this manner the race was preserved. Thus
did Epimetheus, who, not being very wise, forgot that he
had distributed among the brute animals all the qualities
which he had to give,—and when he came to man, who
was still unprovided, he was terribly perplexed. Now, while
he was in this perplexity, Prometheus came to inspect the
distribution, and he found that the other animals were
suitably furnished, but that man alone was naked and
shoeless, and had neither bed nor arms of defence. The appointed hour was approaching when man in his turn was
to go forth into the light of day; and Prometheus, not
knowing how he could devise his salvation, stole the mechanical arts of Hephaestus and Athene, and fire with them
(they could neither have been acquired nor used without

fire), and gave them to man. Thus man had the wisdom necessary to the support of life, but political wisdom he had not; for that was in the keeping of Zeus, and the power of Prometheus did not extend to entering into the citadel of heaven, where Zeus dwelt, who moreover had terrible sentinels; but he did enter by stealth into the common workship of Athene and Hephaestus, in which they used to practise their favourite arts, and carried off Hephaestus' art of working by fire, and also the art of Athene, and gave them to man. And in this way man was supplied with the means of life. But Prometheus is said to have been afterwards prosecuted for theft, owing to the blunder of Epimetheus.

Now man, having a share of the divine attributes, was at first the only one of the animals who had any gods, because he alone was of their kindred; and he would raise altars and images of them. He was not long in inventing articulate speech and names; and he also constructed houses and clothes and shoes and beds, and drew sustenance from the earth. Thus provided, mankind at first lived dispersed, and there were no cities. But the consequence was that they were destroyed by the wild beasts, for they were utterly weak in comparison of them, and their art was only sufficient to provide them with the means of life, and did not enable them to carry on war against the animals: food they had, but not as yet the art of government, of which the art of war is a part. After a while the desire of self-preservation gathered them into cities; but when they were gathered together, having no art of government, they evil entreated one another, and were again in process of dispersion and destruction. Zeus feared that the entire race would be exterminated, and so he sent Hermes to them, bearing reverence and justice to be the ordering principles of cities and the bonds of friendship and conciliation. Hermes asked Zeus how he should impart justice and reverence among men:—Should he distribute them as the arts are distributed; that is to say, to a favoured few only, one skilled individual having enough of medicine or of any other art for many unskilled ones? "Shall this be the manner in which I am to distribute justice and reverence among men, or shall I give them to all?" "To all," said Zeus; "I should like them all to have a share; for cities cannot exist, if a few only share in the virtues, as in the arts. And further, make a law by my order, that he who has no part in reverence and justice shall be put to death, for he is a plague of the State."

And this is the reason, Socrates, why the Athenians and mankind in general, when the question relates to carpentering or any other mechanical art, allow but a few to share in their deliberations; and when any one else interferes, then, as you say, they object, if he be not of the favoured few; which, as I reply, is very natural. But when they meet to deliberate about political virtue, which proceeds only by way of justice and wisdom, they are patient enough of any man who speaks of them, as is also natural, because they think that every man ought to share in this sort of virtue, and that States could not exist if this were otherwise. I have explained to you, Socrates, the reason of this phenomenon.

And that you may not suppose yourself to be deceived in thinking that all men regard every man as having a share of justice or honesty and of every other political virtue, let me give you a further proof, which is this. In other cases, as you are aware, if a man says that he is a good flute-player, or skilful in any other art in which he has no skill, people either laugh at him or are angry with him, and his relations think that he is mad and go and admonish him; but when honesty is in question, or some other political virtue, even if they know that he is dishonest, yet, if the man comes publicly forward and tells the truth about his dishonesty, then, what in the other case was held by them to be good sense, they now deem to be madness. They say that all men ought to profess honesty whether they are honest or not, and that a man is out of his mind who says anything else. Their notion is, that a man must have some degree of honesty; and that if he has none at all he ought not to be in the world.

I have been showing that they are right in admitting every man as a counsellor about this sort of virtue, as they are of opinion that every man is a partaker of it. And I will now endeavour to show further that they do not conceive this virtue to be given by nature, or to grow spontaneously, but to be a thing which may be taught; and which comes to a man by taking pains. No one would instruct, no one would rebuke, or be angry with those whose calamities they suppose to be due to nature or chance; they do not try to punish or to prevent them from being what they are; they do but pity them. Who is so foolish as to chastise or instruct the ugly, or the diminutive, or the feeble? And for this reason. Because he knows that good and evil of this kind is the work of nature and of chance; whereas if a man is wanting in those good qualities which are attained by study and exercise and teaching, and has only the contrary evil qualities, other men are angry with him, and punish and reprove him—of these evil qualities one is impiety, another injustice, and they may be described generally as the very opposite of political virtue. In such cases any man will be angry with another, and reprimand him,—clearly because he thinks that by study and learning, the virtue in which the other is deficient may be acquired. If you will think, Socrates, of the nature of punishment, you will see at once that in the opinion of mankind virtue may be acquired; no one punishes the evildoer under the notion, or for the reason, that he has done wrong,—only the unreasonable fury of a beast acts in that manner. But he who desires to inflict rational punishment does not retaliate for a past wrong which cannot be undone; he has regard to the future, and is desirous that the man who is punished, and he who sees him punished, may be deterred from doing wrong again. He punishes for the sake of prevention, thereby clearly implying that virtue is capable of being taught. This is the notion of all who retaliate upon others either privately or publicly. And the Athenians, too, your own citizens, like other men, punish and take vengeance on all whom they regard as evildoers; and hence, we may infer them to be of the number of those who think that virtue may be acquired and taught. Thus far, Socrates, I have shown you clearly enough, if I am not mistaken, that your countrymen are right in admitting the tinker and the cobbler to advise about politics, and also that they deem virtue to be capable of being taught and acquired.

There yet remains one difficulty which has been raised by you about the sons of good men. What is the reason why good men teach their sons the knowledge which is gained from teachers, and make them wise in that, but do nothing towards improving them in virtues which distinguish themselves? And here, Socrates, I will leave the apologue and resume the argument. Please to consider: Is there or is there not some one quality of which all the citizens must be partakers, if there is to be a city at all? In the answer to this question is contained the only solution of your difficulty; there is no other. For if there be any such quality, and this quality or unity is not the art of the carpenter, or the smith, or the potter, but justice and temperance and holiness and, in a word, manly virtue —if this is the quality of which all men must be partakers, and which is the very condition of their learning or doing anything else, and if he who is wanting in this, whether he be a child only or a grown-up man or woman, must be taught and punished, until by punishment he becomes better, and he who rebels against instruction and punishment is either exiled or condemned to death under the idea that he is incurable—if what I am saying be true, good men

have their sons taught other things and not this, do consider how extraordinary their conduct would appear to be.
For we have shown that they think virtue capable of being
taught and cultivated both in private and public; and,
notwithstanding, they have their sons taught lesser matters,
ignorance of which does not involve the punishment of
death: but greater things, of which the ignorance may cause
death and exile to those who have no training or knowledge
of them—aye, and confiscation as well as death, and, in
a word, may be the ruin of families—those things, I say,
they are supposed not to teach them,—not to take the utmost care that they should learn. How improbable is this,
Socrates!

Education and admonition commence in the first years
of childhood, and last to the very end of life. Mother and
nurse and father and tutor are vying with one another about
the improvement of the child as soon as ever he is able to
understand what is being said to him: he cannot say or
do anything without their setting forth to him that this
is just and that is unjust; this is honourable, that is dishonourable; this is holy, that is unholy; do this and abstain from that. And if he obeys, well and good; if not, he
is straightened by threats and blows, like a piece of bent
or warped wood. At a later stage they send him to teachers,
and enjoin them to see to his manners even more than to
his reading and music; and the teachers do as they are
desired. And when the boy has learned his letters and is
beginning to understand what is written, as before he understood only what was spoken, they put into his hands
the works of great poets, which he reads sitting on a bench
at school; in these are contained many admonitions, and
many tales, and praises, and encomia of ancient famous
men, which he is required to learn by heart, in order that
he may imitate or emulate them and desire to become like
them. Then, again, the teachers of the lyre take similar
care that their young disciple is temperate and gets into

no mischief; and when they have taught him the use of the lyre, they introduce him to the poems of other excellent poets, who are the lyric poets; and these they set to music, and make their harmonies and rhythms quite familiar to the children's souls, in order that they may learn to be more gentle, and harmonious, and rhythmical, and so fitted for speech and action; for the life of man in every part has need of harmony and rhythm. Then they send them to the master of gymnastic, in order that their bodies may better minister to the virtuous mind, and that they may not be compelled through bodily weakness to play the coward in war or on any other occasion. This is what is done by those who have the means, and those who have the means are the rich; their children begin to go to school soonest and leave off latest. When they have done with masters, the State again compels them to learn the laws, and live after the pattern which they furnish, and not after their own fancies; and just as in learning to write, the writing master first draws lines with a style for the use of the young beginner, and gives him the tablet and makes him follow the lines, so the city draws the laws, which were the invention of good lawgivers living in the olden time; these are given to the young man, in order to guide him in his conduct whether he is commanding or obeying; and he who transgresses them is to be corrected, or, in other words, called to account, which is a term used not only in your country, but also in many others, seeing that justice calls men to account. Now, when there is all this care about virtue private and public, why, Socrates, do you still wonder and doubt whether virtue can be taught? Cease to wonder, for the opposite would be far more surprising.

But why then do the sons of good fathers often turn out ill? There is nothing very wonderful in this; for, as I have been saying, the existence of a State implies that virtue is not any man's private possession. If so—and nothing can be truer—then I will further ask you to imagine, as an illustration, some other pursuit or branch of knowledge which may be assumed equally to be the condition of the existence of a State. Suppose that there could be no state unless we were all flute-players, as far as each had the capacity, and everybody was freely teaching everybody the art, both in private and public, and reproving the bad player as freely and openly as every man now teaches justice and the laws, not concealing them as he would conceal the other arts, but imparting them—for all of us have a mutual interest in the justice and virtue of one another, and this is the reason why every one is so ready to teach justice and the laws;—suppose, I say, that there were the same readiness and liberality among us in teaching one another flute-playing, do you imagine, Socrates, that the sons of good flute-players would be more likely to be good than the sons of bad ones? I think not. Would not their sons grow up to be distinguished or undistinguished according to their own natural capacities as flute-players, and the son of a good player would often turn out to be a bad one, and the son of a bad player to be a good one, and all flute-players would be good enough in comparison of those who were ignorant and unacquainted with the art of flute-playing? In like manner I would have you consider that he who appears to you to be the worst of those who have been brought up in laws and humanities, would appear to be a just man and a master of justice if he were to be compared with men who had no education, or courts of justice, or laws, or any restraints upon them which compelled them to practise virtue—with the savages, for example, whom the poet Pherecrates exhibited on the stage at the last year's Lenaean festival. If you were living among men such as the man-haters in his chorus, you would be only too glad to meet with Eurybates and Phrynondas, and you would sorrowfully long to revisit the rascality of this part of the world. And you, Socrates, are discontented, and why? Because all men are teachers of virtue, each one according to his ability; and you say, Where are the teachers? You might as well ask, Who teaches Greek? For of that too there will not be any teachers found. Or you might ask, Who is to teach the sons of our artisans this same art which they have learned of their fathers? He and his fellow-workmen have taught them to the best of their ability,—but who will carry them further in their arts? And you would certainly have a difficulty, Socrates, in finding a teacher of them; but there would be no difficulty in finding a teacher of those who are wholly ignorant. And this is true of virtue or of anything else; if a man is better able than we are to promote virtue ever so little, we must be content with the result. A teacher of this sort I believe myself to be, and above all other men to have the knowledge which makes a man noble and good; and I give my pupils their money's worth, and even more, as they themselves confess. And therefore I have introduced the following mode of payment:—When a man has been my pupil, if he likes he pays my price, but there is no compulsion; and if he does not like, he has only to go into a temple and take an oath of the value of the instructions, and he pays no more than he declares to be their value.

Such is my apologue, Socrates, and such is the argument by which I endeavour to show that virtue may be taught, and that this is the opinion of the Athenians. And I have also attempted to show that you are not to wonder at good fathers having bad sons, or at good sons having bad fathers, of which the sons of Polycleitus afford an example, who are the companions of our friends here, Paralus and Xanthippus, but are nothing in comparison with their father; and this is true of the sons of many other artists. As yet I ought not to say the same of Paralus and Xanthippus themselves, for they are young and there is still hope of them.

Protagoras ended, and in my ear

"So charming left his voice, that I the while
Thought him still speaking; still stood fixed to hear."[1]

At length, when the truth dawned upon me, that he had really finished, not without difficulty I began to collect myself, and looking at Hippocrates, I said to him: O son of Apollodorus, how deeply grateful I am to you for having brought me hither; I would not have missed the speech of Protagoras for a great deal. For I used to imagine that no human care could make men good; but I know better now. Yet I have still one very small difficulty which I am sure that Protagoras will easily explain, as he has already explained so much. If a man were to go and consult Pericles or any of our great speakers about these matters, he might perhaps hear as fine a discourse; but then when one has a question to ask of any of them, like books, they can neither answer nor ask; and if any one challenges the least particular of their speech, they go ringing on in a long harangue, like brazen pots, which when they are struck continue to sound unless some one puts his hand upon them: whereas our friend Protagoras cannot only make a good speech, as he has already shown, but when he is asked a question he can answer briefly; and when he asks he will wait and hear the answer; and this is a very rare gift. Now I, Protagoras, want to ask you a little question, which if you will only answer, I shall be quite satisfied. You were saying that virtue can be taught;—that I will take upon your authority, and there is no one to whom I am more ready to trust. But I marvel at one thing about which I should like to have my mind set at rest. You were speaking of Zeus sending justice and reverence to men; and several times while you were speaking, justice, and temperance, and holiness, and all these qualities, were described by you as if together they made up virtue. Now

[1] Borrowed by Milton, Paradise Lost, viii, 2, 3.

I want you to tell me truly whether virtue is one whole, of which justice and temperance and holiness are parts; or whether all these are only the names of one and the same thing: that is the doubt which still lingers in my mind.

There is no difficulty, Socrates, in answering that the qualities of which you are speaking are the parts of virtue which is one.

And are they parts, I said, in the same sense in which mouth, nose, and eyes, and ears, are the parts of a face; or are they like parts of gold, which differ from the whole and from one another only in being larger or smaller?

I should say that they differed, Socrates, in the first way; they are related to one another as the parts of a face are related to the whole face.

And do men have some one part and some another part of virtue? Or if a man has one part, must he also have all the others?

By no means, he said; for many a man is brave and not just, or just and not wise.

You would not deny, then, that courage and wisdom are also parts of virtue?

Most undoubtedly they are, he answered; and wisdom is the noblest of the parts.

And they are all different from ane another? I said.

Yes.

And has each of them a distinct function like the parts of the face;—the eye, for example, is not like the ear, and has not the same functions; and the other parts are none of them like one another, either in their functions, or in any other way? I want to know whether the comparison holds concerning the parts of virtue. Do they also differ from one another in themselves and in their functions? For that is clearly what the simile would imply.

Yes, Socrates, you are right in supposing that they differ.

Then, I said, no other part of virtue is like knowledge,

or like justice, or like courage, or like temperance, or like holiness?

No, he answered.

Well, then, I said, suppose that you and I enquire into their natures. And first, you would agree with me that justice is of the nature of a thing, would you not? That is my opinion: would it not be yours also?

Mine also, he said.

And suppose that some one were to ask us, saying, "O Protagoras, and you, Socrates, what about this thing which you were calling justice, is it just or unjust?"—and I were to answer, just: would you vote with me or against me?

With you, he said.

Thereupon I should answer to him who asked me, that justice is of the nature of the just: would not you?

Yes, he said.

And suppose that he went on to say: "Well, now, is there also such a thing as holiness?"—we should answer, "Yes," if I am not mistaken?

Yes, he said.

Which you would also acknowledge to be a thing—should we not say so?

He assented.

"And is this sort of thing which is of the nature of the holy, or of the nature of the unholy?" I should be angry at his putting such a question, and should say, "Peace, man; nothing can be holy if holiness is not holy." What would you say? Would you not answer in the same way?

Certainly, he said.

And then after this suppose that he came and asked us, "What were you saying just now? Perhaps I may not have heard you rightly, but you seemed to me to be saying that the parts of virtue were not the same as one another." I should reply, "You certainly heard that said, but not, as you imagine, by me; for I only asked the question; Protagoras gave the answer." And suppose that he turned to

you and said, "Is this true, Protagoras? and do you maintain that one part of virtue is unlike another, and is this
your position?"—how would you answer him?

I could not help acknowledging the truth of what he
said, Socrates.

Well, then, Protagoras, we will assume this; and now
supposing that he proceeded to say further, "Then holiness
is not of the nature of justice, nor justice of the nature of
holiness, but of the nature of unholiness; and holiness is
of the nature of the not just, and therefore of the unjust,
and the unjust is the unholy"; how shall we answer him?
I should certainly answer him on my own behalf that justice is holy, and that holiness is just; and I would say in
like manner on your behalf also, if you would allow me,
that justice is either the same with holiness, or very nearly
the same; and above all I would assert that justice is like
holiness and holiness is like justice; and I wish that you
would tell me whether I may be permitted to give this
answer on your behalf, and whether you would agree with
me.

He replied, I cannot simply agree, Socrates, to the proposition that justice is holy and that holiness is just, for there
appears to me to be a difference between them. But what
matter? if you please I please; and let us assume, if you
will, that justice is holy, and that holiness is just.

Pardon me, I replied; I do not want this "if you wish"
or "if you will" sort of conclusion to be proven, but I want
you and me to be proven: I mean to say that the conclusion will be best proven if there be no "if."

Well, he said, I admit that justice bears a resemblance
to holiness, for there is always some point of view in which
everything is like every other thing; white is in a certain
way like black, and hard is like soft, and the most extreme
opposites have some qualities in common; even the parts
of the face which, as we were saying before, are distinct
and have different functions, are still in a certain point of

view similar, and one of them is like another of them. And you may prove that they are like one another on the same principle that all things are like one another; and yet things which are alike in some particular ought not to be called alike, nor things which are unlike in some particular, however slight, unlike.

And do you think, I said in a tone of surprise, that justice and holiness have but a small degree of likeness?

Certainly not; any more than I agree with what I understand to be your view.

Well, I said, as you appear to have a difficulty about this, let us take another of the examples which you mentioned instead. Do you admit the existence of folly?

I do.

And is not wisdom the very opposite of folly?

That is true, he said.

And when men act rightly and advantageously they seem to you to be temperate?

Yes, he said.

And temperance makes them temperate?

Certainly.

And they who do not act rightly act foolishly, and in acting thus are not temperate?

I agree, he said.

Then to act foolishly is the opposite of acting temperately?

He assented.

And foolish actions are done by folly, and temperate actions by temperance?

He agreed.

And that is done strongly which is done by strength, and that which is weakly done, by weakness?

He assented.

And that which is done with swiftness is done swiftly, and that which is done with slowness, slowly?

He assented again.

And that which is done in the same manner, is done by the same; and that which is done in an opposite manner by the opposite?

He agreed.

Once more, I said, is there anything beautiful?

Yes.

To which the only opposite is the ugly?

There is no other.

And is there anything good?

There is.

To which the only opposite is the evil?

There is no other.

And there is the acute in sound?

True.

To which the only opposite is the grave?

There is no other, he said, but that.

Then every opposite has one opposite only and no more?

He assented.

Then now, I said, let us recapitulate our admissions. First of all we admitted that everything has one opposite and not more than one?

We did so.

And we admitted also that what was done in opposite ways was done by opposites?

Yes.

And that which was done foolishly, as we further admitted, was done in the opposite way to that which was done temperately?

Yes.

And that which was done temperately was done by temperance, and that which was done foolishly by folly?

He agreed.

And that which is done in opposite ways is done by opposites?

Yes.

And one thing is done by temperance, and quite another thing by folly?

Yes.

And in opposite ways?

Certainly.

And therefore by opposites:—then folly is the opposite of temperance?

Clearly.

And do you remember that folly has already been acknowledged by us to be the opposite of wisdom?

He assented.

And we said that everything has only one opposite?

Yes.

Then, Protagoras, which of the two assertions shall we renounce? One says that everything has but one opposite; the other that wisdom is distinct from temperance, and that both of them are parts of virtue; and that they are not only distinct, but dissimilar, both in themselves and in their functions, like the parts of a face. Which of these two assertions shall we renounce? For both of them together are certainly not in harmony; they do not accord or agree: for how can they be said to agree if everything is assumed to have only one opposite and not more than one, and yet folly, which is one, has clearly the two opposites—wisdom and temperance? Is not that true, Protagoras? What else would you say?

He assented, but with great reluctance.

Then temperance and wisdom are the same, as before justice and holiness appeared to us to be nearly the same. And now, Protagoras, I said, we must finish the enquiry, and not faint. Do you think that an unjust man can be temperate in his unjustice?

I should be ashamed, Socrates, he said, to acknowledge this, which nevertheless many may be found to assert.

And shall I argue with them or with you? I replied.

224 THE WORKS OF PLATO

I would rather, he said, that you should argue with the

224   THE   WORKS   OF   PLATO

I would rather, he said, that you should argue with the many first, if you will.

Whichever you please, if you will only answer me and say whether you are of their opinion or not. My object is to test the validity of the argument; and yet the result may be that I who ask and you who answer may both be put on our trial.

Protagoras at first made a show of refusing, as he said that the argument was not encouraging; at length, he consented to answer.

Now then, I said, begin at the beginning and answer me. You think that some men are temperate, and yet unjust?

Yes, he said; let that be admitted.

And temperance is good sense?

Yes.

And good sense is good counsel in doing injustice?
Granted.

If they succeed, I said, or if they do not succeed?

If they succeed.

And you would admit the existence of good?

Yes.

And is the good that which is expedient for man?

Yes, indeed, he said: and there are some things which may be inexpedient, and yet I call them good.

I thought that Protagoras was getting ruffled and excited; he seemed to be setting himself in an attitude of war. Seeing this, I minded my business, and gently said:—

When you say, Protagoras, that things inexpedient are good, do you mean inexpedient for man only, or inexpedient altogether? and do you call the latter good?

Certainly not the last, he replied; for I know of many things,—meats, drinks, medicines, and ten thousand other things, which are inexpedient for man, and some which are expedient; and some which are neither expedient nor inexpedient for man, but only for horses; and some for oxen only, and some for dogs; and some for no animals, but only for trees; and some for the roots of trees and not for their branches, as for example, manure, which is a good thing when laid about the roots of a tree, but utterly destructive if thrown upon the shoots and young branches; or I may instance olive oil, which is mischievous to all plants, and generally most injurious to the hair of every animal with the exception of man, but beneficial to human hair and to the human body generally; and even in this application (so various and changeable is the nature of the benefit), that which is the greatest good to the outward parts of a man, is a very great evil to his inward parts: and for this reason physicians always forbid their patients the use of oil in their food, except in very small quantities, just enough to extinguish the disagreeable sensation of smell in meats and sauces.

When he had given this answer, the company cheered him. And I said: Protagoras, I have a wretched memory, and when any one makes a long speech to me I never remember what he is talking about. As then, if I had been deaf, and you were going to converse with me, you would have had to raise your voice; so now, having such a bad memory, I will ask you to cut your answers shorter, if you would take me with you.

What do you mean? he said: how am I to shorten my answers? shall I make them too short?

Certainly not, I said.

But short enough?

Yes, I said.

Shall I answer what appears to me to be short enough, or what appears to you to be short enough?

I have heard, I said, that you can speak and teach others to speak about the same things at such length that words never seemed to fail, or with such brevity that no one could use fewer of them. Please therefore, if you talk with me, to adopt the latter or more compendious method.

Socrates, he replied, many a battle of words have I fought,

and if I had followed the method of disputation which my adversaries desired, as you want me to do, I should have been no better than another, and the name of Protagoras would have been nowhere.

I saw that he was not satisfied with his previous answers, and that he would not play the part of answerer any more if he could help; and I considered that there was no call upon me to continue the conversation; so I said: Protagoras, I do not wish to force the conversation upon you if you had rather not, but when you are willing to argue with me in such a way that I can follow you, then I will argue with you. Now you, as is said of you by others and as you say yourself, are able to have discussions in shorter forms of speech as well as in longer, for you are a master of wisdom; but I cannot manage these long speeches: I only wish that I could. You, on the other hand, who are capable of either, ought to speak shorter as I beg you, and then we might converse. But I see that you are disinclined, and as I have an engagement which will prevent my staying to hear you at greater length (for I have to be in another place), I will depart; although I should have liked to have heard you.

Thus I spoke, and was rising from my seat, when Callias seized me by the right hand, and in his left hand caught hold of this old cloak of mine. He said: We cannot let you go, Socrates, for if you leave us there will be an end of our discussions: I must therefore beg you to remain, as there is nothing in the world that I should like better than to hear you and Protagoras discourse. Do not deny the company this pleasure.

Now, I had got up, and was in the act of departure. Son of Hipponicus, I replied, I have always admired, and do now heartily applaud and love your philosophical spirit, and I would gladly comply with your request, if I could. But the truth is that I cannot. And what you ask is as great an impossibility to me, as if you bade me run a race with Crison of Himera, when in his prime, or with some one of the long or day course runners. To such a request I should reply that I would fain ask the same of my own legs; but they refuse to comply. And therefore if you want to see Crison and me in the same stadium, you must bid him slacken his speed to mine, for I cannot run quickly, and he can run slowly. And in like manner if you want to hear me and Protagoras discoursing, you must ask him to shorten his answers, and to keep to the point, as he did at first; if not, how can there be any discussion? For discussion is one thing, and making an oration is quite another, in my humble opinion.

But you see, Socrates, said Callias, that Protagoras may fairly claim to speak in his own way, just as you claim to speak in yours.

Here Alcibiades interposed, and said: That, Callias, is not a true statement of the case. For our friend Socrates admits that he cannot make a speech—in this he yields the palm to Protagoras: but I should be greatly surprised if he yielded to any living man in the power of holding and apprehending an argument. Now, if Protagoras will make a similar admission, and confess that he is inferior to Socrates in argumentative skill, that is enough for Socrates; but if he claims superiority in argument as well, let him ask and answer—not, when a question is asked, slipping away from the point, and instead of answering, making a speech at such length that most of his hearers forget the question at issue (not that Socrates is likely to forget—I will be bound for that, although he may pretend in fun that he has a bad memory). And Socrates appears to me to be more in the right than Protagoras; that is my view, and every man ought to say what he thinks.

When Alcibiades had done speaking, some one—Critias, I believe—went on to say: O Prodicus and Hippias, Callias appears to me to be a partisan of Protagoras: and this led Alcibiades, who loves opposition, to take the other side. But we should not be partisans either of Socrates or of Protagoras; let us rather unite in entreating both of them not to break up the discussion.

Prodicus added: That, Critias, seems to me to be well said, for those who are present at such discussions ought to be impartial hearers of both the speakers; remembering, however, that impartiality is not the same as equality, for both sides should be impartially heard, and yet an equal meed should not be assigned to both of them; but to the wiser a higher meed should be given, and a lower to the less wise. And I as well as Critias would beg you, Protagoras and Socrates, to grant our request, which is, that you will argue with one another and not wrangle; for friends argue with friends out of good-will, but only adversaries and enemies wrangle. And then our meeting will be delightful; for in this way you, who are the speakers, will be most likely to win esteem, and not praise only, among us who are your audience; for esteem is a sincere conviction of the hearers' souls, but praise is often an insincere expression of men uttering falsehoods contrary to their conviction. And thus we who are the hearers will be gratified and not pleased; for gratification is of the mind when receiving wisdom and knowledge, but pleasure is of the body when eating or experiencing some other bodily delight. Thus spoke Prodicus, and many of the company applauded his words.

Hippias the sage spoke next. He said: All of you who are here present I reckon to be kinsmen and friends and fellow-citizens, by nature and not by law; for by nature like is akin to like, whereas law is the tyrant of mankind, and often compels us to do many things which are against nature. How great would be the disgrace then, if we, who know the nature of things, and are the wisest of the Hellenes, and such are met together in this city, which is the metropolis of wisdom, and in the greatest and most glorious house of this city, should have nothing to show worthy of this height of dignity, but should only quarrel with one another like the meanest of mankind! I do pray and advise you, Protagoras, and you, Socrates, to agree upon a compromise. Let us be your peacemakers. And do not you, Socrates, aim at this precise and extreme brevity in discourse, if Protagoras objects, but loosen and let go the reins of speech, that your words may be grander and more becoming to you.[1] Neither do you, Protagoras, go forth on the gale with every sail set out of sight of land into an ocean of words, but let there be a mean observed by both of you. Do as I say. And let me also persuade you to choose an arbiter or overseer or president; he will keep watch over your words and will prescribe their proper length.

This proposal was received by the company with universal approval; Callias said that he would not let me off, and they begged me to choose an arbiter. But I said that to choose an umpire of discourse would be unseemly; for if the person chosen was inferior, then the inferior or worse ought not to preside over the better; or if he was equal, neither would that be well; for he who is our equal will do as we do, and what will be the use of choosing him? And if you say, "Let us have a better then,"—to that I answer that you cannot have any one who is wiser than Protagoras. And if you choose another who is not really better, and whom you only say is better, to put another over him as though he were an inferior person would be an unworthy reflection on him; not that, as far as I am concerned, any reflection is of much consequence to me. Let me tell you then what I will do in order that the conversation and discussion may go as you desire. If Protagoras is not disposed to answer let him ask and I will answer; and I will endeavour to show at the same time how, as I maintain, he ought to answer: and when I have answered as many questions as he likes to ask, let him in like manner answer me; and if he seems to be not very ready at answering the precise question asked of him, you and I will unite in entreating him, as you entreated me, not to spoil the discussion. And

[1] Reading ὑμῖν.

this will require no special arbiter—all of you shall be arbiters.

This was generally approved, and Prótagoras, though very much against his will, was obliged to agree that he would ask questions; and when he had put a sufficient number of them, that he would answer in his turn those which he was asked in short replies. He began to put his questions as follows:—

I am of opinion, Socrates, he said, that skill in poetry is the principal part of education; and this I conceive to be the power of knowing what compositions of the poets are correct, and what are not, and how they are to be distinguished, and of explaining when asked the reason of the difference. And I propose to transfer the question which you and I have been discussing to the domain of poetry; we will speak as before of virtue, but in reference to a passage of a poet. Now Simonides says to Scopas the son of Creon the Thessalian:—

"Hardly on the one hand can a man become truly good, built four-square in hands and feet and mind, a work without a flaw."

Do you know the poem? or shall I repeat the whole?

There is no need, I said; for I am perfectly well acquainted with the ode,—I have made a careful study of it.

Very well, he said. And do you think that the ode is a good composition, and true?

Yes, I said, both good and true.

But if there is a contradiction, can the composition be good or true?

No, not in that case, I replied.

And is there not a contradiction? he asked. Reflect.

Well, my friend, I have reflected.

And does not the poet proceed to say, "I do not agree with the word of Pittacus, albeit the utterance of a wise

man: Hardly can a man be good"? Now you will observe
that this is said by the same poet.

I know it.

And do you think, he said, that the two sayings are consistent?

Yes, I said, I think so (at the same time I could not help
fearing that there might be something in what he said).
And you think otherwise?

Why, he said, how can he be consistent in both? First of
all, premising as his own thought, "Hardly can a man become truly good"; and then a little further on in the poem,
forgetting, and blaming Pittacus and refusing to agree with
him, when he says, "Hardly can a man be good," which is
the very same thing. And yet when he blames him who
says the same with himself, he blames himself; so that he
must be wrong either in his first or his second assertion.

Many of the audience cheered and applauded this. And
I felt at first giddy and faint, as if I had received a blow
from the hand of an expert boxer, when I heard his words
and the sounds of cheering; and to confess the truth, I
wanted to get time to think what the meaning of the poet
really was. So I turned to Prodicus and called him. Prodicus,
I said, Simonides is a countryman of yours, and you ought
to come to his aid. I must appeal to you, like the river
Scamander in Homer, who, when beleaguered by Achilles,
summons the Simoïs to aid him, saying:

"Brother dear, let us both together stay the force of the
hero." [1]

And I summon you, for I am afraid that Protagoras will
make an end of Simonides. Now is the time to rehabilitate
Simonides, by the application of your philosophy of syn-
onyms, which enables you to distinguish "will" and "wish,"
and make other charming distinctions like those which you
drew just now. And I should like to know whether you

[1] Il. xxi. 308.

would agree with me; for I am of opinion that there is no contradiction in the words of Simonides. And first of all I wish that you would say whether, in your opinion, Prodicus, "being" is the same as "becoming."

Not the same, certainly, replied Prodicus.

Did not Simonides first set forth, as his own view, that "Hardly can a man become truly good"?

Quite right, said Prodicus.

And then he blames Pittacus, not, as Protagoras imagines, for repeating that which he says himself, but for saying something different from himself. Pittacus does not say as Simonides says, that hardly can a man become good, but hardly can a man be good: and our friend Prodicus would maintain that being, Protagoras, is not the same as becoming; and if they are not the same, then Simonides is not inconsistent with himself. I dare say that Prodicus and many others would say, as Hesiod says,

"On the one hand, hardly can a man become good,
  For the gods have made virtue the reward of toil;
  But on the other hand, when you have climbed the height,
  Then, to retain virtue, however difficult the acquisition,
    is easy."[1]

Prodicus heard and approved; but Protagoras said: Your correction, Socrates, involves a greater error than is contained in the sentence which you are correcting.

Alas! I said, Protagoras; then I am a sorry physician, and do but aggravate a disorder which I am seeking to cure.

Such is the fact, he said.

How so? I asked.

The poet, he replied, could never have made such a mistake as to say that virtue, which in the opinion of all men is the hardest of all things, can be easily retained.

[1] Works and Days, 264 foll.

Well, I said, and how fortunate are we in having Prodicus among us, at the right moment; for he has a wisdom, Protagoras, which, as I imagine, is more than human and of very ancient date, and may be as old as Simonides or even older. Learned as you are in many things, you appear to know nothing of this; but I know, for I am a disciple of his. And now, if I am not mistaken, you do not understand the word "hard" (χαλεπόν) in the sense which Simonides intended; and I must correct you, as Prodicus corrects me when I use the word "awful" (δεινόν) as a term of praise. If I say that Protagoras or any one else is an "awfully" wise man, he asks me if I am not ashamed of calling that which is good "awful"; and then he explains to me that the term "awful" is always taken in a bad sense, and that no one speaks of being "awfully" healthy or wealthy, or of "awful" peace, but of "awful" disease, "awful" war, "awful" poverty, meaning by the term "awful," evil. And I think that Simonides and his countrymen the Ceans, when they spoke of "hard" meant "evil," or something which you do not understand. Let us ask Prodicus, for he ought to be able to answer questions about the dialect of Simonides. What did he mean, Prodicus, by the term "hard"?

Evil, said Prodicus.

And therefore, I said, Prodicus, he blames Pittacus for saying, "Hard is the good" just as if that were equivalent to saying, Evil is the good.

Yes, he said, that was certainly his meaning; and he is twitting Pittacus with ignorance of the use of terms, which in a Lesbian, who has been accustomed to speak a barbarous language, is natural.

Do you hear, Protagoras, I asked, what our friend Prodicus is saying? And have you an answer for him?

You are entirely mistaken, Prodicus, said Protagoras; and I know very well that Simonides in using the word "hard" meant what all of us mean, not evil, but that which is not easy—that which takes a great deal of trouble: of this I am positive.

I said: I also incline to believe, Protagoras, that this was the meaning of Simonides, of which our friend Prodicus was very well aware, but he thought that he would make fun, and try if you could maintain your thesis; for that Simonides could never have meant the other is clearly proved by the context, in which he says that God only has this gift. Now, he cannot surely mean to say that to be good is evil, when he afterwards proceeds to say that God only has this gift, and that this is the attribute of him and of no other. For if this be his meaning, Prodicus would impute to Simonides a character of recklessness which is very unlike his countrymen. And I should like to tell you, I said, what I imagine to be the real meaning of Simonides in this poem, if you will test what, in your way of speaking, would be called my skill in poetry; or, if you would rather, I will be the listener.

To this proposal Protagoras replied: As you please;—and Hippias, Prodicus, and the others told me by all means to do as I proposed.

Then now, I said, I will endeavour to explain to you my opinion about this poem of Simonides. There is a very ancient philosophy which is more cultivated in Crete and Lacedaemon than in any other part of Hellas, and there are more philosophers in those countries than anywhere else in the world. This, however, is a secret which the Lacedaemonians deny; and they pretend to be ignorant, just because they do not wish to have it thought that they rule the world by wisdom, like the Sophists of whom Protagoras was speaking, and not by valour of arms; considering that if the reason of their superiority were disclosed, all men would be practising their wisdom. And this secret of theirs has never been discovered by the imitators of Lacedaemonian fashions in other cities, who go about with their ears bruised in imitation of them, and have the caestus bound

on their arms and are always in training, and wear short
cloaks; for they imagine that these are the practices which
have enabled the Lacedaemonians to conquer the other
Hellenes. Now, when the Lacedaemonians want to unbend
and hold free conversation with their wise men, and are
no longer satisfied with mere secret intercourse, they drive
out all these laconizers, and any other foreigners who may
happen to be in their country, and they hold a philosophical
séance unknown to strangers; and they themselves forbid
their young men to go out into other cities—in this they
are like the Cretans—in order that they might not unlearn
the lessons which they have taught them. And in Lacedaemon and Crete not only men but also women have a pride
in their high cultivation. And hereby you may know that
I am right in attributing to the Lacedaemonians this excellence in philosophy and speculation: If a man converses
with the most ordinary Lacedaemonian, he will find him
seldom good for much in general conversation, but at any
point in the discourse he will be darting out some notable
saying, terse and full of meaning, with unerring aim; and
the person with whom he is talking seems to be like a child
in his hands. And many of our own age and of former ages
have noted that the true Lacedaemonian type of character
has the love of philosophy even stronger than the love of
gymnastics; they are conscious that only a perfectly educated man is capable of uttering such expressions. Such were
Thales of Miletus, and Pittacus of Mitylene, and Bias of
Priene, and our own Solon, and Cleobulus the Lindian, and
Myson the Chenian; and seventh in the catalogue of wise
men was the Lacedaemonian Chilo. All these were lovers
and emulators and disciples of the culture of the Lacedaemonians, and any one may perceive that their wisdom was
of this character; consisting of short memorable sentences,
which they severally uttered. And they met together and
dedicated in the temple of Apollo at Delphi, as the first
fruits of their wisdom, the far-famed inscriptions, which

are in all men's mouths,—"Know thyself," and "Nothing too much."

Why do I say all this? I am explaining that this Lacedaemonian brevity was the style of primitive philosophy. Now there was a saying of Pittacus which was privately circulated and received the approbation of the wise, "Hard is it to be good." And Simonides, who was ambitious of the fame of wisdom, was aware that if he could overthrow this saying, then, as if he had won a victory over some famous athlete, he would carry off the palm among his contemporaries. And if I am not mistaken, he composed the entire poem with the secret intention of damaging Pittacus and his saying.

Let us all unite in examining his words, and see whether I am speaking the truth. Simonides must have been a lunatic, if, in the very first words of the poem, wanting to say only that to become good is hard, he inserted μέν, "on the one hand" ["on the one hand to become good is hard"]; there would be no reason for the introduction of μέν, unless you suppose him to speak with a hostile reference to the words of Pittacus. Pittacus is saying "Hard is it to be good," and he, in refutation of this thesis, rejoins that the truly hard thing, Pittacus, is to become good, not joining "truly" with "good," but with "hard." Not, that the hard thing is to be truly good, as though there were some truly good men, and there were others who were good but not truly good (this would be a very simple observation, and quite unworthy of Simonides); but you must suppose him to make a trajection of the word "truly" (ἀλαθέως), construing the saying of Pittacus thus (and let us imagine Pittacus to be speaking and Simonides answering him): "O my friends," says Pittacus, "hard is it to be good," and Simonides answers, "In that, Pittacus, you are mistaken; the difficulty is not to be good, but on the one hand, to become good, four-square in hands and feet and mind, without a flaw—that is hard truly." This way of reading the passage accounts for the insertion of μέν, "on the one hand," and for the position at the end of the clause of the word "truly," and all that follows shows this to be the meaning A great deal might be said in praise of the details of the poem, which is a charming piece of workmanship, and very finished, but such minutiae would be tedious. I should like, however, to point out the general intention of the poem, which is certainly designed in every part to be a refutation of the saying of Pittacus. For he speaks in what follows a little further on as if he meant to argue that although there is a difficulty in becoming good, yet this is possible for a time, and only for a time. But having become good, to remain in a good state and be good, as you, Pittacus, affirm, is not possible, and is not granted to man; God only has this blessing; "but man cannot help being bad when the force of circumstances overpowers him." Now, whom does the force of circumstances overpower in the command of a vessel? Not the private individual, for he is always overpowered; and as one who is already prostrate cannot be overthrown, and only he who is standing upright but not he who is prostrate can be laid prostrate, so the force of circumstances can only overpower him who, at some time or other, has resources, and not him who is at all times helpless. The descent of a great storm may make the pilot helpless, or the severity of the season the husbandman or the physician; for the good may become bad, as another poet witnesses:—

"The good are sometimes good and sometimes bad."

But the bad does not become bad; he is always bad. So that when the force of circumstances overpowers the man of resources and skill and virtue, then he cannot help being bad. And you, Pittacus, are saying, "Hard is it to be good." Now there is a difficulty in becoming good; and yet this is possible: but to be good is an impossibility—

"For he who does well is the good man, and he who does
ill is the bad."

But what sort of doing is good in letters? and what sort of
doing makes a man good in letters? Clearly the knowing
of them. And what sort of well-doing makes a man a good
physician? Clearly the knowledge of the art of healing the
sick. "But he who does ill is the bad." Now, who becomes
a bad physician? Clearly he who is in the first place a
physician, and in the second place a good physician;
for he may become a bad one also: but none of us
unskilled individuals can by any amount of doing ill become physicians, any more than we can become carpenters
or anything of that sort; and he who by doing ill cannot
become a physician at all, clearly cannot become a bad
physician. In like manner the good may become deteriorated
by time, or toil, or disease, or other accident (the only real
doing ill is to be deprived of knowledge), but the bad man
will never become bad, for he is always bad; and if he were
to become bad, he must previously have been good. Thus
the words of the poem tend to show that on the one hand
a man cannot be continuously good, but that he may become good and may also become bad; and again that

"They are the best for the longest time whom the gods
love."

All this relates to Pittacus, as is further proved by the
sequel. For he adds:—

"Therefore I will not throw away my span of life to no
purpose in searching after the impossible, hoping in vain
to find a perfectly faultless man among those who partake
of the fruit of the broad-bosomed earth: if I find him, I
will send you word."

(this is the vehement way in which he pursues his attack upon Pittacus throughout the whole poem):

"But him who does no evil, voluntarily I praise and love;
—not even the gods war against necessity."

All this has a similar drift, for Simonides was not so ignorant as to say that he praised those who did no evil voluntarily, as though there were some who did evil voluntarily. For no wise man, as I believe, will allow that any human being errs voluntarily, or voluntarily does evil and dishonourable actions; but they are very well aware that all who do evil and dishonourable things do them against their will. And Simonides never says that he praises him who does no evil voluntarily; the word "voluntarily" applies to himself. For he was under the impression that a good man might often compel himself to love and praise another,[1] and to be the friend and approver of another; and that there might be an involuntary love, such as a man might feel to an unnatural father or mother, or country, or the like. Now, bad men, when their parents or country have any defects, look on them with malignant joy, and find fault with them and expose and denounce them to others, under the idea that the rest of mankind will be less likely to take themselves to task and accuse them of neglect; and they blame their defects far more than they deserve, in order that the odium which is necessarily incurred by them may be increased: but the good man dissembles his feelings, and constrains himself to praise them; and if they have wronged him and he is angry, he pacifies his anger and is reconciled, and compels himself to love and praise his own flesh and blood. And Simonides, as is probable, considered that he himself had often had to praise and magnify a tyrant or the like, much against his will, and he also wishes to imply to Pittacus that he does not censure him because he is censorious.

[1] Reading φιλεῖν καὶ ἐπαινεῖν καὶ φίλον τινὶ κ.τ.λ.

"For I am satisfied," he says, "when a man is neither bad nor very stupid; and when he knows justice (which is the health of states), and is of sound mind, I will find no fault with him, for I am not given to finding fault, and there are innumerable fools"

(implying that if he delighted in censure he might have abundant opportunity of finding fault).

"All things are good with which evil is unmingled."

In these latter words he does not mean to say that all things are good which have no evil in them, as you might say "All things are white which have no black in them," for that would be ridiculous; but he means to say that he accepts and finds no fault with the moderate or intermediate state.

["I do not hope," he says, "to find a perfectly blameless man among those who partake of the fruits of the broad-bosomed earth (if I find him, I will send you word); in this sense I praise no man. But he who is moderately good, and does no evil, is good enough for me, who love and approve every one"]

(and here observe that he uses a Lesbian word, ἐπαίνημι [approve], because he is addressing Pittacus,—

"Who love and *approve* every one *voluntarily*, who does no evil":

and that the stop should be put after "voluntarily"); "but there are some whom I involuntarily praise and love. And you, Pittacus, I would never have blamed, if you had spoken what was moderately good and true; but I do blame you because, putting on the appearance of truth, you are speaking falsely about the highest matters."—And this, I said, Prodicus and Protagoras, I take to be the meaning of Simonides in this poem.

Hippias said: I think, Socrates, that you have given a very good explanation of the poem; but I have also an excellent interpretation of my own which I will propound to you, if you will allow me.

Nay, Hippias, said Alcibiades; not now, but at some other time. At present we must abide by the compact which was made between Socrates and Protagoras, to the effect that as long as Protagoras is willing to ask, Socrates should answer; or that if he would rather answer, then that Socrates should ask.

I said: I wish Protagoras either to ask or answer as he is inclined; but I would rather have done with poems and odes, if he does not object, and come back to the question about which I was asking you at first, Protagoras, and by your help make an end of that. The talk about the poets seems to me like a commonplace entertainment to which a vulgar company have recourse; who, because they are not able to converse or amuse one another, while they are drinking, with the sound of their own voices and conversation, by reason of their stupidity, raise the price of flute-girls in the market, hiring for a great sum the voice of a flute instead of their own breath, to be the medium of intercourse among them: but where the company are real gentlemen and men of education, you will see no flute-girls, nor dancing-girls, nor harp-girls; and they have no nonsense or games, but are contented with one another's conversation, of which their own voices are the medium, and which they carry on by turns and in an orderly manner, even though they are very liberal in their potations. And a company like this of ours, and men such as we profess to be do not require the help of another's voice, or of the poets whom you cannot interrogate about the meaning of what they are saying; people who cite them declaring, some that the poet has one meaning, and others that he has another, and the point which is in dispute can never be decided. This sort of entertainment they decline, and prefer to talk with one another, and put one another to the proof in conversation. And these are the models which I desire that you and I should imitate. Leaving the poets, and keeping to ourselves, let us try the mettle of one another and make proof of the truth in conversation. If you have a mind to ask, I am ready to answer; or if you would rather, do you answer, and give me the opportunity of resuming and completing our unfinished argument.

I made these and some similar observations; but Protagoras would not distinctly say which he would do. Thereupon Alcibiades turned to Callias, and said:—Do you think, Callias, that Protagoras is fair in refusing to say whether he will or will not answer? for I certainly think that he is unfair; he ought either to proceed with the argument, or distinctly to refuse to proceed, that we may know his intention; and then Socrates will be able to discourse with some one else, and the rest of the company will be free to talk with one another.

I think that Protagoras was really made ashamed by these words of Alcibiades, and when the prayers of Callias and the company were superadded, he was at last induced to argue, and said that I might ask and he would answer.

So I said: Do not imagine, Protagoras, that I have any other interest in asking questions of you but that of clearing up my own difficulties. For I think that Homer was very right in saying that

"When two go together, one sees before the other," [1]

for all men who have a companion are readier in deed, word, or thought; but if a man

[1] Il. x. 224.

"Sees a thing when he is alone,"

he goes about straightway seeking until he finds some one
to whom he may show his discoveries, and who may confirm him in them. And I would rather hold discourse with
you than with any one, because I think that no man has
a better understanding of most things which a good man
may be expected to understand, and in particular of virtue.
For who is there, but you?—who not only claim to be a
good man and a gentleman, for many are this, and yet have
not the power of making others good—whereas you are not
only good yourself, but also the cause of goodness in others.
Moreover, such confidence have you in yourself, that although other Sophists conceal their profession, you proclaim in the face of Hellas that you are a Sophist or teacher
of virtue and education, and are the first who demanded
pay in return. How then can I do otherwise than invite you
to the examination of these subjects, and ask questions and
consult with you? I must, indeed. And I should like once
more to have my memory refreshed by you about the questions which I was asking you at first, and also to have your
help in considering them. If I am not mistaken the question was this: Are wisdom and temperance and courage and
justice and holiness five names of the same thing? or has
each of the names a separate underlying essence and corresponding thing having a peculiar function, no one of them
being like any other of them? And you replied that the five
names were not the names of the same thing, but that each
of them had a separate object, and that all these objects
were parts of virtue, not in the same way that the parts of
gold are like each other and the whole of which they are
parts, but as the parts of the face are unlike the whole of
which they are parts and one another, and have each of
them a distinct function. I should like to know whether
this is still your opinion; or if not, I will ask you to define
your meaning, and I shall not take you to task if you now

make a different statement. For I dare say that you may have said what you did only in order to make trial of me.

I answer, Socrates, he said, that all these qualities are parts of virtue, and that four out of the five are to some extent similar, and that the fifth of them, which is courage, is very different from the other four, as I prove in this way: You may observe that many men are utterly unrighteous, unholy, intemperate, ignorant, who are nevertheless remarkable for their courage.

Stop, I said; I should like to think about that. When you speak of brave men, do you mean the confident, or another sort of nature?

Yes, he said; I mean the impetuous, ready to go at that which others are afraid to approach.

In the next place, you would affirm virtue to be a good thing, of which good thing you assert yourself to be a teacher.

Yes, he said; I should say the best of all things, if I am in my right mind.

And is it partly good and partly bad, I said, or wholly good?

Wholly good, and in the highest degree.

Tell me, then, who are they who have confidence when diving into a well?

I should say, the divers.

And the reason of this is that they have knowledge?

Yes, that is the reason.

And who have confidence when fighting on horseback—the skilled horsemen or the unskilled?

The skilled.

And who when fighting with light shields—the peltasts or the nonpeltasts?

The peltasts. And that is true of all other things, he said, if that is your point: those who have knowledge are more confident than those who have no knowledge, and they are more confident after they have learned than before.

And have you not seen persons utterly ignorant, I said, of these things, and yet confident about them?

Yes, he said, I have seen such persons far too confident.

And are not these confident persons also courageous?

In that case, he replied, courage would be a base thing, for the men of whom we are speaking are surely madmen.

Then who are the courageous? Are they not the confident?

Yes, he said; to that statement I adhere.

And those, I said, who are thus confident without knowledge are really not courageous, but mad; and in that case the wisest are also the most confident, and being the most confident are also the bravest, and upon that view again wisdom will be courage.

Nay, Socrates, he replied, you are mistaken in your remembrance of what was said by me. When you asked me, I certainly did say that the courageous are the confident; but I was never asked whether the confident are the courageous; if you had asked me, I should have answered "Not all of them": and what I did answer you have not proved to be false, although you proceeded to show that those who have knowledge are more courageous than they were before they had knowledge, and more courageous than others who have no knowledge, and were then led on to think that courage is the same as wisdom. But in this way of arguing you might come to imagine that strength is wisdom. You might begin by asking whether the strong are able, and I should say "Yes"; and then whether those who know how to wrestle are not more able to wrestle than those who do not know how to wrestle, and more able after than before they had learned, and I should assent. And when I had admitted this, you might use my admissions in such a way as to prove that upon my view wisdom is strength; whereas in that case I should not have admitted, any more than in the other, that the able are strong, although I have admitted that the strong are able. For there is a difference between ability and strength; the former is given by knowledge as well as by madness or rage, but strength comes from nature and a healthy state of the body. And in like manner I say of confidence and courage, that they are not the same; and I argue that the courageous are confident, but not all the confident courageous. For confidence may be given to men by art, and also, like ability, by madness and rage; but courage comes to them from nature and the healthy state of the soul.

I said: You would admit, Protagoras, that some men live well and others ill?

He assented.

And do you think that a man lives well who lives in pain and grief?

He does not.

But if he lives pleasantly to the end of his life, will he not in that case have lived well?

He will.

Then to live pleasantly is a good, and to live unpleasantly an evil?

Yes, he said, if the pleasure be good and honourable.

And do you, Protagoras, like the rest of the world, call some pleasant things evil and some painful things good?— for I am rather disposed to say that things are good in as far as they are pleasant, if they have no consequences of another sort, and in as far as they are painful they are bad.

I do not know, Socrates, he said, whether I can venture to assert in that unqualified manner that the pleasant is the good and the painful the evil. Having regard not only to my present answer, but also the whole of my life, I shall be safer, if I am not mistaken, in saying that there are some pleasant things which are not good, and that there are some painful things which are good, and some which are not good, and that there are some which are neither good nor evil.

And you would call pleasant, I said, the things which participate in pleasure or create pleasure?

Certainly, he said.

Then my meaning is, that in as far as they are pleasant they are good; and my question would imply that pleasure is a good in itself.

According to your favourite mode of speech, Socrates, "let us reflect about this," he said; and if the reflection is to the point, and the result proves that pleasure and good are really the same, then we will agree; but, if not, then we will argue.

And would you wish to begin the enquiry? I said; or shall I begin?

You ought to take the lead, he said; for you are the author of the discussion.

May I employ an illustration? I said. Suppose some one who is enquiring into the health or some other bodily quality of another:—he looks at his face and at the tips of his fingers, and then he says, Uncover your chest and back to me that I may have a better view:—that is the sort of thing which I desire in this speculation. Having seen what your opinion is about good and pleasure, I am minded to say to you: Uncover your mind to me, Protagoras, and reveal your opinion about knowledge, that I may know whether you agree with the rest of the world. Now, the rest of the world are of opinion that knowledge is a principle not of strength, or of rule, or of command: their notion is that a man may have knowledge, and yet that the knowledge which is in him may be over-mastered by anger, or pleasure, or pain, or love, or perhaps by fear,—just as if knowledge were a slave, and might be dragged about anyhow. Now, is that your view? or do you think that knowledge is a noble and commanding thing, which cannot be overcome, and will not allow a man, if he only knows the difference of good and evil, to do anything which is contrary to knowledge, but that wisdom will have strength to help him?

I agree with you, Socrates, said Protagoras; and not only so, but I, above all other men, am bound to say that wisdom and knowledge are the highest of human things.

Good, I said, and true. But are you aware that the majority of the world are of another mind; and that men are commonly supposed to know the things which are best, and not to do them when they might? And most persons whom I have asked the reason of this have said that when men act contrary to knowledge they are overcome by pain, or pleasure, or some of those affections which I was just now mentioning.

Yes, Socrates, he replied; and that is not the only point about which mankind are in error.

Suppose, then, that you and I endeavour to instruct and inform them what is the nature of this affection which they call "being overcome by pleasure," and which they affirm to be the reason why they do not always do what is best. When we say to them: Friends, you are mistaken, and are saying what is not true, they would probably reply: Socrates and Protagoras, if this affection of the soul is not to be called "being overcome by pleasure," pray, what is it, and by what name would you describe it?

But why, Socrates, should we trouble ourselves about the opinion of the many, who just say anything that happens to occur to them?

I believe, I said, that they may be of use in helping us to discover how courage is related to the other parts of virtue. If you are disposed to abide by our agreement, that I should show the way in which, as I think, our recent difficulty is most likely to be cleared up, do you follow; but if not, never mind.

You are quite right, he said; and I would have you proceed as you have begun.

Well, then, I said, let me suppose that they repeat their question, What account do you give of that which, in our way of speaking, is termed being overcome by pleasure? I should answer thus: Listen, and Protagoras and I will endeavour to show you. When men are overcome by eating and drinking and other sensual desires which are pleasant, and they, knowing them to be evil, nevertheless indulge in them, would you not say that they were overcome by pleasure? They will not deny this. And suppose that you and I were to go on and ask them again: "In what way do you say that they are evil,—in that they are pleasant and give pleasure at the moment, or because they cause disease and poverty and other like evils in the future? Would they still be evil, if they had no attendant evil consequences, simply because they give the consciousness of pleasure of whatever nature?"—Would they not answer that they are not evil on account of the pleasure which is immediately given by them, but on account of the after consequences—diseases and the like?

I believe, said Protagoras, that the world in general would answer as you do.

And in causing diseases do they not cause pain? and in causing poverty do they not cause pain;—they would agree to that also, if I am not mistaken?

Protagoras assented.

Then I should say to them, in my name and yours: Do you think them evil for any other reason, except because they end in pain and rob us of other pleasures:—there again they would agree?

We both of us thought that they would.

And then I should take the question from the opposite point of view, and say: "Friends, when you speak of goods being painful, do you not mean remedial goods, such as gymnastic exercises, and military service, and the physician's use of burning, cutting, drugging and starving? Are these the things which are good but painful?" They would assent to me?

He agreed.

"And do you call them good because they occasion the greatest immediate suffering and pain; or because, afterwards, they bring health and improvement of the bodily condition and the salvation of States and power over others and wealth?"—they would agree to the latter alternative, if I am not mistaken?

He assented.

"Are these things good for any other reason except that they end in pleasure, and get rid of and avert pain? Are you looking to any other standard but pleasure and pain when you call them good?" They would acknowledge that they were not?

I think so, said Protagoras.

"And do you not pursue after pleasure as a good, and avoid pain as an evil?"

He assented.

"Then you think that pain is an evil and pleasure is a good: and even pleasure you deem an evil, when it robs you of greater pleasures than it gives, or causes pains greater than the pleasure. If, however, you call pleasure an evil in relation to some other end or standard, you will be able to show us that standard. But you have none to show."

I do not think that they have, said Protagoras.

"And have you not a similar way of speaking about pain? You call pain a good when it takes away greater pains than those which it has, or gives pleasures greater than the pains: then if you have some standard other than pleasure and pain to which you refer when you call actual pain a good, you can show what that is. But you cannot."

True, said Protagoras.

Suppose again, I said, that the world says to me: "Why do you spend many words and speak in many ways on this subject?" Excuse me, friends, I should reply; but in the first place there is a difficulty in explaining the meaning of the expression "overcome by pleasure"; and the whole argument turns upon this. And even now, if you see any possible way in which evil can be explained as other than pain, or good as other than pleasure, you may still retract. Are you satisfied, then, at having a life of pleasure which is without pain? If you are, and if you are unable to show any good

or evil which does not end in pleasure and pain, hear the
consequences:—If what you say is true, then the argument
is absurd which affirms that a man often does evil knowingly, when he might abstain, because he is seduced and
overpowered by pleasure; or again, when you say that a
man knowingly refuses to do what is good because he is
overcome at the moment by pleasure. And that this is ridiculous will be evident if only we give up the use of various
names, such as pleasant and painful, and good and evil.
As there are two things, let us call them by two names—
first, good and evil, and then pleasant and painful. Assuming this, let us go on to say that a man does evil knowing
that he does evil. But some one will ask, Why? Because
he is overcome, is the first answer. And by what is he overcome? the enquirer will proceed to ask. And we shall not
be able to reply "By pleasure," for the name of pleasure
has been exchanged for that of good. In our answer, then,
we shall only say that he is overcome. "By what?" he will
reiterate. By the good, we shall have to reply; indeed we
shall. Nay, but our questioner will rejoin with a laugh, if
he be one of the swaggering sort, "This is too ridiculous,
that a man should do what he knows to be evil when he
ought not, because he is overcome by good. Is that," he
will ask, "because the good was worthy or not worthy of
conquering the evil?" And in answer to that we shall clearly
reply, Because it was not worthy; for if it had been worthy,
then he who, as we say, was overcome by pleasure, would
not have been wrong. "But how," he will reply, "can the
good be unworthy of the evil, or the evil of the good?"
Is not the real explanation that they are out of proportion
to one another, either as greater and smaller, or more and
fewer? This we cannot deny. And when you speak of being
overcome—"what do you mean," he will say, "but that you
choose the greater evil in exchange for the lesser good?"
Admitted. And now substitute the names of pleasure and
pain for good and evil, and say, not as before, that a man

does what is evil knowingly, but that he does what is painful knowingly, and because he is overcome by pleasure,
which is unworthy to overcome. What measure is there of
the relations of pleasure to pain other than excess and defect, which means that they become greater and smaller,
and more and fewer, and differ in degree? For if any one
says: "Yes, Socrates, but immediate pleasure differs widely
from future pleasure and pain"—to that I should reply:
And do they differ in anything but in pleasure and pain?
There can be no other measure of them. And do you, like
a skillful weigher, put into the balance the pleasures and
the pains, and their nearness and distance, and weigh them,
and then say which outweighs the other. If you weigh pleasures against pleasures, you of course take the more and
greater; or if you weigh pains against pains, you take the
fewer and the less; or if pleasures against pains, then you
choose that course of action in which the painful is exceeded
by the pleasant, whether the distant by the near or the near
by the distant; and you avoid that course of action in which
the pleasant is exceeded by the painful. Would you not
admit, my friends, that this is true? I am confident that
they cannot deny this.

He agreed with me.

Well, then, I shall say, if you agree so far, be so good
as to answer me a question: Do not the same magnitudes
appear larger to your sight when near, and smaller when
at a distance? They will acknowledge that. And the same
holds of thickness and number; also sounds, which are in
themselves equal, are greater when near, and lesser when
at a distance. They will grant that also. Now suppose happiness to consist in doing or choosing the greater, and in
not doing or in avoiding the less, what would be the saving
principle of human life? Would not the art of measuring be
the saving principle; or would the power of appearance? Is
not the latter that deceiving art which makes us wander
up and down and take the things at one time of which we

repent at another, both in our actions and in our choice of things great and small? But the art of measurement would do away with the effect of appearances, and, showing the truth, would fain teach the soul at last to find rest in the truth, and would thus save our life. Would not mankind generally acknowledge that the art which accomplishes this result is the art of measurement?

Yes, he said, the art of measurement.

Suppose, again, the salvation of human life to depend on the choice of odd and even, and on the knowledge of when a man ought to choose the greater or less, either in reference to themselves or to each other, and whether near or at a distance; what would be the saving principle of our lives? Would not knowledge?—a knowledge of measuring, when the question is one of excess and defect, and a knowledge of number, when the question is of odd and even? The world will assent, will they not?

Protagoras himself thought that they would.

Well, then, my friends, I say to them; seeing that the salvation of human life has been bound to consist in the right choice of pleasures and pains,—in the choice of the more and the fewer, and the greater and the less, and the nearer and remoter, must not this measuring be a consideration of their excess and defect and equality in relation to each other?

This is undeniably true.

And this, as possessing measure, must undeniably also be an art and science?

They will agree, he said.

The nature of that art or science will be a matter of future consideration; but the existence of such a science furnishes a demonstrative answer to the question which you asked of me and Protagoras. At the time when you asked the question, if you remember, both of us were agreeing that there was nothing mightier than knowledge, and that knowledge, in whatever existing, must have the ad-

vantage over pleasure and all other things; and then you
said that pleasure often got the advantage even over a man
who has knowledge; and we refused to allow this, and you
rejoined: O Protagoras and Socrates, what is the meaning
of being overcome by pleasure if not this?—tell us what
you call such a state:—if we had immediately and at the
time answered "Ignorance," you would have laughed at us.
But now, in laughing at us, you will be laughing at yourselves: for you also admitted that men err in their choice of
pleasures and pains; that is, in their choice of good and evil,
from defect of knowledge; and you admitted further, that
they err, not only from defect of knowledge in general, but of
that particular knowledge which is called measuring. And
you are also aware that the erring act which is done without
knowledge is done in ignorance. This, therefore, is the meaning of being overcome by pleasure;—ignorance, and that the
greatest. And our friends Protagoras and Prodicus and Hippias declare that they are the physicians of ignorance; but
you, who are under the mistaken impression that ignorance
is not the cause, and that the art of which I am speaking
cannot be taught, neither go yourselves, nor send your children, to the Sophists, who are the teachers of these things—
you take care of your money and give them none; and the
result is, that you are the worse off both in public and
private life:—Let us suppose this to be our answer to the
world in general: And now I should like to ask you, Hippias,
and you, Prodicus, as well as Protagoras (for the argument
is to be yours as well as ours), whether you think that I
am speaking the truth or not?

They all thought that what I said was entirely true.

Then you agree, I said, that the pleasant is the good, and
the painful evil. And here I would beg my friend Prodicus
not to introduce his distinction of names, whether he is
disposed to say pleasurable, delightful, joyful. However, by
whatever name he prefers to call them, I will ask you, most
excellent Prodicus, to answer in my sense of the words.

Prodicus laughed and assented, as did the others.

Then, my friends, what do you say to this? Are not all actions honourable and useful, of which the tendency is to make life painless and pleasant? The honourable work is also useful and good?

This was admitted.

Then I said, if the pleasant is the good, nobody does anything under the idea or conviction that some other thing would be better and is also attainable, when he might do the better. And this inferiority of a man to himself is merely ignorance, as the superiority of a man to himself is wisdom.

They all assented.

And is not ignorance the having a false opinion and being deceived about important matters?

To this also they unanimously assented.

Then, I said, no man voluntarily pursues evil, or that which he thinks to be evil. To prefer evil to good is not in human nature; and when a man is compelled to choose one of two evils, no one will choose the greater when he may have the less.

All of us agreed to every word of this.

Well, I said, there is a certain thing called fear or terror; and here, Prodicus, I should particularly like to know whether you would agree with me in defining this fear or terror as expectation of evil.

Protagoras and Hippias agreed, but Prodicus said that this was fear and not terror.

Never mind, Prodicus, I said; but let me ask whether, if our former assertions are true, a man will pursue that which he fears when he is not compelled? Would not this be in flat contradiction to the admission which has been already made, that he thinks the things which he fears to be evil; and no one will pursue or voluntarily accept that which he thinks to be evil?

That also was universally admitted.

Then, I said, these, Hippias and Prodicus, are our premises; and I would beg Protagoras to explain to us how he can be right in what he said at first. I do not mean in what he said quite at first, for his first statement, as you may remember, was that whereas there were five parts of virtue none of them was like any other of them; each of them had a separate function. To this, however, I am not referring, but to the assertion which he afterwards made that of the five virtues four were nearly akin to each other, but that the fifth, which was courage, differed greatly from the others. And of this he gave me the following proof. He said: You will find, Socrates, that some of the most impious, and unrighteous, and intemperate, and ignorant of men are among the most courageous; which proves that courage is very different from the other parts of virtue. I was surprised at his saying this at the time, and I am still more surprised now that I have discussed the matter with you. So I asked him whether by the brave he meant the confident. Yes, he replied, and the impetuous or goers. (You may remember, Protagoras, that this was your answer.)

He assented.

Well, then, I said, tell us against what are the courageous ready to go—against the same dangers as the cowards?

No, he answered.

Then against something different?

Yes, he said.

Then do cowards go where there is safety, and the courageous where there is danger?

Yes, Socrates, so men say.

Very true, I said. But I want to know against what do you say that the courageous are ready to go—against dangers, believing them to be dangers, or not against dangers?

No, said he; the former case has been proved by you in the previous argument to be impossible.

That, again, I replied, is quite true. And if this has been rightly proven, then no one goes to meet what he thinks to

be dangers, since the want of self-control, which makes men
rush into dangers, has been shown to be ignorance.

He assented.

And yet the courageous man and the coward alike go
to meet that about which they are confident; so that, in
this point of view, the cowardly and the courageous go to
meet the same things.

And yet, Socrates, said Protagoras, that to which the
coward goes is the opposite of that to which the courageous
goes; the one, for example, is ready to go to battle, and
the other is not ready.

And is going to battle honourable or disgraceful? I said.

Honourable, he replied.

And if honourable, then already admitted by us to be
good; for all honourable actions we have admitted to be
good.

That is true; and to that opinion I shall always adhere

True, I said. But which of the two are they who, as you
say, are unwilling to go to war, which is a good and honourable thing?

The cowards, he replied.

And what is good and honourable, I said, is also pleasant?

It has certainly been acknowledged to be so, he replied.

And do the cowards knowingly refuse to go to the nobler,
and pleasanter, and better?

The admission of that, he replied, would belie our former
admissions.

But does not the courageous man also go to meet the better, and pleasanter, and nobler?

That must be admitted.

And the courageous man has no base fear or base confidence?

True, he replied.

And if not base, then honourable?

He admitted this.

And if honourable, then good?

Yes.

But the fear and confidence of the coward or foolhardy or madman, on the contrary, are base?

He assented.

And these base fears and confidences originate in ignorance and uninstructedness?

True, he said.

Then, as to the motive from which the cowards act, do you call it cowardice or courage?

I should say cowardice, he replied.

And have they not been shown to be cowards through their ignorance of dangers?

Assuredly, he said.

And because of that ignorance they are cowards?

He assented.

And the reason why they are cowards is admitted by you to be cowardice?

He again assented.

Then the ignorance of what is and is not dangerous is cowardice?

He nodded assent.

But surely courage, I said, is opposed to cowardice?

Yes.

Then the wisdom which knows what are and are not dangers is opposed to the ignorance of them?

To that again he nodded assent.

And the ignorance of them is cowardice?

To that he very reluctantly nodded assent.

And the knowledge of that which is and is not dangerous is courage, and is opposed to the ignorance of these things?

At this point he would no longer nod assent, but was silent.

And why, I said, do you neither assent nor dissent, Protagoras?

Finish the argument by yourself, he said.

I only want to ask one more question, I said. I want to
know whether you still think that there are men who are
most ignorant and yet most courageous?

You seem to have a great ambition to make me answer,
Socrates, and therefore I will gratify you, and say, that
this appears to me to be impossible consistently with the
argument.

My only object, I said, in continuing the discussion, has
been the desire to ascertain the nature and relations of virtue; for if this were clear, I am very sure that the other
controversy which has been carried on at great length by
both of us—you affirming and I denying that virtue can be
taught—would also become clear. The result of our discussion appears to me to be singular. For if the argument had
a human voice, that voice would be heard laughing at us
and saying: "Protagoras and Socrates, you are strange
beings; there are you, Socrates, who were saying that virtue cannot be taught, contradicting yourself now by your
attempt to prove that all things are knowledge, including
justice, and temperance, and courage,—which tends to show
that virtue can certainly be taught; for if virtue were other
than knowledge, as Protagoras attempted to prove, then
clearly virtue cannot be taught; but if virtue is entirely
knowledge, as you are seeking to show, then I cannot but
suppose that virtue is capable of being taught. Protagoras,
on the other hand, who started by saying that it might be
taught, is now eager to prove it to be anything rather than
knowledge; and if this is true, it must be quite incapable
of being taught." Now I, Protagoras, perceiving this terrible
confusion of our ideas, have a great desire that they should
be cleared up. And I should like to carry on the discussion
until we ascertain what virtue is, and whether capable of
being taught or not, lest haply Epimetheus should trip us
up and deceive us in the argument, as he forgot us in the
story; I prefer your Prometheus to your Epimetheus, for
of him I make use, whenever I am busy about these ques-

tions, in Promethean care of my own life. And if you have no objection, as I said at first, I should like to have your help in the enquiry.

Protagoras replied: Socrates, I am not of a base nature, and I am the last man in the world to be envious. I cannot but applaud your energy and your conduct of an argument. As I have often said, I admire you above all men whom I know, and far above all men of your age; and I believe that you will become very eminent in philosophy. Let us come back to the subject at some future time; at present we had better turn to something else.

By all means, I said, if that is your wish; for I too ought long since to have kept the engagement of which I spoke before, and only tarried because I could not refuse the request of the noble Callias. So the conversation ended, and we went our way.

PHAEDRUS

PHAEDRUS

PERSONS OF THE DIALOGUE

Socrates.   Phaedrus.

Scene:—Under a plane-tree, by the banks of the Ilissus.

Socrates. My dear Phaedrus, whence come you, and whither are you going?

Phaedrus. I have come from Lysias the son of Cephalus, and I am going to take a walk outside the wall, for I have been sitting with him the whole morning; and our common friend Acumenus tells me that it is much more refreshing to walk in the open air than to be shut up in a cloister.

Soc. There he is right. Lysias then, I suppose, was in the town?

Phaedr. Yes, he was staying with Epicrates, here at the house of Morychus; that house which is near the temple of Olympian Zeus.

Soc. And how did he entertain you? Can I be wrong in supposing that Lysias gave you a feast of discourse?

Phaedr. You shall hear, if you can spare time to accompany me.

Soc. And should I not deem the conversation of you and Lysias "a thing of higher import," as I may say in the words of Pindar, "than any business"?

Phaedr. Will you go on?

Soc. And will you go on with the narration?

Phaedr. My tale, Socrates, is one of your sort, for love was the theme which occupied us—love after a fashion: Lysias has been writing about a fair youth who was being tempted, but not by a lover; and this was the point: he

263

ingeniously proved that the non-lover should be accepted
rather than the lover.

Soc. O that is noble of him! I wish that he would say
the poor man rather than the rich, and the old man rather
than the young one;—then he would meet the case of me
and of many a man; his words would be quite refreshing,
and he would be a public benefactor. For my part, I do so
long to hear his speech, that if you walk all the way to
Megara, and when you have reached the wall come back,
as Herodicus recommends, without going in, I will keep you
company.

Phaedr. What do you mean, my good Socrates? How can
you imagine that my unpractised memory can do justice to
an elaborate work, which the greatest rhetorician of the
age spent a long time in composing? Indeed, I cannot; I
would give a great deal if I could.

Soc. I believe that I know Phaedrus about as well as I
know myself, and I am very sure that the speech of Lysias
was repeated to him, not once only, but again and again;—
he insisted on hearing it many times over and Lysias was
very willing to gratify him; at last, when nothing else would
do, he got hold of the book, and looked at what he most
wanted to see,—this occupied him during the whole morning;—and then when he was tired with sitting, he went out
to take a walk, not until, by the dog, as I believe, he had
simply learned by heart the entire discourse, unless it was
unusually long, and he went to a place outside the wall
that he might practise his lesson. There he saw a certain
lover of discourse who had a similar weakness;—he saw
and rejoiced; now thought he, "I shall have a partner in
my revels." And he invited him to come and walk with him.
But when the lover of discourse begged that he would repeat the tale, he gave himself airs and said, "No, I cannot,"
as if he were indisposed; although, if the hearer had refused, he would sooner or later have been compelled by
him to listen whether he would or no. Therefore, Phaedrus,

bid him do at once what he will soon do whether bidden or not.

Phaedr. I see that you will not let me off until I speak in some fashion or other; verily therefore my best plan is to speak as I best can.

Soc. A very true remark, that of yours.

Phaedr. I will do as I say; but believe me, Socrates, I did not learn the very words—O no; nevertheless I have a general notion of what he said, and will give you a summary of the points in which the lover differed from the non-lover. Let me begin at the beginning.

Soc. Yes, my sweet one; but you must first of all show what you have in your left hand under your cloak, for that roll, as I suspect, is the actual discourse. Now, much as I love you, I would not have you suppose that I am going to have your memory exercised at my expense, if you have Lysias himself here.

Phaedr. Enough; I see that I have no hope of practising my art upon you. But if I am to read, where would you please to sit?

Soc. Let us turn aside and go by the Ilissus; we will sit down at some quiet spot.

Phaedr. I am fortunate in not having my sandals, and as you never have any, I think that we may go along the brook and cool our feet in the water; this will be the easiest way, and at midday and in the summer is far from being unpleasant.

Soc. Lead on, and look out for a place in which we can sit down.

Phaedr. Do you see that tallest plane-tree in the distance?

Soc. Yes.

Phaedr. There are shade and gentle breezes, and grass on which we may either sit or lie down.

Soc. Move forward.

Phaedr. I should like to know, Socrates, whether the

place is not somewhere here at which Boreas is said to have carried off Orithyia from the banks of the Ilissus?

Soc. Such is the tradition.

Phaedr. And is this the exact spot? The little stream is delightfully clear and bright; I can fancy that there might be maidens playing near.

Soc. I believe that the spot is not exactly here, but about a quarter of a mile lower down, where you cross to the temple of Artemis, and there is, I think, some sort of an altar of Boreas at the place.

Phaedr. I have never noticed it; but I beseech you to tell me, Socrates, do you believe this tale?

Soc. The wise are doubtful, and I should not be singular if, like them, I too doubted. I might have a rational explanation that Orithyia was playing with Pharmacia, when a northern gust carried her over the neighbouring rocks; and this being the manner of her death, she was said to have been carried away by Boreas. There is a discrepancy, however, about the locality; according to another version of the story she was taken from the Areopagus, and not from this place. Now I quite acknowledge that these allegories are very nice, but he is not to be envied who has to invent them; much labour and ingenuity will be required of him; and when he has once begun, he must go on and rehabilitate Hippocentaurs and chimeras dire. Gorgons and winged steeds flow in apace, and numberless other inconceivable and portentous natures. And if he is sceptical about them, and would fain reduce them one after another to the rules of probability, this sort of crude philosophy will take up a great deal of time. Now I have no leisure for such enquiries; shall I tell you why? I must first know myself, as the Delphian inscription says; to be curious about that which is not my concern, while I am still in ignorance of my own self, would be ridiculous. And therefore I bid farewell to all this; the common opinion is enough for me. For, as I was saying, I want to know not about this, but about myself:

am I a monster more complicated and swollen with passion than the serpent Typho, or a creature of a gentler and simpler sort, to whom Nature has given a diviner and lowlier destiny? But let me ask you, friend: have we not reached the plane-tree to which you were conducting us?

Phaedr. Yes, this is the tree.

Soc. By Here, a fair resting-place, full of summer sounds and scents. Here is this lofty and spreading plane-tree, and the agnus castus high and clustering, in the fullest blossom and the greatest fragrance; and the stream which flows beneath the plane-tree is deliciously cold to the feet. Judging from the ornaments and images, this must be a spot sacred to Achelous and the Nymphs. How delightful is the breeze: —so very sweet; and there is a sound in the air shrill and summerlike which makes answer to the chorus of the cicadae. But the greatest charm of all is the grass, like a pillow gently sloping to the head. My dear Phaedrus, you have been an admirable guide.

Phaedr. What an incomprehensible being you are, Socrates: when you are in the country, as you say, you really are like some stranger who is led about by a guide. Do you ever cross the border? I rather think that you never venture even outside the gates.

Soc. Very true, my good friend; and I hope that you will excuse me when you hear the reason, which is, that I am a lover of knowledge, and the men who dwell in the city are my teachers, and not the trees or the country. Though I do indeed believe that you have found a spell with which to draw me out of the city into the country, like a hungry cow before whom a bough or a bunch of fruit is waved. For only hold up before me in like manner a book, and you may lead me all round Attica, and over the wide world. And now having arrived, I intend to lie down, and do you choose any posture in which you can read best. Begin.

Phaedr. Listen. You know how matters stand with me; and how, as I conceive, this affair may be arranged for the

advantage of both of us. And I maintain that I ought not
to fail in my suit, because I am not your lover: for lovers
repent of the kindnesses which they have shown when their
passion ceases, but to the non-lovers who are free and not
under any compulsion, no time of repentance ever comes;
for they confer their benefits according to the measure of
their ability, in the way which is most conducive to their
own interest. Then again, lovers consider how by reason of
their love they have neglected their own concerns and rendered service to others: and when to these benefits conferred
they add on the troubles which they have endured, they
think that they have long ago made to the beloved a very
ample return. But the non-lover has no such tormenting rec-
ollections; he has never neglected his affairs or quarrelled
with his relations; he has no troubles to add up or excuses
to invent; and being well rid of all these evils, why should
he not freely do what will gratify the beloved? If you say
that the lover is more to be esteemed, because his love is
thought to be greater; for he is willing to say and do what
is hateful to other men, in order to please his beloved;—
that, if true, is only a proof that he will prefer any future
love to his present, and will injure his old love at the pleasure of the new. And how, in a matter of such infinite importance, can a man be right in trusting himself to one who
is afflicted with a malady which no experienced person would
attempt to cure, for the patient himself admits that he is
not in his right mind, and acknowledges that he is wrong
in his mind, but says that he is unable to control himself?
And if he came to his right mind, would he ever imagine
that the desires were good which he conceived when in his
wrong mind? Once more, there are many more non-lovers
than lovers; and if you choose the best of the lovers, you
will not have many to choose from; but if from the non-
lovers, the choice will be larger, and you will be far more
likely to find among them a person who is worthy of your
friendship. If public opinion be your dread, and you would

avoid reproach, in all probability the lover, who is always thinking that other men are as emulous of him as he is of them, will boast to some one [1] of his successes, and make a show of them openly in the pride of his heart;—he wants others to know that his labour has not been lost; but the non-lover is more his own master, and is desirous of solid good, and not of the opinion of mankind. Again, the lover may be generally noted or seen following the beloved (this is his regular occupation), and whenever they are observed to exchange two words they are supposed to meet about some affair of love either past or in contemplation; but when non-lovers meet, no one asks the reason why, because people know that talking to another is natural, whether friendship or mere pleasure be the motive. Once more, if you fear the fickleness of friendship, consider that in any other case a quarrel might be a mutual calamity; but now, when you have given up what is most precious to you, you will be the greater loser, and therefore, you will have more reason in being afraid of the lover, for his vexations are many, and he is always fancying that every one is leagued against him. Wherefore also he debars his beloved from society; he will not have you intimate with the wealthy, lest they should exceed him in wealth, or with men of education, lest they should be his superiors in understanding; and he is equally afraid of anybody's influence who has any other advantage over himself. If he can persuade you to break with them, you are left without a friend in the world; or if, out of a regard to your own interest, you have more sense than to comply with his desire, you will have to quarrel with him. But those who are non-lovers, and whose success in love is the reward of their merit, will not be jealous of the companions of their beloved, and will rather hate those who refuse to be his associates, thinking that their favourite is slighted by the latter and benefited by the former; for more love than hatred may be expected

[1] Reading τῷ λέγειν; cf. infra, τῷ διαλέγεσθαι.

to come to him out of his friendship with others. Many lovers too have loved the person of a youth before they knew his character or his belongings; so that when their passion has passed away, there is no knowing whether they will continue to be his friends; whereas, in the case of non-lovers who were always friends, the friendship is not lessened by the favours granted; but the recollection of these remains with them, and is an earnest of good things to come. Further, I say that you are likely to be improved by me, whereas the lover will spoil you. For they praise your words and actions in a wrong way; partly, because they are afraid of offending you, and also, their judgment is weakened by passion. Such are the feats which love exhibits; he makes things painful to the disappointed which give no pain to others; he compels the successful lover to praise what ought not to give him pleasure, and therefore the beloved is to be pitied rather than envied. But if you will listen to me, in the first place, I, in my intercourse with you, shall not merely regard present enjoyment, but also future advantage, being not mastered by love, but my own master; nor for small causes taking violent dislikes, but even when the cause is great, slowly laying up little wrath—unintentional offences I shall forgive, and intentional ones I shall try to prevent; and these are the marks of a friendship which will last. Do you think that a lover only can be a firm friend? Reflect: —if this were true, we should set small value on sons, or fathers, or mothers; nor should we ever have loyal friends, for our love of them arises not from passion, but from other associations. Further, if we ought to shower favours on those who are the most eager suitors,—on that principle, we ought always to do good, not to the most virtuous, but to the most needy; for they are the persons who will be most relieved, and will therefore be the most grateful; and when you make a feast you should invite not your friend, but the beggar and the empty soul; for they will love you, and attend you, and come about your doors, and will be the best

pleased, and the most grateful, and will invoke many a blessing on your head. Yet surely you ought not to be granting
favours to those who besiege you with prayer, but to those
who are best able to reward you; nor to the lover only,
but to those who are worthy of love; nor to those who will
enjoy the bloom of your youth, but to those who will share
their possessions with you in age; nor to those who, having
succeeded, will glory in their success to others, but to those
who will be modest and tell no tales; nor to those who care
about you for a moment only, but to those who will continue your friends through life; nor to those who, when
their passion is over, will pick a quarrel with you, but
rather to those who, when the charm of youth has left you,
will show their own virtue. Remember what I have said;
and consider yet this further point: friends admonish the
lover under the idea that his way of life is bad, but no one
of his kindred ever yet censured the non-lover, or thought
that he was ill-advised about his own interests.

"Perhaps you will ask me whether I propose that you
should indulge every non-lover. To which I reply that not
even the lover would advise you to indulge all lovers, for
the indiscriminate favour is less esteemed by the rational
recipient, and less easily hidden by him who would escape
the censure of the world. Now love ought to be for the
advantage of both parties, and for the injury of neither.

"I believe that I have said enough; but if there is anything more which you desire or which in your opinion needs
to be supplied, ask and I will answer."

Now, Socrates, what do you think? Is not the discourse
excellent, more especially in the matter of the language?

Soc. Yes, quite admirable; the effect on me was ravish-
ing. And this I owe to you, Phaedrus, for I observed you
while reading to be in an ecstasy, and thinking that you
are more experienced in these matters than I am, I followed
your example, and, like you, my divine darling, I became
inspired with a phrenzy.

Phaedr. Indeed, you are pleased to be merry.

Soc. Do you mean that I am not in earnest?

Phaedr. Now don't talk in that way, Socrates, but let me have your real opinion; I adjure you, by Zeus, the god of friendship, to tell me whether you think that any Hellene could have said more or spoken better on the same subject.

Soc. Well, but are you and I expected to praise the sentiments of the author, or only the clearness, and roundness, and finish, and tournure of the language? As to the first I willingly submit to your better judgment, for I am not worthy to form an opinion, having only attended to the rhetorical manner; and I was doubting whether this could have been defended even by Lysias himself; I thought, though I speak under correction, that he repeated himself two or three times, either from want of words or from want of pains; and also, he appeared to me ostentatiously to exult in showing how well he could say the same thing[1] in two or three ways.

Phaedr. Nonsense, Socrates; what you call repetition was the especial merit of the speech; for he omitted no topic of which the subject rightly allowed, and I do not think that any one could have spoken better or more exhaustively.

Soc. There I cannot go along with you. Ancient sages, men and women, who have spoken and written of these things, would rise up in judgment against me, if out of complaisance I assented to you.

Phaedr. Who are they, and where did you hear anything better than this?

Soc. I am sure that I must have heard; but at this moment I do not remember from whom; perhaps from Sappho the fair, or Anacreon the wise; or, possibly, from a prose writer. Why do I say so? Why, because I perceive that my bosom is full, and that I could make another speech as good as that of Lysias, and different. Now I am certain that this is not an invention of my own, who am well aware

[1] Reading ταὐτά.

that I know nothing, and therefore I can only infer that I have been filled through the ears, like a pitcher, from the waters of another, though I have actually forgotten in my stupidity who was my informant.

Phaedr. That is grand:—but never mind where you heard the discourse or from whom; let that be a mystery not to be divulged even at n.y earnest desire. Only, as you say, promise[1] to make another and better oration, equal in length and entirely new, on the same subject; and I, like the nine Archons, will promise to set up a golden image at Delphi, not only of myself, but of you, and as large as life.

Soc. You are a dear golden ass if you suppose me to mean that Lysias has altogether missed the mark, and that I can make a speech from which all his arguments are to be excluded. The worst of authors will say something which is to the point. Who, for example, could speak on this thesis of yours without praising the discretion of the non-lover and blaming the indiscretion of the lover? These are the commonplaces of the subject which must come in (for what else is there to be said?) and must be allowed and excused; the only merit is the arrangement of them, for there can be none in the invention; but when you leave the commonplaces, then there may be some originality.

Phaedr. I admit that there is reason in what you say, and I too will be reasonable, and will allow you to start with the premise that the lover is more disordered in his wits than the non-lover; if in what remains you make a longer and better speech than Lysias, and use other arguments, then I say again, that a statue you shall have of beaten gold, and take your place by the colossal offerings of the Cypselids at Olympia.

Soc. How profoundly in earnest is the lover, because to tease him I lay a finger upon his love! And so, Phaedrus, you really imagine that I am going to improve upon the ingenuity of Lysias?

[1] Reading ὑπόσχες εἰπεῖν.

Phaedr. There I have you as you had me, and you must just speak, "as you best can." Do not let us exchange "tu quoque" as in a farce, or compel me to say to you as you said to me, "I know Socrates as well as I know myself, and he was wanting to speak, but he gave himself airs." Rather I woud have you consider that from this place we stir not until you have unbosomed yourself of the speech; for here are we all alone, and I am stronger, remember, and younger than you:—Wherefore perpend, and do not compel me to use violence.

Soc. But, my sweet Phaedrus, how ridiculous it would be of me to compete with Lysias in an extempore speech! He is a master in his art and I am an untaught man.

Phaedr. You see how matters stand; and therefore let there be no more pretences; for, indeed, I know the word that is irresistible.

Soc. Then don't say it.

Phaedr. Yes, but I will; and my word shall be an oath. "I say, or rather swear"—but what good will be the witness of my oath?—"By this plane-tree I swear, that unless you repeat the discourse here in the face of this very plane-tree, I will never tell you another; never let you have word of another!"

Soc. Villain! I am conquered; the poor lover of discourse has no more to say.

Phaedr. Then why are you still at your tricks?

Soc. I am not going to play tricks now that you have taken the oath, for I cannot allow myself to be starved.

Phaedr. Proceed.

Soc. Shall I tell you what I will do?

Phaedr. What?

Soc. I will veil my face and gallop through the discourse as fast as I can, for if I see you I shall feel ashamed and not know what to say.

Phaedr. Only go on and you may do anything else which you please.

Soc. Come, O ye Muses, melodious, as ye are called, whether you have received this name from the character of your strains, or because the Melians[1] are a musical race, help, O help me in the tale which my good friend here desires me to rehearse, in order that his friend whom he always deemed wise may seem to him to be wiser now than ever.

Once upon a time there was a fair boy, or, more properly speaking, a youth; he was very fair and had a great many lovers; and there was one special cunning one, who had persuaded the youth that he did not love him, but he really loved him all the same; and one day when he was paying his addresses to him, he used this very argument—that he ought to accept the non-lover rather than the lover; his words were as follows:—

"All good counsel begins in the same way; a man should know what he is advising about, or his counsel will all come to nought. But people imagine that they know about the nature of things, when they don't know about them, and, not having come to an understanding at first because they think that they know, they end, as might be expected, in contradicting one another and themselves. Now you and I must not be guilty of this fundamental error which we condemn in others; but as our question is whether the lover or non-lover is to be preferred, let us first of all agree in defining the nature and power of love, and then, keeping our eyes upon the definition and to this appealing, let us further enquire whether love brings advantage or disadvantage.

"Every one sees that love is a desire, and we know also that non-lovers desire the beautiful and good. Now in what way is the lover to be distinguished from the non-lover? Let us note that in every one of us there are two guiding and ruling principles which lead us whither they will; one is the natural desire of pleasure, the other is an

[1] In the original, λέγεται, Λίγυες.

acquired opinion which aspires after the best; and these two are sometimes in harmony and then again at war, and sometimes the one, sometimes the other conquers. When opinion by the help of reason leads us to the best, the conquering principle is called temperance; but when desire, which is devoid of reason, rules in us and drags us to pleasure, that power of misrule is called excess. Now excess has many names, and many members, and many forms, and any of these forms when very marked gives a name, neither honourable nor creditable, to the bearer of the name. The desire of eating, for example, which gets the better of the higher reason and the other desires, is called gluttony, and he who is possessed by it is called a glutton; the tyrannical desire of drink, which inclines the possessor of the desire to drink, has a name which is only too obvious, and there can be as little doubt by what name any other appetite of the same family would be called;—it will be the name of that which happens to be dominant. And now I think that you will perceive the drift of my discourse; but as every spoken word is in a manner plainer than the unspoken, I had better say further that the irrational desire which overcomes the tendency of opinion towards right, and is led away to the enjoyment of beauty, and especially of personal beauty, by the desires which are her own kindred—that supreme desire, I say, which by leading [1] conquers and by the force of passion is reinforced, from this very force, receiving a name, is called love (ἐρρωμένω; ἔρως)."

And now, dear Phaedrus, I shall pause for an instant to ask whether you do not think me, as I appear to myself, inspired?

Phaedr. Yes, Socrates, you seem to have a very unusual flow of words.

Soc. Listen to me, then, in silence; for surely the place is holy; so that you must not wonder, if, as I proceed, I

---

[1] Reading ἀγωγῇ.

appear to be in a divine fury, for already I am getting into dithyrambics.

Phaedr. Nothing can be truer.

Soc. The responsibility rests with you. But hear what follows, and perhaps the fit may be averted; all is in their hands above. I will go on talking to my youth. Listen:—

Thus, my friend, we have declared and defined the nature of the subject. Keeping the definition in view, let us now enquire what advantage or disadvantage is likely to ensue from the lover or the non-lover to him who accepts their advances.

He who is the victim of his passions and the slave of pleasure will of course desire to make his beloved as agreeable to himself as possible. Now to him who has a mind diseased anything is agreeable which is not opposed to him, but that which is equal or superior is hateful to him, and therefore the lover will not brook any superiority or equality on the part of his beloved; he is always employed in reducing him to inferiority. And the ignorant is the inferior of the wise, the coward of the brave, the slow of speech of the speaker, the dull of the clever. These, and not these only, are the mental defects of the beloved;— defects which, when implanted by nature, are necessarily a delight to the lover, and, when not implanted, he must contrive to implant them in him, if he would not be deprived of his fleeting joy. And therefore he cannot help being jealous, and will debar his beloved from the advantages of society which would make a man of him, and especially from that society which would have given him wisdom, and thereby he cannot fail to do him great harm. That is to say, in his excessive fear lest he should come to be despised in his eyes he will be compelled to banish from him divine philosophy; and there is no greater injury which he can inflict upon him than this. He will contrive that his beloved shall be wholly ignorant, and in everything shall

look to him; he is to be the delight of the lover's heart, and
a curse to himself. Verily, a lover is a profitable guardian
and associate for him in all that relates to his mind.

Let us next see how his master, whose law of life is pleasure and not good, will keep and train the body of his servant. Will he not choose a beloved who is delicate rather
than sturdy and strong? One brought up in shady bowers
and not in the bright sun, a stranger to manly exercises and
the sweat of toil, accustomed only to a soft and luxurious
diet, instead of the hues of health having the colours of
paint and ornament, and the rest of a piece?—such a life
as any one can imagine and which I need not detail at
length. But I may sum up all that I have to say in a word,
and pass on. Such a person in war, or in any of the great
crises of life, will be the anxiety of his friends and also of
his lover, and certainly not the terror of his enemies; which
nobody can deny.

And now let us tell what advantage or disadvantage the
beloved will receive from the guardianship and society of
his lover in the matter of his property; this is the next point
to be considered. The lover will be the first to see what, indeed, will be sufficiently evident to all men, that he desires
above all things to deprive his beloved of his dearest and
best and holiest possessions, father, mother, kindred, friends,
of all who he thinks may be hinderers or reprovers of their
most sweet converse; he will even cast a jealous eye upon
his gold and silver or other property, because these make
him a less easy prey, and when caught less manageable;
hence he is of necessity displeased at his possession of them
and rejoices at their loss; and he would like him to be wife-
less, childless, homeless, as well; and the longer the better,
for the longer he is all this, the longer he will enjoy him.

There are some sort of animals, such as flatterers, who
are dangerous and mischievous enough, and yet nature has
mingled a temporary pleasure and grace in their composition. You may say that a courtesan is hurtful, and disap-

prove of such creatures and their practices, and yet for
the time they are very pleasant. But the lover is not only
hurtful to his love; he is also an extremely disagreeable
companion. The old proverb says that "birds of a feather
flock together"; I suppose that equality of years inclines
them to the same pleasures, and similarity begets friendship; yet you may have more than enough even of this;
and verily constraint is always said to be grievous. Now the
lover is not only unlike his beloved, but he forces himself
upon him. For he is old and his love is young, and neither
day nor night will he leave him if he can help; necessity
and the sting of desire drive him on, and allure him with
the pleasure which he receives from seeing, hearing, touching, perceiving him in every way. And therefore he is delighted to fasten upon him and to minister to him. But what
pleasure or consolation can the beloved be receiving all this
time? Must he not feel the extremity of disgust when he
looks at an old shrivelled face and the remainder to match,
which even in a description is disagreeable, and quite de-
testable when he is forced into daily contact with his lover?
Moreover he is jealously watched and guarded against everything and everybody, and has to hear misplaced and exagger-
ated praises of himself, and censures equally inappropriate,
which are intolerable when the man is sober, and, besides
being intolerable, are published all over the world in all their
indelicacy and wearisomeness when he is drunk.

And not only while his love continues is he mischievous
and unpleasant, but when his love ceases he becomes a per-
fidious enemy of him on whom he showered his oaths and
prayers and promises, and yet could hardly prevail upon
him to tolerate the tedium of his company even from motives of interest. The hour of payment arrives, and now he
is the servant of another master; instead of love and infatuation, wisdom and temperance are his bosom's lords;
but the beloved has not discovered the change which has
taken place in him, when he asks for a return and recalls

to his recollection former sayings and doings; he believes himself to be speaking to the same person, and the other, not having the courage to confess the truth, and not knowing how to fulfil the oaths and promises which he made when under the dominion of folly, and having now grown wise and temperate, does not want to do as he did or to be as he was before. And so he runs away and is constrained to be a defaulter; the oyster-shell [1] has fallen with the other side uppermost—he changes pursuit into flight, while the other is compelled to follow him with passion and imprecation, not knowing that he ought never from the first to have accepted a demented lover instead of a sensible non-lover; and that in making such a choice he was giving himself up to a faithless, morose, envious, disagreeable being, hurtful to his estate, hurtful to his bodily health, and still more hurtful to the cultivation of his mind, than which there neither is nor ever will be anything more honoured in the eyes both of gods and men. Consider this, fair youth, and know that in the friendship of the lover there is no real kindness; he has an appetite and wants to feed upon you:

"As wolves love lambs so lovers love their loves."

But I told you so, I am speaking in verse, and therefore I had better make an end; enough.

Phaedr. I thought that you were only half-way and were going to make a similar speech about all the advantages of accepting the non-lover. Why do you not proceed?

Soc. Does not your simplicity observe that I have got out of dithyrambics into heroics, when only uttering a censure on the lover? And if I am to add the praises of the non-lover what will become of me? Do you not perceive that I am already overtaken by the Nymphs to whom you have mischievously exposed me? And therefore I will only add

[1] In allusion to a game in which two parties fled or pursued according as an oyster-shell which was thrown into the air fell with the dark or light side uppermost.

that the non-lover has all the advantages in which the lover is accused of being deficient. And now I will say no more; there has been enough of both of them. Leaving the tale to its fate, I will cross the river and make the best of my way home, lest a worse thing be inflicted upon me by you.

Phaedr. Not yet, Socrates; not until the heat of the day has passed; do you not see that the hour is almost noon? There is the midday sun standing still, as people say, in the meridian. Let us rather stay and talk over what has been said, and then return in the cool.

Soc. Your love of discourse, Phaedrus, is superhuman, simply marvellous, and I do not believe that there is any one of your contemporaries who has either made or in one way or another has compelled others to make an equal number of speeches. I would except Simmias the Theban, but all the rest are far behind you. And now I do verily believe that you have been the cause of another.

Phaedr. That is good news. But what do you mean?

Soc. I mean to say that as I was about to cross the stream the usual sign was given to me,—that sign which always forbids, but never bids, me to do anything which I am going to do; and I thought that I heard a voice saying in my ear that I had been guilty of impiety, and that I must not go away until I had made an atonement. Now I am a diviner, though not a very good one, but I have enough religion for my own use, as you might say of a bad writer—his writing is good enough for him; and I am beginning to see that I was in error. O my friend, how prophetic is the human soul! At the time I had a sort of misgiving, and, like Ibycus, "I was troubled; I feared that I might be buying honour from men at the price of sinning against the gods." Now I recognize my error.

Phaedr. What error?

Soc. That was a dreadful speech which you brought with you, and you made me utter one as bad.

Phaedr. How so?

Soc. It was foolish, I say,—to a certain extent, impious; can anything be more dreadful?

Phaedr. Nothing, if the speech was really such as you describe.

Soc. Well, and is not Eros the son of Aphrodite, and a god?

Phaedr. So men say.

Soc. But that was not acknowledged by Lysias in his speech, nor by you in that other speech which you by a charm drew from my lips. For if love be, as he surely is, a divinity, he cannot be evil. Yet this was the error of both the speeches. There was also a simplicity about them which was refreshing; having no truth or honesty in them, nevertheless they pretended to be something, hoping to succeed in deceiving the manikins of earth and gain celebrity among them. Wherefore I must have a purgation. And I bethink me of an ancient purgation of mythological error which was devised, not by Homer, for he never had the wit to discover why he was blind, but by Stesichorus, who was a philosopher and knew the reason why; and therefore, when he lost his eyes, for that was the penalty which was inflicted upon him for reviling the lovely Helen, he at once purged himself. And the purgation was a recantation, which began thus,—

"False is that word of mine—the truth is that thou didst not embark in ships, nor ever go to the walls of Troy";

and when he had completed his poem, which is called "the recantation," immediately his sight returned to him. Now I will be wiser than either Stesichorus or Homer, in that I am going to make my recantation for reviling love before I suffer; and this I will attempt, not as before, veiled and ashamed, but with forehead bold and bare.

Phaedr. Nothing could be more agreeable to me than to hear you say so.

Soc. Only think, my good Phaedrus, what an utter want of delicacy was shown in the two discourses; I mean, in my own and in that which you recited out of the book. Would not any one who was himself of a noble and gentle nature, and who loved or ever had loved a nature like his own, when we tell of the petty causes of lovers' jealousies, and of their exceeding animosities, and of the injuries which they do to their beloved, have imagined that our ideas of love were taken from some haunt of sailors to which good manners were unknown—he would certainly never have ad·· mitted the justice of our censure?

Phaedr. I dare say not, Socrates.

Soc. Therefore, because I blush at the thought of this person, and also because I am afraid of Love himself, I desire to wash the brine out of my ears with water from the spring; and I would counsel Lysias not to delay, but to write another discourse, which shall prove that "ceteris paribus" the lover ought to be accepted rather than the non-lover.

Phaedr. Be assured that he shall. You shall speak the praises of the lover, and Lysias shall be compelled by me to write another discourse on the same theme.

Soc. You will be true to your nature in that, and therefore I believe you.

Phaedr. Speak, and fear not.

Soc. But where is the fair youth whom I was addressing before, and who ought to listen now; lest, if he hear me not, he should accept a non-lover before he knows what he is doing?

Phaedr. He is close at hand, and always at your service.

Soc. Know then, fair youth, that the former discourse was the word of Phaedrus, the son of Vain Man, who dwells in the city of Myrrhina (Myrrhinusius). And this which I am about to utter is the recantation of Stesichorus the son of Godly Man (Euphemus), who comes from the town of Desire (Himera), and is to the following effect: "I told a lie when I said" that the beloved ought to accept the non-lover when he might have the lover, because the one is sane, and the other mad. It might be so if madness were simply an evil; but there is also a madness which is a divine gift, and the source of the chiefest blessings granted to men. For prophecy is a madness, and the prophetess at Delphi and the priestesses at Dodona when out of their senses have conferred great benefits on Hellas, both in public and private life, but when in their senses few or none. And I might also tell you how the Sibyl and other inspired persons have given to many an one many an intimation of the future which has saved them from falling. But it would be tedious to speak of what every one knows.

There will be more reason in appealing to the ancient inventors of names,[1] who would never have connected prophecy (μαντική), which foretells the future and is the noblest of arts, with madness (μανική), or called them both by the same name, if they had deemed madness to be a disgrace or dishonour;—they must have thought that there was an inspired madness which was a noble thing; for the two words, μαντική and μανική, are really the same, and the letter τ is only a modern and tasteless insertion. And this is confirmed by the name which was given by them to the rational investigation of futurity, whether made by the help of birds or of other signs—this, for as much as it is an art which supplies from the reasoning faculty mind (νοῦς) and information (ἱστορία) to human thought (οἴησις), they orignally termed οἰονοιστική, but the word has been lately altered and made sonorous by the modern introduction of the letter Omega (οἰονοιστική and οἰωνιστική), and in proportion as prophecy (μαντική) is more perfect and august than augury, both in name and fact, in the same proportion, as the ancients testify, is madness superior to a sane mind (σωφροσύνη), for the one is only of human, but the other of divine origin. Again, where plagues and mighti-

[1] Cp. Cratylus 388 foll.

est woes have bred in certain families, owing to some ancient blood-guiltiness, there madness has entered with holy
prayers and rites, and by inspired utterances found a way
of deliverance for those who are in need; and he who has
part in this gift, and is truly possessed and duly out of
his mind, is by the use of purifications and mysteries made
whole and exempt from evil, future as well as present, and
has a release from the calamity which was afflicting him.
The third kind is the madness of those who are possessed
by the Muses; which taking hold of a delicate and virgin
soul, and there inspiring frenzy, awakens lyrical and all
other numbers; with these adorning the myriad actions of
ancient heroes for the instruction of posterity. But he who,
having no touch of the Muses' madness in his soul, comes
to the door and thinks that he will get into the temple by
the help of art—he, I say, and his poetry are not admitted;
the sane man disappears and is nowhere when he enters
into rivalry with the madman.

I might tell of many other noble deeds which have sprung
from inspired madness. And therefore, let no one frighten
or flutter us by saying that the temperate friend is to be
chosen rather than the inspired, but let him further show
that love is not sent by the gods for any good to lover or
beloved; if he can do so we will allow him to carry off the
palm. And we, on our part, will prove in answer to him that
the madness of love is the greatest of heaven's blessings,
and the proof shall be one which the wise will receive, and
the witling disbelieve. But first of all, let us view the affections and actions of the soul divine and human, and
try to ascertain the truth about them. The beginning of
our proof is as follows:—

[1] The soul through all her being is immortal, for that
which is ever in motion is immortal; but that which moves
another and is moved by another, in ceasing to move ceases
also to live. Only the self-moving, never leaving self, never

[1] Translated by Cic. Tus. Quaest. s. 24.

ceases to move, and is the fountain and beginning of motion to all that moves besides. Now, the beginning is unbegotten, for that which is begotten has a beginning; but the beginning is begotten of nothing, for if it were begotten of something, then the begotten would not come from a beginning. But if unbegotten, it must also be indestructible; for if beginning were destroyed, there could be no beginning out of anything, nor anything out of a beginning; and all things must have a beginning. And therefore the self-moving is the beginning of motion; and this can neither be destroyed nor begotten, else the whole heavens and all creation would collapse and stand still, and never again have motion or birth. But if the self-moving is proved to be immortal, he who affirms that self-motion is the very idea and essence of the soul will not be put to confusion. For the body which is moved from without is soulless; but that which is moved from within has a soul, for such is the nature of the soul. But if this be true, must not the soul be the self-moving, and therefore of necessity unbegotten and immortal? Enough of the soul's immortality.

Of the nature of the soul, though her true form be ever a theme of large and more than mortal discourse, let me speak briefly, and in a figure. And let the figure be composite—a pair of winged horses and a charioteer. Now the winged horses and the charioteers of the gods are all of them noble and of noble descent, but those of other races are mixed; the human charioteer drives his in a pair; and one of them is noble and of noble breed, and the other is ignoble and of ignoble breed; and the driving of them of necessity gives a great deal of trouble to him. I will endeavour to explain to you in what way the mortal differs from the immortal creature. The soul in her totality has the care of inanimate being everywhere, and traverses the whole heaven in divers forms appearing;—when perfect and fully winged she soars upward, and orders the whole world; whereas the imperfect soul, losing her wings and drooping in her flight, at last settles on the solid ground—there, finding a home, she receives an earthly frame which appears to be self-moved, but is really moved by her power; and this composition of soul and body is called a living and mortal creature. For immortal no such union can be reasonably believed to be; although fancy, not having seen nor surely known the nature of God, may imagine an immortal creature having both a body and also a soul which are united throughout all time. Let that, however, be as God wills, and be spoken of acceptably to him. And now let us ask the reason why the soul loses her wings!

The wing is the corporeal element which is most akin to the divine, and which by nature tends to soar aloft and carry that which gravitates downwards into the upper region, which is the habitation of the gods. The divine is beauty, wisdom, goodness, and the like; and by these the wing of the soul is nourished, and grows apace; but when fed upon evil and foulness and the opposite of good, wastes and falls away. Zeus, the mighty lord, holding the reins of a winged chariot, leads the way in heaven, ordering all and taking care of all; and there follows him the array of gods and demi-gods, marshalled in eleven bands; Hestia alone abides at home in the house of heaven; of the rest they who are reckoned among the princely twelve march in their appointed order. They see many blessed sights in the inner heaven, and there are many ways to and fro, along which the blessed gods are passing, every one doing his own work; he may follow who will and can, for jealousy has no place in the celestial choir. But when they go to banquet and festival, then they move up the steep to the top of the vault of heaven. The chariots of the gods in even poise, obeying the rein, glide rapidly; but the others labour, for the vicious steed goes heavily, weighing down the charioteer to the earth when his steed has not been thoroughly trained:— and this is the hour of agony and extremest conflict for the soul. For the immortals, when they are at the end of their course, go forth and stand upon the outside of heaven, and the revolution of the spheres carries them round, and they behold the things beyond. But of the heaven which is above the heavens, what earthly poet ever did or ever will sing worthily? It is such as I will describe; for I must dare to speak the truth, when truth is my theme. There abides the very being with which true knowledge is concerned; the colourless, formless, intangible essence, visible only to mind, the pilot of the soul. The divine intelligence, being nurtured upon mind and pure knowledge, and the intelligence of every soul which is capable of receiving the food proper to it, rejoices at beholding reality, and once more gazing upon truth, is replenished and made glad, until the revolution of the worlds brings her round again to the same place. In the revolution she beholds justice, and temperance, and knowledge absolute, not in the form of generation or of relation, which men call existence, but knowledge absolute in existence absolute; and beholding the other true existences in like manner, and feasting upon them, she passes down into the interior of the heavens and returns home; and there the charioteer putting up his horses at the stall, gives them ambrosia to eat and nectar to drink.

Such is the life of the gods; but of other souls, that which follows God best and is likest to him lifts the head of the charioteer into the outer world, and is carried round in the revolution, troubled indeed by the steeds, and with difficulty beholding true being; while another only rises and falls, and sees, and again fails to see by reason of the unruliness of the steeds. The rest of the souls are also longing after the upper world and they all follow, but not being strong enough they are carried round below the surface, plunging, treading on one another, each striving to be first; and there is confusion and perspiration and the extremity of effort; and many of them are lamed or have their wings broken through the ill-driving of the charioteers; and all of them after a fruitless toil, not having attained to the mysteries of true being, go away, and feed upon opinion. The reason why the souls exhibit this exceeding eagerness to behold the plain of truth is that pasturage is found there, which is suited to the highest part of the soul; and the wing on which the soul soars is nourished with this. And there is a law of Destiny, that the soul which attains any vision of truth in company with a god is preserved from harm until the next period, and if attaining always is always unharmed. But when she is unable to follow, and fails to behold the truth, and through some ill-hap sinks beneath the double load of forgetfulness and vice, and her wings fall from her and she drops to the ground, then the law ordains that this soul shall at her first birth pass, not into any other animal, but only into man; and the soul which has seen most of truth shall come to the birth as a philosopher, or artist, or some musical and loving nature; that which has seen truth in the second degree shall be some righteous king or warrior chief; the soul which is of the third class shall be a politician, or economist, or trader; the fourth shall be a lover of gymnastic toils, or a physician; the fifth shall lead the life of a prophet or hierophant; to the sixth the character of a poet or some other imitative artist will be assigned; to the seventh the life of an artisan or husbandman; to the eighth that of a sophist or demagogue; to the ninth that of a tyrant;—all these are states of probation, in which he who does righteously improves, and he who does unrighteously, deteriorates his lot.

Ten thousand years must elapse before the soul of each one can return to the place from whence she came, for she cannot grow her wings in less; only the soul of a philosopher, guileless and true, or the soul of a lover, who is not devoid of philosophy, may acquire wings in the third of the recurring periods of a thousand years; he is distinguished from the ordinary good man who gains wings in three thousand years:—and they who choose this life three times in succession have wings given them, and go away at the end of three thousand years. But the others [1] receive judgment when they have completed their first life, and after the judgment they go, some of them to the houses of correction which are under the earth, and are punished; others to some place in heaven whither they are lightly borne by justice, and there they live in a manner worthy of the life which they led here when in the form of men. And at the end of the first thousand years the good souls and also the evil souls both come to draw lots and choose their second life, and they may take any which they please. The soul of a man may pass into the life of a beast, or from the beast return again into the man. But the soul which has never seen the truth will not pass into the human form. For a man must have intelligence of universals, and be able to proceed from the many particulars of sense to one conception of reason;—this is the recollection of those things which our soul once saw while following God—when regardless of that which we now call being she raised her head up towards the true being. And therefore the mind of the philosopher alone has wings; and this is just, for he is always, according to the measure of his abilities, clinging in recollection to those things in which God abides, and in beholding which He is what He is. And he who employs aright these memories is ever being initiated into perfect mysteries and alone becomes truly perfect. But, as he forgets earthly interests and is rapt in the divine, the vulgar deem him mad, and rebuke him; they do not see that he is inspired.

Thus far I have been speaking of the fourth and last kind of madness, which is imputed to him who, when he sees the beauty of earth, is transported with the recollection of the true beauty; he would like to fly away, but he cannot; he is like a bird fluttering and looking upward and careless of the world below; and he is therefore thought to

---

[1] The philosopher alone is not subject to judgment (κρίσις), for he has never lost the vision of truth.

be mad. And I have shown this of all inspirations to be the noblest and highest and the offspring of the highest to him who has or shares in it, and that he who loves the beautiful is called a lover because he partakes of it. For, as has been already said, every soul of man has in the way of nature beheld true being; this was the condition of her passing into the form of man. But all souls do not easily recall the things of the other world; they may have seen them for a short time only, or they may have been unforunate in their earthly lot, and, having had their hearts turned to unrighteousness through some corrupting influence, they may have lost the memory of the holy things which once they saw. Few only retain an adequate remembrance of them; and they, when they behold here any image of that other world, are rapt in amazement; but they are ignorant of what this rapture means, because they do not clearly perceive. For there is no light of justice or temperance or any of the higher ideas which are precious to souls in the earthly copies of them: they are seen through a glass dimly; and there are few who, going to the images, behold in them the realities, and these only with difficulty. There was a time when with the rest of the happy band they saw beauty shining in brightness,—we philosophers following in the train of Zeus, others in company with other gods; and then we beheld the beatific vision and were initiated into a mystery which may be truly called most blessed, celebrated by us in our state of innocence, before we had any experience of evils to come, when we were admitted to the sight of apparitions innocent and simple and calm and happy, which we beheld shining in pure light, pure ourselves and not yet enshrined in that living tomb which we carry about, now that we are imprisoned in the body, like an oyster in his shell. Let me linger over the memory of scenes which have passed away.

But of beauty, I repeat again that we saw her there shining in company with the celestial forms; and coming to earth we find her here too, shining in clearness through the

clearest aperture of sense. For sight is the most piercing of
our bodily senses; though not by that is wisdom seen; her
loveliness would have been transporting if there had been
a visible image of her, and the other ideas, if they had visible
counterparts, would be equally lovely. But this is the privilege of beauty, that being the loveliest she is also the most
palpable to sight. Now he who is not newly initiated or
who has become corrupted, does not easily rise out of this
world to the sight of true beauty in the other; he looks
only at her earthly namesake, and instead of being awed
at the sight of her, he is given over to pleasure, and like
a brutish beast he rushes on to enjoy and beget; he consorts
with wantonness, and is not afraid or ashamed of pursuing pleasure in violation of nature. But he whose initiation is recent, and who has been the spectator of many
glories in the other world, is amazed when he sees any one
having a godlike face or form, which is the expression of
divine beauty; and at first a shudder runs through him,
and again the old awe steals over him; then looking upon
the face of his beloved as of a god he reverences him, and
if he were not afraid of being thought a downright madman,
he would sacrifice to his beloved as to the image of a god;
then while he gazes on him there is a sort of reaction, and
the shudder passes into an unusual heat and perspiration;
for, as he receives the effluence of beauty through the eyes,
the wing moistens and he warms. And as he warms, the
parts out of which the wing grew, and which had been hitherto closed and rigid, and had prevented the wing from
shooting forth, are melted, and as nourishment streams upon
him, the lower end of the wing begins to swell and grow
from the root upwards; and the growth extends under the
whole soul—for once the whole was winged. During this
process the whole soul is all in a state of ebullition and
effervescence,—which may be compared to the irritation
and uneasiness in the gums at the time of cutting teeth,—

bubbles up, and has a feeling of uneasiness and tickling; but when in like manner the soul is beginning to grow wings, the beauty of the beloved meets her eye and she receives the sensible warm motion of particles which flow towards her, therefore called emotion (ἵμερος), and is refreshed and warmed by them, and then she ceases from her pain with joy. But when she is parted from her beloved and her moisture fails, then the orifices of the passage out of which the wing shoots dry up and close, and intercept the germ of the wing; which, being shut up with the emotion, throbbing as with the pulsations of an artery, pricks the aperture which is nearest, until at length the entire soul is pierced and maddened and pained, and at the recollection of beauty is again delighted. And from both of them together the soul is oppressed at the strangeness of her condition, and is in a great strait and excitement, and in her madness can neither sleep by night nor abide in her place by day. And wherever she thinks that she will behold the beautiful one, thither in her desire she runs. And when she has seen him, and bathed herself in the waters of beauty, her constraint is loosened, and she is refreshed, and has no more pangs and pains; and this is the sweetest of all pleasures at the time, and is the reason why the soul of the lover will never forsake his beautiful one, whom he esteems above all; he has forgotten mother and brethren and companions, and he thinks nothing of the neglect and loss of his property; the rules and proprieties of life, on which he formerly prided himself, he now despises, and is ready to sleep like a servant, wherever he is allowed, as near as he can to his desired one, who is the object of his worship, and the physician who can alone assuage the greatness of his pain. And this state, my dear imaginary youth to whom I am talking, is by men called love, and among the gods has a name at which you, in your simplicity, may be inclined to mock; there are two lines in the apocryphal writings of Homer in which the name occurs. One of them is rather outrageous, and not altogether metrical. They are as follows:—

"Mortals call him fluttering love,
But the immortals call him winged one,
Because the growing of wings [1] is a necessity to him."

You may believe this, but not unless you like. At any rate the loves of lovers and their causes are such as I have described.

Now the lover who is taken to be the attendant of Zeus is better able to bear the winged god, and can endure a heavier burden; but the attendants and companions of Ares, when under the influence of love, if they fancy that they have been at all wronged, are ready to kill and put an end to themselves and their beloved. And he who follows in the train of any other god, while he is unspoiled and the impression lasts, honours and imitates him, as far as he is able; and after the manner of his god he behaves in his intercourse with his beloved and with the rest of the world during the first period of his earthly existence. Every one chooses his love from the ranks of beauty according to his character, and this he makes his god, and fashions and adorns as a sort of image which he is to fall down and worship. The followers of Zeus desire that their beloved should have a soul like him; and therefore they seek out some one of a philosophical and imperial nature, and when they have found him and loved him, they do all they can to confirm such a nature in him, and if they have no experience of such a disposition hitherto, they learn of any one who can teach them, and themselves follow in the same way. And they have the less difficulty in finding the nature of their own god in themselves, because they have been compelled to gaze intensely on him; their recollection clings

[1] Or, reading πτερόφοιτον, "the movement of wings."

to him, and they become possessed of him, and receive from him their character and disposition, so far as man can participate in God. The qualities of their god they attribute to the beloved, wherefore they love him all the more, and if, like the Bacchic Nymphs, they draw inspiration from Zeus, they pour out their own fountain upon him, wanting to make him as like as possible to their own god. But those who are the followers of Here seek a royal love, and when they have found him they do just the same with him; and in like manner the followers of Apollo, and of every other god walking in the ways of their god, seek a love who is to be made like him whom they serve, and when they have found him, they themselves imitate their god, and persuade their love to do the same, and educate him into the manner and nature of the god as far as they each can; for no feelings of envy or jealousy are entertained by them towards their beloved, but they do their utmost to create in him the greatest likeness of themselves and of the god whom they honour. Thus fair and blissful to the beloved is the desire of the inspired lover, and the initiation of which I speak into the mysteries of true love, if he be captured by the lover and their purpose is effected. Now the beloved is taken captive in the following manner:—

As I said at the beginning of this tale, I divided each soul into three—two horses and a charioteer; and one of the horses was good and the other bad: the division may remain, but I have not yet explained in what the goodness or badness of either consists, and to that I will now proceed. The right-hand horse is upright and cleanly made; he has a lofty neck and an aquiline nose; his colour is white, and his eyes dark; he is a lover of honour and modesty and temperance, and the follower of true glory; he needs no touch of the whip, but is guided by word and admonition only. The other is a crooked lumbering animal, put together anyhow; he has a short thick neck; he is flat-faced and of a dark colour, with grey eyes and blood-red complexion;[1] the mate of insolence and pride, shag-eared and deaf, hardly yielding to whip and spur. Now when the charioteer beholds the vision of love, and has his whole soul warmed through sense, and is full of the prickings and ticklings of desire, the obedient steed, then as always under the government of shame, refrains from leaping on the beloved; but the other, heedless of the pricks and of the blows of the whip, plunges and runs away, giving all manner of trouble to his companion and the charioteer, whom he forces to approach the beloved and to remember the joys of love. They at first indignantly oppose him and will not be urged on to do terrible and unlawful deeds; but at last, when he persists in plaguing them, they yield and agree to do as he bids them. And now they are at the spot and behold the flashing beauty of the beloved; which when the charioteer sees, his memory is carried to the true beauty, whom he beholds in company with Modesty like an image placed upon a holy pedestal. He sees her, but he is afraid and falls backwards in adoration, and by his fall is compelled to pull back the reins with such violence as to bring both the steeds on their haunches, the one willing and unresisting, the unruly one very unwilling; and when they have gone back a little, the one is overcome with shame and wonder, and his whole soul is bathed in perspiration; the other, when the pain is over which the bridle and the fall had given him, having with difficulty taken breath, is full of wrath and reproaches, which he heaps upon the charioteer and his fellow-steed, for want of courage and manhood, declaring that they have been false to their agreement and guilty of desertion. Again they refuse, and again he urges them on, and will scarce yield to their prayer that he would wait until another time. When the appointed hour comes, they make as if they had forgotten, and he reminds them, fighting and neighing and dragging them on, until at length he on the same thoughts intent, forces them to draw near

[1] Or with grey and blood-shot eyes.

again. And when they are near he stoops his head and puts
up his tail, and takes the bit in his teeth and pulls shame-
lessly. Then the charioteer is worse off than ever; he falls
back like a racer at the barrier, and with a still more violent
wrench drags the bit out of the teeth of the wild steed and
covers his abusive tongue and jaws with blood, and forces
his legs and haunches to the ground and punishes him sorely.
And when this has happened several times and the villain
has ceased from his wanton way, he is tamed and humbled,
and follows the will of the charioteer, and when he sees the
beautiful one he is ready to die of fear. And from that time
forward the soul of the lover follows the beloved in modesty
and holy fear.

And so the beloved who, like a god, has received every
true and loyal service from his lover, not in pretence but in
reality, being also himself of a nature friendly to his admirer,[1] if in former days he has blushed to own his passion
and turned away his lover, because his youthful companions
or others slanderously told him that he would be disgraced,
now as years advance, at the appointed age and time, is
led to receive him into communion. For fate which has ordained that there shall be no friendship among the evil has
also ordained that there shall ever be friendship among
the good. And the beloved when he has received him into
communion and intimacy, is quite amazed at the good-will
of the lover; he recognises that the inspired friend is worth
all other friends or kinsmen; they have nothing of friendship in them worthy to be compared with his. And when
this feeling continues and he is nearer to him and embraces
him, in gymnastic exercises and at other times of meeting,
then the fountain of that stream, which Zeus when he was
in love with Ganymede named Desire, overflows upon the
lover, and some enters into his soul, and some when he is
filled flows out again; and as a breeze or an echo rebounds
from the smooth rocks and returns whence it came, so does

[1] Omitting εἰς ταὐτὸν ἄγει τὴν φιλίαν.

the stream of beauty, passing through the eyes which are
the windows of the soul, come back to the beautiful one;
there arriving and quickening the passages of the wings,
watering them and inclining them to grow, and filling the
soul of the beloved also with love. And thus he loves, but
he knows not what; he does not understand and cannot
explain his own state; he appears to have caught the infection of blindness from another; the lover is his mirror
in whom he is beholding himself, but he is not aware of
this. When he is with the lover, both cease from their pain,
but when he is away then he longs as he is longed for, and
has love's image, love for love (Anteros) lodging in his
breast, which he calls and believes to be not love but friendship only, and his desire is as the desire of the other, but
weaker; he wants to see him, touch him, kiss, embrace him,
and probably not long afterwards his desire is accomplished.
When they meet, the wanton steed of the lover has a word
to say to the charioteer; he would like to have a little pleasure in return for many pains, but the wanton steed of the
beloved says not a word, for he is bursting with passion
which he understands not;—he throws his arms round the
lover and embraces him as his dearest friend; and, when
they are side by side, he is not in a state in which he can
refuse the lover anything, if he ask him; although his fellow-steed and the charioteer oppose him with the arguments
of shame and reason. After this their happiness depends
upon their self-control; if the better elements of the mind
which lead to order and philosophy prevail, then they pass
their life here in happiness and harmony—masters of themselves and orderly—enslaving the vicious and emancipating
the virtuous elements of the soul; and when the end comes,
they are light and winged for flight, having conquered in
one of the three heavenly or truly Olympian victories; nor
can human discipline or divine inspiration confer any
greater blessing on man than this. If, on the other hand,
they leave philosophy and lead the lower life of ambition,

then probably, after wine or in some other careless hour, the two wanton animals take the two souls when off their guard and bring them together, and they accomplish that desire of their hearts which to the many is bliss; and this having once enjoyed they continue to enjoy, yet rarely because they have not the approval of the whole soul. They too are dear, but not so dear to one another as the others, either at the time of their love or afterwards. They consider that they have given and taken from each other the most sacred pledges, and they may not break them and fall into enmity. At last they pass out of the body, unwinged, but eager to soar, and thus obtain no mean reward of love and madness. For those who have once begun the heavenward pilgrimage may not go down again to darkness and the journey beneath the earth, but they live in light always; happy companions in their pilgrimage, and when the time comes at which they receive their wings they have the same plumage because of their love.

Thus great are the heavenly blessings which the friendship of a lover will confer upon you, my youth. Whereas the attachment of the non-lover, which is alloyed with a worldly prudence and has worldly and niggardly ways of doling out benefits, will breed in your soul those vulgar qualities which the populace applaud, will send you bowling round the earth during a period of nine thousand years, and leave you a fool in the world below.

And thus, dear Eros, I have made and paid my recantation, as well and as fairly as I could; more especially in the matter of the poetical figures which I was compelled to use, because Phaedrus would have them.[1] And now forgive the past and accept the present, and be gracious and merciful to me, and do not in thine anger deprive me of sight, or take from me the art of love which thou hast given me, but grant that I may be yet more esteemed in the eyes of the fair. And if Phaedrus or I myself said anything rude

[1] See 234 C.

in our first speeches, blame Lysias, who is the father of the
brat, and let us have no more of his progeny; bid him study
philosophy, like his brother Polemarchus; and then his lover
Phaedrus will no longer halt between two opinions, but will
dedicate himself wholly to love and to philosophical discourses.

Phaedr. I join in the prayer, Socrates, and say with you,
if this be for my good, may your words come to pass. But
why did you make your second oration so much finer than
the first? I wonder why. And I begin to be afraid that I
shall lose conceit of Lysias, and that he will appear tame
in comparison, even if he be willing to put another as fine
and as long as yours into the field, which I doubt. For quite
lately one of your politicians was abusing him on this very
account; and called him a "speech-writer" again and again.
So that a feeling of pride may probably induce him to give
up writing speeches.

Soc. What a very amusing notion! But I think, my young
man, that you are much mistaken in your friend if you
imagine that he is frightened at a little noise; and, possibly, you think that his assailant was in earnest?

Phaedr. I thought, Socrates, that he was. And you are
aware that the greatest and most influential statesmen are
ashamed of writing speeches and leaving them in a written
form, lest they should be called Sophists by posterity.

Soc. You seem to be unconscious, Phaedrus, that the
'sweet elbow'[1] of the proverb is really the long arm of the
Nile. And you appear to be equally unaware of the fact
that this sweet elbow of theirs is also a long arm. For there
is nothing of which our great politicians are so fond as of
writing speeches and bequeathing them to posterity. And
they add their admirers' names at the top of the writing,
out of gratitude to them.

[1] A proverb, like "the grapes are sour," applied to pleasures which
cannot be had, meaning sweet things which, like the elbow, are out
of the reach of the mouth. The promised pleasure turns out to be a
long and tedious affair.

Phaedr. What do you mean? I do not understand.

Soc. Why, do you not know that when a politician writes, he begins with the names of his approvers?

Phaedr. How so?

Soc. Why, he begins in this manner: "Be it enacted by the senate, the people, or both, on the motion of a certain person," who is our author; and so putting on a serious face, he proceeds to display his own wisdom to his admirers in what is often a long and tedious composition. Now what is that sort of thing but a regular piece of authorship?

Phaedr. True.

Soc. And if the law is finally approved, then the author leaves the theatre in high delight; but if the law is rejected and he is done out of his speech-making, and not thought good enough to write, then he and his party are in mourning.

Phaedr. Very true.

Soc. So far are they from despising, or rather so highly do they value the practice of writing.

Phaedr. No doubt.

Soc. And when the king or orator has the power, as Lycurgus or Solon or Darius had, of attaining an immortality of authorship in a State, is he not thought by posterity, when they see his compositions, and does he not think himself, while he is yet alive, to be a god?

Phaedr. Very true.

Soc. Then do you think that any one of this class, however ill-disposed, would reproach Lysias with being an author?

Phaedr. Not upon your view; for according to you he would be casting a slur upon his own favourite pursuit.

Soc. Any one may see that there is no disgrace in the mere fact of writing.

Phaedr. Certainly not.

Soc. The disgrace begins when a man writes not well, but badly.

Phaedr. Clearly.

Soc. And what is well and what is badly—need we ask Lysias, or any other poet or orator, who ever wrote or will write either a political or any other work, in metre or out of metre, poet, or prose writer, to teach us this?

Phaedr. Need we? For what should a man live if not for the pleasures of discourse? Surely not for the sake of bodily pleasures, which almost always have previous pain as a condition of them, and therefore are rightly called slavish.

Soc. There is time enough. And I believe that the grasshoppers chirruping after their manner in the heat of the sun over our heads are talking to one another and looking down at us. What would they say if they saw that we, like the many, are not conversing, but slumbering at mid-day, lulled by their voices, too indolent to think? Would they not have a right to laugh at us? They might imagine that we were slaves, who, coming to rest at a place of resort of theirs, like sheep lie asleep at noon around the well. But if they see us discoursing, and like Odysseus sailing past them, deaf to their siren voices, they may perhaps, out of respect, give us of the gifts which they receive from the gods that they may impart them to men.

Phaedr. What gifts do you mean? I never heard of any.

Soc. A lover of music like yourself ought surely to have heard the story of the grasshoppers, who are said to have been human beings in an age before the Muses. And when the Muses came and song appeared they were ravished with delight; and singing always, never thought of eating and drinking, until at last in their forgetfulness they died. And now they live again in the grasshoppers; and this is the return which the Muses make to them—they neither hunger, nor thirst, but from the hour of their birth are always singing, and never eating or drinking; and when they die they go and inform the Muses in heaven who honours them on earth. They win the love of Terpsichore for the dancers by their report of them; of Erato for the lovers, and of the other Muses for those who do them honour, according to the several ways of honouring them;—of Calliope the eldest Muse and of Urania who is next to her, for the philosophers, of whose music the grasshoppers make report to them; for these are the Muses who are chiefly concerned with heaven and thought, divine as well as human, and they have the sweetest utterance. For many reasons, then, we ought always to talk and not to sleep at mid-day.

Phaedr. Let us talk.

Soc. Shall we discuss the rules of writing and speech as we were proposing?

Phaedr. Very good.

Soc. In good speaking should not the mind of the speaker know the truth of the matter about which he is going to speak?

Phaedr. And yet, Socrates, I have heard that he who would be an orator has nothing to do with true justice, but only with that which is likely to be approved by the many who sit in judgment; nor with the truly good or honourable, but only with opinion about them, and that from opinion comes persuasion, and not from the truth.

Soc. The words of the wise are not to be set aside; for there is probably something in them; and therefore the meaning of this saying is not hastily to be dismissed.

Phaedr. Very true.

Soc. Let us put the matter thus:—Suppose that I persuaded you to buy a horse and go to the wars. Neither of us knew what a horse was like, but I knew that you believed a horse to be of tame animals the one which has the longest ears.

Phaedr. That would be ridiculous.

Soc. There is something more ridiculous coming:—Suppose, further, that in sober earnest I, having persuaded you of this, went and composed a speech in honour of an ass, whom I entitled a horse, beginning: "A noble animal and a most useful possession, especially in war, and you may get on his back and fight, and he will carry baggage or anything."

Phaedr. How ridiculous!

Soc. Ridiculous! Yes; but is not even a ridiculous friend better than a cunning enemy?

Phaedr. Certainly.

Soc. And when the orator instead of putting an ass in the place of a horse, puts good for evil, being himself as ignorant of their true nature as the city on which he imposes is ignorant; and having studied the notions of the multitude, falsely persuades them not about "the shadow of an ass," which he confounds with a horse, but about good which he confounds with evil,—what will be the harvest which rhetoric will be likely to gather after the sowing of that seed?

Phaedr. The reverse of good.

Soc. But perhaps rhetoric has been getting too roughly handled by us, and she might answer: What amazing nonsense you are talking! As if I forced any man to learn to speak in ignorance of the truth! Whatever my advice may be worth, I should have told him to arrive at the truth first, and then come to me. At the same time I boldly assert that mere knowledge of the truth will not give you the art of persuasion.

Phaedr. There is reason in the lady's defence of herself.

Soc. Quite true; if only the other arguments which remain to be brought up bear her witness that she is an art at all. But I seem to hear them arraying themselves on the opposite side, declaring that she speaks falsely, and that rhetoric is a mere routine and trick, not an art. Lo! a Spartan appears, and says that there never is nor ever will be a real art of speaking which is divorced from the truth.

Phaedr. And what are these arguments, Socrates? Bring them out that we may examine them.

Soc. Come out, fair children, and convince Phaedrus, who is the father of similar beauties, that he will never be able to speak about anything as he ought to speak unless he have a knowledge of philosophy. And let Phaedrus answer you.

Phaedr. Put the question.

Soc. Is not rhetoric, taken generally, a universal art of enchanting the mind by arguments; which is practised not only in courts and public assemblies, but in private houses also, having to do with all matters, great as well as small, good and bad alike, and is in all equally right, and equally to be esteemed—that is what you have heard?

Phaedr. Nay, not exactly that; I should say rather that I have heard the art confined to speaking and writing in lawsuits, and to speaking in public assemblies—not extended farther.

Soc. Then I suppose that you have only heard of the rhetoric of Nestor and Odysseus, which they composed in their leisure hours when at Troy, and never of the rhetoric of Palamedes?

Phaedr. No more than of Nestor and Odysseus, unless Gorgias is your Nestor, and Thrasymachus or Theodorus your Odysseus.

Soc. Perhaps that is my meaning. But let us leave them. And do you tell me, instead, what are plaintiff and defendant doing in a law-court—are they not contending?

Phaedr. Exactly so.

Soc. About the just and unjust—that is the matter in dispute?

Phaedr. Yes.

Soc. And a professor of the art will make the same thing appear to the same persons to be at one time just, at another time, if he is so inclined, to be unjust?

Phaedr. Exactly.

Soc. And when he speaks in the assembly, he will make the same things seem good to the city at one time, and at another time the reverse of good?

Phaedr. That is true.

Soc. Have we not heard of the Eleatic Palamedes (Zeno),

who has an art of speaking by which he makes the same things appear to his hearers like and unlike, one and many, at rest and in motion?

Phaedr. Very true.

Soc. The art of disputation, then, is not confined to the courts and the assembly, but is one and the same in every use of language; this is the art, if there be such an art, which is able to find a likeness of everything to which a likeness can be found, and draws into the light of day the likenesses and disguises which are used by others?

Phaedr. How do you mean?

Soc. Let me put the matter thus: When will there be more chance of deception—when the difference is large or small?

Phaedr. When the difference is small.

Soc. And you will be less likely to be discovered in passing by degrees into the other extreme than when you go all at once?

Phaedr. Of course.

Soc. He, then, who would deceive others, and not be deceived, must exactly know the real likenesses and differences of things?

Phaedr. He must.

Soc. And if he is ignorant of the true nature of any subject, how can he detect the greater or less degree of likeness in other things to that of which by the hypothesis he is ignorant?

Phaedr. He cannot.

Soc. And when men are deceived and their notions are at variance with realities, it is clear that the error slips in through resemblances?

Phaedr. Yes, that is the way.

Soc. Then he who would be a master of the art must understand the real nature of everything; or he will never know either how to make the gradual departure from truth into the opposite of truth which is effected by the help of resemblances, or how to avoid it?

Phaedr. He will not.

Soc. He then, who being ignorant of the truth aims at appearances, will only attain an art of rhetoric which is ridiculous and is not an art at all?

Phaedr. That may be expected.

Soc. Shall I propose that we look for examples of art and want of art, according to our notion of them, in the speech of Lysias which you have in your hand, and in my own speech?

Phaedr. Nothing could be better; and indeed I think that our previous argument has been too abstract and wanting in illustrations.

Soc. Yes; and the two speeches happen to afford a very good example of the way in which the speaker who knows the truth may, without any serious purpose, steal away the hearts of his hearers. This piece of good-fortune I attribute to the local deities; and, perhaps, the prophets of the Muses who are singing over our heads may have imparted their inspiration to me. For I do not imagine that I have any rhetorical art of my own.

Phaedr. Granted; if you will only please to get on.

Soc. Suppose that you read me the first words of Lysias' speech.

Phaedr. "You know how matters stand with me, and how, as I conceive, they might be arranged for our common interest; and I maintain that I ought not to fail in my suit, because I am not your lover. For lovers repent——"

Soc. Enough:—Now, shall I point out the rhetorical error of those words?

Phaedr. Yes.

Soc. Every one is aware that about some things we are agreed, whereas about other things we differ.

Phaedr. I think that I understand you; but will you explain yourself?

Soc. When any one speaks of iron and silver, is not the same thing present in the minds of all?

Phaedr. Certainly.

Soc. But when any one speaks of justice and goodness we part company and are at odds with one another and with ourselves?

Phaedr. Precisely.

Soc. Then in some things we agree, but not in others?

Phaedr. That is true.

Soc. In which are we more likely to be deceived, and in which has rhetoric the greater power?

Phaedr. Clearly, in the uncertain class.

Soc. Then the rhetorician ought to make a regular division, and acquire a distinct notion of both classes, as well of that in which the many err, as of that in which they do not err?

Phaedr. He who made such a distinction would have an excellent principle.

Soc. Yes; and in the next place he must have a keen eye for the observation of particulars in speaking, and not make a mistake about the class to which they are to be referred.

Phaedr. Certainly.

Soc. Now to which class does love belong—to the debatable or to the undisputed class?

Phaedr. To the debatable, clearly; for if not, do you think that love would have allowed you to say as you did, that he is an evil both to the lover and the beloved, and also the greatest possible good?

Soc. Capital. But will you tell me whether I defined love at the beginning of my speech? for, having been in an ecstasy, I cannot well remember.

Phaedr. Yes, indeed; that you did, and no mistake.

Soc. Then I perceive that the Nymphs of Achelous and Pan the son of Hermes, who inspired me, were far better rhetoricians than Lysias the son of Cephalus. Alas! how inferior to them he is! But perhaps I am mistaken; and Lysias at the commencement of his lover's speech did insist on our supposing love to be something or other which he fancied him to be, and according to this model he fashioned and framed the remainder of his discourse. Suppose we read his beginning over again:

Phaedr. If you please; but you will not find what you want.

Soc. Read, that I may have his exact words.

Phaedr. "You know how matters stand with me, and how, as I conceive, they might be arranged for our common interest; and I maintain I ought not to fail in my suit because I am not your lover, for lovers repent of the kindnesses which they have shown, when their love is over."

Soc. Here he appears to have done just the reverse of what he ought; for he has begun at the end, and is swimming on his back through the flood to the place of starting. His address to the fair youth begins where the lover would have ended. Am I not right, sweet Phaedrus?

Phaedr. Yes, indeed, Socrates; he does begin at the end.

Soc. Then as to the other topics—are they not thrown down anyhow? Is there any principle in them? Why should the next topic follow next in order, or any other topic? I cannot help fancying in my ignorance that he wrote off boldly just what came into his head, but I dare say that you would recognize a rhetorical necessity in the succession of the several parts of the composition?

Phaedr. You have too good an opinion of me if you think that I have any such insight into his principles of composition.

Soc. At any rate, you will allow that every discourse ought to be a living creature, having a body of its own and a head and feet; there should be a middle, beginning, and end, adapted to one another and to the whole?

Phaedr. Certainly.

Soc. Can this be said of the discourse of Lysias? See whether you can find any more connexion in his words than in the epitaph which is said by some to have been inscribed on the grave of Midas the Phrygian.

Phaedr. What is there remarkable in the epitaph?

Soc. It is as follows:—

"I am a maiden of bronze and lie on the tomb of Midas;
  So long as water flows and tall trees grow,
  So long here on this spot by his sad tomb abiding,
  I shall declare to passers-by that Midas sleeps below."

Now in this rhyme whether a line comes first or comes last, as you will perceive, makes no difference.

Phaedr. You are making fun of that oration of ours.

Soc. Well, I will say no more about your friend's speech lest I should give offence to you; although I think that it might furnish many other examples of what a man ought rather to avoid. But I will proceed to the other speech, which, as I think, is also suggestive to students of rhetoric.

Phaedr. In what way?

Soc. The two speeches, as you may remember, were unlike; the one argued that the lover and the other that the non-lover ought to be accepted.

Phaedr. And right manfully.

Soc. You would rather say "madly"; and madness was the argument of them, for, as I said, "love is a madness."

Phaedr. Yes.

Soc. And of madness there were two kinds; one produced by human infirmity, the other was a divine release of the soul from the yoke of custom and convention.

Phaedr. True.

Soc. The divine madness was subdivided into four kinds, prophetic, initiatory, poetic, erotic, having four gods presiding over them; the first was the inspiration of Apollo, the second that of Dionysus, the third that of the Muses, the fourth that of Aphrodite and Eros. In the description of the last kind of madness, which was also said to be the best, we spoke of the affection of love in a figure, into which we introduced a tolerably credible and possibly true though partly erring myth, which was also a hymn in honour of Love, who is your lord and also mine, Phaedrus, and the guardian of fair children, and to him we sung the hymn in measured and solemn strain.

Phaedr. I know that I had great pleasure in listening to you.

Soc. Let us take this instance and note how the transition was made from blame to praise.

Phaedr. What do you mean?

Soc. I mean to say that the composition was mostly playful. Yet in these chance fancies of the hour were involved two principles of which we should be too glad to have a clearer description if art could give us one.

Phaedr. What are they?

Soc. First, the comprehension of scattered particulars in one idea; as in our definition of love, which whether true or false certainly gave clearness and consistency to the discourse, the speaker should define his several notions and so make his meaning clear.

Phaedr. What is the other principle, Socrates?

Soc. The second principle is that of division into species according to the natural formation, where the joint is, not breaking any part as a bad carver might. Just as our two discourses, alike assumed, first of all, a single form of unreason; and then, as the body which from being one becomes double and may be divided into a left side and a right side, each having parts right and left of the same name—after this manner the speaker proceeded to divide the parts of the left side and did not desist until he found in them an evil or left-handed love which he justly reviled; and the other discourse leading us to the madness which lay on the right side, found another love, also having the same name, but divine, which the speaker held up before us and applauded and affirmed to be the author of the greatest benefits.

Phaedr. Most true.

Soc. I am myself a great lover of these processes of division and generalization; they help me to speak and to think. And if I find any man who is able to see "a One and Many" in nature, him I follow, and "walk in his footsteps as if he were a god." And those who have this art, I have hitherto been in the habit of calling dialecticians; but God knows whether the name is right or not. And I should like to know what name you would give to your or to Lysias' disciples, and whether this may not be that famous art of rhetoric which Thrasymachus and others teach and practise? Skilful speakers they are, and impart their skill to any who is willing to make kings of them and to bring gifts to them.

Phaedr. Yes, they are royal men; but their art is not the same with the art of those whom you call, and rightly, in my opinion, dialecticians:—Still we are in the dark about rhetoric.

Soc. What do you mean? The remains of it, if there be anything remaining which can be brought under rules of art, must be a fine thing; and, at any rate, is not to be despised by you and me. But how much is left?

Phaedr. There is a great deal surely to be found in books of rhetoric?

Soc. Yes; thank you for reminding me:—There is the exordium, showing how the speech should begin, if I remember rightly; that is what you mean—the niceties of the art?

Phaedr. Yes.

Soc. Then follows the statement of facts, and upon that witnesses; thirdly, proofs; fourthly, probabilities are to come; the great Byzantian word-maker also speaks, if I am not mistaken, of confirmation and further confirmation.

Phaedr. You mean the excellent Theodorus.

Soc. Yes; and he tells how refutation or further refutation is to be managed, whether in accusation or defence. I ought also to mention the illustrious Parian, Evenus, who first invented insinuations and indirect praises; and also indirect censures, which according to some he put into verse to help the memory. But shall I "to dumb forgetfulness consign" Tisias and Gorgias, who are not ignorant that probability is superior to truth, and who by force of argument make the little appear great and the great little, disguise the new in old fashions and the old in new fashions, and have discovered forms for everything, either short or going on to infinity? I remember Prodicus laughing when I told him of this; he said that he had himself discovered the true rule of art, which was to be neither long nor short, but of a convenient length.

Phaedr. Well done, Prodicus!

Soc. Then there is Hippias the Elean stranger, who probably agrees with him.

Phaedr. Yes.

Soc. And there is also Polus, who has treasuries of diplasiology, and gnomology, and eikonology, and who teaches in them the names of which Licymnius made him a present; they were to give a polish.

Phaedr. Had not Protagoras something of the same sort?

Soc. Yes, rules of correct diction and many other fine precepts; for the "sorrows of a poor old man," or any other pathetic case, no one is better than the Chalcedonian giant; he can put a whole company of people into a passion and out of one again by his mighty magic, and is first-rate at inventing or disposing of any sort of calumny on any grounds or none. All of them agree in asserting that a speech should end in a recapitulation, though they do not all agree to use the same word.

Phaedr. You mean that there should be a summing up of the arguments in order to remind the hearers of them.

Soc. I have now said all that I have to say of the art of rhetoric: have you anything to add?

Phaedr. Not much; nothing very important.

Soc. Leave the unimportant and let us bring the really important question into the light of day, which is: What power has this art of rhetoric, and when?

Phaedr. A very great power in public meetings.

Soc. It has. But I should like to know whether you have the same feeling as I have about the rhetoricians? To me there seem to be a great many holes in their web.

Phaedr. Give an example.

Soc. I will. Suppose a person to come to your friend Eryximachus, or to his father Acumenus, and to say to him: "I know how to apply drugs which shall have either a heating or a cooling effect, and I can give a vomit and also a purge, and all that sort of thing; and knowing all this, as I do, I claim to be a physician and to make physicians by imparting this knowledge to others,"—what do you suppose that they would say?

Phaedr. They would be sure to ask him whether he knew "to whom" he would give his medicines, and "when," and "how much."

Soc. And suppose that he were to reply: "No; I know nothing of all that; I expect the patient who consults me to be able to do these things for himself"?

Phaedr. They would say in reply that he is a madman or a pedant who fancies that he is a physician because he has read something in a book, or has stumbled on a prescription or two, although he has no real understanding of the art of medicine.

Soc. And suppose a person were to come to Sophocles or Euripides and say that he knows how to make a very long speech about a small matter, and a short speech about a great matter, and also a sorrowful speech, or a terrible, or threatening speech, of any other kind of speech, and in teaching this fancies that he is teaching the art of tragedy—?

Phaedr. They too would surely laugh at him if he fancies

that tragedy is anything but the arranging of these elements in a manner which will be suitable to one another and to the whole.

Soc. But I do not suppose that they would be rude or abusive to him: Would they not treat him as a musician would a man who thinks that he is a harmonist because he knows how to pitch the highest and lowest note? Happening to meet such an one he would not say to him savagely, "Fool, you are mad!" But like a musician, in a gentle and harmonious tone of voice, he would answer: "My good friend, he who would be a harmonist must certainly know this, and yet he may understand nothing of harmony if he has not got beyond your stage of knowledge, for you only know the preliminaries of harmony and not harmony itself."

Phaedr. Very true.

Soc. And will not Sophocles say to the display of the would-be tragedian, that this is not tragedy but the preliminaries of tragedy? and will not Acumenus say the same of medicine to the would-be physician?

Phaedr. Quite true.

Soc. And if Adrastus the mellifluous or Pericles heard of these wonderful arts, brachylogies and eikonologies and all the hard names which we have been endeavouring to draw into the light of day, what would they say? Instead of losing temper and applying uncomplimentary epithets, as you and I have been doing, to the authors of such an imaginary art, their superior wisdom would rather censure us, as well as them. "Have a little patience, Phaedrus and Socrates," they would say; "you should not be in such a passion with those who from some want of dialectical skill are unable to define the nature of rhetoric, and consequently suppose that they have found the art in the preliminary conditions of it, and when these have been taught by them to others, fancy that the whole art of rhetoric has been taught by them; but as to using the several instruments of the art effectively, or making the composition a whole,—an application of it such as this is they regard as an easy thing which their disciples may make for themselves."

Phaedr. I quite admit, Socrates, that the art of rhetoric which these men teach and of which they write is such as you describe—there I agree with you. But I still want to know where and how the true art of rhetoric and persuasion is to be acquired.

Soc. The perfection which is required of the finished orator is, or rather must be, like the perfection of anything else, partly given by nature, but may also be assisted by art. If you have the natural power and add to it knowledge and practice, you will be a distinguished speaker; if you fall short in either of these, you will be to that extent defective. But the art, as far as there is an art, of rhetoric does not lie in the direction of Lysias or Thrasymachus.

Phaedr. In what direction then?

Soc. I conceive Pericles to have been the most accomplished of rhetoricians.

Phaedr. What of that?

Soc. All the great arts require discussion and high speculation about the truths of nature; hence come loftiness of thought and completeness of execution. And this, as I conceive, was the quality which, in addition to his natural gifts, Pericles acquired from his intercourse with Anaxagoras whom he happened to know. He was thus imbued with the higher philosophy, and attained the knowledge of Mind and the negative of Mind, which were favourite themes of Anaxagoras, and applied what suited his purpose to the art of speaking.

Phaedr. Explain.

Soc. Rhetoric is like medicine.

Phaedr. How so?

Soc. Why, because medicine has to define the nature of the body and rhetoric of the soul—if we would proceed, not empirically but scientifically, in the one case to impart health and strength by giving medicine and food, in the other to implant the conviction or virtue which you desire, by the right application of words and training.

Phaedr. There, Socrates, I suspect that you are right.

Soc. And do you think that you can know the nature of the soul intelligently without knowing the nature of the whole?

Phaedr. Hippocrates the Asclepiad says that the nature even of the body can only be understood as a whole.[1]

Soc. Yes, friend, and he was right:—still, we ought not to be content with the name of Hippocrates, but to examine and see whether his argument agrees with his conception of nature.

Phaedr. I agree.

Soc. Then consider what truth as well as Hippocrates says about this or about any other nature. Ought we not to consider first whether that which we wish to learn and to teach is a simple or multiform thing, and if simple, then to enquire what power it has of acting or being acted upon in relation to other things, and if multiform, then to number the forms; and see first in the case of one of them, and then in the case of all of them, what is that power of acting or being acted upon which makes each and all of them to be what they are?

Phaedr. You may very likely be right, Socrates.

Soc. The method which proceeds without analysis is like the groping of a blind man. Yet, surely, he who is an artist ought not to admit of a comparison with the blind, or deaf. The rhetorician, who teaches his pupil to speak scientifically, will particularly set forth the nature of that being to which he addresses his speeches; and this, I conceive, to be the soul.

Phaedr. Certainly.

Soc. His whole effort is directed to the soul; for in that he seeks to produce conviction.

[1] Cp. Charmides, 156 C.

Phaedr. Yes.

Soc. Then clearly, Thrasymachus or any one else who teaches rhetoric in earnest will give an exact description of the nature of the soul; which will enable us to see whether she be single and same, or, like the body, multiform. That is what we should call showing the nature of the soul.

Phaedr. Exactly.

Soc. He will explain, secondly, the mode in which she acts or is acted upon.

Phaedr. True.

Soc. Thirdly, having classified men and speeches, and their kinds and affections, and adapted them to one another, he will tell the reasons of his arrangement, and show why one soul is persuaded by a particular form of argument, and another not.

Phaedr. You have hit upon a very good way.

Soc. Yes, that is the true and only way in which any subject can be set forth or treated by rules of art, whether in speaking or writing. But the writers of the present day, at whose feet you have sat, craftily conceal the nature of the soul which they know quite well. Nor, until they adopt our method of reading and writing, can we admit that they write by rules of art?

Phaedr. What is our method?

Soc. I cannot give you the exact details; but I should like to tell you generally, as far as is in my power, how a man ought to proceed according to rules of art.

Phaedr. Let me hear.

Soc. Oratory is the art of enchanting the soul, and therefore he who would be an orator has to learn the differences of human souls—they are so many and of such a nature, and from them come the differences between man and man. Having proceeded thus far in his analysis, he will next divide speeches into their different classes:—"Such and such persons," he will say, "are affected by this or that kind of speech in this or that way," and he will tell you why. The pupil must have a good theoretical notion of them first, and then he must have experience of them in actual life, and be able to follow them with all his senses about him, or he will never get beyond the precepts of his masters. But when he understands what persons are persuaded by what arguments, and sees the person about whom he was speaking in the abstract actually before him, and knows that it is he, and can say to himself, "This is the man or this is the character who ought to have a certain argument applied to him in order to convince him of a certain opinion";—he who knows all this, and knows also when he should speak and when he should refrain, and when he should use pithy sayings, pathetic appeals, sensational effects, and all the other modes of speech which he has learned;—when, I say, he knows the times and seasons of all these things, then, and not till then, he is a perfect master of his art; but if he fail in any of these points, whether in speaking or teaching or writing them, and yet declares that he speaks by rules of art, he who says "I don't believe you" has the better of him. Well, the teacher will say, is this, Phaedrus and Socrates, your account of the so-called art of rhetoric, or am I to look for another?

Phaedr. He must take this, Socrates, for there is no possibility of another, and yet the creation of such an art is not easy.

Soc. Very true; and therefore let us consider this matter in every light, and see whether we cannot find a shorter and easier road; there is no use in taking a long rough roundabout way if there be a shorter and easier one. And I wish that you would try and remember whether you have heard from Lysias or any one else anything which might be of service to us.

Phaedr. If trying would avail, then I might; but at the moment, I can think of nothing.

Soc. Suppose I tell you something which somebody who knows told me.

Phaedr. Certainly.

Soc. May not "the wolf," as the proverb says, "claim a hearing"?

Phaedr. Do you say what can be said for him.

Soc. He will argue that there is no use in putting a solemn face on these matters, or in going round and round, until you arrive at first principles; for, as I said at first, when the question is of justice and good, or is a question in which men are concerned who are just and good, either by nature or habit, he who would be a skilful rhetorician has no need of truth—for that in courts of law men literally care nothing about truth, but only about conviction: and this is based on probability, to which he who would be a skilful orator should therefore give his whole attention. And they say also that there are cases in which the actual facts, if they are improbable, ought to be withheld, and only the probabilities should be told either in accusation or defence, and that always in speaking, the orator should keep probability in view, and say good-bye to the truth. And the observance of this principle throughout a speech furnishes the whole art.

Phaedr. That is what the professors of rhetoric do actually say, Socrates. I have not forgotten that we have quite briefly touched upon this matter [1] already; with them the point is all-important.

Soc. I dare say that you are familiar with Tisias. Does he not define probability to be that which the many think?

Phaedr. Certainly, he does.

Soc. I believe that he has a clever and ingenious case of this sort:—He supposes a feeble and valiant man to have assaulted a strong and cowardly one, and to have robbed him of his coat or of something or other; he is brought into court, and then Tisias says that both parties should tell lies: the coward should say that he was assaulted by

[1] Cp. 259 E.

more men than one; the other should prove that they were alone, and should argue thus: "How could a weak man like me have assaulted a strong man like him?" The complainant will not like to confess his own cowardice, and will therefore invent some other lie which his adversary will thus gain an opportunity of refuting. And there are other devices of the same kind which have a place in the system. Am I not right, Phaedrus?

Phaedr. Certainly.

Soc. Bless me, what a wonderfully mysterious art is this which Tisias or some other gentleman, in whatever name or country he rejoices, has discovered. Shall we say a word to him or not?

Phaedr. What shall we say to him?

Soc. Let us tell him that, before he appeared, you and I were saying that the probability of which he speaks was engendered in the minds of the many by the likeness of the truth, and we had just been affirming that he who knew the truth would always know best how to discover the resemblances of the truth. If he has anything else to say about the art of speaking we should like to hear him; but if not, we are satisfied with our own view, that unless a man estimates the various characters of his hearers and is able to divide all things into classes and to comprehend them under single ideas, he will never be a skilful rhetorician even within the limits of human power. And this skill he will not attain without a great deal of trouble, which a good man ought to undergo, not for the sake of speaking and acting before men, but in order that he may be able to say what is acceptable to God and always to act acceptably to Him as far as in him lies; for there is a saying of wiser men than ourselves, that a man of sense should not try to please his fellow-servants (at least this should not be his first object) but his good and noble masters; and therefore if the way is long and circuitous, marvel not at this, for, where the end is great, there we may take the longer road, but not for lesser ends such as yours. Truly, the argument may say, Tisias, that if you do not mind going so far, rhetoric has a fair beginning here.

Phaedr. I think, Socrates, that this is admirable, if only practicable.

Soc. But even to fail in an honourable object is honourable.

Phaedr. True.

Soc. Enough appears to have been said by us of a true and false art of speaking.

Phaedr. Certainly.

Soc. But there is something yet to be said of propriety and impropriety of writing.

Phaedr. Yes.

Soc. Do you know how you can speak or act about rhetoric in a manner which will be acceptable to God?

Phaedr. No, indeed. Do you?

Soc. I have heard a tradition of the ancients, whether true or not they only know; although if we had found the truth ourselves, do you think that we should care much about the opinions of men?

Phaedr. Your question needs no answer; but I wish that you would tell me what you say that you have heard.

Soc. At the Egyptian city of Naucratis, there was a famous old god, whose name was Theuth; the bird which is called the Ibis is sacred to him, and he was the inventor of many arts, such as arithmetic and calculation and geometry and astronomy and draughts and dice, but his great discovery was the use of letters. Now in those days the god Thamus was the king of the whole country of Egypt; and he dwelt in that great city of Upper Egypt which the Hellenes call Egyptian Thebes, and the god himself is called by them Ammon. To him came Theuth and showed his inventions, desiring that the other Egyptians might be allowed to have the benefit of them; he enumerated them, and Thamus enquired about their several uses, and praised some of them and censured others, as he approved or disapproved of them. It would take a long time to repeat all that Thamus said to Theuth in praise or blame of the various arts. But when they came to letters, This, said Theuth, will make the Egyptians wiser and give them better memories; it is a specific both for the memory and for the wit. Thamus replied: O most ingenious Theuth, the parent or inventor of an art is not always the best judge of the utility or inutility of his own inventions to the users of them. And in this instance, you who are the father of letters, from a paternal love of your own children have been led to attribute to them a quality which they cannot have; for this discovery of yours will create forgetfulness in the learners' souls, because they will not use their memories; they will trust to the external written characters and not remember of themselves. The specific which you have discovered is an aid not to memory, but to reminiscence, and you give your disciples not truth, but only the semblance of truth; they will be hearers of many things and will have learned nothing; they will appear to be omniscient and will generally know nothing; they will be tiresome company, having the show of wisdom without the reality.

Phaedr. Yes, Socrates, you can easily invent tales of Egypt, or of any other country.

Soc. There was a tradition in the temple of Dodona that oaks first gave prophetic utterances. The men of old, unlike in their simplicity to young philosophy, deemed that if they heard the truth even from "oak or rock," it was enough for them; whereas you seem to consider not whether a thing is or is not true, but who the speaker is and from what country the tale comes.

Phaedr. I acknowledge the justice of your rebuke; and I think that the Theban is right in his view about letters.

Soc. He would be a very simple person, and quite a stranger to the oracles of Thamus or Ammon, who should leave in writing or receive in writing any art under the idea that the written word would be intelligible or certain; or who deemed that writing was at all better than knowledge and recollection of the same matters?

Phaedr. That is most true.

Soc. I cannot help feeling, Phaedrus, that writing is unfortunately like painting; for the creations of the painter have the attitude of life, and yet if you ask them a question they preserve a solemn silence. And the same may be said of speeches. You would imagine that they had intelligence, but if you want to know anything and put a question to one of them, the speaker always gives one unvarying answer. And when they have been once written down they are tumbled about anywhere among those who may or may not understand them, and know not to whom they should reply, to whom not; and, if they are maltreated or abused, they have no parent to protect them; and they cannot protect or defend themselves.

Phaedr. That again is most true.

Soc. Is there not another kind of word or speech far better than this, and having far greater power—a son of the same family, but lawfully begotten?

Phaedr. Whom do you mean, and what is his origin?

Soc. I mean an intelligent word graven in the soul of the learner, which can defend itself, and knows when to speak and when to be silent.

Phaedr. You mean the living word of knowledge which has a soul, and of which the written word is properly no more than an image?

Soc. Yes, of course that is what I mean. And now may I be allowed to ask you a question: Would a husbandman, who is a man of sense, take the seeds, which he values and which he wishes to bear fruit, and in sober seriousness plant them during the heat of summer, in some garden of Adonis, that he may rejoice when he sees them in eight days appearing in beauty? At least he would do so, if at all, only for the sake of amusement and pastime. But when he is in earnest he sows in fitting soil, and practises husbandry, and is satisfied if in eight months the seeds which he has sown arrive at perfection?

Phaedr. Yes, Socrates, that will be his way when he is in earnest; he will do the other, as you say, only in play.

Soc. And can we suppose that he who knows the just and good and honourable has less understanding, than the husbandman, about his own seeds?

Phaedr. Certainly not.

Soc. Then he will not seriously incline to "write" his thoughts "in water" with pen and ink, sowing words which can neither speak for themselves nor teach the truth adequately to others?

Phaedr. No, that is not likely.

Soc. No, that is not likely—in the garden of letters he will sow and plant, but only for the sake of recreation and amusement; he will write them down as memorials to be treasured against the forgetfulness of old age, by himself, or by any other old man who is treading the same path. He will rejoice in beholding the tender growth; and while others are refreshing their souls with banqueting and the like, this will be the pastime in which his days are spent.

Phaedr. A pastime, Socrates, as noble as the other is ignoble, the pastime of a man who can be amused by serious talk, and can discourse merrily about justice and the like.

Soc. True, Phaedrus. But nobler far is the serious pursuit of the dialectician, who, finding a congenial soul, by the help of science sows and plants therein words which are able to help themselves and him who planted them, and are not unfruitful, but have in them a seed which others brought up in different soils render immortal, making the possessors of it happy to the utmost extent of human happiness.

Phaedr. Far nobler, certainly.

Soc. And now, Phaedrus, having agreed upon the premises we may decide about the conclusion.

Phaedr. About what conclusion?

Soc. About Lysias, whom we censured, and his art of

writing, and his discourses, and the rhetorical skill or want of skill which was shown in them—these are the questions which we sought to determine, and they brought us to this point. And I think that we are now pretty well informed about the nature of art and its opposite.

Phaedr. Yes, I think with you; but I wish that you would repeat what was said.

Soc. Until a man knows the truth of the several particulars of which he is writing or speaking, and is able to define them as they are, and having defined them again to divide them until they can be no longer divided, and until in like manner he is able to discern the nature of the soul, and discover the different modes of discourse which are adapted to different natures, and to arrange and dispose them in such a way that the simple form of speech may be addressed to the simpler nature, and the complex and composite to the more complex nature—until he has accomplished all this, he will be unable to handle arguments according to rules of art, as far as their nature allows them to be subjected to art, either for the purpose of teaching or persuading;—such is the view which is implied in the whole preceding argument.

Phaedr. Yes, that was our view, certainly.

Soc. Secondly, as to the censure which was passed on the speaking or writing of discourses, and how they might be rightly or wrongly censured—did not our previous argument show—?

Phaedr. Show what?

Soc. That whether Lysias or any other writer that ever was or will be, whether private man or statesman, proposes laws and so becomes the author of a political treatise, fancying that there is any greater certainty and clearness in his performance, the fact of his so writing is only a disgrace to him, whatever men may say. For not to know the nature of justice and injustice, and good and evil, and not to be able to distinguish the dream from the reality, cannot in truth be

otherwise than disgraceful to him, even though he have the
applause of the whole world.

Phaedr. Certainly.

Soc. But he who thinks that in the written word there is
necessarily much which is not serious, and that neither poetry
nor prose, spoken or written, is of any great value, if, like the
compositions of the rhapsodes, they are only recited in order
to be believed, and not with any view to criticism or instruction; and who thinks that even the best of writings are but
a reminiscence of what we know, and that only in principles
of justice and goodness and nobility taught and communicated orally for the sake of instruction and graven in the
soul, which is the true way of writing, is there clearness and
perfection and seriousness, and that such principles are a
man's own and his legitimate offspring;—being, in the first
place, the word which he finds in his own bosom; secondly,
the brethren and descendants and relations of his idea which
have been duly implanted by him in the souls of others;—
and who cares for them and no others—this is the right sort
or man; and you and I, Phaedrus, would pray that we may
become like him.

Phaedr. That is most assuredly my desire and prayer.

Soc. And now the play is played out; and of rhetoric
enough. Go and tell Lysias that to the fountain and school of
the Nymphs we went down, and were bidden by them to
convey a message to him and to other composers of speeches
—to Homer and other writers of poems, whether set to music
or not; and to Solon and others who have composed writings
in the form of political discourses which they would term
laws—to all of them we are to say that if their compositions
are based on knowledge of the truth, and they can defend or
prove them, when they are put to the test, by spoken arguments, which leave their writings poor in comparison of
them, then they are to be called, not only poets, orators,
legislators, but are worthy of a higher name, befitting the
serious pursuit of their life.

Phaedr. What name would you assign to them?

Soc. Wise, I may not call them; for that is a great name which belongs to God alone,—lovers of wisdom or philosophers is their modest and befitting title.

Phaedr. Very suitable.

Soc. And he who cannot rise above his own compilations and compositions, which he has been long patching and piecing, adding some and taking away some, may be justly called poet or speech-maker or law-maker.

Phaedr. Certainly.

Soc. Now go and tell this to your companion.

Phaedr. But there is also a friend of yours who ought not to be forgotten.

Soc. Who is he?

Phaedr. Isocrates the fair:—What message will you send to him, and how shall we describe him?

Soc. Isocrates is still young, Phaedrus; but I am willing to hazard a prophecy concerning him.

Phaedr. What would you prophesy?

Soc. I think that he has a genius which soars above the orations of Lysias, and that his character is cast in a finer mould. My impression of him is that he will marvellously improve as he grows older, and that all former rhetoricians will be as children in comparison of him. And I believe that he will not be satisfied with rhetoric, but that there is in him a divine inspiration which will lead him to things higher still. For he has an element of philosophy in his nature. This is the message of the gods dwelling in this place, and which I will myself deliver to Isocrates, who is my delight; and do you give the other to Lysias, who is yours.

Phaedr. I will; and now as the heat is abated let us depart.

Soc. Should we not offer up a prayer first of all to the local deities?

Phaedr. By all means.

Soc. Beloved Pan, and all ye other gods who haunt this place, give me beauty in the inward soul; and may the outward and inward man be at one. May I reckon the wise to be the wealthy, and may I have such a quantity of gold as a temperate man and he only can bear and carry.—Anything more? The prayer, I think, is enough for me.

Phaedr. Ask the same for me, for friends should have all things in common.

Soc. Let us go.

SYMPOSIUM

SYMPOSIUM

PERSONS OF THE DIALOGUE

APOLLODORUS, *who repeats to his companion the Dialogue which he had heard from Aristodemus, and had already once narrated to Glaucon.*

PHAEDRUS.
PAUSANIAS.
ERYXIMACHUS.
ARISTOPHANES.
AGATHON.
SOCRATES.
ALCIBIADES.
A TROOP OF REVELLERS.

SCENE: The house of Agathon.

Concerning the things about which you ask to be informed I believe that I am not ill-prepared with an answer. For the day before yesterday I was coming from my own home at Phalerum to the city, and one of my acquaintance, who had caught sight of me from behind, calling out playfully in the distance, said: Apollodorus, O thou Phalerian [1] man, halt! So I did as I was bid; and then he said, I was looking for you, Apollodorus, only just now, that I might ask you about the speeches in praise of love, which were delivered by Socrates, Alcibiades, and others, at Agathon's supper. Phoenix, the son of Philip, told another person who told me of them; his narrative was very indistinct, but he said that you knew, and I wish that you would give me an account of them. Who, if not you, should be the reporter of the words of your friend? And first tell me, he said, were you present at this meeting?

Your informant, Glaucon, I said, must have been very indistinct indeed, if you imagine that the occasion was recent; or that I could have been of the party.

Why, yes, he replied, I thought so.

[1] Probably a play of words on φαλαρός, "bald-headed."

333

Impossible: I said. Are you ignorant that for many years
Agathon has not resided at Athens; and not three have
elapsed since I became acquainted with Socrates, and have
made it my daily business to know all that he says and
does? There was a time when I was running about the
world, fancying myself to be well employed, but I was
really a most wretched being, no better than you are now.
I thought that I ought to do anything rather than be a
philosopher.

Well, he said, jesting apart, tell me when the meeting
occurred.

In our boyhood, I replied, when Agathon won the prize
with his first tragedy, on the day after that on which he
and his chorus offered the sacrifice of victory.

Then it must have been a long while ago, he said; and
who told you—did Socrates?

No, indeed, I replied, but the same person who told
Phoenix;—he was a little fellow, who never wore any shoes,
Aristodemus, of the deme of Cydathenaeum. He had been
at Agathon's feast; and I think that in those days there
was no one who was a more devoted admirer of Socrates.
Moreover, I have asked Socrates about the truth of some
parts of his narrative, and he confirmed them. Then, said
Glaucon, let us have the tale over again; is not the road
to Athens just made for conversation? And so we walked,
and talked of the discourses on love; and therefore, as I
said at first, I am not ill-prepared to comply with your request, and will have another rehearsal of them if you like.
For to speak or to hear others speak of philosophy always
gives me the greatest pleasure, to say nothing of the profit.
But when I hear another strain, especially that of you rich
men and traders, such conversation displeases me; and I
pity you who are my companions, because you think that
you are doing something when in reality you are doing nothing. And I dare say that you pity me in return, whom you
regard as an unhappy creature, and very probably you are

right. But I certainly know of you what you only think of me—there is the difference.

Companion. I see, Apollodorus, that you are just the same —always speaking evil of yourself, and of others; and I do believe that you pity all mankind, with the exception of Socrates, yourself first of all, true in this to your old name, which, however deserved, I know not how you acquired, of Apollodorus the madman; for you are always raging against yourself and everybody but Socrates.

Apollodorus. Yes, friend, and the reason why I am said to be mad, and out of my wits, is just because I have these notions of myself and you; no other evidence is required.

Com. No more of that, Apollodorus; but let me renew my request that you would repeat the conversation.

Apoll. Well, the tale of love was on this wise:—But perhaps I had better begin at the beginning, and endeavour to give you the exact words of Aristodemus:

He said that he met Socrates fresh from the bath and sandalled; and as the sight of the sandals was unusual, he asked him whither he was going that he had been converted into such a beau:—

To a banquet at Agathon's, he replied, whose invitation to his sacrifice of victory I refused yesterday, fearing a crowd, but promising that I would come to-day instead; and so I have put on my finery, because he is such a fine man. What say you to going with me unasked?

I will do as you bid me, I replied.

Follow then, he said, and let us demolish the proverb:—

"To the feasts of inferior men the good unbidden go";

instead of which our proverb will run:—

"To the feasts of the good the good unbidden go";

and this alteration may be supported by the authority of Homer himself, who not only demolishes but literally outrages the proverb. For, after picturing Agamemnon as the most valiant of men, he makes Menelaus, who is but a faint-hearted warrior, come unbidden[1] to the banquet of Agamemnon, who is feasting and offering sacrifices, not the better to the worse, but the worse to the better.

I rather fear, Socrates, said Aristodemus, lest this may still be my case; and that, like Menelaus in Homer, I shall be the inferior person, who

"To the feasts of the wise unbidden goes."

But I shall say that I was bidden of you, and then you will have to make an excuse.

"Two going together,"

he replied, in Homeric fashion, one or other of them may invent an excuse by the way.[2]

This was the style of their conversation as they went along. Socrates dropped behind in a fit of abstraction, and desired Aristodemus, who was waiting, to go on before him. When he reached the house of Agathon he found the doors wide open, and a comical thing happened. A servant coming out met him, and led him at once into the banqueting-hall in which the guests were reclining, for the banquet was about to begin. Welcome, Aristodemus, said Agathon, as soon as he appeared—you are just in time to sup with us; if you come on any other matter put it off, and make one of us, as I was looking for you yesterday and meant to have asked you, if I could have found you. But what have you done with Socrates?

I turned round, but Socrates was nowhere to be seen; and I had to explain that he had been with me a moment before, and that I came by his invitation to the supper.

[1] Iliad ii. 408, and xvii. 588.   [2] Iliad x. 224.

You were quite right in coming, said Agathon; but where is he himself?

He was behind me just now, as I entered, he said, and I cannot think what has become of him.

Go and look for him, boy, said Agathon, and bring him in; and do you, Aristodemus, meanwhile take the place by Eryximachus.

The servant then assisted him to wash, and he lay down, and presently another servant came in and reported that our friend Socrates had retired into the portico of the neighbouring house. "There he is fixed," said he, "and when I call to him he will not stir."

How strange, said Agathon; then you must call him again, and keep calling him.

Let him alone, said my informant; he has a way of stopping anywhere and losing himself without any reason. I believe that he will soon appear; do not therefore disturb him.

Well, if you think so, I will leave him, said Agathon. And then, turning to the servants, he added, "Let us have supper without waiting for him. Serve up whatever you please, for there is no one to give you orders; hitherto I have never left you to yourselves. But on this occasion imagine that you are our hosts, and that I and the company are your guests; treat us well, and then we shall commend you." After this, supper was served, but still no Socrates; and during the meal Agathon several times expressed a wish to send for him, but Aristodemus objected; and at last when the feast was about half over—for the fit, as usual, was not of long duration—Socrates entered. Agathon who was reclining alone at the end of the table, begged that he would take the place next to him; that "I may touch you," he said, "and have the benefit of that wise thought which came into your mind in the portico, and is now in your possession; for I am certain that you would not have come away until you had found what you sought."

How I wish, said Socrates, taking his place as he was desired, that wisdom could be infused by touch, out of the fuller into the emptier man, as water runs through wool out of a fuller cup into an emptier one; if that were so, how greatly should I value the privilege of reclining at your side! For you would have filled me full with a stream of wisdom plenteous and fair; whereas my own is of a very mean and questionable sort, no better than a dream. But yours is bright and full of promise, and was manifested forth in all the splendour of youth the day before yesterday, in the presence of more than thirty thousand Hellenes.

You are mocking, Socrates, said Agathon, and ere long you and I will have to determine who bears off the palm of wisdom—of this Dionysus shall be the judge; but at present you are better occupied with supper.

Socrates took his place on the couch, and supped with the rest; and then libations were offered, and after a hymn had been sung to the god, and there had been the usual ceremonies, they were about to commence drinking, when Pausanias said, And now, my friends, how can we drink with least injury to ourselves? I can assure you that I feel severely the effect of yesterday's potations, and must have time to recover; and I suspect that most of you are in the same predicament, for you were of the party yesterday. Consider then: How can the drinking be made easiest?

I entirely agree, said Aristophanes, that we should, by all means, avoid hard drinking, for I was myself one of those who were yesterday drowned in drink.

I think that you are right, said Eryximachus, the son of Acumenus; but I should still like to hear one other person speak: Is Agathon able to drink hard?

I am not equal to it, said Agathon.

Then, said Eryximachus, the weak heads like myself, Aristodemus, Phaedrus, and others who never can drink, are fortunate in finding that the stronger ones are not in a drinking mood. (I do not include Socrates, who is able either to drink or to abstain, and will not mind, whichever we do.) Well, as none of the company seem disposed to drink much, I may be forgiven for saying, as a physician, that drinking deep is a bad practice, which I never follow, if I can help, and certainly do not recommend to another, least of all to any one who still feels the effects of yesterday's carouse.

I always do what you advise, and especially what you prescribe as a physician, rejoined Phaedrus the Myrrhinusian, and the rest of the company, if they are wise, will do the same.

It was agreed that drinking was not to be the order of the day, but that they were all to drink only so much as they pleased.

Then, said Eryximachus, as you are all agreed that drinking is to be voluntary, and that there is to be no compulsion, I move, in the next place, that the flute-girl, who has just made her appearance, be told to go away and play to herself, or, if she likes, to the women who are within.[1] To-day let us have conversation instead; and, if you will allow me, I will tell you what sort of conversation. This proposal having been accepted, Eryximachus proceeded as follows:—

I will begin, he said, after the manner of Melanippe in Euripides,

"Not mine the word"

which I am about to speak, but that of Phaedrus. For often he says to me in an indignant tone:—"What a strange thing it is, Eryximachus, that, whereas other gods have poems and hymns made in their honour, the great and glorious god, Love, has no encomiast among all the poets who are so many. There are the worthy Sophists too—the excellent Prodicus, for example—who have descanted in prose on the virtues of Heracles and other heroes; and,

[1] Cp. Prot. 347.

what is still more extraordinary, I have met with a philosophical work in which the utility of salt has been made the
theme of an eloquent discourse; and many other like things
have had a like honour bestowed upon them. And only to
think that there should have been an eager interest created
about them, and yet that to this day no one has ever dared
worthily to hymn Love's praises! So entirely has this great
deity been neglected." Now in this Phaedrus seems to me
to be quite right, and therefore I want to offer him a contribution; also I think that at the present moment we who
are here assembled cannot do better than honour the god
Love. If you agree with me, there will be no lack of conversation; for I mean to propose that each of us in turn,
going from left to right, shall make a speech in honour of
Love. Let him give us the best which he can; and Phaedrus,
because he is sitting first on the left hand, and because he
is the father of the thought, shall begin.

No one will vote against you, Eryximachus, said Socrates. How can I oppose your motion, who profess to understand nothing but matters of love? Nor, I presume, will
Agathon and Pausanias; and there can be no doubt of
Aristophanes, whose whole concern is with Dionysus and
Aphrodite; nor will any one disagree of those whom I see
around me. The proposal, as I am aware, may seem rather
hard upon us whose place is last; but we shall be contented
if we hear some good speeches first. Let Phaedrus begin
the praise of Love, and good luck to him. All the company
expressed their assent, and desired him to do as Socrates
bade him.

Aristodemus did not recollect all that was said, nor do
I recollect all that he related to me; but I will tell you
what I thought most worthy of remembrance, and what the
chief speakers said.

Phaedrus began by affirming that Love is a mighty god,
and wonderful among gods and men, but especially wonderful in his birth. For he is the eldest of the gods, which

is an honour to him; and a proof of his claim to this honour is, that of his parents there is no memorial; neither
poet nor prose-writer has ever affirmed that he had any.
As Hesiod says:—

"First Chaos came, and then broad-bosomed Earth,
    The everlasting seat of all that is,
    And Love."

In other words, after Chaos, the Earth and Love, these two,
came into being. Also Parmenides sings of Generation:

"First in the train of gods, he fashioned Love."

And Acusilaus agrees with Hesiod. Thus numerous are the
witnesses who acknowledge Love to be the eldest of the
gods. And not only is he the eldest, he is also the source
of the greatest benefits to us. For I know not any greater
blessing to a young man who is beginning life than a virtuous lover, or to the lover than a beloved youth. For the
principle which ought to be the guide of men who would
nobly live—that principle, I say, neither kindred, nor honour, nor wealth, nor any other motive is able to implant
so well as love. Of what am I speaking? Of the sense of
honour and dishonour, without which neither States nor individuals ever do any good or great work. And I say that
a lover who is detected in doing any dishonourable act, or
submitting through cowardice when any dishonour is done
to him by another, will be more pained at being detected
by his beloved than at being seen by his father, or by his
companions, or by any one else. The beloved too, when he
is found in any disgraceful situation, has the same feeling
about his lover. And if there were only some way of contriving that a State or an army should be made up of lovers
and their loves,[1] they would be the very best governors of

[1] Cp. Rep. v. 468 D.

their own city, abstaining from all dishonour, and emulating one another in honour; and when fighting at each other's side, although a mere handful, they would overcome the world. For what lover would not choose rather to be seen by all mankind than by his beloved, either when abandoning his post or throwing away his arms? He would be ready to die a thousand deaths rather than endure this. Or who would desert his beloved or fail him in the hour of danger? The veriest coward would become an inspired hero, equal to the bravest, at such a time; Love would inspire him. That courage which, as Homer says, the god breathes into the souls of some heroes, Love of his own nature infuses into the lover.

Love will make men dare to die for their beloved—love alone; and women as well as men. Of this, Alcestis, the daughter of Pelias, is a monument to all Hellas; for she was willing to lay down her life on behalf of her husband, when no one else would, although he had a father and mother; but the tenderness of her love so far exceeded theirs, that she made them seem to be strangers in blood to their own son, and in name only related to him; and so noble did this action of hers appear to the gods, as well as to men, that among the many who have done virtuously she is one of the very few to whom, in admiration of her noble action, they have granted the privilege of returning alive to earth; such exceeding honour is paid by the gods to the devotion and virtue of love. But Orpheus, the son of Oeagrus, the harper, they sent empty away, and presented to him an apparition only of her whom he sought, but herself they would not give up, because he showed no spirit; he was only a harp-player, and did not dare like Alcestis to die for love, but was contriving how he might enter Hades alive; moreover, they afterwards caused him to suffer death at the hands of women, as the punishment of his cowardliness. Very different was the reward of the true love of Achilles towards his lover Patroclus—his lover and not his love (the notion that Patroclus was the beloved one is a foolish error into which Aeschylus has fallen, for Achilles was surely the fairer of the two, fairer also than all the other heroes; and, as Homer informs us, he was still beardless, and younger far). And greatly as the gods honour the virtue of love, still the return of love on the part of the beloved to the lover is more admired and valued and rewarded by them, for the lover is more divine; because he is inspired by God. Now Achilles was quite aware, for he had been told by his mother, that he might avoid death and return home, and live to a good old age, if he abstained from slaying Hector. Nevertheless he gave his life to revenge his friend, and dared to die, not only in his defence, but after he was dead. Wherefore the gods honoured him even above Alcestis, and sent him to the Islands of the Blest. These are my reasons for affirming that Love is the eldest and noblest and mightiest of the gods, and the chiefest author and giver of virtue in life, and of happiness after death.

This, or something like this, was the speech of Phaedrus; and some other speeches followed which Aristodemus did not remember; the next which he repeated was that of Pausanias. Phaedrus, he said, the argument has not been set before us, I think, quite in the right form;—we should not be called upon to praise Love in such an indiscriminate manner. If there were only one Love, then what you said would be well enough; but since there are more Loves than one, you should have begun by determining which of them was to be the theme of our praises. I will amend this defect; and first of all I will tell you which Love is deserving of praise, and then try to hymn the praiseworthy one in a manner worthy of him. For we all know that Love is inseparable from Aphrodite, and if there were only one Aphrodite there would be only one Love; but as there are two goddesses there must be two Loves. And am I not right in asserting that there are two goddesses? The elder one, having no mother, who is called the heavenly Aphrodite—she is the daughter of Uranus; the younger, who is the daughter of Zeus and Dione—her we call common; and the Love who is her fellow-worker is rightly named common, as the other love is called heavenly. All the gods ought to have praise given to them, but not without distinction of their natures; and therefore I must try to distinguish the characters of the two Loves. Now actions vary according to the manner of their performance. Take, for example, that which we are now doing, drinking, singing and talking—these actions are not in themselves either good or evil, but they turn out in this or that way according to the mode of performing them; and when well done they are good, and when wrongly done they are evil; and in like manner not every love, but only that which has a noble purpose, is noble and worthy of praise. The Love who is the offspring of the common Aphrodite is essentially common, and has no discrimination, being such as the meaner sort of men feel, and is apt to be of women as well as of youths, and is of the body rather than of the soul—the most foolish beings are the objects of this love which desires only to gain an end, but never thinks of accomplishing the end nobly, and therefore does good and evil quite indiscriminately. The goddess who is his mother is far younger than the other, and she was born of the union of the male and female, and partakes of both. But the offspring of the heavenly Aphrodite is derived from a mother in whose birth the female has no part,—she is from the male only; this is that love which is of youths, and the goddess being older, there is nothing of wantonness in her. Those who are inspired by this love turn to the male, and delight in him who is the more valiant and intelligent nature; any one may recognize the pure enthusiasts in the very character of their attachments. For they love not boys, but intelligent beings whose reason is beginning to be developed, much about the time at which their beards begin to grow. And in choosing young men to be their companions, they mean to be faithful to them, and pass their whole life in company with them, not to take them in their inexperience, and deceive them, and play the fool with them, or run away from one to another of them. But the love of young boys should be forbidden by law, be· cause their future is uncertain; they may turn out good oɪ bad, either in body or soul, and much noble enthusiasm may be thrown away upon them; in this matter the good are a law to themselves, and the coarser sort of lovers ought to be restrained by force, as we restrain or attempt to restrain them from fixing their affections on women of free birth. These are the persons who bring a reproach on love; and some have been led to deny the lawfulness of such attachments because they see the impropriety and evil of them; for surely nothing that is decorously and lawfully done can justly be censured. Now here and in Lacedaemon the rules about love are perplexing, but in most cities they are simple and easily intelligible; in Elis and Boeotia, and in countries having no gifts of eloquence, they are very straightforward; the law is simply in favour of these connexions, and no one, whether young or old, has anything to say to their discredit; the reason being, as I suppose, that they are men of few words in those parts, and therefore the lovers do not like the trouble of pleading their suit. In Ionia and other places, and generally in countries which are subject to the barbarians, the custom is held to be dishonourable; loves of youths share the evil repute in which philosophy and gymnastics are held, because they are inimical to tyranny; for the interests of rulers require that their subjects should be poor in spirit;[1] and that there should be no strong bond of friendship or society among them, which love, above all other motives, is likely to inspire, as our Athenian tyrants learned by experience; for the love of Aristogeiton and the constancy of Harmodius had a strength which undid their power. And, therefore, the ill-repute into which these at-

[1] Cp. Arist. Politics, v. 11. §15.

tachments have fallen is to be ascribed to the evil condition
of those who make them to be ill-reputed; that is to say,
to the self-seeking of the governors and the cowardice of
the governed; on the other hand, the indiscriminate honour
which is given to them in some countries is attributable to
the laziness of those who hold this opinion of them. In our
own country a far better principle prevails, but, as I was
saying, the explanation of it is rather perplexing. For, observe that open loves are held to be more honourable than
secret ones, and that the love of the noblest and highest,
even if their persons are less beautiful than others, is especially honourable. Consider, too, how great is the encouragement which all the world gives to the lover; neither is he
supposed to be doing anything dishonourable; but if he suc-
ceeds he is praised, and if he fail he is blamed. And in the
pursuit of his love the custom of mankind allows him to do
many strange things, which philosophy would bitterly censure if they were done from any motive of interest, or wish
for office or power. He may pray, and entreat, and suppli-
cate, and swear, and lie on a mat at the door, and endure a
slavery worse than that of any slave—in any other case
friends and enemies would be equally ready to prevent him,
but now there is no friend who will be ashamed of him and
admonish him, and no enemy will charge him with meanness
or flattery; the actions of a lover have a grace which en-
nobles them; and custom has decided that they are highly
commendable and that there is no loss of character in them;
and, what is strangest of all, he only may swear and for-
swear himself (so men say), and the gods will forgive his
transgression, for there is no such thing as a lover's oath.
Such is the entire liberty which gods and men have allowed
the lover, according to the custom which prevails in our
part of the world. From this point of view a man fairly argues
that in Athens to love and to be loved is held to be a very
honourable thing. But when parents forbid their sons to
talk with their lovers, and place them under a tutor's care,

who is appointed to see to these things, and their companions and equals cast in their teeth anything of the sort which
they may observe, and their elders refuse to silence the reprovers and do not rebuke them—any one who reflects on
all this will, on the contrary, think that we hold these practices to be most disgraceful. But, as I was saying at first,
the truth as I imagine is, that whether such practices are
honourable or whether they are dishonourable is not a simple
question; they are honourable to him who follows them
honourably, dishonourable to him who follows them dis-
honourably. There is dishonour in yielding to the evil, or
in an evil manner; but there is honour in yielding to the
good, or in an honourable manner. Evil is the vulgar lover
who loves the body rather than the soul, inasmuch as he
is not even stable, because he loves a thing which is in itself
unstable, and therefore when the bloom of youth which he
was desiring is over, he takes wing and flies away, in spite
of all his words and promises; whereas the love of the noble
disposition is lifelong, for it becomes one with the everlasting. The custom of our country would have both of them
proven well and truly, and would have us yield to the one
sort of lover and avoid the other, and therefore encourages
some to pursue, and others to fly; testing both the lover
and beloved in contests and trials, until they show to which
of the two classes they respectively belong. And this is the
why, in the first place, a hasty attachment is held to be
dishonourable, because time is the true test of this as of
most other things; and secondly there is a dishonour in
being overcome by the love of money, or of wealth, or of
political power, whether a man is frightened into surrender
by the loss of them, or, having experienced the benefits of
money and political corruption, is unable to rise above the
seductions of them. For none of these things are of a perma-
nent or lasting nature; not to mention that no generous
friendship ever sprang from them. There remains, then, only
one way of honourable attachment which custom allows in

the beloved, and this is the way of virtue; for as we admitted that any service which the lover does to him is not to be accounted flattery or a dishonour to himself, so the beloved has one way only of voluntary service which is not dishonourable, and this is virtuous service.

For we have a custom, and according to our custom any one who does service to another under the idea that he will be improved by him either in wisdom, or in some other particular of virtue—such a voluntary service, I say, is not to be regarded as a dishonour, and is not open to the charge of flattery. And these two customs, one the love of youth, and the other the practice of philosophy and virtue in general, ought to meet in one, and then the beloved may honourably indulge the lover. For when the lover and beloved come together, having each of them a law, and the lover thinks that he is right in doing any service which he can to his gracious loving one; and the other that he is right in showing any kindness which he can to him who is making him wise and good; the one capable of communicating wisdom and virtue, the other seeking to acquire them with a view to education and wisdom; when the two laws of love are fulfilled and meet in one—then, and then only, may the beloved yield with honour to the lover. Nor when love is of this disinterested sort is there any disgrace in being deceived, but in every other case there is equal disgrace in being or not being deceived. For he who is gracious to his lover under the impression that he is rich, and is disappointed of his gains because he turns out to be poor, is disgraced all the same: for he has done his best to show that he would give himself up to any one's "uses base" for the sake of money; but this is not honourable. And on the same principle, he who gives himself to a lover because he is a good man, and in the hope that he will be improved by his company, shows himself to be virtuous, even though the object of his affection turn out to be a villain, and to have no virtue; and if he is deceived he has committed a noble error. For he has proved that for his part he will do anything for anybody with a view to virtue and improve‐ ment, than which there can be nothing nobler. Thus noble in every case is the acceptance of another for the sake of virtue. This is that love which is the love of the heavenly goddess, and is heavenly, and of great price to individuals and cities, making the lover and the beloved alike eager in the work of their own improvement. But all other loves are the offspring of the other, who is the common goddess. To you, Phaedrus, I offer this my contribution in praise of love, which is as good as I could make extempore.

Pausanias came to a pause—this is the balanced way in which I have been taught by the wise to speak; and Aris‐ todemus said that the turn of Aristophanes was next, but either he had eaten too much, or from some other cause he had the hiccough, and was obliged to change turns with Eryximachus the physician, who was reclining on the couch below him. Eryximachus, he said, you ought either to stop my hiccough, or to speak in my turn until I have left off.

I will do both, said Eryximachus: I will speak in your turn, and do you speak in mine; and while I am speaking let me recommend you to hold your breath, and if after you have done so for some time the hiccough is no better, then gargle with a little water; and if it still continues, tickle your nose with something and sneeze; and if you sneeze once or twice, even the most violent hiccough is sure to go. I will do as you prescribe, said Aristophanes, and now get on.

Eryximachus spoke as follows: Seeing that Pausanias made a fair beginning, and but a lame ending, I must en‐ deavour to supply his deficiency. I think that he has rightly distinguished two kinds of love. But my art further in‐ forms me that the double love is not merely an affection of the soul of man towards the fair, or towards anything, but is to be found in the bodies of all animals and in productions of the earth, and I may say in all that is; such is the con‐ clusion which I seem to have gathered from my own art of medicine, whence I learn how great and wonderful and universal is the deity of love, whose empire extends over all things, divine as well as human. And from medicine I will begin that I may do honour to my art. There are in the human body these two kinds of love, which are confessedly different and unlike, and being unlike, they have loves and desires which are unlike; and the desire of the healthy is one, and the desire of the diseased is another; and as Pausanias was just now saying that to indulge good men is honourable, and bad men dishonourable:—so too in the body the good and healthy elements are to be indulged, and the bad elements and the elements of disease are not to be indulged, but discouraged. And this is what the physician has to do, and in this the art of medicine consists: for medicine may be regarded generally as the knowledge of the loves and desires of the body, and how to satisfy them or not; and the best physician is he who is able to separate fair love from foul, or to convert one into the other; and he who knows how to eradicate and how to implant love, whichever is required, and can reconcile the most hostile elements in the constitution and make them loving friends, is a skillful practitioner. Now the most hostile are the most opposite, such as hot and cold, bitter and sweet, moist and dry, and the like. And my ancestor, Asclepius, knowing how to implant friendship and accord in these elements, was the creator of our art, as our friends the poets here tell us, and I believe them; and not only medicine in every branch, but the arts of gymnastic and husbandry are under his dominion. Any one who pays the least attention to the subject will also perceive that in music there is the same reconciliation of opposites; and I suppose that this must have been the meaning of Heracleitus, although his words are not accurate; for he says that The One is united by disunion, like the harmony of the bow and the lyre. Now there is an absurdity in saying that harmony is discord or is composed of elements which are still in a state of discord.

But what he probably meant was, that harmony is composed of differing notes of higher or lower pitch which disagreed once, but are now reconciled by the art of music; for if the higher and lower notes still disagreed, there could be no harmony,—clearly not. For harmony is a symphony, and symphony is an agreement; but an agreement of disagreements while they disagree there cannot be; you cannot harmonize that which disagrees. In like manner rhythm is compounded of elements short and long, once differing and now in accord; which accordance, as in the former instance, medicine, so in all these other cases, music implants, making love and unison to grow up among them; and thus music, too, is concerned with the principles of love in their application to harmony and rhythm. Again, in the essential nature of harmony and rhythm there is no difficulty in discerning love which has not yet become double. But when you want to use them in actual life, either in the composition of songs or in the correct performance of airs or metres composed already, which latter is called education, then the difficulty begins, and the good artist is needed. Then the old tale has to be repeated of fair and heavenly love—the love of Urania the fair and heavenly muse, and of the duty of accepting the temperate, and those who are as yet intemperate only that they may become temperate, and of preserving their love; and again, of the vulgar Polyhymnia, who must be used with circumspection that the pleasure be enjoyed, but may not generate licentiousness; just as in my own art it is a great matter so to regulate the desires of the epicure that he may gratify his tastes without the attendant evil of disease. Whence I infer that in music, in medicine, in all other things human as well as divine, both loves ought to be noted as far as may be, for they are both present.

The course of the seasons is also full of both these principles; and when, as I was saying, the elements of hot and cold, moist and dry, attain the harmonious love of one an-

other and blend in temperance and harmony, they bring
to men, animals, and plants health and plenty, and do them
no harm; whereas the wanton love, getting the upper hand
and affecting the seasons of the year, is very destructive
and injurious, being the source of pestilence, and bringing
many other kinds of diseases on animals and plants; for
hoarfrost and hail and blight spring from the excesses and
disorders of these elements of love, which to know in relation to the revolutions of the heavenly bodies and the
seasons of the year is termed astronomy. Furthermore, all
sacrifices and the whole province of divination, which is the
art of communion between gods and men—these, I say,
are concerned only with the preservation of the good and
the cure of the evil love. For all manner of impiety is likely
to ensue if, instead of accepting and honouring and reverencing the harmonious love in all his actions, a man honours the other love, whether in his feelings towards gods
or parents, towards the living or the dead. Wherefore the
business of divination is to see to these loves and to heal
them, and divination is the peacemaker of gods and men,
working by a knowledge of the religious or irreligious tenden-
cies which exist in human loves. Such is the great and mighty,
or rather omnipotent force of love in general. And the love,
more especially, which is concerned with the good, and
which is perfected in company with temperance and justice, whether among gods or men, has the greatest power,
and is the source of all our happiness and harmony, and
makes us friends with the gods who are above us, and with
one another. I dare say that I too have omitted several
things which might be said in praise of Love, but this was
not intentional, and you, Aristophanes, may now supply
the omission or take some other line of commendation; for
I perceive that you are rid of the hiccough.

Yes, said Aristophanes, who followed, the hiccough is
gone; not, however, until I applied the sneezing; and I wonder whether the harmony of the body has a love of such

noises and ticklings, for I no sooner applied the sneezing than I was cured.

Eryximachus said: Beware, friend Aristophanes, although you are going to speak, you are making fun of me; and I shall have to watch and see whether I cannot have a laugh at your expense, when you might speak in peace.

You are quite right, said Aristophanes, laughing. I will unsay my words; but do you please not to watch me, as I fear that in the speech which I am about to make, instead of others laughing with me, which is to the manner born of our muse and would be all the better, I shall only be laughed at by them.

Do you expect to shoot your bolt and escape, Aristophanes? Well, perhaps if you are very careful and bear in mind that you will be called to account, I may be induced to let you off.

Aristophanes professed to open another vein of discourse; he had a mind to praise Love in another way, unlike that either of Pausanias or Eryximachus. Mankind, he said, judging by their neglect of him, have never, as I think, at all understood the power of Love. For if they had understood him they would surely have built noble temples and altars, and offered solemn sacrifices in his honour; but this is not done, and most certainly ought to be done: since of all the gods he is the best friend of men, the helper and the healer of the ills which are the great impediment to the happiness of the race. I will try to describe his power to you, and you shall teach the rest of the world what I am teaching you. In the first place, let me treat of the nature of man and what has happened to it; for the original human nature was not like the present, but different. The sexes were not two as they are now, but originally three in number; there was man, woman, and the union of the two, having a name corresponding to this double nature, which had once a real existence, but is now lost, and the word "Androgynous" is only preserved as a term of reproach. In

the second place, the primeval man was round, his back
and sides forming a circle; and he had four hands and four
feet, one head with two faces, looking opposite ways, set
on a round neck and precisely alike; also four ears, two
privy members, and the remainder to correspond. He could
walk upright as men now do, backwards or forwards as
he pleased, and he could also roll over and over at a great
pace, turning on his four hands and four feet, eight in all,
like tumblers going over and over with their legs in the air;
this was when he wanted to run fast. Now, the sexes were
three, and such as I have described them; because the sun,
moon, and earth are three; and the man was originally the
child of the sun, the woman of the earth, and the man-
woman of the moon, which is made up of sun and earth,
and they were all round and moved round and round like
their parents. Terrible was their might and strength, and
the thoughts of their hearts were great, and they made an
attack upon the gods; of them is told the tale of Otys and
Ephialtes who, as Homer says, dared to scale heaven, and
would have laid hands upon the gods. Doubt reigned in the
celestial councils. Should they kill them and annihilate the
race with thunderbolts, as they had done the giants, then
there would be an end of the sacrifices and worship which
men offered to them; but, on the other hand, the gods could
not suffer their insolence to be unrestrained. At last, after
a good deal of reflection, Zeus discovered a way. He said:
"Methinks I have a plan which will humble their pride and
improve their manners; men shall continue to exist, but I
will cut them in two and then they will be diminished in
strength and increased in numbers; this will have the advantage of making them more profitable to us. They shall
walk upright on two legs, and if they continue insolent and
will not be quiet, I will split them again and they shall hop
about on a single leg." He spoke and cut men in two, like
a sorb-apple which is halved for pickling, or as you might
divide an egg with a hair; and as he cut them one after

another, he bade Apollo give the face and the half of the
neck a turn in order that the man might contemplate the
section of himself: he would thus learn a lesson of humility.
Apollo was also bidden to heal their wounds and compose
their forms. So he gave a turn to the face and pulled the
skin from the sides all over that which in our language is
called the belly, like the purses which draw in, and he made
one mouth at the centre, which he fastened in a knot (the
same which is called the navel); he also moulded the breast
and took out most of the wrinkles, much as a shoemaker
might smooth leather upon a last; he left a few, however, in
the region of the belly and navel, as a memorial of the
primeval state. After the division the two parts of man,
each desiring his other half, came together, and throwing
their arms about one another, entwined in mutual embraces,
longing to grow into one; they were on the point of dying
from hunger and self-neglect, because they did not like to
do anything apart; and when one of the halves died and
the other survived, the survivor sought another mate, man
or woman, as we call them,—being the sections of entire
men or women,—and clung to that. They were being destroyed, when Zeus in pity of them invented a new plan:
he turned the parts of generation round to the front, for
this had not been always their position, and they sowed the
seed no longer as hitherto like grasshoppers in the ground,
but in one another; and after the transposition the male
generated in the female in order that by mutual embraces
of man and woman they might breed, and the race might
continue; or if man came to man they might be satisfied,
and rest, and go their ways to the business of life: so ancient
is the desire of one another which is implanted in us, re-
uniting our original nature, making one of two, and healing the state of man. Each of us when separated, having
one side only, like a flat fish, is but the indenture of a man,
and he is always looking for his other half. Men who are
a section of that double nature which was once called An-

drogynous are lovers of women; adulterers are generally of
this breed, and also adulterous women who lust after men:
the women who are a section of the woman do not care for
men, but have female attachments; the female companions
are of this sort. But they who are a section of the male,
follow the male, and while they are young, being slices of
the original man, they hang about men and embrace them,
and they are themselves the best of boys and youths, because they have the most manly nature. Some indeed assert
that they are shameless, but this is not true; for they do
not act thus from any want of shame, but because they are
valiant and manly, and have a manly countenance, and
they embrace that which is like them. And these when they
grow up become our statesmen, and these only, which is a
great proof of the truth of what I am saying. When they
reach manhood they are lovers of youth, and are not naturally inclined to marry or beget children,—if at all, they do
so only in obedience to the law; but they are satisfied if
they may be allowed to live with one another unwedded;
and such a nature is prone to love and ready to return love,
always embracing that which is akin to him. And when
one of them meets with his other half, the actual half of
himself, whether he be a lover of youth or a lover of another sort, the pair are lost in an amazement of love and
friendship and intimacy, and one will not be out of the
other's sight, as I may say, even for a moment: these are
the people who pass their whole lives together; yet they
could not explain what they desire of one another. For the
intense yearning which each of them has towards the other
does not appear to be the desire of lover's intercourse, but
of something else which the soul of either evidently desires
and cannot tell, and of which she has only a dark and doubtful presentiment. Suppose Hephaestus, with his instruments,
to come to the pair who are lying side by side and to say
to them, "What do you people want of one another?" they
would be unable to explain. And suppose further, that when

he saw their perplexity he said: "Do you desire to be wholly one; always day and night to be in one another's company? for if this is what you desire, I am ready to melt you into one and let you grow together, so that being two you shall become one, and while you live live a common life as if you were a single man, and after your death in the world below still be one departed soul instead of two—I ask whether this is what you lovingly desire, and whether you are satisfied to attain this?"—there is not a man of them who when he heard the proposal would deny or would not acknowledge that this meeting and melting into one another, this becoming one instead of two, was the very expression of his ancient need.[1] And the reason is that human nature was originally one and we were a whole, and the desire and pursuit of the whole is called love. There was a time, I say, when we were one, but now because of the wickedness of mankind God has dispersed us, as the Arcadians were dispersed into villages by the Lacedaemonians.[2] And if we are not obedient to the gods, there is a danger that we shall be split up again and go about in *basso-rilievo*, like the profile figures having only half a nose which are sculptured on monuments, and that we shall be like tallies. Wherefore let us exhort all men to piety, that we may avoid evil, and obtain the good, of which Love is to us the lord and minister; and let no one oppose him—he is the enemy of the gods who opposes him. For if we are friends of the god and at peace with him we shall find our own true loves, which rarely happens in this world at present. I am serious, and therefore I must beg Eryximachus not to make fun or to find any allusion in what I am saying to Pausanias and Agathon, who, as I suspect, are both of the manly nature, and belong to the class which I have been describing. But my words have a wider application—they include men and women everywhere; and I believe that if our loves were perfectly accomplished, and each one returning to his primeval

[1] Cp. Arist. Pol. ii. 4, § 6.   [2] Cp. Arist. Pol. ii. 2, § 3.

nature had his original true love, then our race would be happy. And if this would be best of all, the best in the next degree and under present circumstances must be the nearest approach to such an union; and that will be the attainment of a congenial love. Wherefore, if we would praise him who has given to us the benefit, we must praise the god Love, who is our greatest benefactor, both leading us in this life back to our own nature, and giving us high hopes for the future, for he promises that if we are pious, he will restore us to our original state, and heal us and make us happy and blessed. This, Eryximachus, is my discourse of love, which, although different to yours, I must beg you to leave unassailed by the shafts of your ridicule, in order that each may have his turn; each, or rather either, for Agathon and Socrates are the only ones left.

Indeed, I am not going to attack you, said Eryximachus, for I thought your speech charming, and did I not know that Agathon and Socrates are masters in the art of love, I should be really afraid that they would have nothing to say, after the world of things which have been said already. But, for all that, I am not without hopes.

Socrates said: You played your part well, Eryximachus; but if you were as I am now, or rather as I shall be when Agathon has spoken, you would, indeed, be in a great strait.

You want to cast a spell over me, Socrates, said Agathon, in the hope that I may be disconcerted at the expectation raised among the audience that I shall speak well.

I should be strangely forgetful, Agathon, replied Socrates, of the courage and magnanimity which you showed when your own compositions were about to be exhibited, and you came upon the stage with the actors and faced the vast theatre altogether undismayed, if I thought that your nerves could be fluttered at a small party of friends.

Do you think, Socrates, said Agathon, that my head is so full of the theatre as not to know how much more for-

midable to a man of sense a few good judges are than
many fools?

Nay, replied Socrates, I should be very wrong in attributing to you, Agathon, that or any other want of refinement.
And I am quite aware that if you happened to meet with
any whom you thought wise, you would care for their opinion much more than for that of the many. But then we,
having been a part of the foolish many in the theatre, cannot be regarded as the select wise; though I know that if
you chanced to be in the presence, not of one of ourselves,
but of some really wise man, you would be ashamed of dis-
gracing yourself before him—would you not?

Yes, said Agathon.

But before the many you would not be ashamed, if you
thought that you were doing something disgraceful in their
presence?

Here Phaedrus interrupted them, saying: Do not answer
him, my dear Agathon; for if he can only get a partner with
whom he can talk, especially a good-looking one, he will no
longer care about the completion of our plan. Now, I love
to hear him talk; but just at present I must not forget the
encomium on Love which I ought to receive from him and
from every one. When you and he have paid your tribute
to the god, then you may talk.

Very good, Phaedrus, said Agathon; I see no reason why
I should not proceed with my speech, as I shall have many
other opportunities of conversing with Socrates. Let me say
first how I ought to speak, and then speak:—

The previous speakers, instead of praising the god Love,
or unfolding his nature, appear to have congratulated mankind on the benefits which he confers upon them. But I
would rather praise the god first, and then speak of his
gifts; this is always the right way of praising everything.
May I say without impiety or offence, that of all the blessed
gods he is the most blessed because he is the fairest and

best? And he is the fairest: for, in the first place, he is the youngest, and of his youth he is himself the witness, fleeing out of the way of age, who is swift enough, swifter truly than most of us like:—Love hates him and will not come near him; but youth and love live and move together —like to like, as the proverb says. Many things were said by Phaedrus about Love in which I agree with him; but I cannot agree that he is older than Iapetus and Cronos:— not so; I maintain him to be the youngest of the gods, and youthful ever. The ancient doings among the gods of which Hesiod and Parmenides spoke, if the tradition of them be true, were done of Necessity and not of Love; had Love been in those days, there would have been no chaining or mutilation of the gods, or other violence, but peace and sweetness, as there is now in heaven, since the rule of Love began. Love is young and also tender; he ought to have a poet like Homer to describe his tenderness, as Homer says of Ate, that she is a goddess and tender:—

"Her feet are tender, for she sets her steps,
    Not on the ground but on the heads of men":

herein is an excellent proof of her tenderness,—that she walks not upon the hard but upon the soft. Let us adduce a similar proof of the tenderness of Love; for he walks not upon the earth, nor yet upon the skulls of men, which are not so very soft, but in the hearts and souls of both gods and men, which are of all things the softest: in them he walks and dwells and makes his home. Not in every soul without exception, for where there is hardness he departs, where there is softness there he dwells; and nestling always with his feet and in all manner of ways in the softest of soft places, how can he be other than the softest of all things? Of a truth he is the tenderest as well as the youngest, and also he is of flexile form; for if he were hard and without flexure he could not enfold all things, or wind his way into and out of every soul of man undiscovered. And a proof of his flexibility and symmetry of form is his grace, which is universally admitted to be in an especial manner the attribute of Love; ungrace and love are always at war with one another. The fairness of his complexion is revealed by his habitation among the flowers; for he dwells not amid bloomless or fading beauties, whether of body or soul or aught else, but in the place of flowers and scents, there he sits and abides. Concerning the beauty of the god I have said enough; and yet there remains much more which I might say. Of his virtue I have now to speak: his greatest glory is that he can neither do nor suffer wrong to or from any god or any man; for he suffers not by force if he suffers; force comes not near him, neither when he acts does he act by force. For all men in all things serve him of their own free will, and where there is voluntary agreement, there, as the laws which are the lords of the city say, is justice. And not only is he just but exceedingly temperate, for Temperance is the acknowledged ruler of the pleasures and desires, and no pleasure ever masters Love; he is their master and they are his servants; and if he conquers them he must be temperate indeed. As to courage, even the God of War is no match for him; he is the captive and Love is the lord, for love, the love of Aphrodite, masters him, as the tale runs; and the master is stronger than the servant. And if he conquers the bravest of all others, he must be himself the bravest. Of his courage and justice and temperance I have spoken, but I have yet to speak of his wisdom; and according to the measure of my ability I must try to do my best. In the first place, he is a poet (and here, like Eryximachus, I magnify my art), and he is also the source of poesy in others, which he could not be if he were not himself a poet. And at the touch of him every one becomes a poet,[1] even though he had no music in him before;[1] this also is a proof that Love is a good poet and accomplished

[1] A fragment of the Stenoboea of Euripides.

In all the fine arts; for no one can give to another that which he has not himself, or teach that of which he has no knowledge. Who will deny that the creation of the animals is his doing? Are they not all the works of his wisdom, born and begotten of him? And as to the artists, do we not know that he only of them whom love inspires has the light of flame? —he whom Love touches not walks in darkness. The arts of medicine and archery and divination were discovered by Apollo, under the guidance of love and desire; so that he too is a disciple of Love. Also the melody of the Muses, the metallurgy of Hephaestus, the weaving of Athene, the empire of Zeus over gods and men, are all due to Love, who was the inventor of them. And so Love set in order the empire of the gods—the love of beauty, as is evident, for with deformity Love has no concern. In the days of old, as I began by saying, dreadful deeds were done among the gods, for they were ruled by Necessity; but now since the birth of Love, and from the love of the beautiful, has sprung every good in heaven and earth. Therefore, Phaedrus, I say of Love that he is the fairest and best in himself, and the cause of what is fairest and best in all other things. And there comes into my mind a line of poetry in which he is said to be the god who

"Gives peace on earth and calms the stormy deep,
    Who stills the winds and bids the sufferer sleep."

This is he who empties men of disaffection and fills them with affection, who makes them to meet together at banquets such as these: in sacrifices, feasts, dances, he is our lord—who sends courtesy and sends away discourtesy, who gives kindness ever and never gives unkindness; the friend of the good, the wonder of the wise, the amazement of the gods; desired by those who have no part in him, and precious to those who have the better part in him; parent of delicacy, luxury, desire, fondness, softness, grace; regardful of the good, regardless of the evil: in every word, work, wish, fear—saviour, pilot, comrade, helper; glory of gods and men, leader best and brightest: in whose footsteps let every man follow, sweetly singing in his honour and join-ing in that sweet strain with which love charms the souls of gods and men. Such is the speech, Phaedrus, half-playful, yet having a certain measure of seriousness, which, accord-ing to my ability, I dedicate to the god.

When Agathon had done speaking, Aristodemus said that there was a general cheer; the young man was thought to have spoken in a manner worthy of himself, and of the god. And Socrates, looking at Eryximachus, said: Tell me, son of Acumenus, was there not reason in my fears? and was I not a true prophet when I said that Agathon would make a wonderful oration, and that I should be in a strait?

The part of the prophecy which concerns Agathon, re-plied Eryximachus, appears to me to be true; but not the other part—that you will be in a strait.

Why, my dear friend, said Socrates, must not I or any one be in a strait who has to speak after he has heard such a rich and varied discourse? I am especially struck with the beauty of the concluding words—who could listen to them without amazement? When I reflected on the im-measurable inferiority of my own powers, I was ready to run away for shame, if there had been a possibility of es-cape. For I was reminded of Gorgias, and at the end of his speech I fancied that Agathon was shaking at me the Gor-ginian or Gorgonian head of the great master of rhetoric, which was simply to turn me and my speech into stone, as Homer says,[1] and strike me dumb. And then I perceived how foolish I had been in consenting to take my turn with you in praising love, and saying that I too was a master of the art, when I really had no conception how anything ought to be praised. For in my simplicity I imagined that the topics of praise should be true, and that this being

[1] Odyssey, λ. 632.

presupposed, out of the true the speaker was to choose the best and set them forth in the best manner. And I felt quite proud, thinking that I knew the nature of true praise, and should speak well. Whereas I now see that the intention was to attribute to Love every species of greatness and glory, whether really belonging to him or not, without regard to truth or falsehood—that was no matter; for the original proposal seems to have been not that each of you should really praise Love, but only that you should appear to praise him. And so you attribute to Love every imaginable form of praise which can be gathered anywhere; and you say that "he is all this," and "the cause of all that," making him appear the fairest and best of all to those who know him not, for you cannot impose upon those who know him. And a noble and solemn hymn of praise have you rehearsed. But as I misunderstood the nature of the praise when I said that I would take my turn, I must beg to be absolved from the promise which I made in ignorance, and which (as Euripides would say[1]) was a promise of the lips and not of the mind. Farewell then to such a strain: for I do not praise in that way; no, indeed, I cannot. But if you like to hear the truth about love, I am ready to speak in my own manner, though I will not make myself ridiculous by entering into any rivalry with you. Say then, Phaedrus, whether you would like to have the truth about love, spoken in any words and in any order which may happen to come into my mind at the time. Will that be agreeable to you?

Aristodemus said that Phaedrus and the company bid him speak in any manner which he thought best. Then, he added, let me have your permission first to ask Agathon a few more questions, in order that I may take his admissions as the premises of my discourse.

I grant the permission, said Phaedrus: put your questions. Socrates then proceeded as follows:—

In the magnificent oration which you have just uttered,

[1] Eurip. Hyppolytus, l. 612.

I think that you were right, my dear Agathon, in proposing to speak of the nature of Love first and afterwards of his works—that is a way of beginning which I very much approve. And as you have spoken so eloquently of his nature, may I ask you further, Whether love is the love of something or of nothing? And here I must explain myself: I do not want you to say that love is the love of a father or the love of a mother—that would be ridiculous; but to answer as you would, if I asked is a father a father of something? to which you would find no difficulty in replying, of a son or daughter: and the answer would be right.

Very true, said Agathon.

And you would say the same of a mother?

He assented.

Yet let me ask you one more question in order to illustrate my meaning: Is not a brother to be regarded essentially as a brother of something?

Certainly, he replied.

That is, of a brother or sister?

Yes, he said.

And now, said Socrates, I will ask about Love:—Is Love of something or of nothing?

Of something, surely, he replied.

Keep in mind what this is, and tell me what I want to know—whether Love desires that of which love is.

Yes, surely.

And does he possess, or does he not possess, that which he loves and desires?

Probably not, I should say.

Nay, replied Socrates, I would have you consider whether "necessarily" is not rather the word. The inference that he who desires something is in want of something, and that he who desires nothing is in want of nothing, is in my judgment, Agathon, absolutely and necessarily true. What do you think?

I agree with you, said Agathon.

Very good. Would he who is great, desire to be great, or he who is strong, desire to be strong?

That would be inconsistent with our previous admissions.

True. For he who is anything cannot want to be that which he is?

Very true.

And yet, added Socrates, if a man being strong desired to be strong, or being swift desired to be swift, or being healthy desired to be healthy, in that case he might be thought to desire something which he already has or is. I give the example in order that we may avoid misconception. For the possessors of these qualities, Agathon, must be supposed to have their respective advantages at the time, whether they choose or not; and who can desire that which he has? Therefore, when a person says, I am well and wish to be well, or I am rich and wish to be rich, and I desire simply to have what I have—to him we shall reply: "You, my friend, having wealth and health and strength, want to have the continuance of them; for at this moment, whether you choose or no, you have them. And when you say, I desire that which I have and nothing else, is not your meaning that you want to have what you now have in the future?" He must agree with us—must he not?

He must, replied Agathon.

Then, said Socrates, he desires that what he has at present may be preserved to him in the future, which is equivalent to saying that he desires something which is non-existent to him, and which as yet he has not got?

Very true, he said.

Then he and every one who desires, desires that which he has not already, and which is future and not present, and which he has not, and is not, and of which he is in want; —these are the sort of things which love and desire seek?

Very true, he said.

Then now, said Socrates, let us recapitulate the argument. First, is not love of something, and of something too which is wanting to a man?

Yes, he replied.

Remember further what you said in your speech, or if you do not remember I will remind you: you said that the love of the beautiful set in order the empire of the gods, for that of deformed things there is no love—did you not say something of that kind?

Yes, said Agathon.

Yes, my friend, and the remark was a just one. And if this is true, Love is the love of beauty and not of deformity?

He assented.

And the admission has been already made that Love is of something which a man wants and has not?

True, he said.

Then Love wants and has not beauty?

Certainly, he replied.

And would you call that beautiful which wants and does not possess beauty?

Certainly not.

Then would you still say that love is beautiful?

Agathon replied: I fear that I did not understand what I was saying.

You made a very good speech, Agathon, replied Socrates; but there is yet one small question which I would fain ask:—Is not the good also the beautiful?

Yes.

Then in wanting the beautiful, love wants also the good?

I cannot refute you, Socrates, said Agathon:—Let us assume that what you say is true.

Say rather, beloved Agathon, that you cannot refute the truth; for Socrates is easily refuted.

And now, taking my leave of you, I will rehearse a tale of love which I heard from Diotima of Mantineia,[1] a woman wise in this and in many other kinds of knowledge, who in

---

[1] Cp. I. Alcibiades.

the days of old, when the Athenians offered sacrifice before the coming of the plague, delayed the disease ten years.
She was my instructress in the art of love, and I shall repeat to you what she said to me, beginning with the admissions made by Agathon, which are nearly if not quite
the same which I made to the wise woman when she ques-
tioned me: I think that this will be the easiest way, and I
shall take both parts myself as well as I can.[1] As you,
Agathon, suggested,[2] I must speak first of the being and
nature of Love, and then of his works. First I said to her
in nearly the same words which he used to me, that Love
was a mighty god, and likewise fair; and she proved to me
as I proved to him that, by my own showing, Love was
neither fair nor good. "What do you mean, Diotima," I
said, "is Love then evil and foul?" "Hush," she cried; "must
that be foul which is not fair?" "Certainly," I said. "And
is that which is not wise, ignorant? Do you not see that
there is a mean between wisdom and ignorance?" "And what
may that be?" I said. "Right opinion," she replied; "which,
as you know, being incapable of giving a reason, is not
knowledge (for how can knowledge be devoid of reason?
nor again, ignorance, for neither can ignorance attain the
truth), but is clearly something which is a mean between
ignorance and wisdom." "Quite true," I replied. "Do not
then insist," she said, "that what is not fair is of necessity
foul, or what is not good evil; or infer that because Love
is not fair and good he is therefore foul and evil; for he is
in a mean between them." "Well," I said, "Love is surely
admitted by all to be a great god." "By those who know or by
those who do not know?" "By all." "And now, Socrates,"
she said with a smile, "can Love be acknowledged to be a
great god by those who say that he is not a god at all?"
"And who are they?" I said. "You and I are two of them,"
she replied. "How can that be?" I said. "It is quite intelligible," she replied; "for you yourself would acknowledge

[1] Cp. Gorgias, 505 E.   [2] Supra, 195 A.

that the gods are happy and fair—of course you would—
would you dare to say that any god was not?" "Certainly
not," I replied. "And you mean by the happy, those who
are the possessors of things good or fair?" "Yes." "And
you admitted that Love, because he was in want, desires
those good and fair things of which he is in want?" "Yes,
I did." "But how can he be a god who has no portion in
what is either good or fair?" "Impossible." "Then you see
that you also deny the divinity of Love."

"What then is Love?" I asked. "Is he mortal?" "No."
"What then?" "As in the former instance, he is neither
mortal nor immortal, but in a mean between the two."
"What is he, Diotima?" "He is a great spirit (δαίμων),
and like all spirits he is intermediate between the divine
and the mortal." "And what," I said, "is his power?" "He
interprets," she replied, "between gods and men, conveying
and taking across to the gods the prayers and sacrifices of
men, and to men the commands and replies of the gods;
he is the mediator who spans the chasm which divides them,
and therefore in him all is bound together, and through
him the arts of the prophet and the priest, their sacrifices
and mysteries and charms, and all prophecy and incanta-
tion, find their way. For God mingles not with man; but
through Love all the intercourse and converse of God with
man, whether awake or asleep, is carried on. The wisdom
which understands this is spiritual; all other wisdom, such
as that of arts and handicrafts, is mean and vulgar. Now
these spirits or intermediate powers are many and diverse,
and one of them is Love." "And who," I said, "was his
father, and who his mother?" "The tale," she said, "will
take time; nevertheless I will tell you. On the birthday of
Aphrodite there was a feast of the gods, at which the god
Poros, or Plenty, who is the son of Metis, or Discretion,
was one of the guests. When the feast was over, Penia or
Poverty, as the manner is on such occasions, came about
the doors to beg. Now Plenty, who was the worse for nectar

(there was no wine in those days), went into the garden of Zeus and fell into a heavy sleep; and Poverty considering her own straitened circumstances, plotted to have a child by him, and accordingly she lay down at his side and conceived Love, who partly because he is naturally a lover of the beautiful, and because Aphrodite is herself beautiful, and also because he was born on her birthday, is her follower and attendant. And as his parentage is, so also are his fortunes. In the first place he is always poor, and anything but tender and fair, as the many imagine him; and he is rough and squalid, and has no shoes, nor a house to dwell in; on the bare earth exposed he lies under the open heaven, in the streets, or at the doors of houses, taking his rest; and like his mother he is always in distress. Like his father too, whom he also partly resembles, he is always plotting against the fair and good; he is bold, enterprising, strong, a mighty hunter, always weaving some intrigue or other, keen in the pursuit of wisdom, fertile in resources; a philosopher at all times, terrible as an enchanter, sorcerer, sophist. He is by nature neither mortal nor immortal, but alive and flourishing at one moment when he is in plenty, and dead at another moment, and again alive by reason of his father's nature. But that which is always flowing in is always flowing out, and so he is never in want and never in wealth; and, further, he is in a mean between ignorance and knowledge: The truth of the matter is this: No god is a philosopher or seeker after wisdom, for he is wise already; nor does any man who is wise seek after wisdom. Neither do the ignorant seek after wisdom. For herein is the evil of ignorance, that he who is neither good nor wise is nevertheless satisfied with himself: he has no desire for that of which he feels no want." "But who, then, Diotima," I said, "are the lovers of wisdom, if they are neither the wise nor the foolish?" "A child may answer that question," she replied; "they are those who are in a mean between the two; Love is one of them. For wisdom is a most beautiful thing, and Love is of the beautiful; and therefore Love is also a philosopher, or lover of wisdom, and being a lover of wisdom is in a mean between the wise and the ignorant. And of this too his birth is the cause; for his father is wealthy and wise, and his mother poor and foolish. Such, my dear Socrates, is the nature of the spirit Love. The error in your conception of him was very natural, and as I imagine from what you say, has arisen out of a confusion of love and the beloved, which made you think that love was all beautiful. For the beloved is the truly beautiful, and delicate, and perfect, and blessed; but the principle of love is of another nature, and is such as I have described."

I said: "O thou stranger woman, thou sayest well; but, assuming Love to be such as you say, what is the use of him to men?" "That, Socrates," she replied, "I will attempt to unfold: of his nature and birth I have already spoken; and you acknowledge that love is of the beautiful. But some one will say: Of the beautiful in what, Socrates and Diotima?—or rather let me put the question more clearly, and ask: When a man loves the beautiful, what does he desire?" I answered her, "That the beautiful may be his." "Still," she said, "the answer suggests a further question: What is given by the possession of beauty?" "To what you have asked," I replied, "I have no answer ready." "Then," she said, "let me put the word 'good' in the place of the beautiful, and repeat the question once more: If he who loves the good, what is it then that he loves?" "The possession of the good," I said. "And what does he gain who possesses the good?" "Happiness," I replied; "there is less difficulty in answering that question." "Yes," she said, "the happy are made happy by the acquisition of good things. Nor is there any need to ask why a man desires happiness; the answer is already final." "You are right," I said. "And is this wish and this desire common to all? and do all men always desire their own good, or only some men?—what say you?" "All men," I replied; "the desire is common to all."

"Why, then," she rejoined, "are not all men, Socrates, said to love, but only some of them? whereas you say that all men are always loving the same things." "I myself wonder," I said, "why this is." "There is nothing to wonder at," she replied; "the reason is that one part of love is separated off and receives the name of the whole, but the other parts have other names." "Give an illustration," I said. She answered me as follows: "There is poetry, which, as you know, is complex and manifold. All creation or passage of non-being into being is poetry or making, and the processes of all art are creative; and the masters of arts are all poets or makers." "Very true." "Still," she said, "you know that they are not called poets, but have other names; only that portion of the art which is separated off from the rest, and is concerned with music and metre, is termed poetry, and they who possess poetry in this sense of the word are called poets." "Very true," I said. "And the same holds of love. For you may say generally that all desire of good and happiness is only the great and subtle power of love; but they who are drawn towards him by any other path, whether the path of money-making or gymnastics or philosophy, are not called lovers—the name of the whole is appropriated to those whose affection takes one form only—they alone are said to love, or to be lovers." "I dare say," I replied, "that you are right." "Yes," she added, "and you hear people say that lovers are seeking for their other half; but I say that they are seeking neither for the half of themselves, nor for the whole, unless the half or the whole be also a good. And they will cut off their own hands and feet and cast them away, if they are evil; for they love not what is their own, unless perchance there be some one who calls what belongs to him the good, and what belongs to another the evil. For there is nothing which men love but the good. Is there anything?" "Certainly, I should say, that there is nothing." "Then," she said, "the simple truth is, that men love the good." "Yes," I said. "To which must be added that they love the possession of the good?" "Yes, that must be added." "And not only the possession, but the everlasting possession of the good?" "That must be added too." "Then love," she said, "may be described generally as the love of the everlasting possession of the good?" "That is most true."

"Then if this be the nature of love, can you tell me further," she said, "what is the manner of the pursuit? what are they doing who show all this eagerness and heat which is called love? and what is the object which they have in view? Answer me." "Nay, Diotima," I replied, "if I had known, I should not have wondered at your wisdom, neither should I have come to learn from you about this very matter." "Well," she said, "I will teach you:—The object which they have in view is birth in beauty, whether of body or soul." "I do not understand you," I said; "the oracle requires an explanation." "I will make my meaning clearer," she replied. "I mean to say, that all men are bringing to the birth in their bodies and in their souls. There is a certain age at which human nature is desirous of procreation—procreation which must be in beauty and not in deformity; and this procreation is the union of man and woman, and is a divine thing; for conception and generation are an immortal principle in the mortal creature, and in the inharmonious they can never be. But the deformed is always inharmonious with the divine, and the beautiful harmonious. Beauty, then, is the destiny or goddess of parturition who presides at birth, and therefore, when approaching beauty, the conceiving power is propitious, and diffusive, and benign, and begets and bears fruit: at the sight of ugliness she frowns and contracts and has a sense of pain, and turns away, and shrivels up, and not without a pang refrains from conception. And this is the reason why, when the hour of conception arrives, and the teeming nature is full, there is such a flutter and ecstasy about beauty whose approach is the alleviation of the pain of travail. For love, Socrates, is not, as you imagine, the love of the beautiful only." "What then?" "The love of generation and of birth in beauty." "Yes," I said. "Yes, indeed," she replied. "But why of generation?" "Because to the mortal creature, generation is a sort of eternity and immortality," she replied; "and if, as has been already admitted, love is of the everlasting possession of the good, all men will necessarily desire immortality together with good: Wherefore love is of immortality."

All this she taught me at various times when she spoke of love. And I remember her once saying to me, "What is the cause, Socrates, of love, and the attendant desire? See you not how all animals, birds, as well as beasts, in their desire of procreation, are in agony when they take the infection of love, which begins with the desire of union; whereto is added the care of offspring, on whose behalf the weakest are ready to battle against the strongest even to the uttermost, and to die for them, and will let themselves be tormented with hunger or suffer anything in order to maintain their young? Man may be supposed to act thus from reason; but why should animals have these passionate feelings? Can you tell me why?" Again I replied that I did not know. She said to me: "And do you expect ever to become a master in the art of love, if you do not know this?" "But I have told you already, Diotima, that my ignorance is the reason why I come to you; for I am conscious that I want a teacher; tell me then the cause of this and of the other mysteries of love." "Marvel not," she said, "if you believe that love is of the immortal, as we have several times acknowledged; for here again, and on the same principle too, the mortal nature is seeking as far as is possible to be everlasting and immortal: and this is only to be attained by generation, because generation always leaves behind a new existence in the place of the old. Nay, even in the life of the same individual there is succession and not absolute unity: a man is called the same, and yet in the short interval which elapses between youth and age, and in which every animal is said to have life and identity, he is under-going a perpetual process of loss and reparation—hair, flesh, bones, blood, and the whole body are always chang-ing. Which is true not only of the body, but also of the soul, whose habits, tempers, opinions, desires, pleasures, pains, fears, never remain the same in any one of us, but are always coming and going; and equally true of knowl-edge, and what is still more surprising to us mortals, not only do the sciences in general spring up and decay, so that in respect of them we are never the same; but each of them individually experiences a like change. For what is implied in the word 'recollection,' but the departure of knowledge, which is ever being forgotten, and is renewed and preserved by recollection, and appears to be the same although in reality new, according to that law of succession by which all mortal things are preserved, not absolutely the same, but by substitution, the old worn-out mortality leaving another new and similar existence behind—unlike the divine, which is always the same and not another? And in this way, Soc-rates, the mortal body, or mortal anything, partakes of im-mortality; but the immortal in another way. Marvel not then at the love which all men have of their offspring; for that universal love and interest is for the sake of immor-tality."

I was astonished at her words, and said: "Is this really true, O thou wise Diotima?" And she answered with all the authority of an accomplished Sophist: "Of that, Socrates, you may be assured;—think only of the ambition of men, and you will wonder at the senselessness of their ways, un-less you consider how they are stirred by the love of an immortality of fame. They are ready to run all risks greater far than they would have run for their children, and to spend money and undergo any sort of toil, and even to die, for the sake of leaving behind them a name which shall be eternal. Do you imagine that Alcestis would have died to save Admetus, or Achilles to avenge Patroclus, or your own Codrus in order to preserve the kingdom for his sons, if they had not imagined that the memory of their virtues, which still survives among us, would be immortal? Nay," she said, "I am persuaded that all men do all things, and the better they are the more they do them, in hope of the glorious fame of immortal virtue; for they desire the immortal.

"Those who are pregnant in the body only, betake themselves to women and beget children—this is the character of their love; their offspring, as they hope, will preserve their memory and give them the blessedness and immortality which they desire in the future. But souls which are pregnant—for there certainly are men who are more creative in their souls than in their bodies -conceive that which is proper for the soul to conceive or contain. And what are these conceptions?—wisdom and virtue in general. And such creators are poets and all artists who are deserving of the name inventor. But the greatest and fairest sort of wisdom by far is that which is concerned with the ordering of states and families, and which is called temperance and justice. And he who in youth has the seed of these implanted in him and is himself inspired, when he comes to maturity desires to beget and generate. He wanders about seeking beauty that he may beget offspring—for in deformity he will beget nothing—and naturally embraces the beautiful rather than the deformed body; above all, when he finds a fair and noble and well-nurtured soul, he embraces the two in one person, and to such an one he is full of speech about virtue and the nature and pursuits of a good man; and he tries to educate him; and at the touch of the beautiful which is ever present to his memory, even when absent, he brings forth that which he had conceived long before, and in company with him tends that which he brings forth; and they are married by a far nearer tie and have a closer friendship than those who beget mortal children, for the children who are their common offspring are fairer

and more immortal. Who, when he thinks of Homer and
Hesiod and other great poets, would not rather have their
children than ordinary human ones? Who would not emulate them in the creation of children such as theirs, which
have preserved their memory and given them everlasting
glory? Or who would not have such children as Lycurgus
left behind him to be the saviours, not only of Lacedaemon,
but of Hellas, as one may say? There is Solon, too, who
is the revered father of Athenian laws; and many others
there are in many other places, both among Hellenes and
barbarians, who have given to the world many noble works,
and have been the parents of virtue of every kind; and
many temples have been raised in their honour for the
sake of children such as theirs; which were never raised in
honour of any one, for the sake of his mortal children.

"These are the lesser mysteries of love, into which even
you, Socrates, may enter; to the greater and more hidden
ones which are the crown of these, and to which, if you pursue them in a right spirit, they will lead, I know not whether
you will be able to attain. But I will do my utmost to inform you, and do you follow if you can. For he who would
proceed aright in this matter should begin in youth to visit
beautiful forms; and first, if he be guided by his instructor
aright, to love one such form only—out of that he should
create fair thoughts; and soon he will of himself perceive
that the beauty of one form is akin to the beauty of another; and then if beauty of form in general is his pursuit,
how foolish would he be not to recognize that the beauty in
every form is one and the same! And when he perceives this
he will abate his violent love of the one, which he will despise
and deem a small thing, and will become a lover of all
beautiful forms; in the next stage he will consider that the
beauty of the mind is more honourable than the beauty of
the outward form. So that if a virtuous soul have but a
little comeliness, he will be content to love and tend him,
and will search out and bring to the birth thoughts which

may improve the young, until he is compelled to contemplate
and see the beauty of institutions and laws, and to understand that the beauty of them all is of one family, and
that personal beauty is a trifle; and after laws and institutions he will go on to the sciences, that he may see their
beauty, being not like a servant in love with the beauty of
one youth or man or institution, himself a slave mean and
narrow-minded, but drawing towards and contemplating the
vast sea of beauty, he will create many fair and noble
thoughts and notions in boundless love of wisdom; until
on that shore he grows and waxes strong, and at last the
vision is revealed to him of a single science, which is the
science of beauty everywhere.   To this I will proceed;
please to give me your very best attention:

"He who has been instructed thus far in the things of
love, and who has learned to see the beautiful in due order
and succession, when he comes towards the end will suddenly
perceive a nature of wondrous beauty (and this, Socrates,
is the final cause of all our former toils)—a nature which
in the first place is everlasting, not growing and decaying,
or waxing and waning; secondly, not fair in one point of
view and foul in another, or at one time or in one relation
or at one place fair, at another time or in another relation or
at another place foul, as if fair to some and foul to others,
or in the likeness of a face or hands or any other part of the
bodily frame, or in any form of speech or knowledge, or
existing in any other being, as, for example, in an animal,
or in heaven, or in earth, or in any other place but beauty
absolute, separate, simple, and everlasting, which without
diminution and without increase, or any change, is imparted
to the ever-growing and perishing beauties of all other things.
He who from these ascending under the influence of true
love, begins to perceive that beauty, is not far from the
end. And the true order of going, or being led by another,
to the things of love, is to begin from the beauties of earth
and mount upwards for the sake of that other beauty, using

these as steps only, and from one going on to two, and from two to all fair forms, and from fair forms to fair practices, and from fair practices to fair notions, until from fair notions he arrives at the notion of absolute beauty, and at last knows what the essence of beauty is. This, my dear Socrates," said the stranger of Mantineia, "is that life above all others which man should live, in the contemplation of beauty absolute; a beauty which if you once beheld, you would see not to be after the measure of gold, and garments, and fair boys and youths, whose presence now entrances you; and you and many an one would be content to live seeing them only and conversing with them without meat or drink, if that were possible—you only want to look at them and to be with them. But what if the man had eyes to see the true beauty—the divine beauty, I mean, pure and clear and unalloyed, not clogged with the pollutions of mortality and all the colours and vanities of human life— thither looking, and holding converse with the true beauty simple and divine? Remember how in that communion only, beholding beauty with the eye of the mind, he will be enabled to bring forth, not images of beauty, but realities (for he has hold not of an image but of a reality), and bring- ing forth and nourishing true virtue to become the friend of God and be immortal, if mortal man may. Would that be an ignoble life?"

Such, Phaedrus—and I speak not only to you, but to all of you—were the words of Diotima; and I am persuaded of their truth. And being persuaded of them, I try to per- suade others, that in the attainment of this end human nature will not easily find a helper better than love. And therefore, also, I say that every man ought to honour him as I myself honour him, and walk in his ways, and exhort others to do the same, and praise the power and spirit of love according to the measure of my ability now and ever.

The words which I have spoken, you, Phaedrus, may call an encomium of love, or anything else which you please.

When Socrates had done speaking, the company applauded, and Aristophanes was beginning to say something
in answer to the allusion which Socrates had made to his
own speech, when suddenly there was a great knocking at
the door of the house, as of revellers, and the sound of a
flute-girl was heard. Agathon told the attendants to go and
see who were the intruders. "If they are friends of ours,"
he said, "invite them in, but if not, say that the drinking is
over." A little while afterwards they heard the voice of
Alcibiades resounding in the court; he was in a great state
of intoxication, and kept roaring and shouting "Where is
Agathon? Lead me to Agathon," and at length, supported
by the flute-girl and some of his attendants, he found his
way to them. "Hail, friends," he said, appearing at the door
crowned with a massive garland of ivy and violets, his head
flowing with ribands. "Will you have a very drunken man
as a companion of your revels? Or shall I crown Agathon,
which was my intention in coming, and go away? For I was
unable to come yesterday, and therefore I am here to-day,
carrying on my head these ribands, that taking them from
my own head, I may crown the head of this fairest and
wisest of men, as I may be allowed to call him. Will you
laugh at me because I am drunk? Yet I know very well that
I am speaking the truth, although you may laugh. But first
tell me; if I come in shall we have the understanding of
which I spoke? Will you drink with me or not?"

The company were vociferous in begging that he would
take his place among them, and Agathon specially invited
him. Thereupon he was led in by the people who were with
him; and as he was being led, intending to crown Agathon,
he took the ribands from his own head and held them in
front of his eyes; he was thus prevented from seeing Socrates, who made way for him, and Alcibiades took the
vacant place between Agathon and Socrates, and in taking
the place he embraced Agathon and crowned him. Take

off his sandals, said Agathon, and let him make a third on the same couch.

By all means; but who makes the third partner in our revels? said Alcibiades, turning round and starting up as he caught sight of Socrates. By Heracles, he said, what is this? here is Socrates always lying in wait for me, and always, as his way is, coming out at all sorts of unsuspected places: and now, what have you to say for yourself, and why are you lying here, where I perceive that you have contrived to find a place, not by a joker or lover of jokes, like Aristoph-anes, but by the fairest of the company.

Socrates turned to Agathon and said: I must ask you to protect me, Agathon; for the passion of this man has grown quite a serious matter to me. Since I became his admirer I have never been allowed to speak to any other fair one, or so much as to look at them. If I do, he goes wild with envy and jealousy, and not only abuses me but can hardly keep his hands off me, and at this moment he may do me some harm. Please to see to this, and either reconcile me to him, or, if he attempts violence, protect me, as I am in bodily fear of his mad and passionate attempts.

There can never be reconciliation between you and me, said Alcibiades; but for the present I will defer your chas-tisement. And I must beg you, Agathon, to give me back some of the ribands that I may crown the marvellous head of this universal despot—I would not have him complain of me for crowning you, and neglecting him, who in con-versation is the conqueror of all mankind; and this not only once, as you were the day before yesterday, but always. Whereupon, taking some of the ribands, he crowned Soc-rates, and again reclined.

Then he said: You seem, my friends, to be sober, which is a thing not to be endured; you must drink—for that was the agreement under which I was admitted—and I elect myself master of the feast until you are well drunk. Let

us have a large goblet, Agathon, or rather, he said, addressing the attendant, bring me that wine-cooler. The wine-
cooler which had caught his eye was a vessel holding more
than two quarts—this he filled and emptied, and bade the
attendant fill it again for Socrates. Observe, my friends,
said Alcibiades, that this ingenious trick of mine will have
no effect on Socrates, for he can drink any quantity of
wine and not be at all nearer being drunk. Socrates drank
the cup which the attendant filled for him.

Eryximachus said: What is this, Alcibiades? Are we to
have neither conversation nor singing over our cups; but
simply to drink as if we were thirsty?

Alcibiades replied: Hail, worthy son of a most wise and
worthy sire!

The same to you, said Eryximachus; but what shall we do?

That I leave to you, said Alcibiades.

"The wise physician skilled our wounds to heal"[1]

shall prescribe and we will obey. What do you want?

Well, said Eryximachus, before you appeared we had
passed a resolution that each one of us in turn should make
a speech in praise of love, and as good a one as he could:
the turn was passed round from left to right; and as all of
us have spoken, and you have not spoken but have well
drunken, you ought to speak, and then impose upon Socrates any task which you please, and he on his right-hand
neighbour, and so on.

That is good, Eryximachus, said Alcibiades; and yet the
comparison of a drunken man's speech with those of sober
men is hardly fair; and I should like to know, sweet friend,
whether you really believe what Socrates was just now
saying; for I can assure you that the very reverse is the
fact, and that if I praise any one but himself in his presence,
whether God or man, he will hardly keep his hands off me.

For shame, said Socrates.

[1] From Pope's Homer, Il. xi. 514.

Hold your tongue, said Alcibiades, for by Poseidon, there is no one else whom I will praise when you are of the company.

Well, then, said Eryximachus, if you like, praise Socrates.

What do you think, Eryximachus? said Alcibiades: shall I attack him and inflict the punishment before you all?

What are you about? said Socrates; are you going to raise a laugh at my expense? Is that the meaning of your praise?

I am going to speak the truth, if you will permit me.

I not only permit, but exhort you to speak the truth.

Then I will begin at once, said Alcibiades, and if I say anything which is not true, you may interrupt me if you will, and say "That is a lie," though my intention is to speak the truth. But you must not wonder if I speak anyhow as things come into my mind; for the fluent and orderly enumeration of all your singularities is not a task which is easy to a man in my condition.

And now, my boys, I shall praise Socrates in a figure which will appear to him to be a caricature, and yet I speak, not to make fun of him, but only for the truth's sake. I say, that he is exactly like the busts of Silenus, which are set up in the statuaries' shops, holding pipes and flutes in their mouths; and they are made to open in the middle, and have images of gods inside them. I say also that he is like Marsyas the satyr. You yourself will not deny, Socrates, that your face is like that of a satyr. Aye, and there is a resemblance in other points too. For example, you are a bully, as I can prove by witnesses, if you will not confess. And are you not a flute-player? That you are, and a performer far more wonderful than Marsyas. He indeed with instruments used to charm the souls of men by the power of his breath, and the players of his music do so still: for the melodies of Olympus[1] are derived from Marsyas who taught them, and these,

[1] Cp. Arist. Pol. viii. 5. 16.

whether they are played by a great master or by a miserable flute-girl, have a power which no others have; they alone possess the soul and reveal the wants of those who have need of gods and mysteries, because they are divine. But you produce the same effect with your words only, and do not require the flute: that is the difference between you and him. When we hear any other speaker, even a very good one, he produces absolutely no effect upon us, or not much, whereas the mere fragments of you and your words, even at second-hand, and however imperfectly repeated, amaze and possess the souls of every man, woman, and child who comes within hearing of them. And if I were not afraid that you would think me hopelessly drunk, I would have sworn as well as spoken to the influence which they have always had and still have over me. For my heart leaps within me more than that of any Corybantian reveller, and my eyes rain tears when I hear them. And I observe that many others are affected in the same manner. I have heard Pericles and other great orators, and I thought that they spoke well, but I never had any similar feeling; my soul was not stirred by them, nor was I angry at the thought of my own slavish state. But this Marsyas has often brought me to such a pass, that I have felt as if I could hardly endure the life which I am leading (this, Socrates, you will admit); and I am conscious that if I did not shut my ears against him, and fly as from the voice of the siren, my fate would be like that of others,—he would transfix me, and I should grow old sitting at his feet. For he makes me confess that I ought not to live as I do, neglecting the wants of my own soul, and busying myself with the concerns of the Athenians; therefore I hold my ears and tear myself away from him. And he is the only person who ever made me ashamed, which you might think not to be in my nature, and there is no one else who does the same. For I know that I cannot answer him or say that I ought not to do as he bids, but when I leave his presence the love of popularity gets the better of

me. And therefore I run away and fly from him, and when I
see him I am ashamed of what I have confessed to him.
Many a time have I wished that he were dead, and yet I
know that I should be much more sorry than glad, if he were
to die: so that I am at my wit's end.

And this is what I and many others have suffered from
the flute-playing of this satyr. Yet hear me once more while
I show you how exact the image is, and how marvellous his
power. For let me tell you; none of you know him; but I
will reveal him to you; having begun, I must go on. See you
how fond he is of the fair? He is always with them and is
always being smitten by them, and then again he knows
nothing and is ignorant of all things—such is the appearance
which he puts on. Is he not like a Silenus in this? To be sure
he is: his outer mask is the carved head of the Silenus; but,
O my companions in drink, when he is opened, what temperance there is residing within! Know you that beauty and
wealth and honour, at which the many wonder, are of no
account with him, and are utterly despised by him: he regards not at all the persons who are gifted with them; mankind are nothing to him; all his life is spent in mocking
and flouting at them. But when I opened him, and looked
within at his serious purpose, I saw in him divine and golden
images of such fascinating beauty that I was ready to do
in a moment whatever Socrates commanded: they may have
escaped the observation of others, but I saw them. Now I
fancied that he was seriously enamoured of my beauty, and
I thought that I should therefore have a grand opportunity
of hearing him tell what he knew, for I had a wonderful
opinion of the attractions of my youth. In the prosecution
of this design, when I next went to him, I sent away the
attendant who usually accompanied me (I will confess the
whole truth, and beg you to listen; and if I speak falsely,
do you, Socrates, expose the falsehood). Well, he and I were
alone together, and I thought that when there was nobody
with us, I should hear him speak the language which lovers

use to their loves when they are by themselves, and I was delighted. Nothing of the sort; he conversed as usual, and spent the day with me and then went away. Afterwards I challenged him to the palaestra; and he wrestled and closed with me several times when there was no one present; I fancied that I might succeed in this manner. Not a bit; I made no way with him. Lastly, as I had failed hitherto, I thought that I must take stronger measures and attack him boldly, and, as I had begun, not give him up, but see how matters stood between him and me. So I invited him to sup with me, just as if he were a fair youth, and I a designing lover. He was not easily persuaded to come; he did, however, after a while accept the invitation, and when he came the first time, he wanted to go away at once as soon as supper was over, and I had not the face to detain him. The second time, still in pursuance of my design, after we had supped, I went on conversing far into the night, and when he wanted to go away, I pretended that the hour was late and that he had much better remain. So he lay down on the couch next to me, the same on which he had supped, and there was no one but ourselves sleeping in the apartment. All this may be told without shame to any one. But what follows I could hardly tell you if I were sober. Yet as the proverb says, "In vino veritas," whether with boys, or without them;[1] and therefore I must speak. Nor, again, should I be justified in concealing the lofty actions of Socrates when I come to praise him. Moreover, I have felt the serpent's sting; and he who has suffered, as they say, is willing to tell his fellow-sufferers only, as they alone will be likely to understand him, and will not be extreme in judging of the sayings or doings which have been wrung from his agony. For I have been bitten by a more than viper's tooth; I have known in my soul, or in my heart, or in some other part, that worst of pangs, more violent in ingenuous youth than any serpent's

[1] In allusion to the two proverbs, οἶνος καὶ παῖδες ἀληθεῖς, and οἶνος καὶ ἀλήθεια.

tooth, the pang of philosophy, which will make a man say
or do anything. And you whom I see around me, Phaedrus
and Agathon and Eryximachus and Pausanias and Aristodemus and Aristophanes, all of you, and I need not say Socrates himself, have had experience of the same madness and
passion in your longing after wisdom. Therefore listen and
excuse my doings then and my sayings now. But let the
attendants and other profane and unmannered persons close
up the doors of their ears.

When the lamp was put out and the servants had gone
away, I thought that I must be plain with him and have no
more ambiquity. So I gave him a shake, and I said: "Socrates, are you asleep?" "No," he said. "Do you know what
I am meditating?" "What are you meditating?" he said.
"I think," I replied, "that of all the lovers whom I have
ever had you are the only one who is worthy of me, and you
appear to be too modest to speak. Now I feel that I should
be a fool to refuse you this or any other favour, and therefore I come to lay at your feet all that I have and all that
my friends have, in the hope that you will assist me in the
way of virtue, which I desire above all things, and in which
I believe that you can help me better than any one else.
And I should certainly have more reason to be ashamed of
what wise men would say if I were to refuse a favour to such
as you, than of what the world, who are mostly fools, would
say of me if I granted it." To these words he replied in the
ironical manner which is so characteristic of him:—"O
Alcibiades, my friend, you have indeed an elevated aim if
what you say is true, and if there really is in me any power
by which you may become better; truly you must see in
me some rare beauty of a kind infinitely higher than any
which I see in you. And therefore, if you mean to share with
me and to exchange beauty for beauty, you will have greatly
the advantage of me; you will gain true beauty in return for
appearance—like Diomede, gold in exchange for brass. But
look again, sweet friend, and see whether you are not de-

ceived in me. The mind begins to grow critical when the bodily eye fails, and it will be a long time before you get old." Hearing this, I said: "I have told you my purpose, which is quite serious, and do you consider what you think best for you and me." "That is good," he said; "at some other time then we will consider and act as seems best about this and about other matters." Whereupon, I fancied that he was smitten, and that the words which I had uttered like arrows had wounded him, and so without waiting to hear more I got up, and throwing my coat about him crept under his threadbare cloak, as the time of year was winter, and there I lay during the whole night having this wonderful monster in my arms. This again, Socrates, will not be denied by you. And yet, notwithstanding all, he was so superior to my solicitations, so contemptuous and derisive and disdainful of my beauty—which really, as I fancied, had some attractions—hear, O judges; for judges you shall be of the haughty virtue of Socrates—nothing more happened, but in the morning when I awoke (let all the gods and goddesses be my witnesses) I arose as from the couch of a father or an elder brother.

What do you suppose must have been my feelings, after this rejection, at the thought of my own dishonour? And yet I could not help wondering at his natural temperance and self-restraint and manliness. I never imagined that I could have met with a man such as he is in wisdom and endurance. And therefore I could not be angry with him or renounce his company, any more than I could hope to win him. For I well knew that if Ajax could not be wounded by steel, much less he by money; and my only chance of captivating him by my personal attractions had failed. So I was at my wit's end: no one was ever more hopelessly enslaved by another. All this happened before he and I went on the expedition to Potidaea; there we messed together, and I had the opportunity of observing his extraordinary power of sustaining fatigue. His endurance was simply marvellous

when, being cut off from our supplies, we were compelled to
go without food—on such occasions, which often happen
in time of war, he was superior not only to me but to everybody; there was no one to be compared to him. Yet at a
festival he was the only person who had any real powers of
enjoyment; though not willing to drink, he could if compelled beat us all at that,—wonderful to relate! no human
being had ever seen Socrates drunk; and his powers, if I
am not mistaken, will be tested before long. His fortitude
in enduring cold was also surprising. There was a severe
frost, for the winter in that region is really tremendous, and
everybody else either remained indoors, or if they went out
had on an amazing quantity of clothes, and were well shod,
and had their feet swathed in felt and fleeces: in the midst
of this, Socrates with his bare feet on the ice and in his
ordinary dress marched better than the other soldiers who
had shoes, and they looked daggers at him because he seemed
to despise them.

I have told you one tale, and now I must tell you another,
which is worth hearing,

"Of the doings and sufferings of the enduring man"

while he was on the expedition. One morning he was thinking
about something which he could not resolve; he would not
give it up, but continued thinking from early dawn until
noon—there he stood fixed in thought; and at noon attention
was drawn to him, and the rumour ran through the wondering crowd that Socrates had been standing and thinking
about something ever since the break of day. At last, in the
evening after supper, some Ionians out of curiosity (I should
explain that this was not in winter but in summer), brought
out their mats and slept in the open air that they might
watch him and see whether he would stand all night. There
he stood until the following morning; and with the return
of light he offered up a prayer to the sun, and went his

way. I will also tell, if you please—and indeed I am bound
to tell—of his courage in battle; for who but he saved my
life? Now this was the engagement in which I received the
prize of valour: for I was wounded and he would not leave
me, but he rescued me and my arms; and he ought to have
received the prize of valour which the generals wanted to
confer on me partly on account of my rank, and I told them
so (this, again, Socrates will not impeach or deny), but he
was more eager than the generals that I and not he should
have the prize. There was another occasion on which his
behaviour was very remarkable—in the flight of the army
after the battle of Delium, where he served among the
heavy-armed,—I had a better opportunity of seeing him
than at Potidaea, for I was myself on horseback, and therefore comparatively out of danger. He and Laches were re-
treating, for the troops were in flight, and I met them and
told them not to be discouraged, and promised to remain
with them; and there you might see him, Aristophanes, as
you describe,[1] just as he is in the streets of Athens, stalking
like a pelican, and rolling his eyes, calmly contemplating
enemies as well as friends, and making very intelligible to
anybody, even from a distance, that whoever attacked him
would be likely to meet with a stout resistance; and in this
way he and his companion escaped—for this is the sort of
man who is never touched in war; those only are pursued
who are running away headlong. I particularly observed
how superior he was to Laches in presence of mind. Many
are the marvels which I might narrate in praise of Socrates;
most of his ways might perhaps be paralleled in another
man, but his absolute unlikeness to any human being that
is or ever has been is perfectly astonishing. You may imagine
Brasidas and others to have been like Achilles; or you may
imagine Nestor and Antenor to have been like Pericles; and
the same may be said of other famous men, but of this
strange being you will never be able to find any likeness,

[1] Aristoph. Clouds, 362.

however remote, either among men who now are or who ever have been—other than that which I have already suggested of Silenus and the satyrs; and they represent in a figure not only himself, but his words. For, although I forgot to mention this to you before, his words are like the images of Silenus which open; they are ridiculous when you first hear them; he clothes himself in language that is like the skin of the wanton satyr—for his talk is of pack-asses and smiths and cobblers and curriers, and he is always repeating the same things in the same words,[1] so that any ignorant or inexperienced person might feel disposed to laugh at him; but he who opens the bust and sees what is within will find that they are the only words which have a meaning in them, and also of the most divine, abounding in fair images of virtue, and of the widest comprehension, or rather extending to the whole duty of a good and honourable man.

This, friends, is my praise of Socrates. I have added my blame of him for his ill-treatment of me; and he has ill-treated not only me, but Charmides the son of Glaucon, and Euthydemus the son of Diocles, and many others in the same way—beginning as their lover he has ended by making them pay their addresses to him. Wherefore I say to you, Agathon, "Be not deceived by him; learn from me and take warning, and do not be a fool and learn by experience, as the proverb says."

When Alcibiades had finished, there was a laugh at his outspokenness; for he seemed to be still in love with Socrates. You are sober, Alcibiades, said Socrates, or you would never have gone so far about to hide the purpose of your satyr's praises, for all this long story is only an ingenious circumlocution, of which the point comes in by the way at the end; you want to get up a quarrel between me and Agathon, and your notion is that I ought to love you and nobody else, and that you and you only ought to love Agathon. But the plot of this Satyric or Silenic drama has

[1] Cp. Gorg. 490, 491, 517.

been detected, and you must not allow him, Agathon, to set us at variance.

I believe you are right, said Agathon, and I am disposed to think that his intention in placing himself between you and me was only to divide us; but he shall gain nothing by that move; for I will go and lie on the couch next to you.

Yes, yes, replied Socrates, by all means come here and lie on the couch below me.

Alas, said Alcibiades, how I am fooled by this man; he is determined to get the better of me at every turn. I do beseech you, allow Agathon to lie between us.

Certainly not, said Socrates; as you praised me, and I in turn ought to praise my neighbour on the right, he will be out of order in praising me again when he ought rather to be praised by me, and I must entreat you to consent to this, and not be jealous, for I have a great desire to praise the youth.

Hurrah! cried Agathon, I will rise instantly, that I may be praised by Socrates.

The usual way, said Alcibiades; where Socrates is, no one else has any chance with the fair; and now how readily has he invented a specious reason for attracting Agathon to himself.

Agathon arose in order that he might take his place on the couch by Socrates, when suddenly a band of revellers entered, and spoiled the order of the banquet. Some one who was going out having left the door open, they had found their way in, and made themselves at home; great confusion ensued, and every one was compelled to drink large quantities of wine. Aristodemus said that Eryximachus, Phaedrus, and others went away—he himself fell asleep, and as the nights were long took a good rest: he was awakened towards daybreak by a crowing of cocks, and when he awoke, the others were either asleep, or had gone away; there remained only Socrates, Aristophanes, and Agathon, who were drinking out of a large goblet which they passed round, and Socrates was discoursing to them. Aristodemus was only half awake, and he did not hear the beginning of the discourse; the chief thing which he remembered was Socrates compelling the other two to acknowledge that the genius of comedy was the same with that of tragedy, and that the true artist in tragedy was an artist in comedy also. To this they were constrained to assent, being drowsy, and not quite following the argument. And first of all Aristophanes dropped off, then, when the day was already dawning, Agathon. Socrates, having laid them to sleep, rose to depart; Aristodemus, as his manner was, following him. At the Lyceum he took a bath, and passed the day as usual. In the evening he retired to rest at his own home.

THE REPUBLIC

THE REPUBLIC

BOOK V

Such is the good and true City or State, and the good and true man is of the same pattern; and if this is right every other is wrong; and the evil is one which affects not only the ordering of the State, but also the regulation of the individual soul, and is exhibited in four forms.

What are they? he said.

I was proceeding to tell the order in which the four evil forms appeared to me to succeed one another, when Polemarchus, who was sitting a little way off, just beyond Adeimantus, began to whisper to him: stretching forth his hand, he took hold of the upper part of his coat by the shoulder, and drew him towards him, leaning forward himself so as to be quite close and saying something in his ear, of which I only caught the words, "Shall we let him off, or what shall we do?"

Certainly not, said Adeimantus, raising his voice.

Who is it, I said, whom you are refusing to let off?

You, he said.

I repeated,[1] Why am I especially not to be let off?

Why, he said, we think that you are lazy, and mean to cheat us out of a whole chapter which is a very important part of the story; and you fancy that we shall not notice your airy way of proceeding; as if it were self-evident to everybody, that in the matter of women and children "friends have all things in common."

And was I not right, Adeimantus?

Yes, he said; but what is right in this particular case, like

[1] Reading ἔτι ἐγὼ εἶπον.

everything else, requires to be explained; for community may be of many kinds. Please, therefore, to say what sort of community you mean. We have been long expecting that you would tell us something about the family life of your citizens—how they will bring children into the world, and rear them when they have arrived, and, in general, what is the nature of this community of women and children—for we are of opinion that the right or wrong management of such matters will have a great and paramount influence on the State for good or for evil. And now, since the question is still undetermined, and you are taking in hand another State, we have resolved, as you heard, not to let you go until you give an account of all this.

To that resolution, said Glaucon, you may regard me as saying Agreed.

And without more ado, said Thrasymachus, you may consider us all to be equally agreed.

I said, You know not what you are doing in thus assailing me: What an argument are you raising about the State! Just as I thought that I had finished, and was only too glad that I had laid this question to sleep, and was reflecting how fortunate I was in your acceptance of what I then said, you ask me to begin again at the very foundation, ignorant of what a hornet's nest of words you are stirring. Now I foresaw this gathering trouble, and avoided it.

For what purpose do you conceive that we have come here, said Thrasymachus,—to look for gold, or to hear discourse?

Yes, but discourse should have a limit.

Yes, Socrates, said Glaucon, and the whole of life is the only limit which wise men assign to the hearing of such discourses. But never mind about us; take heart yourself and answer the question in your own way: What sort of community of women and children is this which is to prevail among our guardians? and how shall we manage the period between birth and education, which seems to require the greatest care? Tell us how these things will be.

Yes, my simple friend, but the answer is the reverse of easy; many more doubts arise about this than about our previous conclusions. For the practicability of what is said may be doubted; and looked at in another point of view, whether the scheme, if ever so practicable, would be for the best, is also doubtful. Hence I feel a reluctance to approach the subject, lest our aspiration, my dear friend, should turn out to be a dream only.

Fear not, he replied, for your audience will not be hard upon you; they are not sceptical or hostile.

I said: My good friend, I suppose that you mean to encourage me by these words.

Yes, he said.

Then let me tell you that you are doing just the reverse; the encouragement which you offer would have been all very well had I myself believed that I knew what I was talking about: to declare the truth about matters of high interest which a man honours and loves among wise men who love him need occasion no fear of faltering in his mind; but to carry on an argument when you are yourself only a hesitating enquirer, which is my condition, is a dangerous and slippery thing; and the danger is not that I shall be laughed at (of which the fear would be childish), but that I shall miss the truth where I have most need to be sure of my footing, and drag my friends after me in my fall. And I pray Nemesis not to visit upon me the words which I am going to utter. For I do indeed believe that to be an involuntary homicide is a less crime than to be a deceiver about beauty or goodness or justice in the matter of laws.[1] And that is a risk which I would rather run among enemies than among friends, and therefore you do well to encourage me.[2]

[1] Or inserting καὶ before νομίμων: "a deceiver about beauty or goodness or principles of justice or law."
[2] Reading ὥστε εὖ με παραμυθεῖ.

Glaucon laughed and said: Well, then, Socrates, in case you and your argument do us any serious injury you shall be acquitted beforehand of the homicide, and shall not be held to be a deceiver; take courage then and speak.

Well, I said, the law says that when a man is acquitted he is free from guilt, and what holds at law may hold in argument.

Then why should you mind?

Well, I replied, I suppose that I must retrace my steps and say what I perhaps ought to have said before in the proper place. The part of the men has been played out, and now properly enough comes the turn of the women. Of them I will proceed to speak, and the more readily since I am invited by you.

For men born and educated like our citizens, the only way, in my opinion, of arriving at a right conclusion about the possession and use of women and children is to follow the path on which we originally started, when we said that the men were to be the guardians and watchdogs of the herd.

True.

Let us further suppose the birth and education of our women to be subject to similar or nearly similar regulations; then we shall see whether the result accords with our design.

What do you mean?

What I mean may be put into the form of a question, I said: Are dogs divided into hes and shes, or do they both share equally in hunting and in keeping watch and in the other duties of dogs? or do we entrust to the males the entire and exclusive care of the flocks, while we leave the females at home, under the idea that the bearing and suckling their puppies is labour enough for them?

No, he said, they share alike; the only difference between them is that the males are stronger and the females weaker.

But can you use different animals for the same purpose, unless they are bred and fed in the same way?

You cannot.

Then, if women are to have the same duties as men, they must have the same nurture and education?

Yes.

The education which was assigned to the men was music and gymnastic.

Yes.

Then women must be taught music and gymnastic and also the art of war, which they must practise like the men?

That is the inference, I suppose.

I should rather expect, I said, that several of our proposals, if they are carried out, being unusual, may appear ridiculous.

No doubt of it.

Yes, and the most ridiculous thing of all will be the sight of women naked in the palaestra, exercising with the men, especially when they are no longer young; they certainly will not be a vision of beauty, any more than the enthusiastic old men who in spite of wrinkles and ugliness continue to frequent the gymnasia.

Yes, indeed, he said: according to present notions the proposal would be thought ridiculous.

But then, I said, as we have determined to speak our minds, we must not fear the jests of the wits which will be directed against this sort of innovation; how they will talk of women's attainments both in music and gymnastic, and above all about their wearing armour and riding upon horseback!

Very true, he replied.

Yet having begun we must go forward to the rough places of the law; at the same time begging of these gentlemen for once in their life to be serious. Not long ago, as we shall remind them, the Hellenes were of the opinion, which is still generally received among the barbarians, that the sight of a naked man was ridiculous and improper; and when first the Cretans and then the Lacedaemonians introduced the custom, the wits of that day might equally have ridiculed the innovation.

No doubt.

But when experience showed that to let all things be uncovered was far better than to cover them up, and the ludicrous effect to the outward eye vanished before the better principle which reason asserted, then the man was perceived to be a fool who directs the shafts of his ridicule at any other sight but that of folly and vice, or seriously inclines to weigh the beautiful by any other standard but that of the good.[1]

Very true, he replied.

First, then, whether the question is to be put in jest or in earnest, let us come to an understanding about the nature of woman: Is she capable of sharing either wholly or partially in the actions of men, or not at all? And is the art of war one of those arts in which she can or can not share? That will be the best way of commencing the enquiry, and will probably lead to the fairest conclusion.

That will be much the best way.

Shall we take the other side first and begin by arguing against ourselves; in this manner the adversary's position will not be undefended.

Why not? he said.

Then let us put a speech into the mouths of our opponents. They will say: "Socrates and Glaucon, no adversary need convict you, for you yourselves, at the first foundation of the State, admitted the principle that everybody was to do the one work suited to his own nature." And certainly, if I am not mistaken, such an admission was made by us. "And do not the natures of men and women differ very much indeed?" And we shall reply: Of course they do. Then we shall be asked, "Whether the tasks assigned to men and to women should not be different, and such as are agreeable to their different natures?" Certainly they should. "But if so,

[1] Reading with Paris A. καὶ καλοῦ . . .

have you not fallen into a serious inconsistency in saying
that men and women, whose natures are so entirely different,
ought to perform the same actions?"—What defence will
you make for us, my good sir, against any one who offers
these objections?

That is not an easy question to answer when asked
suddenly; and I shall and I do beg of you to draw out the
case on our side.

These are the objections, Glaucon, and there are many
others of a like kind, which I foresaw long ago; they made
me afraid and reluctant to take in hand any law about the
possession and nurture of women and children.

By Zeus, he said, the problem to be solved is anything but
easy.

Why, yes, I said, but the fact is that when a man is out
of his depth, whether he has fallen into a little swimming-
bath or into mid-ocean, he has to swim all the same.

Very true.

And must not we swim and try to reach the shore: we will
hope that Arion's dolphin or some other miraculous help
may save us?

I suppose so, he said.

Well, then, let us see if any way of escape can be found.
We acknowledged—did we not?—that different natures
ought to have different pursuits, and that men's and women's
natures are different. And now what are we saying?—that
different natures ought to have the same pursuits,—this is
the inconsistency which is charged upon us.

Precisely.

Verily, Glaucon, I said, glorious is the power of the art
of contradiction!

Why do you say so?

Because I think that many a man falls into the practice
against his will. When he thinks that he is reasoning he is
really disputing, just because he cannot define and divide,

and so know that of which he is speaking; and he will pursue a merely verbal opposition in the spirit of contention and not of fair discussion.

Yes, he replied, such is very often the case; but what has that to do with us and our argument?

A great deal; for there is certainly a danger of our getting unintentionally into a verbal opposition.

In what way?

Why, we valiantly and pugnaciously insist upon the verbal truth, that different natures ought to have different pursuits, but we never considered at all what was the meaning of sameness or difference of nature, or why we distinguished them when we assigned different pursuits to different natures and the same to the same natures.

Why, no, he said, that was never considered by us.

I said: Suppose that by way of illustration we were to ask the question whether there is not an opposition in nature between bald men and hairy men; and if this is admitted by us, then, if bald men are cobblers, we should forbid the hairy men to be cobblers and conversely?

That would be a jest, he said.

Yes, I said, a jest; and why? because we never meant when we constructed the State, that the opposition of natures should extend to every difference, but only to those differences which affected the pursuit in which the individual is engaged; we should have argued, for example, that a physician and one who is in mind a physician[1] may be said to have the same nature.

True.

Whereas the physician and the carpenter have different natures?

Certainly.

And if, I said, the male and female sex appear to differ in their fitness for any art or pursuit, we should say that such pursuit or art ought to be assigned to one or the other

---

[1] Reading ἰατρὸν μὲν καὶ ἰατρικὸν τὴν ψυχὴν ὄντα.

of them; but if the difference consist only in women bearing and men begetting children, this does not amount to a proof that a woman differs from a man in respect of the sort of education she should receive; and we shall therefore continue to maintain that our guardians and their wives ought to have the same pursuits.

Very true, he said.

Next, we shall ask our opponent how, in reference to any of the pursuits or arts of civic life, the nature of a woman differs from that of a man?

That will be quite fair.

And perhaps he, like yourself, will reply that to give a sufficient answer on the instant is not easy; but after a little reflection there is no difficulty.

Yes, perhaps.

Suppose, then, that we invite him to accompany us in the argument, and then we may hope to show him that there is nothing peculiar in the constitution of women which would affect them in the administration of the State.

By all means.

Let us say to him: Come, now, and we will ask you a question:—when you spoke of a nature gifted or not gifted in any respect, did you mean to say that one man will acquire a thing easily, another with difficulty; a little learning will lead the one to discover a great deal; whereas the other, after much study and application, no sooner learns than he forgets; or again, did you mean, that the one has a body which is a good servant to his mind, while the body of the other is a hindrance to him?—would not these be the sort of differences which distinguish the man gifted by nature from the one who is ungifted?

No one will deny that.

And can you mention any pursuit of mankind in which the male sex has not all these gifts and qualities in a higher degree than the female? Need I waste time in speaking of the art of weaving, and the management of pancakes and preserves, in which womankind does really appear to be great, and in which for her to be beaten by a man is of all things the most absurd?

You are quite right, he replied, in maintaining the general inferiority of the female sex: although many women are in many things superior to many men, yet on the whole what you say is true.

And if so, my friend, I said, there is no special faculty of administration in a State which a woman has because she is a woman, or which a man has by virtue of his sex, but the gifts of nature are alike diffused in both; all the pursuits of men are the pursuits of women also, but in all of them a woman is inferior to a man.

Very true.

Then are we to impose all our enactments on men and none of them on women?

That will never do.

One woman has a gift of healing, another not; one is a musician, and another has no music in her nature?

Very true.

And one woman has a turn for gymnastic and military exercises, and another is unwarlike and hates gymnastics?

Certainly.

And one woman is a philosopher, and another is an enemy of philosophy; one has spirit, and another is without spirit?

That is also true.

Then one woman will have the temper of a guardian, and another not. Was not the selection of the male guardians determined by differences of this sort?

Yes.

Men and women alike possess the qualities which make a guardian; they differ only in their comparative strength or weakness.

Obviously.

And those women who have such qualities are to be selected as the companions and colleagues of men who have similar qualities and whom they resemble in capacity and in character?

Very true.

And ought not the same natures to have the same pursuits?

They ought.

Then, as we were saying before, there is nothing unnatural in assigning music and gymnastic to the wives of the guardians—to that point we come round again.

Certainly not.

The law which we then enacted was agreeable to nature, and therefore not an impossibility or mere aspiration; and the contrary practice, which prevails at present, is in reality a violation of nature.

That appears to be true.

We had to consider, first, whether our proposals were possible, and secondly whether they were the most beneficial?

Yes.

And the possibility had been acknowledged?

Yes.

The very great benefit has next to be established?

Quite so.

You will admit that the same education which makes a man a good guardian will make a woman a good guardian; for their original nature is the same?

Yes.

I should like to ask you a question.

What is it?

Would you say that all men are equal in excellence, or is one man better than another?

The latter.

And in the commonwealth which we were founding do you conceive the guardians who have been brought up on our model system to be more perfect men, or the cobblers whose education has been cobbling?

What a ridiculous question!

You have answered me, I replied: Well, and may we not further say that our guardians are the best of our citizens?

By far the best.

And will not their wives be the best women?

Yes, by far the best.

And can there be anything better for the interests of the State than that the men and women of a State should be as good as possible?

There can be nothing better.

And this is what the arts of music and gymnastic, when present in such manner as we have described, will accomplish?

Certainly.

Then we have made an enactment not only possible but in the highest degree beneficial to the State?

True.

Then let the wives of our guardians strip, for their virtue will be their robe, and let them share in the toils of war and the defence of their country; only in the distribution of labours the lighter are to be assigned to the women, who are the weaker natures, but in other respects their duties are to be the same. And as for the man who laughs at naked women exercising their bodies from the best of motives, in his laughter he is plucking

"A fruit of unripe wisdom,"

and he himself is ignorant of what he is laughing at, or what he is about;—for that is, and ever will be, the best of sayings, *That the useful is the noble and the hurtful is the base.*

Very true.

Here, then, is one difficulty in our law about women, which we may say that we have now escaped; the wave has not swallowed us up alive for enacting that the guardians of either sex should have all their pursuits in common; to the utility and also to the possibility of this arrangement the consistency of the argument with itself bears witness.

Yes, that was a mighty wave which you have escaped.

Yes, I said, but a greater is coming; you will not think much of this when you see the next.

Go on; let me see.

The law, I said, which is the sequel of this and of all that has preceded, is to the following effect,—"that the wives of our guardians are to be common, and their children are to be common, and no parent is to know his own child, nor any child his parent."

Yes, he said, that is a much greater wave than the other; and the possibility as well as the utility of such a law are far more questionable.

I do not think, I said, that there can be any dispute about the very great utility of having wives and children in common; the possibility is quite another matter, and will be very much disputed.

I think that a good many doubts may be raised about both.

You imply that the two questions must be combined, I replied. Now I meant that you should admit the utility; and in this way, as I thought, I should escape from one of them, and then there would remain only the possibility.

But that little attempt is detected, and therefore you will please to give a defence of both.

Well, I said, I submit to my fate. Yet grant me a little favour: let me feast my mind with the dream as day-dreamers are in the habit of feasting themselves when they are walking alone; for before they have discovered any means of effecting their wishes—that is a matter which never troubles them—they would rather not tire themselves by thinking about possibilities; but assuming that what they desire is already granted to them, they proceed with their plan, and delight in detailing what they mean to do when their wish has come true—that is a way which they have of not doing much good to a capacity which was never good for much. Now I myself am beginning to lose heart, and I should like, with your permission, to pass over the question of possibilities at present. Assuming therefore the possibility of the proposal, I shall now proceed to enquire how the rulers will carry out these arrangements, and I shall demonstrate that our plan, if executed, will be of the greatest benefit to the State and to the guardians. First of all, then, if you have no objection, I will endeavour with your help to consider the advantages of the measure; and hereafter the question of possibility.

I have no objection; proceed.

First, I think that if our rulers and their auxiliaries are to be worthy of the name which they bear, there must be willingness to obey in the one and the power of command in the other; the guardians must themselves obey the laws, and they must also imitate the spirit of them in any details which are entrusted to their care.

That is right, he said.

You, I said, who are their legislator, having selected the men, will now select the women and give them to them;— they must be as far as possible of like natures with them; and they must live in common houses and meet at common meals. None of them will have anything specially his or her own; they will be together, and will be brought up together, and will associate at gymnastic exercises. And so they will be drawn by a necessity of their natures to have intercourse with each other—necessity is not too strong a word, I think?

Yes, he said;—necessity, not geometrical, but another sort of necessity which lovers know, and which is far more convincing and constraining to the mass of mankind.

True, I said; and this, Glaucon, like all the rest, must proceed after an orderly fashion; in a city of the blessed, licentiousness is an unholy thing which the rulers will forbid.

Yes, he said, and it ought not to be permitted.

Then clearly the next thing will be to make matrimony sacred in the highest degree, and what is most beneficial will be deemed sacred?

Exactly.

And how can marriages be made most beneficial?—that is a question which I put to you, because I see in your house dogs for hunting, and of the nobler sort of birds not a few. Now, I beseech you, do tell me, have you ever attended to their pairing and breeding?

In what particulars?

Why, in the first place, although they are all of a good sort, are not some better than others?

True.

And do you breed from them all indifferently, or do you take care to breed from the best only?

From the best.

And do you take the oldest or the youngest, or only those of ripe age?

I choose only those of ripe age.

And if care was not taken in the breeding, your dogs and birds would greatly deteriorate?

Certainly.

And the same of horses and of animals in general?

Undoubtedly.

Good heavens! my dear friend, I said, what consummate skill will our rulers need if the same principle holds of the human species!

Certainly, the same principle holds; but why does this involve any particular skill?

Because, I said, our rulers will often have to practise upon the body corporate with medicines. Now you know that when patients do not require medicines, but have only to be put under a regimen, the inferior sort of practitioner is deemed to be good enough; but when medicine has to be given, then the doctor should be more of a man.

That is quite true, he said; but to what are you alluding?

I mean, I replied, that our rulers will find a considerable dose of falsehood and deceit necessary for the good of their subjects: we were saying that the use of all these things regarded as medicines might be of advantage.

And we were very right.

And this lawful use of them seems likely to be often needed in the regulations of marriages and births.

How so?

Why, I said, the principle has been already laid down that the best of either sex should be united with the best as often, and the inferior with the inferior, as seldom as possible; and that they should rear the offspring of the one sort of union, but not of the other, if the flock is to be maintained in first-rate condition. Now these goings-on must be a secret which the rulers only know, or there will be a further danger of our herd, as the guardians may be termed, breaking out into rebellion.

Very true.

Had we not better appoint certain festivals at which we will bring together the brides and bridegrooms, and sacrifices will be offered and suitable hymeneal songs composed by our poets: the number of weddings is a matter which must be left to the discretion of the rulers, whose aim will be to preserve the average of population? There are many other things which they will have to consider, such as the effects of wars and diseases and any similar agencies, in order as far as this is possible to prevent the State from becoming either too large or too small.

Certainly, he replied.

We shall have to invent some ingenious kind of lots which the less worthy may draw on each occasion of our bringing them together, and then they will accuse their own ill-luck and not the rulers.

To be sure, he said.

And I think that our braver and better youth, besides their other honours and rewards, might have greater facilities of intercourse with women given them; their bravery will be a reason, and such fathers ought to have as many sons as possible.

True.

And the proper officers, whether male or female or both, for offices are to be held by women as well as by men—

Yes—

The proper officers will take the offspring of the good parents to the pen or fold, and there they will deposit them with certain nurses who dwell in a separate quarter; but the offspring of the inferior, or of the better when they chance to be deformed, will be put away in some mysterious, unknown place, as they should be.

Yes, he said, that must be done if the breed of the guardians is to be kept pure.

They will provide for their nurture, and will bring the mothers to the fold when they are full of milk, taking the greatest possible care that no mother recognizes her own child; and other wet nurses may be engaged if more are required. Care will also be taken that the process of suckling shall not be protracted too long; and the mothers will have no getting up at night or other trouble, but will hand over all this sort of thing to the nurses and attendants.

You suppose the wives of our guardians to have a fine easy time of it when they are having children.

Why, said I, and so they ought. Let us, however, proceed with our scheme. We were saying that the parents should be in the prime of life?

Very true.

And what is the prime of life? May it not be defined as a period of abouty twenty years in a woman's life, and thirty in a man's?

Which years do you mean to include?

A woman, I said, at twenty years of age may begin to bear children to the State, and continue to bear them until forty; a man may begin at five-and-twenty, when he has passed the point at which the pulse of life beats quickest, and continue to beget children until he be fifty-five.

Certainly, he said, both in men and women those years are the prime of physical as well as of intellectual vigour.

Any one above or below the prescribed ages who takes part in the public hymeneals shall be said to have done an unholy and unrighteous thing; the child of which he is the father, if it steals into life, will have been conceived under auspices very unlike the sacrifices and prayers, which at each hymeneal priestesses and priests and the whole city will offer, that the new generation may be better and more useful than their good and useful parents, whereas his child will be the offspring of darkness and strange lust.

Very true, he replied.

And the same law will apply to any one of those within the prescribed age who forms a connexion with any woman in the prime of life without the sanction of the rulers; for we shall say that he is raising up a bastard to the State, un-certified and unconsecrated.

Very true, he replied.

This applies, however, only to those who are within the specified age: after that we allow them to range at will, ex-cept that a man may not marry his daughter or his daugh-ter's daughter, or his mother or his mother's mother; and women, on the other hand, are prohibited from marrying their sons or fathers, or son's son or father's father, and so on in either direction. And we grant all this, accompanying the permission with strict orders to prevent any embryo which may come into being from seeing the light; and if any force a way to the birth, the parents must understand that the offspring of such an union cannot be maintained, and arrange accordingly.

That also, he said, is a reasonable proposition. But how will they know who are fathers and daughters, and so on?

They will never know. The way will be this:—dating

from the day of the hymeneal, the bridegroom who was then married will call all the male children who are born in the seventh and tenth month afterwards his sons, and the female children his daughters, and they will call him father, and he will call their children his grandchildren, and they will call the elder generation grandfathers and grandmothers. All who were begotten at the time when their fathers and mothers came together will be called their brothers and sisters, and these, as I was saying, will be forbidden to intermarry. This, however, is not to be understood as an absolute prohibition of the marriage of brothers and sisters; if the lot favours them, and they receive the sanction of the Pythian oracle, the law will allow them.

Quite right, he replied.

Such is the scheme, Glaucon, according to which the guardians of our State are to have their wives and families in common. And now you would have the argument show that this community is consistent with the rest of our polity, and also that nothing can be better—would you not?

Yes, certainly.

Shall we try to find a common basis by asking of ourselves what ought to be the chief aim of the legislator in making laws and in the organization of a State,—what is the greatest good, and what is the greatest evil, and then consider whether our previous description has the stamp of the good or of the evil?

By all means.

Can there be any greater evil than discord and distraction and plurality where unity ought to reign? or any greater good than the bond of unity?

There cannot.

And there is unity where there is community of pleasures and pains—where all the citizens are glad or grieved on the same occasions of joy and sorrow?

No doubt.

Yes; and where there is no common but only private feeling a State is disorganized—when you have one half of the world triumphing and the other plunged in grief at the same events happening to the city or the citizens?

Certainly.

Such differences commonly originate in a disagreement about the use of the terms "mine" and "not mine," "his" and "not his."

Exactly so.

And is not that the best-ordered State in which the greatest number of persons apply the terms "mine" and "not mine" in the same way to the same thing?

Quite true.

Or that again which most nearly approaches to the condition of the individual—as in the body, when but a finger of one of us is hurt, the whole frame, drawn towards the soul as a centre and forming one kingdom under the ruling power therein, feels the hurt and sympathizes all together with the part affected, and we say that the man has a pain in his finger; and the same expression is used about any other part of the body, which has a sensation of pain at suffering or of pleasure at the alleviation of suffering?

Very true, he replied; and I agree with you that in the best-ordered State there is the nearest approach to this common feeling which you describe.

Then when any one of the citizens experiences any good or evil, the whole State will make his case their own, and will either rejoice or sorrow with him?

Yes, he said, that is what will happen in a well-ordered State.

It will now be time, I said, for us to return to our State and see whether this or some other form is most in accordance with these fundamental principles.

Very good.

Our State like every other has rulers and subjects?

True.

All of whom will call one another citizens?

Of course.

But is there not another name which people give to their rulers in other States?

Generally they call them masters, but in democratic States they simply call them rulers.

And in our State what other name besides that of citizens do the people give the rulers?

They are called saviours and helpers, he replied.

And what do the rulers call the people?

Their maintainers and foster-fathers.

And what do they call them in other States?

Slaves.

And what do the rulers call one another in other States?

Fellow-rulers.

And what in ours?

Fellow-guardians.

Did you ever know an example in any other State of a ruler who would speak of one of his colleagues as his friend and of another as not being his friend?

Yes, very often.

And the friend he regards and describes as one in whom he has an interest, and the other as a stranger in whom he has no interest?

Exactly.

But would any of your guardians think or speak of any other guardian as a stranger?

Certainly he would not; for every one whom they meet will be regarded by them either as a brother or sister, or father or mother, or son or daughter, or as the child or parent of those who are thus connected with him.

Capital, I said; but let me ask you once more: Shall they be a family in name only; or shall they in all their actions be true to the name? For example, in the use of the word "father," would the care of a father be implied and the filial reverence and duty and obedience to him which the law commands; and is the violator of these duties to be regarded as an impious and unrighteous person who is not likely to receive much good either at the hands of God or of man? Are these to be or not to be the strain which the children will hear repeated in their ears by all the citizens about those who are intimated to them to be their parents and the rest of the kinsfolk?

These, he said, and none other; for what can be more ridiculous than for them to utter the names of family ties with the lips only and not to act in the spirit of them?

Then in our city the language of harmony and concord will be more often heard than in any other. As I was describing before, when any one is well or ill, the universal word will be "with me it is well" or "it is ill."

Most true.

And agreeably to this mode of thinking and speaking, were we not saying that they will have their pleasures and pains in common?

Yes, and so they will.

And they will have a common interest in the same thing which they will alike call "my own," and having this common interest they will have a common feeling of pleasure and pain?

Yes, far more so than in other States.

And the reason of this, over and above the general constitution of the State, will be that the guardians will have a community of women and children?

That will be the chief reason.

And this unity of feeling we admitted to be the greatest good, as was implied in our own comparison of a well-ordered State to the relation of the body and the members, when affected by pleasure or pain?

That we acknowledged, and very rightly.

Then the community of wives and children among our citizens is clearly the source of the greatest good to the State?

Certainly.

And this agrees with the other principle which we were

affirming,—that the guardians were not to have houses or lands or any other property; their pay was to be their food, which they were to receive from the other citizens, and they were to have no private expenses; for we intended them to preserve their true character of guardians.

Right, he replied.

Both the community of property and the community of families, as I am saying, tend to make them more truly guardians; they will not tear the city in pieces by differing about "mine" and "not mine"; each man dragging any acquisition which he has made into a separate house of his own, where he has a separate wife and children and private pleasures and pains; but all will be affected as far as may be by the same pleasures and pains because they are all of one opinion about what is near and dear to them, and therefore they all tend towards a common end.

Certainly, he replied.

And as they have nothing but their persons which they can call their own, suits and complaints will have no existence among them; they will be delivered from all those quarrels of which money or children or relations are the occasion.

Of course they will.

Neither will trials for assault or insult ever be likely to occur among them. For that equals should defend themselves against equals we shall maintain to be honourable and right; we shall make the protection of the person a matter of necessity.

That is good, he said.

Yes; and there is a further good in the law; namely, that if a man has a quarrel with another he will satisfy his resentment then and there, and not proceed to more dangerous lengths.

Certainly.

To the elder shall be assigned the duty of ruling and chastising the younger.

Clearly.

Nor can there be a doubt that the younger will not strike or do any other violence to an elder, unless the magistrates command him; nor will he slight him in any way. For there are two guardians, shame and fear, mighty to prevent him: shame, which makes men refrain from laying hands on those who are to them in the relation to parents; fear, that the injured one will be succoured by the others who are his brothers, sons, fathers.

That is true, he replied.

Then in every way the laws will help the citizens to keep the peace with one another?

Yes, there will be no want of peace.

And as the guardians will never quarrel among themselves there will be no danger of the rest of the city being divided either against them or against one another.

None whatever.

I hardly like even to mention the little meannesses of which they will be rid, for they are beneath notice: such, for example, as the flattery of the rich by the poor, and all the pains and pangs which men experience in bringing up a family, and in finding money to buy necessaries for their household, borrowing and then repudiating, getting how they can, and giving the money into the hands of women and slaves to keep—the many evils of so many kinds which people suffer in this way are mean enough and obvious enough, and not worth speaking of.

Yes, he said, a man has no need of eyes in order to perceive that.

And from all these evils they will be delivered, and their life will be blessed as the life of Olympic victors and yet more blessed.

How so?

The Olympic victor, I said, is deemed happy in receiving a part only of the blessedness which is secured to our citizens, who have won a more glorious victory and have a more complete maintenance at the public cost. For the victory which they have won is the salvation of the whole State; and the crown with which they and their children are crowned is the fullness of all that life needs; they receive rewards from the hands of their country while living, and after death have an honourable burial.

Yes, he said, and glorious rewards they are.

Do you remember, I said, how in the course of the previous discussion some one who shall be nameless accused us of making our guardians unhappy—they had nothing and might have possessed all things—to whom we replied that, if an occasion offered, we might perhaps hereafter consider this question, but that, as at present advised, we would make our guardians truly guardians, and that we were fashioning the State with a view to the greatest happiness, not of any particular class, but of the whole?

Yes, I remember.

And what do you say, now that the life of our protectors is made out to be far better and nobler than that of Olympic victors—is the life of shoemakers, or any other artisans, or of husbandmen, to be compared with it?

Certainly not.

At the same time, I ought here to repeat what I have said elsewhere, that if any of our guardians shall try to be happy in such a manner that he will cease to be a guardian, and is not content with this safe and harmonious life, which, in our judgment, is of all lives best, but infatuated by some youthful conceit of happiness which gets up into his head shall seek to appropriate the whole State to himself, then he will have to learn how wisely Hesiod spoke, when he said, "Half is more than the whole."

If he were to consult me, I should say to him: Stay where you are, when you have the offer of such a life.

You agree, then, I said, that men and women are to have a common way of life such as we have described—common education, common children; and they are to watch over the citizens in common whether abiding in the city or going out to war; they are to keep watch together, and to hunt together like dogs; and always and in all things, as far as they are able, women are to share with the men? And in so doing they will do what is best, and will not violate, but preserve the natural relation of the sexes.

I agree with you, he replied.

The enquiry, I said, has yet to be made, whether such a community will be found possible—as among other animals, so also among men—and if possible, in what way possible?

You have anticipated the question which I was about to suggest.

There is no difficulty, I said, in seeing how war will be carried on by them.

How?

Why, of course they will go on expeditions together; and will take with them any of their children who are strong enough, that, after the manner of the artisan's child, they may look on at the work which they will have to do when they are grown up; and besides looking on they will have to help and be of use in war, and to wait upon their fathers and mothers. Did you never observe in the arts how the potters' boys look on and help, long before they touch the wheel?

Yes, I have.

And shall potters be more careful in educating their children and in giving them the opportunity of seeing and practising their duties than our guardians will be?

The idea is ridiculous, he said.

There is also the effect on the parents, with whom, as with other animals, the presence of their young ones will be the greatest incentive to valour.

That is quite true, Socrates; and yet if they are defeated, which may often happen in war, how great the danger is! the children will be lost as well as their parents, and the State will never recover.

True, I said; but would you never allow them to run any risk?

I am far from saying that.

Well, but if they are ever to run a risk, should they not do so on some occasion when, if they escape disaster, they will be the better for it?

Clearly.

Whether the future soldiers do or do not see war in the days of their youth is a very important matter, for the sake of which some risk may fairly be incurred.

Yes, very important.

This then must be our first step,—to make our children spectators of war; but we must also contrive that they shall be secured against danger; then all will be well.

True.

Their parents may be supposed not to be blind to the risks of war, but to know, as far as human foresight can, what expeditions are safe and what dangerous?

That may be assumed.

And they will take them on the safe expeditions and be cautious about the dangerous ones?

True.

And they will place them under the command of experienced veterans who will be their leaders and teachers?

Very properly.

Still, the dangers of war cannot be always foreseen; there is a good deal of chance about them?

True.

Then against such chances the children must be at once furnished with wings, in order that in the hour of need they may fly away and escape.

What do you mean? he said.

I mean that we must mount them on horses in their earliest youth, and when they have learnt to ride, take them on horseback to see war: the horses must not be spirited and warlike, but the most tractable and yet the swiftest that can be had. In this way they will get an excellent view of what is hereafter to be their own business; and if there is danger they have only to follow their elder leaders and escape.

I believe that you are right, he said.

Next, as to war; what are to be the relations of your soldiers to one another and to their enemies? I should be inclined to propose that the soldier who leaves his rank or throws away his arms, or is guilty of any other act of cowardice, should be degraded into the rank of husbandman or artisan. What do you think?

By all means, I should say.

And he who allows himself to be taken prisoner may as well be made a present of to his enemies; he is their lawful prey, and let them do what they like with him.

Certainly.

But the hero who has distinguished himself, what shall be done to him? In the first place, he shall receive honour in the army from his youthful comrades; every one of them in succession shall crown him. What do you say?

I approve.

And what do you say to his receiving the right hand of fellowship?

To that too, I agree.

But you will hardly agree to my next proposal.

What is your proposal?

That he should kiss and be kissed by them.

Most certainly, and I should be disposed to go further, and say: Let no one whom he has a mind to kiss refuse to be kissed by him while the expedition lasts. So that if there be a lover in the army, whether his love be youth or maiden, he may be more eager to win the prize of valour.

Capital, I said. That the brave man is to have more wives than others has been already determined: and he is to have first choice in such matters more than others, in order that he may have as many children as possible?

Agreed.

Again, there is another manner in which, according to

Homer, brave youths should be honoured; for he tells how Ajax,[1] after he had distinguished himself in battle, was rewarded with long chines, which seem to be a compliment appropriate to a hero in the flower of his age, being not only a tribute to honour but also a very strengthening thing.

Most true, he said.

Then in this, I said, Homer shall be our teacher; and we too, at sacrifices and on the like occasions, will honour the brave according to the measure of their valour, whether men or women, with hymns and those other distinctions which we were mentioning; also with

"seats of precedence, and meats and full cups";[2]

and in honouring them, we shall be at the same time training them.

That, he replied, is excellent.

Yes, I said; and when a man dies gloriously in war shall we not say, in the first place, that he is of the golden race?

To be sure.

Nay, have we not the authority of Hesiod for affirming that when they are dead

"They are holy angels upon the earth, authors of good, averters of evil, the guardians of speech-gifted men"?[3]

Yes; and we accept his authority.

We must learn of the god how we are to order the sepulture of divine and heroic personages, and what is to be their special distinction; and we must do as he bids?

By all means.

And in ages to come we will reverence them and kneel before their sepulchres as at the graves of heroes. And not only they but any who are deemed pre-eminently good,

---

[1] Iliad, vii. 321.   [2] Iliad, viii. 162.
[3] Probably Works and Days, 121 foll.

whether they die from age, or in any other way, shall be admitted to the same honours.

That is very right, he said.

Next, how shall our soldiers treat their enemies? What about this?

In what respect do you mean?

First of all, in regard to slavery? Do you think it right that Hellenes should enslave Hellenic States, or allow others to enslave them, if they can help? Should not their custom be to spare them, considering the danger which there is that the whole race may one day fall under the yoke of the barbarians?

To spare them is infinitely better.

Then no Hellene should be owned by them as a slave; that is a rule which they will observe and advise the other Hellenes to observe.

Certainly, he said; they will in this way be united against the barbarians and will keep their hands off one another.

Next as to the slain; ought the conquerors, I said, to take anything but their armour? Does not the practice of despoiling an enemy afford an excuse for not facing the battle? Cowards skulk about the dead, pretending that they are fulfilling a duty, and many an army before now has been lost from this love of plunder.

Very true.

And is there not illiberality and avarice in robbing a corpse, and also a degree of meanness and womanishness in making an enemy of the dead body when the real enemy has flown away and left only his fighting gear behind him,—is not this rather like a dog who cannot get at his assailant, quarrelling with the stones which strike him instead?

Very like a dog, he said.

Then we must abstain from spoiling the dead or hindering their burial?

Yes, he replied, we most certainly must.

Neither shall we offer up arms at the temples of the gods,

least of all the arms of Hellenes, if we care to maintain good feeling with other Hellenes; and, indeed, we have reason to fear that the offering of spoils taken from kinsmen may be a pollution unless commanded by the god himself?

Very true.

Again, as to the devastation of Hellenic territory or the burning of houses, what is to be the practice?

May I have the pleasure, he said, of hearing your opinion?

Both should be forbidden, in my judgment; I would take the annual produce and no more. Shall I tell you why?

Pray do.

Why, you see, there is a difference in the names "discord" and "war," and I imagine that there is also a difference in their natures; the one is expressive of what is internal and domestic, the other of what is external and foreign; and the first of the two is termed discord, and only the second, war.

That is a very proper distinction, he replied.

And may I not observe with equal propriety that the Hellenic race is all united together by ties of blood and friendship, and alien and strange to the barbarians?

Very good, he said.

And therefore when Hellenes fight with barbarians and barbarians with Hellenes, they will be described by us as being at war when they fight, and by nature enemies, and this kind of antagonism should be called war; but when Hellenes fight with one another we shall say that Hellas is then in a state of disorder and discord, they being by nature friends; and such enmity is to be called discord.

I agree.

Consider then, I said, when that which we have acknowledged to be discord occurs, and a city is divided, if both parties destroy the lands and burn the houses of one another, how wicked does the strife appear! No true lover of his country would bring himself to tear in pieces his own nurse and mother: There might be reason in the conqueror depriving the conquered of their harvest, but still they would have the idea of peace in their hearts and would not mean to go on fighting for ever.

Yes, he said, that is a better temper than the other.

And will not the city, which you are founding, be an Hellenic city?

It ought to be, he replied.

Then will not the citizens be good and civilized?

Yes, very civilized.

And will they not be lovers of Hellas, and think of Hellas as their own land, and share in the common temples?

Most certainly.

And any difference which arises among them will be regarded by them as discord only—a quarrel among friends, which is not to be called a war?

Certainly not.

Then they will quarrel as those who intend some day to be reconciled?

Certainly.

They will use friendly correction, but will not enslave or destroy their opponents; they will be correctors, not enemies?

Just so.

And as they are Hellenes themselves they will not devastate Hellas, nor will they burn houses, nor ever suppose that the whole population of a city—men, women, and children—are equally their enemies, for they know that the guilt of war is always confined to a few persons and that the many are their friends. And for all these reasons they will be unwilling to waste their lands and raze their houses; their enmity to them will only last until the many innocent sufferers have compelled the guilty few to give satisfaction?

I agree, he said, that our citizens should thus deal with their Hellenic enemies; and with barbarians as the Hellenes now deal with one another.

Then let us enact this law also for our guardians:—that they are neither to devastate the lands of Hellenes nor to burn their houses.

Agreed; and we may agree also in thinking that these, like all our previous enactments, are very good.

But still I must say, Socrates, that if you are allowed to go on in this way you will entirely forget the other question which at the commencement of this discussion you thrust aside:—Is such an order of things possible, and how, if at all? For I am quite ready to acknowledge that the plan which you propose, if only feasible, would do all sorts of good to the State. I will add, what you have omitted, that your citizens will be the bravest of warriors, and will never leave their ranks, for they will all know one another, and each will call the other father, brother, son; and if you suppose the women to join their armies, whether in the same rank or in the rear, either as a terror to the enemy, or as auxiliaries in case of need, I know that they will then be absolutely invincible; and there are many domestic advantages which might also be mentioned and which I also fully acknowledge: but, as I admit all these advantages and as many more as you please, if only this State of yours were to come into existence, we need say no more about them; assuming then the existence of the State, let us now turn to the question of possibility and ways and means—the rest may be left.

If I loiter[1] for a moment, you instantly make a raid upon me, I said, and have no mercy; I have hardly escaped the first and second waves, and you seem not to be aware that you are now bringing upon me the third, which is the greatest and heaviest. When you have seen and heard the third wave, I think you will be more considerate and will acknowledge that some fear and hesitation was natural respecting a proposal so extraordinary as that which I have now to state and investigate.

The more appeals of this sort which you make, he said, the more determined are we that you shall tell us how such a State is possible: speak out and at once.

---

[1] Reading στραγγευομένῳ.

Let me begin by reminding you that we found our way hither in the search after justice and injustice.

True, he replied; but what of that?

I was only going to ask whether, if we have discovered them, we are to require that the just man should in nothing fail of absolute justice; or may we be satisfied with an approximation, and the attainment in him of a higher degree of justice than is to be found in other men?

The approximation will be enough.

We were enquiring into the nature of absolute justice and into the character of the perfectly just, and into injustice and the perfectly unjust, that we might have an ideal. We were to look at these in order that we might judge of our own happiness and unhappiness according to the standard which they exhibited and the degree in which we resembled them, but not with any view of showing that they could exist in fact.

True, he said.

Would a painter be any the worse because, after having delineated with consummate art an ideal of a perfectly beautiful man, he was unable to show that any such man could ever have existed?

He would be none the worse.

Well, and were we not creating an ideal of a perfect State?

To be sure.

And is our theory a worse theory because we are unable to prove the possibility of a city being ordered in the manner described?

Surely not, he replied.

That is the truth, I said. But if, at your request, I am to try to show how and under what conditions the possibility is highest, I must ask you, having this in view, to repeat your former admissions.

What admissions?

I want to know whether ideals are ever fully realized in language? Does not the word express more than the fact, and must not the actual, whatever a man may think, always, in the nature of things, fall short of the truth? What do you say?

I agree.

Then you must not insist on my proving that the actual State will in every respect coincide with the ideal: if we are only able to discover how a city may be governed nearly as we proposed, you will admit that we have discovered the possibility which you demand; and will be contented. I am sure that I should be contented—will not you?

Yes, I will.

Let me next endeavour to show what is that fault in States which is the cause of their present maladministration, and what is the least change which will enable a State to pass into the truer form; and let the change, if possible, be of one thing only, or, if not, of two; at any rate, let the changes be as few and slight as possible.

Certainly, he replied.

I think, I said, that there might be a reform of the State if only one change were made, which is not a slight or easy though still a possible one.

What is it? he said.

Now then, I said, I go to meet that which I liken to the greatest of the waves; yet shall the word be spoken, even though the wave break and drown me in laughter and dishonour; and do you mark my words.

Proceed.

I said: *Until philosophers are kings, or the kings and princes of this world have the spirit and power of philosophy, and political greatness and wisdom meet in one, and those commoner natures who pursue either to the exclusion of the other are compelled to stand aside, cities will never have rest from their evils,—no, nor the human race, as I believe,—and then only will this our State have a possibility of life and behold the light of day.* Such was the thought, my dear Glaucon, which I would fain have uttered if it had not seemed too extravagant; for to be convinced that in no other State can there be happiness private or public is indeed a hard thing.

Socrates, what do you mean? I would have you consider that the word which you have uttered is one at which numerous persons, and very respectable persons too, in a figure pulling off their coats all in a moment, and seizing any weapon that comes to hand, will run at you might and main, before you know where you are, intending to do heaven knows what; and if you don't prepare an answer, and put yourself in motion, you will be "pared by their fine wits," and no mistake.

You got me into the scrape, I said.

And I was quite right; however, I will do all I can to get you out of it; but I can only give you good-will and good advice, and, perhaps, I may be able to fit answers to your questions better than another—that is all. And now, having such an auxiliary, you must do your best to show the unbelievers that you are right.

I ought to try, I said, since you offer me such invaluable assistance. And I think that, if there is to be a chance of our escaping, we must explain to them whom we mean when we say that philosophers are to rule in the State; then we shall be able to defend ourselves: There will be discovered to be some natures who ought to study philosophy and to be leaders in the State; and others who are not born to be philosophers, and are meant to be followers rather than leaders.

Then now for a definition, he said.

Follow me, I said, and I hope that I may in some way or other be able to give you a satisfactory explanation.

Proceed.

I dare say that you remember, and therefore I need not remind you, that a lover, if he is worthy of the name, ought to show his love, not to some one part of that which he loves, but to the whole.

I really do not understand, and therefore beg of you to assist my memory.

Another person, I said, might fairly reply as you do; but a man of pleasure like yourself ought to know that all who are in the flower of youth do somehow or other raise a pang or emotion in a lover's breast, and are thought by him to be worthy of his affectionate regards. Is not this a way which you have with the fair: one has a snub nose, and you praise his charming face; the hook nose of another has, you say, a royal look; while he who is neither snub or hooked has the grace of regularity: the dark visage is manly, the fair are children of the gods; and as to the sweet "honey pale," as they are called, what is the very name but the invention of a lover who talks in diminutives, and is not averse to paleness if appearing on the cheek of youth? In a word, there is no excuse which you will not make, and nothing which you will not say, in order not to lose a single flower that blooms in the springtime of youth.

If you make me an authority in matters of love, for the sake of the argument, I assent.

And what do you say of lovers of wine? Do you not see them doing the same? They are glad of any pretext of drinking any wine.

Very good.

And the same is true of ambitious men; if they cannot command an army, they are willing to command a file; and if they cannot be honoured by really great and important persons, they are glad to be honoured by lesser and meaner people,—but honour of some kind they must have.

Exactly.

Once more let me ask: Does he who desires any class of goods, desire the whole class or a part only?

The whole.

And may we not say of the philosopher that he is a lover, not of a part of wisdom only, but of the whole?

Yes, of the whole.

And he who dislikes learning, especially in youth, when

he has no power of judging what is good and what is not, such an one we maintain not to be a philosopher or a lover of knowledge, just as he who refuses his food is not hungry, and may be said to have a bad appetite and not a good one?

Very true, he said.

Whereas he who has a taste for every sort of knowledge and who is curious to learn and is never satisfied, may be justly termed a philosopher? Am I not right?

Glaucon said: If curiosity makes a philosopher, you will find many a strange being will have a title to the name. All the lovers of sights have a delight in learning, and must therefore be included. Musical amateurs, too, are a folk strangely out of place among philosophers, for they are the last persons in the world who would come to anything like a philosophical discussion, if they could help, while they run about at the Dionysiac festivals as if they had let out their ears to hear every chorus; whether the performance is in town or country—that makes no difference—they are there. Now, are we to maintain that all these and any who have similar tastes, as well as the professors of quite minor arts, are philosophers?

Certainly not, I replied; they are only an imitation.

He said: Who then are the true philosophers?

Those, I said, who are lovers of the vision of truth.

That is also good, he said; but I should like to know what you mean?

To another, I replied, I might have a difficulty in explaining; but I am sure that you will admit a proposition which I am about to make.

What is the proposition?

That since beauty is the opposite of ugliness, they are two? Certainly.

And inasmuch as they are two, each of them is one?

True again.

And of just and unjust, good and evil, and of every other class, the same remark holds: taken singly, each of them is one; but from the various combinations of them with actions and things and with one another, they are seen in all sorts of lights and appear many?

Very true.

And this is the distinction which I draw between the sight-loving, art-loving, practical class and those of whom I am speaking, and who are alone worthy of the name of philosophers.

How do you distinguish them? he said.

The lovers of sounds and sights, I replied, are, as I conceive, fond of fine tones and colours and forms and all the artificial products that are made out of them, but their mind is incapable of seeing or loving absolute beauty.

True, he replied.

Few are they who are able to attain to the sight of this.

Very true.

And he who, having a sense of beautiful things has no sense of absolute beauty, or who, if another lead him to a knowledge of that beauty is unable to follow—of such an one I ask, Is he awake or in a dream only? Reflect: is not the dreamer, sleeping or waking, one who likens dissimilar things, who puts the copy in the place of the real object?

I should certainly say that such an one was dreaming.

But take the case of the other, who recognizes the existence of absolute beauty and is able to distinguish the idea from the objects which participate in the idea, neither putting the objects in the place of the idea nor the idea in the place of the objects—is he a dreamer, or is he awake?

He is wide awake.

And may we not say that the mind of the one who knows has knowledge, and that the mind of the other, who opines only, has opinion?

Certainly.

But suppose that the latter should quarrel with us and dispute our statement, can we administer any soothing cordial or advice to him, without revealing to him that there is sad disorder in his wits?

We must certainly offer him some good advice, he replied.

Come, then, and let us think of something to say to him. Shall we begin by assuring him that he is welcome to any knowledge which he may have, and that we are rejoiced at his having it? But we should like to ask him a question: Does he who has knowledge know something or nothing? (You must answer for him.)

I answer that he knows something.

Something that is or is not?

Something that is; for how can that which is not ever be known?

And are we assured, after looking at the matter from many points of view, that absolute being is or may be absolutely known, but that the utterly non-existent is utterly unknown?

Nothing can be more certain.

Good. But if there be anything which is of such a nature as to be and not to be, that will have a place intermediate between pure being and the absolute negation of being?

Yes, between them.

And, as knowledge corresponded to being and ignorance of necessity to not-being, for that intermediate between being and not-being there has to be discovered a corresponding intermediate between ignorance and knowledge, if there be such?

Certainly.

Do we admit the existence of opinion?

Undoubtedly.

As being the same with knowledge, or another faculty?

Another faculty.

Then opinion and knowledge have to do with different kinds of matter corresponding to this difference of faculties?

Yes.

And knowledge is relative to being and knows being. But before I proceed further I will make a division.

What division?

I will begin by placing faculties in a class by themselves: they are powers in us, and in all other things, by which we do as we do. Sight and hearing, for example, I should call faculties. Have I clearly explained the class which I mean?

Yes, I quite understand.

Then let me tell you my view about them. I do not see them, and therefore the distinctions of figure, colour, and the like, which enable me to discern the differences of some things, do not apply to them. In speaking of a faculty I think only of its sphere and its result; and that which has the same sphere and the same result I call the same faculty, but that which has another sphere and another result I call different. Would that be your way of speaking?

Yes.

And will you be so very good as to answer one more question? Would you say that knowledge is a faculty, or in what class would you place it?

Certainly knowledge is a faculty, and the mightiest of all faculties.

And is opinion also a faculty?

Certainly, he said; for opinion is that with which we are able to form an opinion.

And yet you were acknowledging a little while ago that knowledge is to know the nature of being?

Why, yes, he said: how can any reasonable being ever identify that which is infallible with that which errs?

An excellent answer, proving, I said, that we are quite conscious of a distinction between them.

Yes.

Then knowledge and opinion having distinct powers have also distinct spheres or subject-matters?

That is certain.

Being is the sphere or subject-matter of knowledge, and knowledge is to know the nature of being?

Yes.

And opinion is to have an opinion?

Yes.

And do we know what we opine? or is the subject-matter of opinion the same as the subject-matter of knowledge?

Nay, he replied, that has been already disproven; if difference in faculty implies difference in the sphere or subject-matter, and if, as we were saying, opinion and knowledge are distinct faculties, then the sphere of knowledge and of opinion cannot be the same.

Then if being is the subject-matter of knowledge, something else must be the subject-matter of opinion?

Yes, something else.

Well, then, is not-being the subject-matter of opinion? or, rather, how can there be an opinion at all about not-being? Reflect: when a man has an opinion, has he not an opinion about something? Can he have an opinion which is an opinion about nothing?

Impossible.

He who has an opinion has an opinion about some one thing?

Yes.

And not-being is not one thing but, properly speaking, nothing?

True.

Of not-being, ignorance was assumed to be the necessary correlative; of being, knowledge?

True, he said.

Then opinion is not concerned either with being or with not-being?

Not with either.

And can therefore neither be ignorance nor knowledge?

That seems to be true.

But is opinion to be sought without and beyond either of them, in a greater clearness than knowledge, or in a greater darkness than ignorance?

In neither.

Then I suppose that opinion appears to you to be darker than knowledge, but lighter than ignorance?

Both; and in no small degree.

And also to be within and between them?

Yes.

Then you would infer that opinion is intermediate?

No question.

But were we not saying before, that if anything appeared to be of a sort which is and is not at the same time, that sort of thing would appear also to lie in the interval between pure being and absolute not-being; and that the corresponding faculty is neither knowledge nor ignorance, but will be found in the interval between them?

True.

And in that interval there has now been discovered something which we call opinion?

There has.

Then what remains to be discovered is the object which partakes equally of the nature of being and not-being, and cannot rightly be termed either, pure and simple; this unknown term, when discovered, we may truly call the subject of opinion, and assign each to their proper faculty,— the extremes to the faculties of the extremes and the mean to the faculty of the mean.

True.

This being premised, I would ask the gentleman who is of opinion that there is no absolute or unchangeable idea of beauty—in whose opinion the beautiful is the manifold— he, I say, your lover of beautiful sights, who cannot bear to be told that the beautiful is one, and the just is one, or that anything is one—to him I would appeal, saying, Will you be so very kind, sir, as to tell us whether, of all these beautiful things, there is one which will not be found ugly; or of the just, which will not be found unjust; or of the holy, which will not also be unholy?

No, he replied; the beautiful will in some point of

view be found ugly; and the same is true of the rest.

And may not the many which are doubles be also halves?
—doubles, that is, of one thing, and halves of another?

Quite true.

And things great and small, heavy and light, as they are
termed, will not be denoted by these any more than by the
opposite names?

True; both these and the opposite names will always attach to all of them.

And can any one of those many things which are called by
particular names be said to be this rather than not to be
this?

He replied: They are like the punning riddles which are
asked at feasts or the children's puzzle about the eunuch
aiming at the bat, with what he hit him, as they say in the
puzzle, and upon what the bat was sitting. The individual
objects of which I am speaking are also a riddle, and have
a double sense: nor can you fix them in your mind, either
as being or not-being, or both, or neither.

Then what will you do with them? I said. Can they have
a better place than between being and not-being? For they
are clearly not in greater darkness or negation than not-
being, or more full of light and existence than being.

That is quite true, he said.

Thus then we seem to have discovered that the many ideas
which the multitude entertain about the beautiful and about
all other things are tossing about in some region which is
half-way between pure being and pure not-being.

We have.

Yes; and we had before agreed that anything of this kind
which we might find was to be described as matter of opinion, and not as matter of knowledge; being the intermediate
flux which is caught and detained by the intermediate faculty.

Quite true.

Then those who see the many beautiful, and who yet
neither see absolute beauty, nor can follow any guide who

points the way thither; who see the many just, and not absolute justice, and the like,—such persons may be said to have opinion but not knowledge?

That is certain.

But those who see the absolute and eternal and immutable may be said to know, and not to have opinion only?

Neither can that be denied.

The one love and embrace the subjects of knowledge, the other those of opinion? The latter are the same, as I dare say you will remember, who listened to sweet sounds and gazed upon fair colours, but would not tolerate the existence of absolute beauty.

Yes, I remember.

Shall we then be guilty of any impropriety in calling them lovers of opinion rather than lovers of wisdom, and will they be very angry with us for thus describing them?

I shall tell them not to be angry; no man should be angry at what is true.

But those who love the truth in each thing are to be called lovers of wisdom and not lovers of opinion.

Assuredly.

BOOK VI

And thus, Glaucon, after the argument has gone a weary way, the true and the false philosophers have at length appeared in view.

I do not think, he said, that the way could have been shortened.

I suppose not, I said; and yet I believe that we might have had a better view of both of them if the discussion could have been confined to this one subject and if there were not many other questions awaiting us, which he who desires to see in what respect the life of the just differs from that of the unjust must consider.

And what is the next question? he asked.

Surely, I said, the one which follows next in order. Inasmuch as philosophers only are able to grasp the eternal and unchangeable, and those who wander in the region of the many and variable are not philosophers, I must ask you which of the two classes should be the rulers of our State?

And how can we rightly answer that question?

Whichever of the two are best able to guard the laws and institutions of our State—let them be our guardians.

Very good.

Neither, I said, can there be any question that the guardian who is to keep anything should have eyes rather than no eyes?

There can be no question of that.

And are not those who are verily and indeed wanting in the knowledge of the true being of each thing, and who have in their souls no clear pattern, and are unable as with a painter's eye to look at the absolute truth and to that original to repair, and having perfect vision of the other world to order the laws about beauty, goodness, justice in this, if not already ordered, and to guard and preserve the order of them —are not such persons, I ask, simply blind?

Truly, he replied, they are much in that condition.

And shall they be our guardians when there are others who, besides being their equals in experience and falling short of them in no particular of virtue, also know the very truth of each thing?

There can be no reason, he said, for rejecting those who have this greatest of all great qualities; they must always have the first place unless they fail in some other respect.

Suppose then, I said, that we determine how far they can unite this and the other excellences.

By all means.

In the first place, as we began by observing, the nature of the philosopher has to be ascertained. We must come to an understanding about him, and, when we have done so, then, if I am not mistaken, we shall also acknowledge that such an union of qualities is possible, and that those in whom they are united, and those only, should be rulers in the State.

What do you mean?

Let us suppose that philosophical minds always love knowledge of a sort which shows them the eternal nature not varying from generation and corruption.

Agreed.

And further, I said, let us agree that they are lovers of all true being; there is no part whether greater or less, or more or less honourable, which they are willing to renounce; as we said before of the lover and the man of ambition.

True.

And if they are to be what we were describing, is there not another quality which they should also possess?

What quality?

Truthfulness: they will never intentionally receive into their mind falsehood, which is their detestation, and they will love the truth.

Yes, that may be safely affirmed of them.

"May be," my friend, I replied, is not the word; say rather, "must be affirmed": for he whose nature is amorous of anything cannot help loving all that belongs or is akin to the object of his affections.

Right, he said.

And is there anything more akin to wisdom than truth?

How can there be?

Can the same nature be a lover of wisdom and a lover of falsehood?

Never.

The true lover of learning then must from his earliest youth, as far as in him lies, desire all truth?

Assuredly.

But then again, as we know by experience, he whose desires are strong in one direction will have them weaker in others; they will be like a stream which has been drawn off into another channel.

True.

He whose desires are drawn towards knowledge in every form will be absorbed in the pleasures of the soul, and will hardly feel bodily pleasure—I mean, if he be a true philosopher and not a sham one.

That is most certain.

Such an one is sure to be temperate and the reverse of covetous; for the motives which have another man desirous of having and spending, have no place in his character.

Very true.

Another criterion of the philosophical nature has also to be considered.

What is that?

There should be no secret corner of illiberality; nothing can be more antagonistic than meanness to a soul which is ever longing after the whole of things both divine and human.

Most true, he replied.

Then how can he who has magnificence of mind and is the spectator of all time and all existence, think much of human life?

He cannot.

Or can such an one account death fearful?

No, indeed.

Then the cowardly and mean nature has no part in true philosophy?

Certainly not.

Or again: can he who is harmoniously constituted, who is not covetous or mean, or a boaster, or a coward—can he, I say, ever be unjust or hard in his dealings?

Impossible.

Then you will soon observe whether a man is just and gentle, or rude and unsociable; these are the signs which distinguish even in youth the philosophical nature from the unphilosophical.

True.

There is another point which should be remarked.

What point?

Whether he has or has not a pleasure in learning; for no one will love that which gives him pain, and in which after much toil he makes little progress.

Certainly not.

And again, if he is forgetful and retains nothing of what he learns, will he not be an empty vessel?

That is certain.

Labouring in vain, he must end in hating himself and his fruitless occupation?

Yes.

Then a soul which forgets cannot be ranked among genuine philosophic natures; we must insist that the philosopher should have a good memory?

Certainly.

And once more, the inharmonious and unseemly nature can only tend to disproportion?

Undoubtedly.

And do you consider truth to be akin to proportion or to disproportion?

To proportion.

Then, besides other qualities, we must try to find a naturally well-proportioned and gracious mind, which will move spontaneously towards the true being of everything.

Certainly.

Well, and do not all these qualities, which we have been enumerating, go together, and are they not, in a manner, necessary to a soul, which is to have a full and perfect participation of being?

They are absolutely necessary, he replied.

And must not that be a blameless study which he only can pursue who has the gift of a good memory, and is quick to learn,—noble, gracious, the friend of truth, justice, courage, temperance, who are his kindred?

The god of jealousy himself, he said, could find no fault with such a study.

And to men like him, I said, when perfected by years and education, and to these only you will entrust the State.

Here Adeimantus interposed and said: To these statements, Socrates, no one can offer a reply; but when you talk in this way, a strange feeling passes over the minds of your hearers: They fancy that they are led astray a little at each step in the argument, owing to their own want of skill in asking and answering questions; these littles accumulate, and at the end of the discussion they are found to have sustained a mighty overthrow and all their former notions appear to be turned upside down. And as unskilful players of draughts are at last shut up by their more skilful adversaries and have no piece to move, so they too find themselves shut up at last; for they have nothing to say in this new game of which words are the counters; and yet all the time they are in the right. The observation is suggested to me by what is now occurring. For any one of us might say, that although in words he is not able to meet you at each step of the argument, he sees as a fact that the votaries of philosophy, when they carry on the study, not only in youth as a part of education, but as the pursuit of their maturer years, most of them become strange monsters, not to say utter rogues, and that those who may be considered the best of them are made useless to the world by the very study which you extol.

Well, and do you think that those who say so are wrong?

I cannot tell, he replied; but I should like to know what is your opinion.

Hear my answer; I am of opinion that they are quite right.

Then how can you be justified in saying that cities will not cease from evil until philosophers rule in them, when philosophers are acknowledged by us to be of no use to them?

You ask a question, I said, to which a reply can only be given in a parable.

Yes, Socrates; and that is a way of speaking to which you are not at all accustomed, I suppose.

I perceive, I said, that you are vastly amused at having

plunged me into such a hopeless discussion; but now hear the parable, and then you will be still more amused at the meagreness of my imagination: for the manner in which the best men are treated in their own States is so grievous that no single thing on earth is comparable to it; and therefore, if I am to plead their cause, I must have recourse to fiction, and put together a figure made up of many things, like the fabulous unions of goats and stags which are found in pictures. Imagine then a fleet or a ship in which there is a captain who is taller and stronger than any of the crew, but he is a little deaf and has a similar infirmity in sight, and his knowledge of navigation is not much better. The sailors are quarrelling with one another about the steering—every one is of opinion that he has a right to steer, though he has never learned the art of navigation and cannot tell who taught him or when he learned, and will further assert that it cannot be taught, and they are ready to cut in pieces any one who says the contrary. They throng about the captain, begging and praying him to commit the helm to them; and if at any time they do not prevail, but others are preferred to them, they kill the others or throw them overboard, and, having first chained up the noble captain's senses with drink or some narcotic drug, they mutiny and take possession of the ship and make free with the stores; thus, eating and drinking, they proceed on their voyage in such manner as might be expected of them. Him who is their partisan and cleverly aids them in their plot for getting the ship out of the captain's hands into their own whether by force or persuasion, they compliment with the name of sailor, pilot, able seaman, and abuse the other sort of man, whom they call a good-for-nothing; but that the true pilot must pay attention to the year and seasons and sky and stars and winds, and whatever else belongs to his art, if he intends to be really qualified for the command of a ship, and that he must and will be the steerer, whether other people like or not—the possibility of this union of authority with the steerer's art has never seriously entered into their thoughts or been made part of their calling.[1] Now in vessels which are in a state of mutiny and by sailors who are mutineers, how will the true pilot be regarded? Will he not be called by them a prater, a stargazer, a good-for-nothing?

Of course, said Adeimantus.

Then you will hardly need, I said, to hear the interpretation of the figure, which describes the true philosopher in the relation to the State; for you understand already.

Certainly.

Then suppose you now take this parable to the gentleman who is surprised at finding that philosophers have no honour in their cities; explain it to him and try to convince him that their having honour would be far more extraordinary.

I will.

Say to him, that, in deeming the best votaries of philosophy to be useless to the rest of the world, he is right; but also tell him to attribute their uselessness to the fault of those who will not use them, and not to themselves. The pilot should not humbly beg the sailors to be commanded by him—that is not the order of nature; neither are "the wise to go to the doors of the rich"—the ingenious author of this saying told a lie—but the truth is, that, when a man is ill, whether he be rich or poor, to the physician he must go, and he who wants to be governed, to him who is able to govern. The ruler who is good for anything ought not to beg his subjects to be ruled by him; although the present governors of mankind are of a different stamp; they may be justly compared to the mutinous sailors, and the true helmsmen to those who are called by them good-for-nothings and stargazers.

Precisely so, he said.

For these reasons, and among men like these, philosophy, the noblest pursuit of all, is not likely to be much esteemed

---

[1] Or, applying ὅπως δὲ κυβερνήσει to the mutineers, "But only understanding (ἐπαΐοντας) that he (the mutinous pilot) must rule in spite of other people, never considering that there is an art of command which may be practised in combination with the pilot's art."

by those of the opposite faction; not that the greatest and most lasting injury is done to her by her opponents, but by her own professing followers, the same of whom you suppose the accuser to say, that the greater number of them are arrant rogues, and the best are useless; in which opinion I agreed.

Yes.

And the reason why the good are useless has now been explained?

True.

Then shall we proceed to show that the corruption of the majority is also unavoidable, and that this is not to be laid to the charge of philosophy any more than the other?

By all means.

And let us ask and answer in turn, first going back to the description of the gentle and noble nature. Truth, as you will remember, was his leader, whom he followed always and in all things; failing in this, he was an impostor, and had no part or lot in true philosophy.

Yes, that was said.

Well, and is not this one quality, to mention no others, greatly at variance with present notions of him?

Certainly, he said.

And have we not a right to say in his defence, that the true lover of knowledge is always striving after being—that is his nature; he will not rest in the multiplicity of individuals which is an appearance only, but will go on—the keen edge will not be blunted, nor the force of his desire abate until he have attained the knowledge of the true nature of every essence by a sympathetic and kindred power in the soul, and by that power drawing near and mingling and becoming incorporate with very being, having begotten mind and truth, he will have knowledge and will live and grow truly, and then, and not till then, will he cease from his travail.

Nothing, he said, can be more just than such a description of him.

And will the love of a lie be any part of a philosopher's nature? Will he not utterly hate a lie?

He will.

And when truth is the captain, we cannot suspect any evil of the band which he leads?

Impossible.

Justice and health of mind will be of the company, and temperance will follow after?

True, he replied.

Neither is there any reason why I should again set in array the philosopher's virtue, as you will doubtless remember that courage, magnificence, apprehension, memory, were his natural gifts. And you objected that, although no one could deny what I then said, still, if you leave words and look at facts, the persons who are thus described are some of them manifestly useless, and the greater number utterly depraved; we were then led to enquire into the grounds of these accusations, and have now arrived at the point of asking why are the majority bad, which question of necessity brought us back to the examination and definition of true philosopher.

Exactly.

And we have next to consider the corruptions of the philosophic nature, why so many are spoiled and so few escape spoiling—I am speaking of those who were said to be useless but not wicked—and, when we have done with them, we will speak of the imitators of philosophy, what manner of men are they who aspire after a profession which is above them and of which they are unworthy, and then, by their manifold inconsistencies, bring upon philosophy, and upon all philosophers, that universal reprobation of which we speak.

What are these corruptions? he said.

I will see if I can explain them to you. Every one will admit that a nature having in perfection all the qualities which we required in a philosopher, is a rare plant which is seldom seen among men.

Rare indeed.

And what numberless and powerful causes tend to destroy these rare natures!

What causes?

In the first place there are their own virtues, their courage, temperance, and the rest of them, every one of which praiseworthy qualities (and this is a most singular circumstance) destroys and distracts from philosophy the soul which is the possessor of them.

That is very singular, he replied.

Then there are all the ordinary goods of life—beauty, wealth, strength, rank, and great connexions in the State—you understand the sort of things—these also have a corrupting and distracting effect.

I understand; but I should like to know more precisely what you mean about them.

Grasp the truth as a whole, I said, and in the right way; you will then have no difficulty in apprehending the preceding remarks, and they will no longer appear strange to you.

And how am I to do so? he asked.

Why, I said, we know that all germs or seeds, whether vegetable or animal, when they fail to meet with proper nutriment or climate or soil, in proportion to their vigour, are all the more sensitive to the want of a suitable environment, for evil is a greater enemy to what is good than to what is not.

Very true.

There is reason in supposing that the finest natures, when under alien conditions, receive more injury than the inferior, because the contrast is greater.

Certainly.

And may we not say, Adeimantus, that the most gifted minds, when they are ill-educated, become pre-eminently bad? Do not great crimes and the spirit of pure evil spring out of a fullness of nature ruined by education rather than from any inferiority, whereas weak natures are scarcely capable of any very great good or very great evil?

There I think that you are right.

And our philosopher follows the same analogy—he is like a plant which, having proper nurture, must necessarily grow and mature into all virtue, but, if sown and planted in an alien soil, becomes the most noxious of all weeds, unless he be preserved by some divine power. Do you really think, as people so often say, that our youth are corrupted by Sophists, or that private teachers of the art corrupt them in any degree worth speaking of? Are not the public who say these things the greatest of all Sophists? And do they not educate to perfection young and old, men and women alike, and fashion them after their own hearts?

When is this accomplished? he said.

When they meet together, and the world sits down at an assembly, or in a court of law, or a theatre, or a camp, or in any other popular resort, and there is a great uproar, and they praise some things which are being said or done, and blame other things, equally exaggerating both, shouting and clapping their hands, and the echo of the rocks and the place in which they are assembled redoubles the sound of the praise or blame—at such a time will not a young man's heart, as they say, leap within him? Will any private training enable him to stand firm against the overwhelming flood of popular opinion? or will he be carried away by the stream? Will he not have the notions of good and evil which the public in general have—he will do as they do, and as they are, such will he be?

Yes, Socrates; necessity will compel him.

And yet, I said, there is a still greater necessity, which has not been mentioned.

What is that?

The gentle force of attainder or confiscation or death, which, as you are aware, these new Sophists and educators, who are the public, apply when their words are powerless.

Indeed they do; and in right good earnest.

Now what opinion of any other Sophist, or of any private

person, can be expected to overcome in such an unequal contest?

None, he replied.

No, indeed, I said, even to make the attempt is a great piece of folly; there neither is, nor has been, nor is ever likely to be, any different type of character [1] which has had no other training in virtue but that which is supplied by public opinion[1]—I speak, my friend, of human virtue only; what is more than human, as the proverb says, is not included: for I would not have you ignorant that, in the present evil state of governments, whatever is saved and comes to good is saved by the power of God, as we may truly say.

I quite assent, he replied.

Then let me crave your assent also to a further observation.

What are you going to say?

Why, that all those mercenary individuals, whom the many call Sophists and whom they deem to be their adversaries, do, in fact, teach nothing but the opinion of the many, that is to say, the opinions of their assemblies; and this is their wisdom. I might compare them to a man who should study the tempers and desires of a mighty strong beast who is fed by him—he would learn how to approach and handle him, also at what times and from what causes he is dangerous or the reverse, and what is the meaning of his several cries and by what sounds, when another utters them, he is soothed or infuriated; and you may suppose further, that when, by continually attending upon him, he has become perfect in all this, he calls his knowledge wisdom, and makes of it a system or art, which he proceeds to teach, although he has no real notion of what he means by the principles or passions of which he is speaking, but calls this honourable and that dishonourable, or good or evil, or just or unjust, all in accordance with the tastes and tempers of the great brute. Good

[1] Or, taking παρὰ in another sense, "trained to virtue on their principles."

he pronounces to be that in which the beast delights and evil to be that which he dislikes; and he can give no other account of them except that the just and noble are the necessary, having never himself seen, and having no power of explaining to others the nature of either, or the difference between them, which is immense. By heaven, would not such an one be a rare educator?

Indeed he would.

And in what way does he who thinks that wisdom is the discernment of the tempers and tastes of the motley multitude, whether in painting or music, or, finally, in politics, differ from him whom I have been describing? For when a man consorts with the many, and exhibits to them his poem or other work of art or the service which he has done the State, making them his judges [1] when he is not obliged, the so-called necessity of Diomede will oblige him to produce whatever they praise. And yet the reasons are utterly ludicrous which they give in confirmation of their own notions about the honourable and good. Did you ever hear of them which were not?

No, nor am I likely to hear.

You recognize the truth of what I have been saying? Then let me ask you to consider further whether the world will ever be induced to believe in the existence of absolute beauty rather than of the many beautiful, or of the absolute in each kind rather than of the many in each kind?

Certainly not.

Then the world cannot possibly be a philosopher?

Impossible.

And therefore philosophers must inevitably fall under the censure of the world?

They must.

And of individuals who consort with the mob and seek to please them?

That is evident.

[1] Putting a comma after τῶυ ἀναγκαίων.

Then, do you see any way in which the philosopher can be preserved in his calling to the end? and remember what we were saying of him, that he was to have quickness and memory and courage and magnificence—these were admitted by us to be the true philosopher's gifts.

Yes.

Will not such an one from his early childhood be in all things first among all, especially if his bodily endowments are like his mental ones?

Certainly, he said.

And his friends and fellow-citizens will want to use him as he gets older for their own purposes?

No question.

Falling at his feet, they will make requests to him and do him honour and flatter him, because they want to get into their hands now, the power which he will one day possess.

That often happens, he said.

And what will a man such as he is be likely to do under such circumstances, especially if he be a citizen of a great city, rich and noble, and a tall, proper youth? Will he not be full of boundless aspirations, and fancy himself able to manage the affairs of Hellenes and of barbarians, and having got such notions into his head will he not dilate and elevate himself in the fullness of vain pomp and senseless pride?

To be sure he will.

Now, when he is in this state of mind, if some one gently comes to him and tells him that he is a fool and must get understanding, which can only be got by slaving for it, do you think that, under such adverse circumstances, he will be easily induced to listen?

Far otherwise.

And even if there be some one who through inherent goodness or natural reasonableness has had his eyes opened a little and is humbled and taken captive by philosophy, how will his friends behave when they think that they are likely to lose the advantage which they were hoping to reap from

his companionship? Will they not do and say anything to
prevent·him from yielding to his better nature and to render
his teacher powerless, using to this end private intrigues as
well as public prosecutions?

There can be no doubt of it.

And how can one who is thus circumstanced ever become
a philosopher?

Impossible.

Then were we not right in saying that even the very qualities which make a man a philosopher may, if he be ill-educated; divert him from philosophy, no less than riches and
their accompaniments and the other so-called goods of life?

We were quite right.

Thus, my excellent friend, is brought about all that ruin
and failure which I have been describing of the natures
best adapted to the best of all pursuits; they are natures
which we maintain to be rare at any time; this being the
class out of which come the men who are the authors of the
greatest evil to States and individuals; and also of the greatest good when the tide carries them in that direction; but a
small man never was the doer of any great thing either to
individuals or to States.

That is most true, he said.

And so philosophy is left desolate, with her marriage rite
incomplete: for her own have fallen away and forsaken her,
and while they are leading a false and unbecoming life, other
unworthy persons, seeing that she has no kinsmen to be her
protectors, enter in and dishonour her; and fasten upon her
the reproaches which, as you say, her reprovers utter, who
affirm of her votaries that some are good for nothing, and
that the greater number deserve the severest punishment.

That is certainly what people say.

Yes; and what else would you expect, I said, when you
think of the puny creatures who, seeing this land open to
them—a land well stocked with fair names and showy titles
—like prisoners running out of prison into a sanctuary, take

a leap out of their trades into philosophy; those who do so being probably the cleverest hands at their own miserable crafts? For, although philosophy be in this evil case, still there remains a dignity about her which is not to be found in the arts. And many are thus attracted by her whose natures are imperfect and whose souls are maimed and disfigured by their meannesses, as their bodies are by their trades and crafts. Is not this unavoidable?

Yes.

Are they not exactly like a bald little tinker who has just got out of durance and come into a fortune; he takes a bath and puts on a new coat, and is decked out as a bridegroom going to marry his master's daughter, who is left poor and desolate?

A most exact parallel.

What will be the issue of such marriages? Will they not be vile and bastard?

There can be no question of it.

And when persons who are unworthy of education approach philosophy and make an alliance with her who is in a rank above them, what sort of ideas and opinions are likely to be generated? [1] Will they not be sophisms captivating to the ear,[1] having nothing in them genuine, or worthy of or akin to true wisdom?

No doubt, he said.

Then, Adeimantus, I said, the worthy disciples of philosophy will be but a small remnant: perchance some noble and well-educated person, detained by exile in her service, who in the absence of corrupting influences remains devoted to her; or some lofty soul born in a mean city, the politics of which he contemns and neglects; and there may be a gifted few who leave the arts, which they justly despise, and come to her;—or peradventure there are some who are restrained by our friend Theages' bridle; for everything in the life of Theages conspired to divert him from philosophy; but ill-

_____
[1] Or "will they not deserve to be called sophisms," . . .

health kept him away from politics. My own case of the
internal sign is hardly worth mentioning, for rarely, if ever,
has such a monitor been given to any other man. Those who
belong to this small class have tasted how sweet and blessed
a possession philosophy is, and have also seen enough of the
madness of the multitude; and they know that no politician
is honest, nor is there any champion of justice at whose side
they may fight and be saved. Such an one may be compared
to a man who has fallen among wild beasts—he will not join
in the wickedness of his fellows, but neither is he able singly
to resist all their fierce natures, and therefore seeing that he
would be of no use to the State or to his friends, and reflecting that he would have to throw away his life without doing
any good either to himself or others, he holds his peace, and
goes his own way. He is like one who, in the storm of dust
and sleet which the driving wind hurries along, retires under
the shelter of a wall; and seeing the rest of mankind full of
wickedness, he is content, if only he can live his own life
and be pure from evil or unrighteousness, and depart in peace
and good-will, with bright hopes.

Yes, he said, and he will have done a great work before
he departs.

A great work—yes; but not the greatest, unless he find a
State suitable to him; for in a State which is suitable to him,
he will have a larger growth and be the saviour of his country, as well as of himself.

The causes why philosophy is in such an evil name have
now been sufficiently explained: the injustice of the charges
against her has been shown—is there anything more which
you wish to say?

Nothing more on that subject, he replied; but I should
like to know which of the governments now existing is in
your opinion the one adapted to her.

Not any of them, I said; and that is precisely the accusation which I bring against them—not one of them is worthy
of the philosophic nature, and hence that nature is warped

and estranged;—as the exotic seed which is sown in a foreign land becomes denaturalized, and is wont to be overpowered and to lose itself in the new soil, even so this growth
of philosophy, instead of persisting, degenerates and receives
another character. But if philosophy ever finds in the State
that perfection which she herself is, then will be seen that
she is in truth divine, and that all other things, whether
natures of men or institutions, are but human;—and now, I
know, that you are going to ask, What that State is:

No, he said; there you are wrong, for I was going to ask
another question—whether it is the State of which we are
the founders and inventors, or some other?

Yes, I replied, ours in most respects; but you may remember my saying before, that some living authority would always be required in the State having the same idea of the
constitution which guided you when as legislator you were
laying down the laws.

That was said, he replied.

Yes, but not in a satisfactory manner; you frightened us
by interposing objections, which certainly showed that the
discussion would be long and difficult; and what still remains is the reverse of easy.

What is there remaining?

The question how the study of philosophy may be so ordered as not to be the ruin of the State: All great attempts
are attended with risk; "hard is the good," as men say.

Still, he said, let the point be cleared up, and the enquiry
will then be complete.

I shall not be hindered, I said, by any want of will, but,
if at all, by a want of power: my zeal you may see for yourselves; and please to remark in what I am about to say how
boldly and unhesitatingly I declare that States should pursue
philosophy, not as they do now, but in a different spirit.

In what manner?

At present, I said, the students of philosophy are quite
young; beginning when they are hardly past childhood, they

devote only the time saved from moneymaking and house-keeping to such pursuits; and even those of them who are reputed to have most of the philosophic spirit, when they come within sight of the great difficulty of the subject, I mean dialectic, take themselves off. In after life when invited by some one else, they may, perhaps, go and hear a lecture, and about this they make much ado, for philosophy is not considered by them to be their proper business: at last, when they grow old, in most cases they are extinguished more truly than Heracleitus' sun, inasmuch as they never light up again.[1]

But what ought to be their course?

Just the opposite. In childhood and youth their study, and what philosophy they learn, should be suited to their tender years: during this period while they are growing up towards manhood, the chief and special care should be given to their bodies that they may have them to use in the service of philosophy; as life advances and the intellect begins to mature, let them increase the gymnastics of the soul; but when the strength of our citizens fails and is past civil and military duties, then let them range at will and engage in no serious labour, as we intend them to live happily here, and to crown this life with a similar happiness in another.

How truly in earnest you are, Socrates! he said; I am sure of that; and yet most of your hearers, if I am not mistaken, are likely to be still more earnest in their opposition to you, and will never be convinced; Thrasymachus least of all.

Do not make a quarrel, I said, between Thrasymachus and me, who have recently become friends, although, indeed, we were never enemies; for I shall go on striving to the utmost until I either convert him and other men, or do something which may profit them against the day when they live again, and hold the like discourse in another state of existence.

You are speaking of a time which is not very near.

Rather, I replied, of a time which is as nothing in com-

---

[1] Heracleitus said that the sun was extinguished every evening and relighted every morning.

parison with eternity. Nevertheless, I do not wonder that the many refuse to believe; for they have never seen that of which we are now speaking realized; they have seen only a conventional imitation of philosophy, consisting of words artificially brought together, not like these of ours having a natural unity. But a human being who in word and work is perfectly moulded, as far as he can be, into the proportion and likeness of virtue—such a man ruling in a city which bears the same image, they have never yet seen, neither one nor many of them—do you think that they ever did?

No, indeed.

No, my friend, and they have seldom, if ever, heard free and noble sentiments; such as men utter when they are earnestly and by every means in their power seeking after truth for the sake of knowledge, while they look coldly on the subtleties of controversy, of which the end is opinion and strife, whether they meet with them in the courts of law or in society.

They are strangers, he said, to the words of which you speak.

And this was what we foresaw, and this was the reason why truth forced us to admit, not without fear and hesitation, that neither cities nor States nor individuals will ever attain perfection unless the small class of philosophers whom we termed useless but not corrupt are providentially compelled, whether they will or not, to take care of the State, and until a like necessity be laid on the State to obey them;[1] or until kings, or if not kings, the sons of kings or princes, are divinely inspired with a true love of true philosophy. That either or both of these alternatives are impossible, I see no reason to affirm: if they were so, we might indeed be justly ridiculed as dreamers and visionaries. Am I not right?

Quite right.

If then, in the countless ages of the past, or at the present hour in some foreign clime which is far away and beyond our

[1] Reading κατηκόῳ or κατηκόοις.

ken, the perfected philosopher is or has been or hereafter shall be compelled by a superior power to have the charge of the State, we are ready to assert to the death, that this our constitution has been, and is—yea, and will be whenever the Muse of Philosophy is queen. There is no impossibility in all this; that there is a difficulty, we acknowledge ourselves.

My opinion agrees with yours, he said.

But do you mean to say that this is not the opinion of the multitude?

I should imagine not, he replied.

O my friend, I said, do not attack the multitude: they will change their minds, if, not in an aggressive spirit, but gently and with the view of soothing them and removing their dislike of overeducation, you show them your philosophers as they really are and describe as you were just now doing their character and profession, and then mankind will see that he of whom you are speaking is not such as they supposed—if they view him in this new light, they will surely change their notion of him, and answer in another strain.[1] Who can be at enmity with one who loves them, who that is himself gentle and free from envy will be jealous of one in whom there is no jealousy? Nay, let me answer for you, that in a few this harsh temper may be found but not in the majority of mankind.

I quite agree with you, he said.

And do you not also think, as I do, that the harsh feeling which the many entertain towards philosophy originates in the pretenders, who rush in uninvited, and are always abusing them, and finding fault with them, who make persons instead of things the theme of their conversation? And nothing can be more unbecoming in philosophers than this.

It is most unbecoming.

For he, Adeimantus, whose mind is fixed upon true being,

[1] Reading ἤ καὶ ἐὰν οὕτω θεῶνται without a question, and ἀλλοίαν τοι: or, retaining the question and taking ἀλλοίαν δόξαν in a new sense: "Do you mean to say really that, viewing him in this light, they will be of another mind from yours, and answer in another strain?"

has surely no time to look down upon the affairs of earth, or to be filled with malice and envy, contending against men; his eye is ever directed towards things fixed and immutable, which he sees neither injuring nor injured by one another, but all in order moving according to reason; these he imitates, and to these he will, as far as he can, conform himself. Can a man help imitating that with which he holds reverential converse?

Impossible.

And the philosopher, holding converse with the divine order, becomes orderly and divine, as far as the nature of man allows; but like every one else, he will suffer from detraction.

Of course.

And if a necessity be laid upon him of fashioning, not only himself, but human nature generally, whether in States or individuals, into that which he beholds elsewhere, will he, think you, be an unskilful artificer of justice, temperance, and every civil virtue?

Anything but unskilful.

And if the world perceives that what we are saying about him is the truth, will they be angry with philosophy? Will they disbelieve us, when we tell them that no State can be happy which is not designed by artists who imitate the heavenly pattern?

They will not be angry if they understand, he said. But how will they draw out the plan of which you are speaking?

They will begin by taking the State and the manners of men, from which, as from a tablet, they will rub out the picture, and leave a clean surface. This is no easy task. But whether easy or not, herein will lie the difference between them and every other legislator,—they will have nothing to do either with individual or State, and will inscribe no laws, until they have either found, or themselves made, a clean surface.

They will be very right, he said.

Having effected this, they will proceed to trace an outline of the constitution?

No doubt.

And when they are filling in the work, as I conceive, they will often turn their eyes upwards and downwards: I mean that they will first look at absolute justice and beauty and temperance, and again at the human copy; and will mingle and temper the various elements of life into the image of a man; and this they will conceive according to that other image, which, when existing among men, Homer calls the form and likeness of God.

Very true, he said.

And one feature they will erase, and another they will put in, until they have made the ways of men, as far as possible, agreeable to the ways of God?

Indeed, he said, in no way could they make a fairer picture.

And now, I said, are we beginning to persuade those whom you described as rushing at us with might and main, that the painter of constitutions is such an one as we were praising; at whom they were so very indignant because to his hands we committed the State; and are they growing a little calmer at what they have just heard?

Much calmer, if there is any sense in them.

Why, where can they still find any ground for objection? Will they doubt that the philosopher is a lover of truth and being?

They would not be so unreasonable.

Or that his nature, being such as we have delineated, is akin to the highest good?

Neither can they doubt this.

But again, will they tell us that such a nature, placed under favourable circumstances, will not be perfectly good and wise if any ever was? Or will they prefer those whom we have rejected?

Surely not.

Then will they still be angry at our saying, that, until

philosophers bear rule, States and individuals will have no rest from evil, nor will this our imaginary State ever be realized?

I think that they will be less angry.

Shall we assume that they are not only less angry but quite gentle, and that they have been converted and for very shame, if for no other reason, cannot refuse to come to terms?

By all means, he said.

Then let us suppose that the reconciliation has been effected. Will any one deny the other point, that there may be sons of kings or princes who are by nature philosophers?

Surely no man, he said.

And when they have come into being will any one say that they must of necessity be destroyed; that they can hardly be saved is not denied even by us; but that in the whole course of ages no single one of them can escape—who will venture to affirm this?

Who indeed!

But, said I, one is enough; let there be one man who has a city obedient to his will, and he might bring into existence the ideal polity about which the world is so incredulous.

Yes, one is enough.

The ruler may impose the laws and institutions which we have been describing, and the citizens may possibly be willing to obey them?

Certainly.

And that others should approve, of what we approve, is no miracle or impossibility?

I think not.

But we have sufficiently shown, in what has preceded, that all this, if only possible, is assuredly for the best.

We have.

And now we say not only that our laws, if they could be enacted, would be for the best, but also that the enactment of them, though difficult, is not impossible.

Very good.

And so with pain and toil we have reached the end of one subject, but more remains to be discussed;—how and by what studies and pursuits will the saviours of the constitution be created, and at what ages are they to apply themselves for their several studies?

Certainly.

I omitted the troublesome business of the possession of women, and the procreation of children, and the appointment of the rulers, because I knew that the perfect State would be eyed with jealousy and was difficult of attainment; but that piece of cleverness was not of much service to me, for I had to discuss them all the same. The women and children are now disposed of, but the other question of the rulers must be investigated from the very beginning. We were saying, as you will remember, that they were to be lovers of their country, tried by the test of pleasures and pains, and neither in hardships, nor in dangers, nor at any other critical moment were to lose their patriotism—he was to be rejected who failed, but he who always came forth pure, like gold tried in the refiner's fire, was to be made a ruler, and to receive honours and rewards in life and after death. This was the sort of thing which was being said, and then the argument turned aside and veiled her face; not liking to stir the question which has now arisen.

I perfectly remember, he said.

Yes, my friend, I said, and I then shrank from hazarding the bold word; but now let me dare to say—that the perfect guardian must be a philosopher.

Yes, he said, let that be affirmed.

And do not suppose that there will be many of them; for the gifts which were deemed by us to be essential rarely grow together; they are mostly found in shreds and patches.

What do you mean? he said.

You are aware, I replied, that quick intelligence, memory, sagacity, cleverness, and similar qualities, do not often grow together, and that persons who possess them and are at the same time high-spirited and magnanimous are not so constituted by nature as to live orderly and in a peaceful and settled manner; they are driven any way by their impulses, and all solid principle goes out of them.

Very true, he said.

On the other hand, those steadfast natures which can better be depended upon, which in a battle are impregnable to fear and immovable, are equally immovable when there is anything to be learned; they are always in a torpid state, and are apt to yawn and go to sleep over any intellectual toil.

Quite true.

And yet we were saying that both qualities were necessary in those to whom the higher education is to be imparted, and who are to share in any office or command.

Certainly, he said.

And will they be a class which is rarely found?

Yes, indeed.

Then the aspirant must not only be tested in those labours and dangers and pleasures which we mentioned before, but there is another kind of probation which we did not mention—he must be exercised also in many kinds of knowledge, to see whether the soul will be able to endure the highest of all, or will faint under them, as in any other studies and exercises.

Yes, he said, you are quite right in testing him. But what do you mean by the highest of all knowledge?

You may remember, I said, that we divided the soul into three parts; and distinguished the several natures of justice temperance, courage, and wisdom?

Indeed, he said, if I had forgotten, I should not deserve to hear more.

And do you remember the word of caution which preceded the discussion of them?

To what do you refer?

We were saying, if I am not mistaken, that he who wanted

to see them in their perfect beauty must take a longer and more circuitous way, at the end of which they would appear; but that we could add on a popular exposition of them on a level with the discussion which had preceded. And you replied that such an exposition would be enough for you, and so the enquiry was continued in what to me seemed to be a very inaccurate manner; whether you were satisfied or not, it is for you to say.

Yes, he said, I thought and the others thought that you gave us a fair measure of truth.

But, my friend, I said, a measure of such things which in any degree falls short of the whole truth is not fair measure; for nothing imperfect is the measure of anything, although persons are too apt to be contented and think that they need search no further.

Not an uncommon case when people are indolent.

Yes, I said; and there cannot be any worse fault in a guardian of the State and of the laws.

True.

The guardian, then, I said, must be required to take the longer circuit, and toil at learning as well as at gymnastics, or he will never reach the highest knowledge of all which, as we were just now saying, is his proper calling.

What, he said, is there a knowledge still higher than this —higher than justice and the other virtues?

Yes, I said, there is. And of the virtues too we must behold not the outline merely, as at present—nothing short of the most finished picture should satisfy us. When little things are elaborated with an infinity of pains, in order that they may appear in their full beauty and utmost clearness, how ridiculous that we should not think the highest truths worthy of attaining the highest accuracy!

A right noble thought;[1] but do you suppose that we shall refrain from asking you what is this highest knowledge?

[1] Or, separating καὶ μάλα from ἄξιον, "True, he said, and a noble thought": or ἄξιον τὸ διανόημα may be a gloss.

Nay, I said, ask if you will; but I am certain that you have heard the answer many times, and now you either do not understand me or, as I rather think, you are disposed to be troublesome; for you have often been told that the idea of good is the highest knowledge, and that all other things become useful and advantageous only by their use of this. You can hardly be ignorant that of this I was about to speak, concerning which, as you have often heard me say, we know so little; and, without which, any other knowledge or possession of any kind will profit us nothing. Do you think that the possession of all other things is of any value if we do not possess the good? or the knowledge of all other things if we have no knowledge of beauty and goodness?

Assuredly not.

You are further aware that most people affirm pleasure to be the good, but the finer sort of wits say it is knowledge?

Yes.

And you are aware too that the latter cannot explain what they mean by knowledge, but are obliged after all to say knowledge of the good?

How ridiculous!

Yes, I said, that they should begin by reproaching us with our ignorance of the good, and then presume our knowledge of it—for the good they define to be knowledge of the good, just as if we understood them when they use the term "good" —this is of course ridiculous.

Most true, he said.

And those who make pleasure their good are in equal perplexity; for they are compelled to admit that there are bad pleasures as well as good.

Certainly.

And therefore to acknowledge that bad and good are the same?

True.

There can be no doubt about the numerous difficulties in which this question is involved.

There can be none.

Further, do we not see that many are willing to do or to have or to seem to be what is just and honourable without the reality; but no one is satisfied with the appearance of good—the reality is what they seek; in the case of the good, appearance is despised by every one.

Very true, he said.

Of this then, which every soul of man pursues and makes the end of all his actions, having a presentiment that there is such an end, and yet hesitating because neither knowing the nature nor having the same assurance of this as of other things, and therefore losing whatever good there is in other things,—of a principle such and so great as this ought the best men in our State, to whom everything is entrusted, to be in the darkness of ignorance?

Certainly not, he said.

I am sure, I said, that he who does not know how the beautiful and the just are likewise good will be but a sorry guardian of them; and I suspect that no one who is ignorant of the good will have a true knowledge of them.

That, he said, is a shrewd suspicion of yours.

And if we only have a guardian who has this knowledge our State will be perfectly ordered?

Of course, he replied; but I wish that you would tell me whether you conceive this supreme principle of the good to be knowledge or pleasure, or different from either?

Aye, I said, I knew all along that a fastidious gentleman [1] like you would not be contented with the thoughts of other people about these matters.

True, Socrates; but I must say that one who like you has passed a lifetime in the study of philosophy should not be always repeating the opinions of others, and never telling his own.

---

[1] Reading ἀνὴρ καλός: or reading ἀνὴρ καλῶς, "I quite well knew from the very first, that you," etc.

Well, but has any one a right to say positively what he does not know?

Not, he said, with the assurance of positive certainty; he has no right to do that: but he may say what he thinks, as a matter of opinion.

And do you not know, I said, that all mere opinions are bad, and the best of them blind? You would not deny that those who have any true notion without intelligence are only like blind men who feel their way along the road?

Very true.

And do you wish to behold what is blind and crooked and base, when others will tell you of brightness and beauty?

Still, I must implore you, Socrates, said Glaucon, not to turn away just as you are reaching the goal; if you will only give such an explanation of the good as you have already given of justice and temperance and the other virtues, we shall be satisfied.

Yes, my friend, and I shall be at least equally satisfied, but I cannot help fearing that I shall fail, and that my indiscreet zeal will bring ridicule upon me. No, sweet sirs, let us not at present ask what is the actual nature of the good, for to reach what is now in my thoughts would be an effort too great for me. But of the child of the good who is likest him, I would fain speak, if I could be sure that you wished to hear—otherwise, not.

By all means, he said, tell us about the child, and you shall remain in our debt for the account of the parent.

I do indeed wish, I replied, that I could pay, and you receive, the account of the parent, and not, as now, of the offspring only; take, however, this latter by way of interest,[1] and at the same time have a care that I do not render a false account, although I have no intention of deceiving you.

Yes, we will take all the care that we can: proceed.

Yes, I said, but I must first come to an understanding with

[1] A play upon τόκος, which means both "offspring" and "interest."

you, and remind you of what I have mentioned in the course of this discussion, and at many other times.

What?

The old story, that there is a many beautiful and a many good, and so of other things which we describe and define; to all of them the term "many" is applied.

True, he said.

And there is an absolute beauty and an absolute good, and of other things to which the term "many" is applied there is an absolute; for they may be brought under a single idea, which is called the essence of each.

Very true.

The many, as we say, are seen but not known, and the ideas are known but not seen.

Exactly.

And what is the organ with which we see the visible things?

The sight, he said.

And with the hearing, I said, we hear, and with the other senses perceive the other objects of sense?

True.

But have you remarked that sight is by far the most costly and complex piece of workmanship which the artificer of the senses ever contrived?

No, I never have, he said.

Then reflect: has the ear or voice need of any third or additional nature in order that the one may be able to hear and the other to be heard?

Nothing of the sort.

No, indeed, I replied; and the same is true of most, if not all, the other senses—you would not say that any of them requires such an addition?

Certainly not.

But you see that without the addition of some other nature there is no seeing or being seen?

How do you mean?

Sight being, as I conceive, in the eyes, and he who has eyes wanting to see; colour being also present in them, still unless there be a third nature specially adapted to the purpose, the owner of the eyes will see nothing and the colours will be invisible.

Of what nature are you speaking?

Of that which you term light, I replied.

True, he said.

Noble, then, is the bond which links together sight and visibility, and great beyond other bonds by no small difference of nature; for light is their bond, and light is no ignoble thing?

Nay, he said, the reverse of ignoble.

And which, I said, of the gods in heaven would you say was the lord of this element? Whose is that light which makes the eye to see perfectly and the visible to appear?

You mean the sun, as you and all mankind say.

May not the relation of sight to this deity be described as follows?

How?

Neither sight nor the eye in which sight resides is the sun?

No.

Yet of all the organs of sense the eye is the most like the sun?

By far the most like.

And the power which the eye possesses is a sort of effluence which is dispensed from the sun?

Exactly.

Then the sun is not sight, but the author of sight who is recognized by sight?

True, he said.

And this is he whom I call the child of the good, whom the good begat in his own likeness, to be in the visible world, in relation to sight and the things of sight, what the good is in the intellectual world in relation to mind and the things of mind:

Will you be a little more explicit? he said.

Why, you know, I said, that the eyes, when a person directs them towards objects on which the light of day is no longer shining, but the moon and stars only, see dimly, and are nearly blind; they seem to have no clearness of vision in them?

Very true.

But when they are directed towards objects on which the sun shines, they see clearly and there is sight in them?

Certainly.

And the soul is like the eye: when resting upon that on which truth and being shine, the soul perceives and understands, and is radiant with intelligence; but when turned towards the twilight of becoming and perishing, then she has opinion only, and goes blinking about, and is first of one opinion and then of another, and seems to have no intelligence?

Just so.

Now, that which imparts truth to the known and the power of knowing to the knower is what I would have you term the idea of good, and this you will deem to be the cause of science,[1] and of truth in so far as the latter becomes the subject of knowledge; beautiful too, as are both truth and knowledge, you will be right in esteeming this other nature as more beautiful than either; and, as in the previous instance, light and sight may be truly said to be like the sun, and yet not to be the sun, so in this other sphere, science and truth may be deemed to be like the good, but not the good; the good has a place of honour yet higher.

What a wonder of beauty that must be, he said, which is the author of science and truth, and yet surpasses them in beauty; for you surely cannot mean to say that pleasure is the good?

God forbid, I replied; but may I ask you to consider the image in another point of view?

[1] Reading διανοοῦ.

In what point of view?

You would say, would you not, that the sun is not only the author of visibility in all visible things, but of generation and nourishment and growth, though he himself is not generation?

Certainly.

In like manner the good may be said to be not only the author of knowledge to all things known, but of their being and essence, and yet the good is not essence, but far exceeds essence in dignity and power.

Glaucon said, with a ludicrous earnestness: By the light of heaven, how amazing!

Yes, I said, and the exaggeration may be set down to you; for you made me utter my fancies.

And pray continue to utter them; at any rate let us hear if there is anything more to be said about the similitude of the sun.

Yes, I said, there is a great deal more.

Then omit nothing, however slight.

I will do my best, I said; but I should think that a great deal will have to be omitted.

I hope not, he said.

You have to imagine, then, that there are two ruling powers, and that one of them is set over the intellectual world, the other over the visible. I do not say heaven, lest you should fancy that I am playing upon the name (οὐρανός ὁρατός). May I suppose that you have this distinction of the visible and intelligible fixed in your mind?

I have.

Now take a line which has been cut into two unequal[1] parts, and divide each of them again in the same proportion, and suppose the two main divisions to answer, one to the visible and the other to the intelligible, and then compare the subdivisions in respect of their clearness and want of clearness, and you will find that the first section in the sphere

[1] Reading ἄνισα.

of the visible consists of images. And by images I mean, in the first place, shadows, and in the second place, reflections in water and in solid, smooth and polished bodies and the like: Do you understand?

Yes, I understand.

Imagine, now, the other section, of which this is only the the resemblance, to include the animals which we see, and everything that grows or is made.

Very good.

Would you not admit that both the sections of this division have different degrees of truth, and that the copy is to the original as the sphere of opinion is to the sphere of knowledge?

Most undoubtedly.

Next proceed to consider the manner in which the sphere of the intellectual is to be divided.

In what manner?

Thus:—There are two subdivisions, in the lower of which the soul uses the figures given by the former division as images; the enquiry can only be hypothetical, and instead of going upwards to a principle descends to the other end; in the higher of the two, the soul passes out of hypotheses, and goes up to a principle which is above hypotheses, making no use of images[1] as in the former case, but proceeding only in and through the ideas themselves.

I do not quite understand your meaning, he said.

Then I will try again; you will understand me better when I have made some preliminary remarks. You are aware that students of geometry, arithmetic, and the kindred sciences assume the odd and the even and the figures and three kinds of angles and the like in their several branches of science; these are their hypotheses, which they and everybody are supposed to know, and therefore they do not deign to give any account of them either to themselves or others; but they

---

[1] Reading ὧνπερ ἐκεῖνο εἰκόνων.

begin with them, and go on until they arrive at last, and in a consistent manner, at their conclusion?

Yes, he said, I know.

And do you not know also that although they make use of the visible forms and reason about them, they are thinking not of these, but of the ideals which they resemble; not of the figures which they draw, but of the absolute square and the absolute diameter, and so on—the forms which they draw or make, and which have shadows and reflections in water of their own, are converted by them into images, but they are really seeking to behold the things themselves, which can only be seen with the eye of the mind?

That is true.

And of this kind I spoke as the intelligible, although in the search after it the soul is compelled to use hypotheses; not ascending to a first principle, because she is unable to rise above the region of hypothesis, but employing the objects of which the shadows below are resemblances in their turn as images, they having in relation to the shadows and reflections of them a greater distinctness, and therefore a higher value.

I understand, he said, that you are speaking of the province of geometry and the sister arts.

And when I speak of the other division of the intelligible, you will understand me to speak of that other sort of knowledge which reason herself attains by the power of dialectic, using the hypotheses not as first principles, but only as hypotheses—that is to say, as steps and points of departure into a world which is above hypotheses, in order that she may soar beyond them to the first principle of the whole; and clinging to this and then to that which depends on this, by successive steps she descends again without the aid of any sensible object, from ideas, through ideas, and in ideas she ends.

I understand you, he replied; not perfectly, for you seem

to me to be describing a task which is really tremendous; but, at any rate, I understand you to say that knowledge and being, which the science of dialectic contemplates, are clearer than the notions of the arts, as they are termed, which proceed from hypotheses only: these are also contemplated by the understanding, and not by the senses: yet, because they start from hypotheses and do not ascend to a principle, those who contemplate them appear to you not to exercise the higher reason upon them, although when a first principle is added to them they are cognizable by the higher reason. And the habit which is concerned with geometry and the cognate sciences I suppose that you would term understanding and not reason, as being intermediate between opinion and reason.

You have quite conceived my meaning, I said; and now, corresponding to these four divisions, let there be four faculties in the soul—reason answering to the highest, understanding to the second, faith (or conviction) to the third, and perception of shadows to the last—and let there be a scale of them, and let us suppose that the several faculties have clearness in the same degree that their objects have truth.

I understand, he replied, and give my assent, and accept your arrangement.

THEAETETUS

THEAETETUS

PERSONS OF THE DIALOGUE

SOCRATES.   THEODORUS.   THEAETETUS.

Euclid and Terpsion meet in front of Euclid's house in Megara; they
enter the house, and the dialogue is read to them by a servant.

Euclid. Have you only just arrived from the country,
Terpsion?

Terpsion. No, I came some time ago: and I have been in
the Agora looking for you, and wondering that I could not
find you.

Euc. But I was not in the city.

Terp. Where then?

Euc. As I was going down to the harbour, I met Theaetetus
—he was being carried up to Athens from the army at
Corinth.

Terp. Was he alive or dead?

Euc. He was scarcely alive, for he has been badly wounded;
but he was suffering even more from the sickness which has
broken out in the army.

Terp. The dysentery, you mean?

Euc. Yes.

Terp. Alas! what a loss he will be!

Euc. Yes, Terpsion, he is a noble fellow; only to-day I
heard some people highly praising his behaviour in this very
battle.

Terp. No wonder; I should rather be surprised at hearing
anything else of him. But why did he go on, instead of stopping at Megara?

Euc. He wanted to get home: although I entreated and
advised him to remain, he would not listen to me; so I set

him on his way, and turned back, and then I remembered
what Socrates had said of him, and thought how remarkably
this, like all his predictions, had been fulfilled. I believe that
he had seen him a little before his own death, when Theaetetus was a youth, and he had a memorable conversation
with him, which he repeated to me when I came to Athens;
he was full of admiration of his genius, and said that he
would most certainly be a great man, if he lived.

Terp. The prophecy has certainly been fulfilled; but what
was the conversation? Can you tell me?

Euc. No, indeed, not offhand; but I took notes of it as
soon as I got home; these I filled up from memory, writing
them out at leisure; and whenever I went to Athens, I asked
Socrates about any point which I had forgotten, and on my
return I made corrections; thus I have nearly the whole conversation written down.

Terp. I remember—you told me; and I have always been
intending to ask you to show me the writing, but have put
off doing so; and now, why should we not read it through?—
having just come from the country, I should greatly like
to rest.

Euc. I too shall be very glad of a rest, for I went with
Theaetetus as far as Erineum. Let us go in, then, and, while
we are reposing, the servant shall read to us.

Terp. Very good.

Euc. Here is the roll, Terpsion; I may observe that I have
introduced Socrates, not as narrating to me, but as actually
conversing with the persons whom he mentioned—these were,
Theodorus the geometrician (of Cyrene), and Theaetetus. I
have omitted, for the sake of convenience, the interlocutory
words "I said," "I remarked," which he used when he spoke
of himself, and again, "he agreed," or "disagreed," in the
answer, lest the repetition of them should be troublesome.

Terp. Quite right, Euclid.

Euc. And now, boy, you may take the roll and read.

Euclid's servant reads.

Socrates. If I cared enough about the Cyrenians, Theo-dorus, I would ask you whether there are any rising geome-tricians or philosophers in that part of the world. But I am more interested in our own Athenian youth, and I would rather know who among them are likely to do well. I observe them as far as I can myself, and I enquire of any one whom they follow, and I see that a great many of them follow you, in which they are quite right, considering your eminence in geometry and in other ways. Tell me then, if you have met with any one who is good for anything.

Theodorus. Yes, Socrates, I have become acquainted with one very remarkable Athenian youth, whom I commend to you as well worthy of your attention. If he had been a beauty I should have been afraid to praise him, lest you should suppose that I was in love with him; but he is no beauty, and you must not be offended if I say that he is very like you; for he has a snub nose and projecting eyes, although these features are less marked in him than in you. Seeing, then, that he has no personal attractions, I may freely say, that in all my acquaintance, which is very large, I never knew any one who was his equal in natural gifts: for he has a quickness of apprehension which is almost unrivalled, and he is exceedingly gentle, and also the most courageous of men; there is a union of qualities in him such as I have never seen in any other, and should scarcely have thought pos-sible; for those who, like him, have quick and ready and retentive wits, have generally also quick tempers; they are ships without ballast, and go darting about, and are mad rather than courageous; and the steadier sort, when they have to face study, prove stupid and cannot remember. Whereas he moves surely and smoothly and successfully in the path of knowledge and enquiry; and he is full of gentle-ness, flowing on silently like a river of oil; at his age, it is wonderful.

Soc. That is good news; whose son is he?

Theod. The name of his father I have forgotten, but the youth himself is the middle one of those who are approaching us; he and his companions have been anointing themselves in the outer court, and now they seem to have finished, and are coming towards us. Look and see whether you know him.

Soc. I know the youth, but I do not know his name; he is the son of Euphronius the Sunian, who was himself an eminent man, and such another as his son is, according to your account of him; I believe that he left a considerable fortune.

Theod. Theaetetus, Socrates, is his name; but I rather think that the property disappeared in the hands of trustees; notwithstanding which he is wonderfully liberal.

Soc. He must be a fine fellow; tell him to come and sit by me.

Theod. I will. Come hither, Theaetetus, and sit by Socrates.

Soc. By all means, Theaetetus, in order that I may see the reflection of myself in your face, for Theodorus says that we are alike; and yet if each of us held in his hands a lyre, and he said they were tuned alike, should we at once take his word, or should we ask whether he who said so was or was not a musician?

Theaetetus. We should ask.

Soc. And if we found that he was, we should take his word; and if not, not?

Theaet. True.

Soc. And if this supposed likeness of our faces is a matter of any interest to us, we should enquire whether he who says that we are alike is a painter or not?

Theaet. Certainly we should.

Soc. And is Theodorus a painter?

Theaet. I never heard that he was.

Soc. Is he a geometrician?

Theaet. Of course he is, Socrates.

Soc. And is he an astronomer and calculator and musician, and in general an educated man?

Theaet. I think so.

Soc. If, then, he remarks on a similarity in our persons, either by way of praise or blame, there is no particular reason why we should attend to him.

Theaet. I should say not.

Soc. But if he praises the virtue or wisdom which are the mental endowments of either of us, then he who hears the praises will naturally desire to examine him who is praised: and he again should be willing to exhibit himself.

Theaet. Very true, Socrates.

Soc. Then now is the time, my dear Theaetetus, for me to examine, and for you to exhibit; since although Theodorus has praised many a citizen and stranger in my hearing, never did I hear him praise any one as he has been praising you.

Theaet. I am glad to hear it, Socrates; but what if he was only in jest?

Soc. Nay, Theodorus is not given to jesting; and I cannot allow you to retract your consent on any such pretence as that. If you do, he will have to swear to his words; and we are perfectly sure that no one will be found to impugn him. Do not be shy then, but stand to your word.

Theaet. I suppose I must, if you wish it.

Soc. In the first place, I should like to ask what you learn of Theodorus: something of geometry, perhaps?

Theaet. Yes.

Soc. And astronomy and harmony and calculation?

Theaet. I do my best.

Soc. Yes, my boy, and so do I; and my desire is to learn of him, or of anybody who seems to understand these things. And I get on pretty well in general; but there is a little difficulty which I want you and the company to aid me in investigating. Will you answer me a question: "Is not learning growing wiser about that which you learn?"

Theaet. Of course.

Soc. And by wisdom the wise are wise?

Theaet. Yes.

Soc. And is that different in any way from knowledge?

Theaet. What?

Soc. Wisdom; are not men wise in that which they know?

Theaet. Certainly they are.

Soc. Then wisdom and knowledge are the same?

Theaet. Yes.

Soc. Herein lies the difficulty which I can never solve to my satisfaction—What is knowledge? Can we answer that question? What say you? which of us will speak first? Whoever misses shall sit down, as at a game of ball, and shall be donkey, as the boys say; he who lasts out his competitors in the game without missing, shall be our king, and shall have the right of putting to us any questions which he pleases . . . Why is there no reply? I hope, Theodorus, that I am not betrayed into rudeness by my love of conversation? I only want to make us talk and be friendly and sociable.

Theod. The reverse of rudeness, Socrates: but I would rather that you would ask one of the young fellows; for the truth is, that I am unused to your game of question and answer, and I am too old to learn; the young will be more suitable, and they will improve more than I shall, for youth is always able to improve. And so having made a beginning with Theaetetus, I would advise you to go on with him and not let him off.

Soc. Do you hear, Theaetetus, what Theodorus says? The philosopher, whom you would not like to disobey, and whose word ought to be a command to a young man, bids me interrogate you. Take courage, then, and nobly say what you think that knowledge is.

Theaet. Well, Socrates, I will answer as you and he bid me; and if I make a mistake, you will doubtless correct me.

Soc. We will, if we can.

Theaet. Then, I think that the sciences which I learn from Theodorus—geometry, and those which you just now mentioned—are knowledge; and I would include the art of the cobbler and other craftsmen; these, each and all of them, are knowledge.

Soc. Too much, Theaetetus, too much; the nobility and liberality of your nature make you give many and diverse things, when I am asking for one simple thing.

Theaet. What do you mean, Socrates?

Soc. Perhaps nothing. I will endeavour, however, to explain what I believe to be my meaning: When you speak of cobbling, you mean the art or science of making shoes?

Theaet. Just so.

Soc. And when you speak of carpentering, you mean the art of making wooden implements?

Theaet. I do.

Soc. In both cases you define the subject-matter of each of the two arts?

Theaet. True.

Soc. But that, Theaetetus, was not the point of my question: we wanted to know not the subjects, nor yet the number of the arts or sciences, for we were not going to count them, but we wanted to know the nature of knowledge in the abstract. Am I not right?

Theaet. Perfectly right.

Soc. Let me offer an illustration: Suppose that a person were to ask about some very trivial and obvious thing—for example, What is clay? and we were to reply, that there is a clay of potters, there is a clay of oven-makers, there is a clay of brick-makers; would not the answer be ridiculous?

Theaet. Truly.

Soc. In the first place, there would be an absurdity in assuming that he who asked the question would understand from our answer the nature of "clay," merely because we added "of the image-makers," or of any other workers. How can a man understand the name of anything, when he does not know the nature of it?

Theaet. He cannot.

Soc. Then he who does not know what science or knowledge is, has no knowledge of the art or science of making shoes?

Theaet. None.

Soc. Nor of any other science?

Theaet. No.

Soc. And when a man is asked what science or knowledge is, to give in answer the name of some art or science is ridiculous; for the question is, "What is knowledge?" and he replies, "A knowledge of this or that."

Theaet. True.

Soc. Moreover, he might answer shortly and simply, but he makes an enormous circuit. For example, when asked about the clay, he might have said simply, that clay is moistened earth—what sort of clay is not to the point.

Theaet. Yes, Socrates, there is no difficulty as you put the question. You mean, if I am not mistaken, something like what occurred to me and to my friend here, your namesake, Socrates, in a recent discussion.

Soc. What was that, Theaetetus?

Theaet. Theodorus was writing out for us something about roots, such as the roots of three or five, showing that they are incommensurable by the unit: he selected other examples up to seventeen—there he stopped. Now as there are innumerable roots, the notion occurred to us of attempting to include them all under one name or class.

Soc. And did you find such a class?

Theaet. I think that we did; but I should like to have your opinion.

Soc. Let me hear.

Theaet. We divided all numbers into two classes: those which are made up of equal factors multiplying into one another, which we compared to square figures and called square or equilateral numbers;—that was one class.

Soc. Very good.

Theaet. The intermediate numbers, such as three and five, and every other number which is made up of unequal factors, either of a greater multiplied by a less, or of a less multiplied by a greater, and when regarded as a figure, is contained in unequal sides;—all these we compared to oblong figures, and called them oblong numbers.

Soc. Capital; and what followed?

Theaet. The lines, or sides, which have for their squares the equilateral plane numbers, were called by us lengths or magnitudes; and the lines which are the roots of (or whose squares are equal to) the oblong numbers, were called powers or roots; the reason of this latter name being, that they are commensurable with the former [i. e. with the so-called lengths or magnitudes] not in linear measurement, but in the value of the superficial content of their squares; and the same about solids.

Soc. Excellent, my boy; I think that you fully justify the praises of Theodorus, and that he will not be found guilty of false witness.

Theaet. But I am unable, Socrates, to give you a similar answer about knowledge, which is what you appear to want; and therefore Theodorus is a deceiver after all.

Soc. Well, but if some one were to praise you for running, and to say that he never met your equal among boys, and afterwards you were beaten in a race by a grown-up man, who was a great runner—would the praise be any the less true?

Theaet. Certainly not.

Soc. And is the discovery of the nature of knowledge so small a matter, as I just now said? Is it not one which would task the powers of men perfect in every way?

Theaet. By heaven, they should be the top of all perfection!

Soc. Well, then, be of good cheer; do not say that Theodorus was mistaken about you, but do your best to ascertain the true nature of knowledge, as well as of other things.

Theaet. I am eager enough, Socrates, if that would bring to light the truth.

Soc. Come, you made a good beginning just now; let your

own answer about roots be your model, and as you comprehended them all in one class, try and bring the many sorts of
knowledge under one definition.

Theaet. I can assure you, Socrates, that I have tried very
often, when the report of questions asked by you was brought
to me; but I can neither persuade myself that I have a satisfactory answer to give, nor hear of any one who answers as
you would have him; and I cannot shake off a feeling of
anxiety.

Soc. These are the pangs of labour, my dear Theaetetus;
you have something within you which you are bringing to
the birth.

Theaet. I do not know, Socrates; I only say what I feel.

Soc. And have you never heard, simpleton, that I am the
son of a midwife, brave and burly, whose name was Phae-
narete?

Theaet. Yes, I have.

Soc. And that I myself practise midwifery?

Theaet. No, never.

Soc. Let me tell you that I do though, my friend: but you
must not reveal the secret, as the world in general have not
found me out; and therefore they only say of me, that I am
the strangest of mortals and drive men to their wits' end.
Did you ever hear that too?

Theaet. Yes.

Soc. Shall I tell you the reason?

Theaet. By all means.

Soc. Bear in mind the whole business of the midwives, and
then you will see my meaning better:—No woman, as you
are probably aware, who is still able to conceive and bear,
attends other women, but only those who are past bearing.

Theaet. Yes, I know.

Soc. The reason of this is said to be that Artemis—the
goddess of childbirth—is not a mother, and she honours those
who are like herself; but she could not allow the barren to be
midwives, because human nature cannot know the mystery

of an art without experience; and therefore she assigned this office to those who are too old to bear.

Theaet. I dare say.

Soc. And I dare say too, or rather I am absolutely certain, that the midwives know better than others who is pregnant and who is not?

Theaet. Very true.

Soc. And by the use of potions and incantations they are able to arouse the pangs and to soothe them at will; they can make those bear who have a difficulty in bearing, and if they think fit they can smother the embryo in the womb.

Theaet. They can.

Soc. Did you ever remark that they are also most cunning matchmakers, and have a thorough knowledge of what unions are likely to produce a brave brood?

Theaet. No, never.

Soc. Then let me tell you that this is their greatest pride, more than cutting the umbilical cord. And if you reflect, you will see that the same art which cultivates and gathers in the fruits of the earth, will be most likely to know in what soils the several plants or seeds should be deposited.

Theaet. Yes, the same art.

Soc. And do you suppose that with women the case is otherwise?

Theaet. I should think not.

Soc. Certainly not; but midwives are respectable women who have a character to lose, and they avoid this department of their profession, because they are afraid of being called procuresses, which is a name given to those who join together man and woman in an unlawful and unscientific way; and yet the true midwife is also the true and only matchmaker.

Theaet. Clearly.

Soc. Such are the midwives, whose task is a very important one, but not so important as mine; for women do not bring into the world at one time real children, and at another time counterfeits which are with difficulty distinguished from

them; if they did, then the discernment of the true and false
birth would be the crowning achievement of the art of
midwifery—you would think so?

Theaet. Indeed I should.

Soc. Well, my art of midwifery is in most respects like
theirs; but differs, in that I attend men and not women, and
I look after their souls when they are in labour, and not
after their bodies: and the triumph of my art is in thoroughly
examining whether the thought which the mind of the young
man brings forth is a false idol or a noble and true birth.
And like the midwives, I am barren, and the reproach which
is often made against me, that I ask questions of others
and have not the wit to answer them myself, is very just—
the reason is, that the god compels me to be a midwife,
but does not allow me to bring forth. And therefore I am
not myself at all wise, nor have I anything to show which is
the invention or birth of my own soul, but those who converse
with me profit. Some of them appear dull enough at first, but
afterwards, as our acquaintance ripens, if the god is gracious
to them, they all make astonishing progress; and this in the
opinion of others as well as in their own. It is quite clear that
they never learned anything from me; the many fine discoveries to which they cling are of their own making. But to
me and the god they owe their delivery. And the proof of my
words is, that many of them in their ignorance, either in their
self-conceit despising me, or falling under the influence of
others,[1] have gone away too soon; and have not only lost the
children of whom I had previously delivered them by an ill
bringing up, but have stifled whatever else they had in them
by evil communication, being fonder of lies and shams than
of the truth; and they have at last ended by seeing themselves,
as others see them, to be great fools. Aristeides, the son of
Lysimachus, is one of them, and there are many others. The
truants often return to me, and beg that I would consort with
them again—they are ready to go to me on their knees—and

---

[1] Reading with the Bodleian MS. ἢ αὐτοὶ ὑἢ ἄλλων πεισθέντες.

then, if my familiar allows, which is not always the case, I receive them, and they begin to grow again. Dire are the pangs which my art is able to arouse and to allay in those who consort with me, just like the pangs of women in child-birth; night and day they are full of perplexity and travail which is even worse than that of the women. So much for them. And there are others, Theaetetus, who come to me apparently having nothing in them; and as I know that they have no need of my art, I coax them into marrying some one, and by the grace of God I can generally tell who is likely to do them good. Many of them I have given away to Prodicus, and many to other inspired sages. I tell you this long story, friend Thaetetus, because I suspect, as indeed you seem to think yourself, that you are in labour—great with some conception. Come then to me, who am a midwife's son and myself a midwife, and do your best to answer the questions which I will ask you. And if I abstract and expose your first-born, because I discover upon inspection that the conception which you have formed is a vain shadow, do not quarrel with me on that account, as the manner of women is when their first children are taken from them. For I have actually known some who were ready to bite me when I deprived them of a darling folly; they did not perceive that I acted from good-will, not knowing that no god is the enemy of man—that was not within the range of their ideas; neither am I their enemy in all this, but it would be wrong for me to admit falsehood, or to stifle the truth. Once more, then, Theaetetus, I repeat my old question, "What is knowledge?" —and do not say that you cannot tell; but quit yourself like a man, and by the help of God you will be able to tell.

Theaet. At any rate, Socrates, after such an exhortation I should be ashamed of not trying to do my best. Now he who knows perceives what he knows, and, as far as I can see at present, knowledge is perception.

Soc. Bravely said, boy; that is the way in which you should express your opinion. And now, let us examine together this conception of yours, and see whether it is a true birth or a mere wind-egg:—You say that knowledge is perception?

Theaet. Yes.

Soc. Well, you have delivered yourself of a very important doctrine about knowledge; it is indeed the opinion of Protagoras, who has another way of expressing it. Man, he says, is the measure of all things, of the existence of things that are, and of the non-existence of things that are not:—You have read him?

Theaet. O yes, again and again.

Soc. Does he not say that things are to you such as they appear to you, and to me such as they appear to me, and that you and I are men?

Theaet. Yes, he says so.

Soc. A wise man is not likely to talk nonsense. Let us try to understand him: the same wind is blowing, and yet one of us may be cold and the other not, or one may be slightly and the other very cold?

Theaet. Quite true.

Soc. Now is the wind, regarded not in relation to us but absolutely, cold or not; or are we to say, with Protagoras, that the wind is cold to him who is cold, and not to him who is not?

Theaet. I suppose the last.

Soc. Then it must appear so to each of them?

Theaet. Yes.

Soc. And "appears to him" means the same as "he perceives."

Theaet. True.

Soc. Then appearing and perceiving coincide in the case of hot and cold, and in similar instances; for things appear, or may be supposed to be, to each one such as he perceives them?

Theaet. Yes.

Soc. Then perception is always of existence, and being the same as knowledge is unerring?

Theaet. Clearly.

Soc. In the name of the Graces, what an almighty wise man Protagoras must have been! He spoke these things in a parable to the common herd, like you and me, but told the truth, "his Truth,"[1] in secret to his own disciples.

Theaet. What do you mean, Socrates?

Soc. I am about to speak of a high argument, in which all things are said to be relative; you cannot rightly call anything by any name, such as great or small, heavy or light, for the great will be small and the heavy light—there is no single thing or quality, but out of motion and change and admixture all things are becoming relatively to one another, which "becoming" is by us incorrectly called being, but is really becoming, for nothing ever is, but all things are becoming. Summon all philosophers—Protagoras, Heracleitus, Empedocles, and the rest of them, one after another, and with the exception of Parmenides they will agree with you in this. Summon the great masters of either kind of poetry—Epicharmus, the prince of Comedy, and Homer of Tragedy; when the latter sings of

"Ocean whence sprang the gods, and mother Tethys,"

does he not mean that all things are the offspring of flux and motion?

Theaet. I think so.

Soc. And who could take up arms against such a great army having Homer for its general, and not appear ridiculous?[2]

Theaet. Who indeed, Socrates?

Soc. Yes, Theaetetus; and there are plenty of other proofs which will show that motion is the source of what is called being and becoming, and inactivity of not-being and destruction; for fire and warmth, which are supposed to be the parent and guardian of all other things, are born of move-

[1] In allusion to a book of Protagoras' which bore this title.
[2] Cp. Cratylus 401 E. ff.

ment and of friction, which is a kind of motion; [1]—is not this the origin of fire?

Theaet. It is.

Soc. And the race of animals is generated in the same way?

Theaet. Certainly.

Soc. And is not the bodily habit spoiled by rest and idleness, but preserved for a long time [2] by motion and exercise?

Theaet. True.

Soc. And what of the mental habit? Is not the soul informed, and improved, and preserved by study and attention, which are motions; but when at rest, which in the soul only means want of attention and study, is uninformed, and speedily forgets whatever she has learned?

Theaet. True.

Soc. Then motion is a good, and rest an evil, to the soul as well as to the body?

Theaet. Clearly.

Soc. I may add, that breathless calm, stillness and the like waste and impair, while wind and storm preserve; and the palmary argument of all, which I strongly urge, is the golden chain in Homer, by which he means the sun, thereby indicating that so long as the sun and the heavens go round in their orbits, all things human and divine are and are preserved, but if they were chained up and their motions ceased, then all things would be destroyed, and, as the saying is, turned upside down.

Theaet. I believe, Socrates, that you have truly explained his meaning.

Soc. Then now apply his doctrine to perception, my good friend, and first of all to vision; that which you call white colour is not in your eyes, and is not a distinct thing which exists out of them. And you must not assign any place to it: for if it had position it would be, and be at rest, and there would be no process of becoming.

[1] Reading τοῦτο δὲ κίνησις.
[2] Reading ἐπὶ πολύ.

Theaet. Then what is colour?

Soc. Let us carry out the principle which has just been affirmed, that nothing is self-existent, and then we shall see that white, black, and every other colour, arises out of the eye meeting the appropriate motion, and that what we call a colour is in each case neither the active nor the passive element, but something which passes between them, and is peculiar to each percipient; are you quite certain that the several colours appear to a dog or to any animal whatever as they appear to you?

Theaet. Far from it.

Soc. Or that anything appears the same to you as to another man? Are you so profoundly convinced of this? Rather would it not be true that it never appears exactly the same to you, because you are never exactly the same?

Theaet. The latter.

Soc. And if that with which I compare myself in size,[1] or which I apprehend by touch, were great or white or hot, it could not become different by mere contract with another unless it actually changed; nor again, if the comparing or apprehending subject were great or white or hot, could this, when unchanged from within, become changed by any approximation or affection of any other thing. The fact is that in our ordinary way of speaking we allow ourselves to be driven into most ridiculous and wonderful contradictions, as Protagoras and all who take his line of argument would remark.

Theaet. How? and of what sort do you mean?

Soc. A little instance will sufficiently explain my meaning: Here are six dice, which are more by a half when compared with four, and fewer by a half than twelve—they are more and also fewer. How can you or any one maintain the contrary?

Theaet. Very true.

Soc. Well, then, suppose that Protagoras or some one asks

---

[1] Reading with the MSS. ᾧ παραμετρούμεθα.

whether anything can become greater or more if not by increasing, how would you answer him, Theaetetus?

Theaet. I should say 'No,' Socrates, if I were to speak my mind in reference to this last question, and if I were not afraid of contradicting my former answer.

Soc. Capital! excellent! spoken like an oracle, my boy! And if you reply 'Yes,' there will be a case for Euripides; for our tongue will be unconvinced, but not our mind.[1]

Theaet. Very true.

Soc. The thoroughbred Sophists, who know all that can be known about the mind, and argue only out of the superfluity of their wits, would have had a regular sparring-match over this, and would have knocked their arguments together finely. But you and I, who have no professional aims, only desire to see what is the mutual relation of these principles,— whether they are consistent with each other or not.

Theaet. Yes, that would be my desire.

Soc. And mine too. But since this is our feeling, and there is plenty of time, why should we not calmly and patiently review our own thoughts, and thoroughly examine and see what these appearances in us really are? If I am not mistaken, they will be described by us as follows:—first, that nothing can become greater or less, either in number or magnitude, while remaining equal to itself—you would agree?

Theaet. Yes.

Soc. Secondly, that without addition or subtraction there is no increase or diminution of anything, but only equality.

Theaet. Quite true.

Soc. Thirdly, that what was not before cannot be afterwards, without becoming and having become.

Theaet. Yes, truly.

Soc. These three axioms, if I am not mistaken, are fighting with one another in our minds in the case of the dice, or, again, in such a case as this—if I were to say that I, who

---

[1] In allusion to the well-known line of Euripides, Hippol. 612:
ἡ γλῶσσ' ὀμώμοχ', ἡ δὲ φρὴν ἀνώμοτος.

am of a certain height and taller than you, may within a
year, without gaining or losing in height, be not so tall—
not that I should have lost, but that you would have increased. In such a case, I am afterwards what I once was
not, and yet I have not become; for I could not have become
without becoming, neither could I have become less without
losing somewhat of my height; and I could give you ten
thousand examples of similar contradictions, if we admit
them at all. I believe that you follow me, Theaetetus; for
I suspect that you have thought of these questions before
now.

Theaet. Yes, Socrates, and I am amazed when I think of
them; by the gods I am! and I want to know what on earth
they mean; and there are times when my head quite swims
with the contemplation of them.

Soc. I see, my dear Theaetetus, that Theodorus had a true
insight into your nature when he said that you were a
philosopher, for wonder is the feeling of a philosopher, and
philosophy begins in wonder. He was not a bad genealogist
who said that Iris (the messenger of heaven) is the child
of Thaumas (wonder). But do you begin to see what is
the explanation of this perplexity on the hypothesis which
we attribute to Protagoras?

Theaet. Not as yet.

Soc. Then you will be obliged to me if I help you to un-
earth the hidden "truth" of a famous man or school.

Theaet. To be sure, I shall be very much obliged.

Soc. Take a look round, then, and see that none of the
uninitiated are listening. Now by the uninitiated I mean the
people who believe in nothing but what they can grasp in
their hands, and who will not allow that action or generation
or anything invisible can have real existence.

Theaet. Yes, indeed, Socrates, they are very hard and im-
penetrable mortals.

Soc. Yes, my boy, outer barbarians. Far more ingenious
are the brethren whose mysteries I am about to reveal to you.

Their first principle is, that all is motion, and upon this all the affections of which we were just now speaking are supposed to depend: there is nothing but motion, which has two forms, one active and the other passive, both in endless number; and out of the union and friction of them there is generated a progeny endless in number, having two forms, sense and the object of sense, which are ever breaking forth and coming to the birth at the same moment. The senses are variously named hearing, seeing, smelling; there is the sense of heat, cold, pleasure, pain, desire, fear, and many more which have names, as well as innumerable others which are without them; each has its kindred object,—each variety of colour has a corresponding variety of sight, and so with sound and hearing, and with the rest of the senses and the objects akin to them. Do you see, Theaetetus, the bearings of this tale on the preceding argument?

Theaet. Indeed I do not.

Soc. Then attend, and I will try to finish the story. The purport is that all these things are in motion, as I was saying, and that this motion is of two kinds, a slower and a quicker; and the slower elements have their motions in the same place and with reference to things near them, and so they beget; but what is begotten is swifter, for it is carried to and fro, and moves from place to place. Apply this to sense:—When the eye and the appropriate object meet together and give birth to whiteness and the sensation connatural with it, which could not have been given by either of them going elsewhere, then, while the sight is flowing from the eye, whiteness proceeds from the object which combines in producing the colour; and so the eye is fulfilled with sight, and really sees, and becomes, not sight, but a seeing eye; and the object which combined to form the colour is fulfilled with whiteness, and becomes not whiteness but a white thing, whether wood or stone or whatever the object may be which happens to be coloured white.[1] And this is true of all sensible objects, hard,

[1] Reading ὁτιοῦν or ὁτφοῦν and omitting χρῶμα.

warm, and the like, which are similarly to be regarded, as I was saying before, not as having any absolute existence, but as being all of them of whatever kind generated by motion in their intercourse with one another; for of the agent and patient, as existing in separation, no trustworthy conception, as they say, can be formed, for the agent has no existence until united with the patient, and the patient has no existence until united with the agent; and that which by uniting with something becomes an agent, by meeting with some other thing is converted into a patient. And from all these considerations, as I said at first, there arises a general reflection, that there is no one self-existent thing, but everything is becoming and in relation; and being must be altogether abolished, although from habit and ignorance we are compelled even in this discussion to retain the use of the term. But great philosophers tell us that we are not to allow either the word "something," or "belonging to something," or "to me," or "this" or "that," or any other detaining name to be used; in the language of nature all things are being created and destroyed, coming into being and passing into new forms; nor can any name fix or detain them; he who attempts to fix them is easily refuted. And this should be the way of speaking, not only of particulars but of aggregates; such aggregates as are expressed in the word "man," or "stone," or any name of an animal or of a class. O Theaetetus, are not these speculations sweet as honey? And do you not like the taste of them in the mouth?

Theaet. I do not know what to say, Socrates; for, indeed, I cannot make out whether you are giving your own opinion or only wanting to draw me out.

Soc. You forget, my friend, that I neither know, nor profess to know, anything of these matters; you are the person who is in labour, I am the barren midwife; and this is why I soothe you, and offer you one good thing after another, that you may taste them. And I hope that I may at last help to bring your own opinion into the light of day: when this has been accomplished, then we will determine whether what you have brought forth is only a wind-egg or a real and genuine birth. Therefore, keep up your spirits, and answer like a man what you think.

Theaet. Ask me.

Soc. Then once more: Is it your opinion that nothing is but what becomes?—the good and the noble, as well as all the other things which we were just now mentioning?

Theaet. When I hear you discoursing in this style, I think that there is a great deal in what you say, and I am very ready to assent.

Soc. Let us not leave the argument unfinished, then; for there still remains to be considered an objection which may be raised about dreams and disease, in particular about madness, and the various illusions of hearing and sight, or of other senses. For you know that in all these cases the *esse-percipi* theory appears to be unmistakably refuted, since in dreams and illusions we certainly have false perceptions; and far from saying that everything is which appears, we should rather say that nothing is which appears.

Theaet. Very true, Socrates.

Soc. But then, my boy, how can any one contend that knowledge is perception, or that to every man what appears is?

Theaet. I am afraid to say, Socrates, that I have nothing to answer, because you rebuked me just now for making this excuse; but I certainly cannot undertake to argue that madmen or dreamers think truly, when they imagine, some of them that they are gods, and others that they can fly, and are flying in their sleep.

Soc. Do you see another question which can be raised about these phenomena, notably about dreaming and waking?

Theaet. What question?

Soc. A question which I think that you must often have heard persons ask:—How can you determine whether at this moment we are sleeping, and all our thoughts are a dream;

or whether we are awake, and talking to one another in the waking state?

Theaet. Indeed, Socrates, I do not know how to prove the one any more than the other, for in both cases the facts precisely correspond; and there is no difficulty in supposing that during all this discussion we have been talking to one another in a dream; and when in a dream[1] we seem to be narrating dreams, the resemblance of the two states is quite astonishing.

Soc. You see, then, that a doubt about the reality of sense is easily raised, since there may even be a doubt whether we are awake or in a dream. And as our time is equally divided between sleeping and waking, in either sphere of existence the soul contends that the thoughts which are present to our minds at the time are true; and during one half of our lives we affirm the truth of the one, and, during the other half, of the other; and are equally confident of both.

Theaet. Most true.

Soc. And may not the same be said of madness and other disorders? the difference is only that the times are not equal.

Theaet. Certainly.

Soc. And is truth or falsehood to be determined by duration of time?

Theaet. That would be in many ways ridiculous.

Soc. But can you certainly determine by any other means which of these opinions is true?

Theat. I do not think that I can.

Soc. Listen, then, to a statement of the other side of the argument, which is made by the champions of appearance. They would say, as I imagine: Can that which is wholly other than something, have the same quality as that from which it differs? And observe, Theaetetus, that the word "other" means not "partially," but "wholly other."

Theaet. Certainly, putting the question as you do, that which is wholly other cannot either potentially or in any other way be the same.

---

[1] Or perhaps, reading ὕπαρ, "in our waking state."

Soc. And must therefore be admitted to be unlike?

Theaet. True.

Soc. If, then, anything happens to become like or unlike itself or another, when it becomes like we call it the same—when unlike, other?

Theaet. Certainly.

Soc. Were we not saying that there are agents many and infinite, and patients many and infinite?

Theaet. Yes.

Soc. And also that different combinations will produce results which are not the same, but different?

Theaet. Certainly.

Soc. Let us take you and me, or anything as an example:—There is Socrates in health, Socrates sick: Are they like or unlike?

Theaet. You mean to compare Socrates in health as a whole, and Socrates in sickness as a whole?

Soc. Exactly; that is my meaning.

Theaet. I answer, they are unlike.

Soc. And if unlike, they are other?

Theaet. Certainly.

Soc. And would you not say the same of Socrates sleeping and waking, or in any of the states which we were mentioning?

Theaet. I should.

Soc. All agents have a different patient in Socrates, accordingly as he is well or ill.

Theaet. Of course.

Soc. And I who am the patient, and that which is the agent, will produce something different in each of the two cases?

Theaet. Certainly.

Soc. The wine which I drink when I am in health, appears sweet and pleasant to me?

Theaet. True.

Soc. For, as has been already acknowledged, the patient

and agent meet together and produce sweetness and a perception of sweetness, which are in simultaneous motion, and the perception which comes from the patient makes the tongue percipient, and the quality of sweetness which arises out of and is moving about the wine, makes the wine both to be and to appear sweet to the healthy tongue.

Theaet. Certainly; that has been already acknowledged.

Soc. But when I am sick, the wine really acts upon another and a different person?

Theaet. Yes.

Soc. The combination of the draught of wine, and the Socrates who is sick, produces quite another result; which is the sensation of bitterness in the tongue, and the motion and creation of bitterness in and about the wine, which becomes not bitterness but something bitter; as I myself become not perception but percipient?

Theaet. True.

Soc. There is no other object of which I shall ever have the same perception, for another object would give another perception, and would make the percipient other and different; nor can that object which affects me, meeting another subject, produce the same, or become similar, for that too will produce another result from another subject, and become different.

Theaet. True.

Soc. Neither can I by myself, have this sensation, nor the object by itself, this quality.

Theaet. Certainly not.

Soc. When I perceive I must become percipient of something—there can be no such thing as perceiving and perceiving nothing; the object, whether it become sweet, bitter, or of any other quality, must have relation to a percipient; nothing can become sweet which is sweet to no one.

Theaet. Certainly not.

Soc. Then the inference is, that we [the agent and patient] are or become in relation to one another; there is a law which binds us one to the other, but not to any other existence, nor each of us to himself; and therefore we can only be bound to one another; so that whether a person says that a thing is or becomes, he must say that it is or becomes to or of or in relation to something else; but he must not say or allow any one else to say that anything is or becomes absolutely:—such is our conclusion.

Theaet. Very true, Socrates.

Soc. Then, if that which acts upon me has relation to me and to no other, I and no other am the percipient of it?

Theaet. Of course.

Soc. Then my perception is true to me, being inseparable from my own being; and, as Protagoras says, to myself I am judge of what is and what is not to me.

Theaet. I suppose so.

Soc. How then, if I never err, and if my mind never trips in the conception of being or becoming, can I fail of knowing that which I perceive?

Theaet. You cannot.

Soc. Then you were quite right in affirming that knowledge is only perception; and the meaning turns out to be the same, whether with Homer and Heracleitus, and all that company, you say that all is motion and flux, or with the great sage Protagoras, that man is the measure of all things; or with Theaetetus, that, given these premises, perception is knowledge. Am I not right, Theaetetus, and is not this your new-born child, of which I have delivered you? What say you?

Theaet. I cannot but agree, Socrates.

Soc. Then this is the child, however he may turn out, which you and I have with difficulty brought into the world. And now that he is born, we must run round the hearth with him, and see whether he is worth rearing, or is only a wind-egg and a sham. Is he to be reared in any case, and not exposed? or will you bear to see him rejected, and not get into a passion if I take away your first-born?

Theod. Theaetetus will not be angry, for he is very good-natured. But tell me, Socrates, in heaven's name, is this, after all, not the truth?

Soc. You, Theodorus, are a lover of theories, and now you innocently fancy that I am a bag full of them, and can easily pull one out which will overthrow its predecessor. But you do not see that in reality none of these theories come from me; they all come from him who talks with me. I only know just enough to extract them from the wisdom of another, and to receive them in a spirit of fairness. And now I shall say nothing myself, but shall endeavour to elicit something from our young friend.

Theod. Do as you say, Socrates; you are quite right.

Soc. Shall I tell you, Theodorus, what amazes me in your acquaintance Protagoras.

Theod. What is it?

Soc. I am charmed with his doctrine, that what appears is to each one, but I wonder that he did not begin his book on Truth with a declaration that a pig or a dog-faced baboon, or some other yet stranger monster which has sensation, is the measure of all things; then he might have shown a magnificent contempt for our opinion of him by informing us at the outset that while we were reverencing him like a god for his wisdom he was no better than a tadpole, not to speak of his fellow-men—would not this have produced an overpowering effect? For if truth is only sensation, and no man can discern another's feelings better than he, or has any superior right to determine whether his opinion is true or false, but each, as we have several times repeated, is to himself the sole judge, and everything that he judges is true and right, why, my friend, should Protagoras be preferred to the place of wisdom and instruction, and deserve to be well paid, and we poor ignoramuses have to go to him, if each one is the measure of his own wisdom? Must he not be talking "ad captandum" in all this? I say nothing of the ridiculous predicament in which my own midwifery and the whole art of dialectic is placed; for the attempt to supervise or refute the notions or opinions of others would be a tedious and enormous piece of folly, if to each man his own are right; and this must be the case if Protagoras' Truth is the real truth, and the philosopher is not merely amusing himself by giving oracles out of the shrine of his book.

Theod. He was a friend of mine, Socrates, as you were saying, and therefore I cannot have him refuted by my lips, nor can I oppose you when I agree with you; please, then, to take Theaetetus again; he seemed to answer very nicely.

Soc. If you were to go into a Lacedaemonian palaestra, Theodorus, would you have a right to look on at the naked wrestlers, some of them making a poor figure, if you did not strip and give them an opportunity of judging of your own person?

Theod. Why not, Socrates, if they would allow me, as I think you will, in consideration of my age and stiffness? Let some more supple youth try a fall with you, and do not drag me into the gymnasium.

Soc. Your will is my will, Theodorus, as the proverbial philosophers say, and therefore I will return to the sage Theaetetus: Tell me, Theaetetus, in reference to what I was saying, are you not lost in wonder, like myself, when you find that all of a sudden you are raised to the level of the wisest of men, or indeed of the gods?—for you would assume the measure of Protagoras to apply to the gods as well as men?

Theaet. Certainly I should, and I confess to you that I am lost in wonder. At first hearing, I was quite satisfied with the doctrine, that whatever appears is to each one, but now the face of things has changed.

Soc. Why, my dear boy, you are young, and therefore your ear is quickly caught and your mind influenced by popular arguments. Protagoras, or some one speaking on his behalf, will doubtless say in reply,—Good people, young and old, you meet and harangue, and bring in the gods, whose existence or non-existence I banish from writing and speech, or you talk about the reason of man being degraded to the level of the brutes, which is a telling argument with the multitude, but not one word of proof or demonstration do you offer. All is probability with you, and yet surely you and Theodorus had better reflect whether you are disposed to admit of probability and figures of speech in matters of such importance. He or any other mathematician who argued from probabilities and likelihoods in geometry, would not be worth an ace.

Theaet. But neither you nor we, Socrates, would be satisfied with such arguments.

Soc. Then you and Theodorus mean to say that we must look at the matter in some other way?

Theaet. Yes, in quite another way.

Soc. And the way will be to ask whether perception is or is not the same as knowledge; for this was the real point of our argument, and with a view to this we raised (did we not?) those many strange questions.

Theaet. Certainly.

Soc. Shall we say that we know every thing which we see and hear? For example, shall we say that not having learned, we do not hear the language of foreigners when they speak to us? or shall we say that we not only hear, but know what they are saying? Or again, if we see letters which we do not understand, shall we say that we do not see them? or shall we aver that, seeing them, we must know them?

Theaet. We shall say, Socrates, that we know what we actually see and hear of them—that is to say, we see and know the figure and colour of the letters, and we hear and know the elevation or depression of the sound of them; but we do not perceive by sight and hearing, or know, that which grammarians and interpreters teach about them.

Soc. Capital, Theaetetus; and about this there shall be no dispute, because I want you to grow; but there is another difficulty coming, which you will also have to repulse.

Theaet. What is it?

Soc. Some one will say, Can a man who has ever known anything, and still has and preserves a memory of that which he knows, not know that which he remembers at the time when he remembers? I have, I fear, a tedious way of putting a simple question, which is only, whether a man who has learned, and remembers, can fail to know?

Theaet. Impossible, Socrates; the supposition is monstrous.

Soc. Am I talking nonsense, then? Think: is not seeing perceiving, and is not sight perception?

Theaet. True.

Soc. And if our recent definition holds, every man knows that which he has seen?

Theaet. Yes.

Soc. And would you admit that there is such a thing as memory?

Theaet. Yes.

Soc. And is memory of something or of nothing?

Theaet. Of something, surely.

Soc. Of things learned and perceived, that is?

Theaet. Certainly.

Soc. Often a man remembers that which he has seen?

Theaet. True.

Soc. And if he closed his eyes, would he forget?

Theaet. Who, Socrates, would dare to say so?

Soc. But we must say so, if the previous argument is to be maintained.

Theaet. What do you mean? I am not quite sure that I understand you, though I have a strong suspicion that you are right.

Soc. As thus: he who sees knows, as we say, that which he sees; for perception and sight and knowledge are admitted to be the same.

Theaet. Certainly.

Soc. But he who saw, and has knowledge of that which he

saw, remembers, when he closes his eyes, that which he no longer sees.

Theaet. True.

Soc. And seeing is knowing, and therefore not-seeing is not-knowing?

Theaet. Very true.

Soc. Then the inference is, that a man may have attained the knowledge of something, which he may remember and yet not know, because he does not see; and this has been affirmed by us to be a monstrous supposition.

Theaet. Most true.

Soc. Thus, then, the assertion that knowledge and perception are one, involves a manifest impossibility?

Theaet. Yes.

Soc. Then they must be distinguished?

Theaet. I suppose that they must.

Soc. Once more we shall have to begin, and ask "What is knowledge?" and yet, Theaetetus, what are we going to do?

Theaet. About what?

Soc. Like a good-for-nothing cock, without having won the victory, we walk away from the argument and crow.

Theaet. How do you mean?

Soc. After the manner of disputers,[1] we were satisfied with mere verbal consistency, and were well pleased if in this way we could gain an advantage. Although professing not to be mere Eristics, but philosophers, I suspect that we have unconsciously fallen into the error of that ingenious class of persons.

Theaet. I do not as yet understand you.

Soc. Then I will try to explain myself: just now we asked the question, whether a man who had learned and remembered could fail to know, and we showed that a person who had seen might remember when he had his eyes shut and could not see, and then he would at the same time remember and not know. But this was an impossibility. And so the

[1] Lys. 216 A: Phaedo 90 B. 101 E; Rep. V, 453 E ff.

Protagorean fable came to nought, and yours also, who maintained that knowledge is the same as perception.

Theaet. True.

Soc. And yet, my friend, I rather suspect that the result would have been different if Protagoras, who was the father of the first of the two brats, had been alive; he would have had a great deal to say on their behalf. But he is dead, and we insult over his orphan child; and even the guardians whom he left, and of whom our friend Theodorus is one, are unwilling to give any help, and therefore I suppose that I must take up his cause myself, and see justice done?

Theod. Not I, Socrates, but rather Callias, the son of Hipponicus, is guardian of his orphans. I was too soon diverted from the abstractions of dialectic to geometry. Nevertheless, I shall be grateful to you if you assist him.

Soc. Very good, Theodorus; you shall see how I will come to the rescue. If a person does not attend to the meaning of terms as they are commonly used in argument, he may be involved even in greater paradoxes than these. Shall I explain this matter to you or to Theaetetus?

Theod. To both of us, and let the younger answer; he will incur less disgrace if he is discomfited.

Soc. Then now let me ask the awful question, which is this:—Can a man know and also not know that which he knows?

Theod. How shall we answer, Theaetetus?

Theaet. He cannot, I should say.

Soc. He can, if you maintain that seeing is knowing. When you are imprisoned in a well, as the saying is, and the self-assured adversary closes one of your eyes with his hand, and asks whether you can see his cloak with the eye which he has closed, how will you answer the inevitable man?

Theaet. I should answer, "Not with that eye but with the other."

Soc. Then you see and do not see the same thing at the same time.

Theaet. Yes, in a certain sense.

Soc. None of that, he will reply; I do not ask or bid you answer in what sense you know, but only whether you know that which you do not know. You have been proved to see that which you do not see; and you have already admitted that seeing is knowing, and that not-seeing is not-knowing: I leave you to draw the inference.

Theaet. Yes; the inference is the contradictory of my assertion.

Soc. Yes, my marvel, and there might have been yet worse things in store for you, if an opponent had gone on to ask whether you can have a sharp and also a dull knowledge, and whether you can know near, but not at a distance, or know the same thing with more or less intensity, and so on without end. Such questions might have been put to you by a light-armed mercenary, who argued for pay. He would have lain in wait for you, and when you took up the position, that sense is knowledge, he would have made an assault upon hearing, smelling, and the other senses;—he would have shown you no mercy; and while you were lost in envy and admiration of his wisdom, he would have got you into his net, out of which you would not have escaped until you had come to an understanding about the sum to be paid for your release. Well, you ask, and how will Protagoras reinforce his position? Shall I answer for him?

Theaet. By all means.

Soc. He will repeat all those things which we have been urging on his behalf, and then he will close with us in disdain, and say:—The worthy Socrates asked a little boy, whether the same man could remember and not know the same thing, and the boy said No, because he was frightened, and could not see what was coming, and then Socrates made fun of poor me. The truth is, O slatternly Socrates, that when you ask questions about any assertion of mine, and the person asked is found tripping, if he has answered as I should have answered, then I am refuted, but if he answers something else, then he is refuted and not I. For do you really suppose that any one would admit the memory which a man has of an impression which has passed away to be the same with that which he experienced at the time? Assuredly not. Or would he hesitate to acknowledge that the same man may know and not know the same thing? Or, if he is afraid of making this admission, would he ever grant that one who has become unlike is the same as before he became unlike? Or would he admit that a man is one at all, and not rather many and infinite as the changes which take place in him? I ask by the card in order to avoid entanglements of words. But, O my good sir, he will say, come to the argument in a more generous spirit; and either show, if you can, that our sensations are not relative and individual, or, if you admit them to be so, prove that this does not involve the consequence that the appearance becomes, or, if you will have the word, is, to the individual only. As to your talk about pigs and baboons, you are yourself behaving like a pig, and you teach your hearers to make sport of my writings in the same ignorant manner; but this is not to your credit. For I declare that the truth is as I have written, and that each of us is a measure of existence and of non-existence. Yet one man may be a thousand times better than another in proportion as different things are and appear to him. And I am far from saying that wisdom and the wise man have no existence; but I say that the wise man is he who makes the evils which appear and are to a man, into goods which are and appear to him. And I would beg you not to press my words in the letter, but to take the meaning of them as I will explain them. Remember what has been already said,— that to the sick man his food appears to be and is bitter, and to the man in health the opposite of bitter. Now I cannot conceive that one of these men can be or ought to be made wiser than the other: nor can you assert that the sick man because he has one impression is foolish, and the healthy man because he has another is wise; but the one state requires

to be changed into the other, the worse into the better. As
in education, a change of state has to be effected, and the
Sophist accomplishes by words the change which the physician works by the aid of drugs. Not that any one ever made
another think truly, who previously thought falsely. For no
one can think what is not, or think anything different from
that which he feels; and this is always true. But as the inferior habit of mind has thoughts of a kindred nature, so I
conceive that a good mind causes men to have good thoughts;
and these which the inexperienced call true, I maintain to
be only better, and not truer than others. And, O my dear
Socrates, I do not call wise men tadpoles: far from it; I
say that they are the physicians of the human body, and the
husbandmen of plants—for the husbandmen also take away
the evil and disordered sensation of plants, and infuse into
them good and healthy sensations—aye and true ones,[1] and
the wise and good rhetoricians make the good instead of the
evil to seem just to states; for whatever appears to a state
to be just and fair, so long as it is regarded as such, is
just and fair to it; but the teacher of wisdom causes the
good to take the place of the evil, both in appearance and in
reality. And in like manner the Sophist who is able to train
his pupils in this spirit is a wise man, and deserves to be
well paid by them. And so one man is wiser than another;
and no one thinks falsely, and you, whether you will or not,
must endure to be a measure. On these foundations the
argument stands firm, which you, Socrates, may, if you
please, overthrow by an opposite argument, or if you like
you may put questions to me—a method to which no intelligent person will object, quite the reverse. But I must beg you
to put fair questions: for there·is great inconsistency in saying that you have a zeal for virtue, and then always behaving
unfairly in argument. The unfairness of which I complain
is that you do not distinguish between mere disputation
and dialectic: the disputer may trip up his opponent as often

---

[1] Reading ἀληθεῖς, but? Cp. supra 167 A: ταῦτα δὲ ἀεὶ ἀληθῆ.

as he likes, and make fun; but the dialectician will be in earnest, and only correct his adversary when necessary, telling him the errors into which he has fallen through his own fault, or that of the company which he has previously kept. If you do so, your adversary will lay the blame of his own confusion and perplexity on himself, and not on you. He will follow and love you, and will hate himself, and escape from himself into philosophy, in order that he may become different from what he was. But the other mode of arguing, which is practised by the many, will have just the opposite effect upon him; and as he grows older, instead of turning philosopher, he will come to hate philosophy. I would recommend you, therefore, as I said before, not to encourage yourself in this polemical and controversial temper, but to find out, in a friendly and congenial spirit, what we really mean when we say that all things are in motion, and that to every individual and state what appears, is. In this manner you will consider whether knowledge and sensation are the same or different, but you will not argue, as you were just now doing, from the customary use of names and words, which the vulgar pervert in all sorts of ways, causing infinite perplexity to one another. Such, Theodorus, is the very slight help which I am able to offer to your old friend; [1] had he been living, he would have helped himself in a far more gloriose style.

Theod. You are jesting, Socrates; indeed, your defence of him has been most valorous.

Soc. Thank you, friend; and I hope that you observed Protagoras bidding us be serious, as the text, "Man is the measure of all things," was a solemn one; and he reproached us with making a boy the medium of discourse, and said that the boy's timidity was made to tell against his argument; he also declared that we made a joke of him.

Theod. How could I fail to observe all that, Socrates?

Soc. Well, and shall we do as he says?

[1] Reading προσήρκεσα.

Theod. By all means.

Soc. But if his wishes are to be regarded, you and I must take up the argument, and in all seriousness,[1] and ask and answer one another, for you see that the rest of us are nothing but boys. In no other way can we escape the imputation, that in our fresh analysis of his thesis we are making fun with boys.

Theod. Well, but is not Theaetetus better able to follow a philosophical enquiry than a great many men who have long beards?

Soc. Yes, Theodorus, but not better than you; and therefore please not to imagine that I am to defend by every means in my power your departed friend; and that you are to defend nothing and nobody. At any rate, my good man, do not sheer off until we know whether you are a true measure of diagrams, or whether all men are equally measures and. sufficient for themselves in astronomy and geometry, and the other branches of knowledge in which you are supposed to excel them.

Theod. He who is sitting by. you, Socrates, will not easily avoid being drawn into an argument; and when I said just now that you would excuse me, and not, like the Lacedaemonians, compel me to strip and fight, I was talking nonsense—I should rather compare you to Scirrhon, who threw travellers from the rocks; for the Lacedaemonian rule is "strip or depart," but you seem to go about your work more after the fashion of Antaeus: you will not allow any one who approaches you to depart until you have stripped him, and he has been compelled to try a fall with you in argument.

Soc. There, Theodorus, you have hit off precisely the nature of my complaint; but I am even more pugnacious than the giants of old, for I have met with no end of heroes; many a Heracles, many a Theseus, mighty in words, has broken my head; nevertheless I am always at this rough exercise, which inspires me like a passion. Please, then, to try a fall,

[1] Reading αὐτοῦ τῶν λόγων.

with me, whereby you will do yourself good as well as me.

Theod. I consent; lead me whither you will, for I know that you are like destiny; no man can escape from any argument which you may weave for him. But I am not disposed to go further than you suggest.

Soc. Once will be enough; and now take particular care that we do not again unwittingly expose ourselves to the reproach of talking childishly.

Theod. I will do my best to avoid that error.

Soc. In the first place, let us return to our old objection, and see whether we were right in blaming and taking offence at Protagoras on the ground that he assumed all to be equal and sufficient in wisdom; although he admitted that there was a better and worse, and that in respect of this, some who as he said were the wise excelled others.

Theod. Very true.

Soc. Had Protagoras been living and answered for himself, instead of our answering for him, there would have been no need of our reviewing or reinforcing the argument. But as he is not here, and some one may accuse us of speaking without authority on his behalf, had we not better come to a clearer agreement about his meaning, for a great deal may be at stake?

Theod. True.

Soc. Then let us obtain, not through any third person, but from his own statement and in the fewest words possible, the basis of agreement.

Theod. In what way?

Soc. In this way:—His words are, "What seems to a man is to him."

Theod. Yes, so he says.

Soc. And are not we, Protagoras, uttering the opinion of man, or rather of all mankind, when we say that every one thinks himself wiser than other men in some things, and their inferior in others? In the hour of danger, when they are in perils of war, or of the sea, or of sickness, do they not look up to their commanders as if they were gods, and expect salvation from them, only because they excel them in knowledge? Is not the world full of men in their several employments, who are looking for teachers and rulers of themselves and of the animals? And there are plenty who think that they are able to teach and able to rule. Now, in all this is implied that ignorance and wisdom exist among them, at least in their own opinion.

Theod. Certainly.

Soc. And wisdom is assumed by them to be true thought, and ignorance to be false opinion.

Theod. Exactly.

Soc. How then, Protagoras, would you have us treat the argument? Shall we say that the opinions of men are always true, or sometimes true and sometimes false? In either case, the result is the same, and their opinions are not always true, but sometimes true and sometimes false. For tell me, Theodorus, do you suppose that you yourself, or any other follower of Protagoras, would contend that no one deems another ignorant or mistaken in his opinion?

Theod. The thing is incredible, Socrates.

Soc. And yet that absurdity is necessarily involved in the thesis which declares man to be the measure of all things.

Theod. How so?

Soc. Why, suppose that you determine in your own mind something to be true, and declare your opinion to me; let us assume, as he argues, that this is true to you. Now, if so, you must either say that the rest of us are not the judges of this opinion or judgment of yours, or that we judge you always to have a true opinion? But are there not thousands upon thousands who, whenever you form a judgment, take up arms against you and are of an opposite judgment and opinion, deeming that you judge falsely?

Theod. Yes, indeed, Socrates, thousands and tens of thousands, as Homer says, who give me a world of trouble.

Soc. Well, but are we to assert that what you think is true to you and false to the ten thousand others?

Theod. No other inference seems to be possible.

Soc. And how about Protagoras himself? If neither he nor the multitude thought, as indeed they do not think, that man is the measure of all things, must it not follow that the truth of which Protagoras wrote would be true to no one? But if you suppose that he himself thought this, and that the multitude does not agree with him, you must begin by allowing that in whatever proportion the many are more than one, in that proportion his truth is more untrue than true.

Theod. That would follow if the truth is supposed to vary with individual opinion.

Soc. And the best of the joke is, that he acknowledges the truth of their opinion who believe his own opinion to be false; for he admits that the opinions of all men are true.

Theod. Certainly.

Soc. And does he not allow that his own opinion is false, if he admits that the opinion of those who think him false is true?

Theod. Of course.

Soc. Whereas the other side do not admit that they speak falsely?

Theod. They do not.

Soc. And he, as may be inferred from his writings, agrees that this opinion is also true.

Theod. Clearly.

Soc. Then all mankind, beginning with Protagoras, will contend, or rather, I should say that he will allow, when he concedes that his adversary has a true opinion—Protagoras, I say, will himself allow that neither a dog nor any ordinary man is the measure of anything which he has not learned— am I not right?

Theod. Yes.

Soc. And the truth of Protagoras being doubted by all, will be true neither to himself nor to any one else?

Theod. I think, Socrates, that we are running my old friend too hard.

Soc. But I do not know that we are going beyond the truth. Doubtless, as he is older, he may be expected to be wiser than we are. And if he could only just get his head out of the world below, he would have overthrown both of us again and again, me for talking nonsense and you for assenting to me, and have been off and underground in a trice. But as he is not within call, we must make the best use of our own faculties, such as they are, and speak out what appears to us to be true. And one thing which no one will deny is, that there are great differences in the understand· ings of men.

Theod. In that opinion, I quite agree.

Soc. And is there not most likely to be firm ground in the distinction which we were indicating on behalf of Protagoras, viz., that most things, and all immediate sensations, such as hot, dry, sweet, are only such as they appear; if however difference of opinion is to be allowed at all, surely we must allow it in respect of health or disease? For every woman, child, or living creature has not such a knowledge of what conduces to health as to enable them to cure themselves.

Theod. I quite agree.

Soc. Or again, in politics, while affirming that just and unjust, honourable and disgraceful, holy and unholy, are in reality to each State such as the State thinks and makes lawful, and that in determining these matters no individual or State is wiser than another, still the followers of Protagoras will not deny that in determining what is or is not expedient for the community one State is wiser and one counsellor better than another—they will scarcely venture to maintain, that what a city enacts in the belief that it is expedient will always be really expedient. But in the other case, I mean when they speak of justice and injustice, piety and impiety, they are confident that in nature these have no existence or essence of their own—the truth is that which is agreed on at the time of the agreement, and as long as the agreement lasts; and this is the philosophy of many who do not altogether go along with Protagoras. Here arises a new question, Theodorus, which threatens to be more serious than the last.

Theod. Well, Socrates, we have plenty of leisure.

Soc. That is true, and your remark recalls to my mind an observation which I have often made, that those who have passed their days in the pursuit of philosophy are ridiculously at fault when they have to appear and speak in court. How natural is this!

Theod. What do you mean?

Soc. I mean to say, that those who have been trained in philosophy and liberal pursuits are as unlike those who from their youth upwards have been knocking about in the courts and such places, as a freeman is in breeding unlike a slave.

Theod. In what is the difference seen?

Soc. In the leisure spoken of by you, which a freeman can always command: he has his talk out in peace, and, like ourselves, he wanders at will from one subject to another, and from a second to a third,—if the fancy takes him, he begins again, as we are doing now, caring not whether his words are many or few; his only aim is to attain the truth. But the lawyer is always in a hurry; there is the water of the clepsydra driving him on, and not allowing him to expatiate at will: and there is his adversary standing over him, enforcing his rights; the indictment, which in their phraseology is termed the affidavit, is recited at the time: and from this he must not deviate. He is a servant, and is continually disputing about a fellow-servant before his master, who is seated, and has the cause in his hands; the trial is never about some indifferent matter, but always concerns himself; and often the race is for his life. The consequence has been, that he has become keen and shrewd; he has learned how to flatter his master in word and indulge him in deed; but his soul is small and unrighteous. His condition, which has been that of a slave from his youth upwards, has deprived him of growth and uprightness and independence; dangers and fears, which were too much for his truth and honesty, came upon him in early years, when the tenderness of youth was unequal to them, and he has been driven into crooked ways; from the first he has practised deception and retaliation, and has become stunted and warped. And so he has passed out of youth into manhood, having no soundness in him; and is now, as he thinks, a master in wisdom. Such is the lawyer, Theodorus. Will you have the companion picture of the philosopher, who is of our brotherhood; or shall we return to the argument? Do not let us abuse the freedom of digression which we claim.

Theod. Nay, Socrates, not until we have finished what we are about; for you truly said that we belong to a brotherhood which is free, and are not the servants of the argument; but the argument is our servant, and must wait our leisure. Who is our judge? Or where is the spectator having any right to censure or control us, as he might the poets?

Soc. Then, as this is your wish, I will describe the leaders; for there is no use in talking about the inferior sort. In the first place, the lords of philosophy have never, from their youth upwards, known their way to the Agora, or the dicastery, or the council, or any other political assembly; they neither see nor hear the laws or decrees, as they are called, of the State written or recited; the eagerness of political societies in the attainment of offices—clubs, and banquets, and revels, and singing-maidens,—do not enter even into their dreams. Whether any event has turned out well or ill in the city, what disgrace may have descended to any one from his ancestors, male or female, are matters of which the philosopher no more knows than he can tell, as they say, how many pints are contained in the ocean. Neither is he conscious of his ignorance. For he does not hold aloof in order that he may gain a reputation; but the truth is, that the outer form of him only is in the city: his mind, disdaining the littlenesses and nothingnesses of human things, is "flying all abroad" as Pindar says, measuring earth and heaven and the things which are under and on the earth and above the heaven, interrogating the whole nature of each and all in their entirety, but not condescending to anything which is within reach.

Theod. What do you mean, Socrates?

Soc. I will illustrate my meaning, Theodorus, by the jest which the clever witty Thracian handmaid is said to have made about Thales, when he fell into a well as he was looking up at the stars. She said, that he was so eager to know what was going on in heaven, that he could not see what was before his feet. This is a jest which is equally applicable to all philosophers. For the philosopher is wholly unacquainted with his next-door neighbour; he is ignorant, not only of what he is doing, but he hardly knows whether he is a man or an animal; he is searching into the essence of man, and busy in enquiring what belongs to such a nature to do or suffer different from any other;—I think that you understand me, Theodorus?

Theod. I do, and what you say is true.

Soc. And thus, my friend, on every occasion, private as well as public, as I said at first, when he appears in a law-court, or in any place in which he has to speak of things which are at his feet and before his eyes, he is the jest, not only of Thracian handmaids but of the general herd, tumbling into wells and every sort of disaster through his inexperience. His awkwardness is fearful, and gives the impression of imbecility. When he is reviled, he has nothing personal to say in answer to the civilities of his adversaries, for he knows no scandals of any one, and they do not interest him; and therefore he is laughed at for his sheepishness; and when others are being praised and glorified, in the simplicity of his heart he cannot help going into fits of laughter, so that he seems to be a downright idiot. When he hears a tyrant or king eulogized, he fancies that he is listening to the praises of some keeper of cattle—a swineherd, or shepherd, or perhaps a cowherd, who is congratulated on the quantity of milk which he squeezes from them; and he remarks that the creature whom they tend, and out of whom they squeeze the wealth, is of a less tractable and more insidious nature. Then, again, he observes that the great man is of necessity as ill-mannered and uneducated as any shepherd—for he has no leisure, and he is surrounded by a wall, which is his mountain-pen. Hearing of enormous landed proprietors of ten thousand acres and more, our philosopher deems this to be a trifle, because he has been accustomed to think of the whole earth; and when they sing the praises of family, and say that some one is a gentleman because he can show seven generations of wealthy ancestors, he thinks that their sentiments only betray a dull and narrow vision in those who utter them, and who are not educated enough to look at the whole, nor to consider that every man has had thousands and ten thousands of progenitors, and among them have been rich and poor, kings and slaves, Hellenes and barbarians, innumerable. And when people pride themselves on having a pedigree of twenty-five ancestors, which goes back to Heracles, the son of Amphitryon, he cannot understand their poverty of ideas. Why are they unable to calculate that Amphitryon had a twenty-fifth ancestor, who might have been anybody, and was such as fortune made him, and he had a fiftieth, and so on? He amuses himself with the notion that they cannot count, and thinks that a little arithmetic would have got rid of their senseless vanity. Now, in all these cases our philosopher is derided by the vulgar, partly because he is thought to despise them, and also because he is ignorant of what is before him, and always at a loss.

Theod. That is very true, Socrates.

Soc. But, O my friend, when he draws the other into upper air, and gets him out of his pleas and rejoinders into the contemplation of justice and injustice in their own nature and in their difference from one another and from all other things; or from the commonplaces about the happiness of a king or a rich man to the consideration of government, and of human happiness and misery in general—what they are, and how a man is to attain the one and avoid the other—when that narrow, keen, little legal mind is called to account about all this, he gives the philosopher his revenge; for dizzied by the height at which he is hanging, whence he looks down into space, which is a strange experience to him, he being dismayed, and lost, and stammering broken words, is laughed at, not by Thracian handmaidens or any other un-educated persons, for they have no eye for the situation, but by every man who has not been brought up a slave. Such are the two characters, Theodorus: the one of the freeman, who has been trained in liberty and leisure, whom you call the philosopher,—him we cannot blame because he appears simple and of no account when he has to perform some menial task, such as packing up bed-clothes, or flavouring a sauce or fawning speech; the other character is that of the man who is able to do all this kind of service smartly and neatly, but knows not how to wear his cloak like a gentleman; still less with the music of discourse can he hymn the true life aright which is lived by immortals or men blessed of heaven.

Theod. If you could only persuade everybody, Socrates, as you do me, of the truth of your words, there would be more peace and fewer evils among men.

Soc. Evils, Theodorus, can never pass away; for there must always remain something which is antagonistic to good. Having no place among the gods in heaven, of necessity they hover around the mortal nature, and this earthly sphere. Wherefore we ought to fly away from earth to heaven as quickly as we can; and to fly away is to become like God, as far as this is possible; and to become like him, is to become holy, just, and wise. But, O my friend, you cannot easily convince mankind that they should pursue virtue or avoid vice, not merely in order that a man may seem to be good, which is the reason given by the world, and in my judgment is only a repetition of an old wives' fable. Whereas, the truth is that God is never in any way unrighteous—he is perfect righteousness; and he of us who is the most righteous is most like him. Herein is seen the true cleverness of a man, and also his nothingness and want of manhood. For to know this is true wisdom and virtue, and ignorance of this is manifest folly and vice. All other kinds of wisdom or cleverness, which seem only, such as the wisdom of politicians, or the wisdom of the arts, are coarse and vulgar. The unrighteous man, or the sayer and doer of unholy things, had far better not be encouraged in the illusion that his roguery is clever; for men glory in their shame—they fancy that they hear others saying of them, "These are not mere good-for-nothing persons, mere burdens of the earth, but such as men should be who mean to dwell safely in a State." Let us tell them that they are all the more truly what they do not think they are because they do not know it; for they do not know the penalty of injustice, which above all things they ought to know—not stripes and death, as they suppose, which evil-doers often escape, but a penalty which cannot be escaped.

Theod. What is that?

Soc. There are two patterns eternally set before them; the one blessed and divine, the other godless and wretched: but they do not see them, or perceive that in their utter folly and infatuation they are growing like the one and unlike the other, by reason of their evil deeds; and the penalty is, that they lead a life answering to the pattern which they are growing like. And if we tell them, that unless they depart from their cunning, the place of innocence will not receive them after death; and that here on earth, they will live ever in the likeness of their own evil selves, and with evil friends— when they hear this they in their superior cunning will seem to be listening to the talk of idiots.

Theod. Very true, Socrates.

Soc. Too true, my friend, as I well know; there is, however, one peculiarity in their case: when they begin to reason in private about their dislike of philosophy, if they have the courage to hear the argument out, and do not run away, they grow at last strangely discontented with themselves; their rhetoric fades away, and they become helpless as children. These however are digressions from which we must now desist, or they will overflow, and drown the original argument; to which, if you please, we will now return.

Theod. For my part, Socrates, I would rather have the digressions, for at my age I find them easier to follow; but if you wish, let us go back to the argument.

Soc. Had we not reached the point at which the partisans of the perpetual flux, who say that things are as they seem to each one, were confidently maintaining that the ordinances which the State commanded and thought just, were just to the State which imposed them, while they were in force; this was especially asserted of justice; but as to the good, no one had any longer the hardihood to contend of any ordinances which the State thought and enacted to be good that these, while they were in force, were really good;—he who said so would be playing with the name "good," and would not touch the real question—it would be a mockery, would it not?

Theod. Certainly it would.

Soc. He ought not to speak of the name, but of the thing which is contemplated under the name.

Theod. Right.

Soc. Whatever be the term used, the good or expedient, is the aim of legislation, and as far as she has an opinion, the State imposes all laws with a view to the greatest expediency; can legislation have any other aim?

Theod. Certainly not.

Soc. But is the aim attained always? do not mistakes often happen?

Theod. Yes, I think that there are mistakes.

Soc. The possibility of error will be more distinctly recognized, if we put the question in reference to the whole class under which the good or expedient falls. That whole class has to do with the future, and laws are passed under the idea that they will be useful in after-time; which, in other words, is the future.

Theod. Very true.

Soc. Suppose now, that we ask Protagoras, or one of his disciples, a question:—O Protagoras, we will say to him, Man is, as you declare, the measure of all things—white, heavy, light: of all such things he is the judge; for he has the criterion of them in himself, and when he thinks that things are such as he experiences them to be, he thinks what is and is true to himself. Is it not so?

Theod. Yes.

Soc. And do you extend your doctrine, Protagoras (as we shall further say), to the future as well as to the present; and has he the criterion not only of what in his opinion is but of what will be, and do things always happen to him as he expected? For example, take the case of heat:—When an ordinary man thinks that he is going to have a fever, and that this kind of heat is coming on, and another person, who is a physician, thinks the contrary, whose opinion is likely to prove right? Or are they both right?—he will have a heat and fever in his own judgment, and not have a fever in the physician's judgment?

Theod. How ludicrous!

Soc. And the vinegrower, if I am not mistaken, is a better judge of the sweetness or dryness of the vintage which is not yet gathered than the harp-player?

Theod. Certainly.

Soc. And in musical composition the musician will know better than the training master what the training master himself will hereafter think harmonious or the reverse?

Theod. Of course.

Soc. And the cook will be a better judge than the guest, who is not a cook, of the pleasure to be derived from the dinner which is in preparation; for of present or past pleasure we are not as yet arguing; but can we say that every one will be to himself the best judge of the pleasure which will seem to be and will be to him in the future?—nay, would not you, Protagoras, better guess which arguments in a court would convince any one of us than the ordinary man?

Theod. Certainly, Socrates, he used to profess in the strongest manner that he was the superior of all men in this respect.

Soc. To be sure, friend: who would have paid a large sum for the privilege of talking to him, if he had really[1] persuaded his visitors that neither a prophet nor any other man was better able to judge what will be and seem to be in the future than every one could for himself?

Theod. Who indeed?

Soc. And legislation and expediency are all concerned with the future; and every one will admit that States, in passing laws, must often fail of their highest interests?

Theod. Quite true.

Soc. Then we may fairly argue against your master, that he must admit one man to be wiser than another, and that the wiser is a measure: but I, who know nothing, am not at all obliged to accept the honour which the advocate of Protagoras was just now forcing upon me, whether I would or not, of being a measure of anything.

Theod. That is the best refutation of him, Socrates; although he is also caught when he ascribes truth to the opinions of others, who give the lie direct to his own opinion.

Soc. There are many ways, Theodorus, in which the doctrine that every opinion of every man is true may be refuted; but there is more difficulty in proving that states of feeling, which are present to a man, and out of which arise sensations and opinions in accordance with them, are also untrue. And very likely I have been talking nonsense about them; for they may be unassailable, and those who say that there is clear

[1] Reading δή.

evidence of them, and that they are matters of knowledge, may probably be right; in which case our friend Theaetetus was not so far from the mark when he identified perception and knowledge. And therefore let us draw nearer, as the advocate of Protagoras desires, and give the truth of the universal flux a ring: is the theory sound or not? at any rate, no small war is raging about it, and there are combatants not a few.

Theod. No small war, indeed, for in Ionia the sect makes rapid strides; the disciples of Heracleitus are most energetic upholders of the doctrine.

Soc. Then we are the more bound, my dear Theodorus, to examine the question from the foundation as it is set forth by themselves.

Theod. Certainly we are. About these speculations or Heracleitus, which, as you say, are as old as Homer, or even older still, the Ephesians themselves, who profess to know them, are downright mad, and you cannot talk with them on the subject. For in accordance with their text-books, they are always in motion; but as for dwelling upon an argument or a question, and quietly asking and answering in turn, they can no more do so than they can fly; or rather, the determination of these fellows not to have a particle of rest in them is more than the utmost powers of negation can express. If you ask any of them a question, he will produce, as from a quiver, sayings brief and dark, and shoot them at you; and if you enquire the reason of what he has said, you will be hit by some other new-fangled word, and will make no way with any of them, nor they with one another; their great care is, not to allow of any settled principle either in their arguments or in their minds, conceiving, as I imagine, that any such principle would be stationary; for they are at war with the stationary, and do what they can to drive it out everywhere.

Soc. I suppose, Theodorus, that you have only seen them when they were fighting, and have never stayed with them in time of peace, for they are no friends of yours; and their peace doctrines are only communicated by them at leisure, as I imagine, to those disciples of theirs whom they want to make like themselves.

Theod. Disciples! My good sir, they have none; men of their sort are not one another's disciples, but they grow up at their own sweet will, and get their inspiration anywhere, each of them saying of his neighbour that he knows nothing. From these men, then, as I was going to remark, you will never get a reason, whether with their will or without their will; we must take the question out of their hands, and make the analysis ourselves, as if we were doing a geometrical problem.

Soc. Quite right too; but as touching the aforesaid problem, have we not heard from the ancients, who concealed their wisdom from the many in poetical figures, that Oceanus and Tethys, the origin of all things, are streams, and that nothing is at rest? And now the moderns, in their superior wisdom, have declared the same openly, that the cobbler too may hear and learn of them, and no longer foolishly imagine that some things are at rest and others in motion—having learned that all is motion, he will duly honour his teachers. I had almost forgotten the opposite doctrine, Theodorus,

"Alone Being remains unmoved, which is the name for the all."

This is the language of Parmenides, Melissus, and their followers, who stoutly maintain that all being is one and self-contained, and has no place in which to move. What shall we do, friend, with all these people; for, advancing step by step, we have imperceptibly got between the combatants, and, unless we can protect our retreat, we shall pay the penalty of our rashness—like the players in the palaestra who are caught upon the line, and are dragged different ways by the two parties. Therefore I think that we had better begin by considering those whom we first accosted, "the river-gods," and, if we find any truth in them, we will help them to pull us over, and try to get away from the others. But if the partisans of "the whole" appear to speak more truly, we will fly off from the party which would move the immovable, to them. And if we find that neither of them have anything reasonable to say, we shall be in a ridiculous position, having so great a conceit of our own poor opinion and rejecting that of ancient and famous men. O Theodorus, do you think that there is any use in proceeding when the danger is so great?

Theod. Nay, Socrates, not to examine thoroughly what the two parties have to say would be quite intolerable.

Soc. Then examine we must, since you, who were so reluctant to begin, are so eager to proceed. The nature of motion appears to be the question with which we begin. What do they mean when they say that all things are in motion? Is there only one kind of motion, or, as I rather incline to think, two? I should like to have your opinion upon this point in addition to my own, that I may err, if I must err, in your company; tell me, then, when a thing changes from one place to another, or goes round in the same place, is not that what is called motion?

Theod. Yes.

Soc. Here then we have one kind of motion. But when a thing, remaining on the same spot, grows old, or becomes black from being white, or hard from being soft, or undergoes any other change, may not this be properly called motion of another kind?

Theod. I think so.

Soc. Say rather that it must be so. Of motion then there are these two kinds, "change," and "motion in place."[1]

Theod. You are right.

Soc. And now, having made this distinction, let us address ourselves to those who say that all is motion, and ask them whether all things according to them have the two kinds of motion, and are changed as well as move in place, or is one thing moved in both ways, and another in one only?

[1] Reading φοράν: Lib. περιφοράν.

Theod. Indeed, I do not know what to answer; but I think they would say that all things are moved in both ways.

Soc. Yes, comrade; for, if not, they would have to say that the same things are in motion and at rest, and there would be no more truth in saying that all things are in motion, than that all things are at rest.

Theod. To be sure.

Soc. And if they are to be in motion, and nothing is to be devoid of motion, all things must always have every sort of motion?

Theod. Most true.

Soc. Consider a further point: did we not understand them to explain the generation of heat, whiteness, or anything else, in some such manner as the following:—were they not saying that each of them is moving between the agent and the patient, together with a perception, and that the patient ceases to be a perceiving power and becomes a percipient, and the agent a quale instead of a quality? I suspect that quality may appear a strange and uncouth term to you, and that you do not understand the abstract expression. Then I will take concrete instances: I mean to say that the producing power or agent becomes neither heat nor whiteness, but hot and white, and the like of other things. For I must repeat what I said before, that neither the agent nor patient have any absolute existence, but when they come together and generate sensations and their objects, the one becomes a thing of a certain quality, and the other a percipient. You remember?

Theod. Of course.

Soc. We may leave the details of their theory unexamined, but we must not forget to ask them the only question with which we are concerned: Are all things in motion and flux?

Theod. Yes, they will reply.

Soc. And they are moved in both those ways which we distinguished; that is to say, they move in place and are also changed?

Theod. Of course, if the motion is to be perfect.

Soc. If they only moved in place and were not changed, we should be able to say what is the nature of the things which are in motion and flux?

Theod. Exactly.

Soc. But now, since not even white continues to flow white, and whiteness itself is a flux or change which is passing into another colour, and is never to be caught standing still, can the name of any colour be rightly used at all?

Theod. How is that possible, Socrates, either in the case of this or of any other quality—if while we are using the word the object is escaping in the flux?

Soc. And what would you say of perceptions, such as sight and hearing, or any other kind of perception? Is there any stopping in the act of seeing and hearing?

Theod. Certainly not, if all things are in motion.

Soc. Then we must not speak of seeing any more than of not-seeing, nor of any other perception more than of any non-perception, if all things partake of every kind of motion?

Theod. Certainly not.

Soc. Yet perception is knowledge: so at least Theaetetus and I were saying.

Theod. Very true.

Soc. Then when we were asked what is knowledge, we no more answered what is knowledge than what is not knowledge?

Theod. I suppose not.

Soc. Here, then, is a fine result: we corrected our first answer in our eagerness to prove that nothing is at rest. But if nothing is at rest, every answer upon whatever subject is equally right: you may say that a thing is or is not thus; or, if you prefer, "becomes" thus; and if we say "becomes," we shall not then hamper them with words expressive of rest.

Theod. Quite true.

Soc. Yes, Theodorus, except in saying "thus" and "not thus." But you ought not to use the word "thus," for there is no motion in "thus" or in "not thus." The maintainers of the doctrine have as yet no words in which to express themselves, and must get a new language. I know of no word that will suit them, except perhaps "no how," which is perfectly indefinite.

Theod. Yes, that is a manner of speaking in which they will be quite at home.

Soc. And so, Theodorus, we have got rid of your friend without assenting to his doctrine, that every man is the measure of all things—a wise man only is a measure; neither can we allow that knowledge is perception, certainly not on the hypothesis of a perpetual flux, unless perchance our friend Theaetetus is able to convince us that it is.

Theod. Very good, Socrates; and now that the argument about the doctrine of Protagoras has been completed, I am absolved from answering; for this was the agreement.

Theaet. Not, Theodorus, until you and Socrates have discussed the doctrine of those who say that all things are at rest, as you were proposing.

Theod. You, Theaetetus, who are a young rogue, must not instigate your elders to a breach of faith, but should prepare to answer Socrates in the remainder of the argument.

Theaet. Yes, if he wishes; but I would rather have heard about the doctrine of rest.

Theod. Invite Socrates to an argument—invite horsemen to the open plain; do but ask him, and he will answer.

Soc. Nevertheless, Theodorus, I am afraid that I shall not be able to comply with the request of Theaetetus.

Theod. Not comply! for what reason?

Soc. My reason is that I have a kind of reverence; not so much for Melissus and the others, who say that "All is one and at rest," as for the great leader himself, Parmenides, venerable and awful, as in Homeric language he may be called; —him I should be ashamed to approach in a spirit unworthy of him. I met him when he was an old man, and I was a mere youth, and he appeared to me to have a glorious depth of mind. And I am afraid that we may not understand his words, and may be still further from understanding his meaning; above all I fear that the nature of knowledge, which is the main subject of our discussion, may be thrust out of sight by the unbidden guests who will come pouring in upon our feast of discourse, if we let them in—besides, the question which is now stirring is of immense extent, and will be treated unfairly if only considered by the way; or if treated adequately and at length, will put into the shade the other question of knowledge. Neither the one nor the other can be allowed; but I must try by my art of midwifery to deliver Theaetetus of his conceptions about knowledge.

Theaet. Very well; do so if you will.

Soc. Then now, Theaetetus, take another view of the subject: you answered that knowledge is perception?

Theaet. I did.

Soc. And if any one were to ask you: With what does a man see black and white colours? and with what does he hear high and low sounds?—you would say, if I am not mistaken, "With the eyes and with the ears."

Theaet. I should.

Soc. The free use of words and phrases, rather than minute precision, is generally characteristic of a liberal education, and the opposite is pedantic; but sometimes precision is necessary, and I believe that the answer which you have just given is open to the charge of incorrectness; for which is more correct, to say that we see or hear with the eyes and with the ears, or through the eyes and through the ears?

Theaet. I should say "through," Socrates, rather than "with."

Soc. Yes, my boy, for no one can suppose that in each of us, as in a sort of Trojan horse, there are perched a number of unconnected senses, which do not at all meet in some one nature, the mind, or whatever we please to call it, of which they are the instruments, and with which through them we perceive objects of sense.

Theaet. I agree with you in that opinion.

Soc. The reason why I am thus precise is, because I want to know whether, when we perceive black and white through the eyes, and again, other qualities through other organs, we do not perceive them with one and the same part of ourselves, and, if you were asked, you might refer all such perceptions to the body. Perhaps, however, I had better allow you to answer for yourself and not interfere. Tell me, then, are not the organs through which you perceive warm and hard and light and sweet, organs of the body?

Theaet. Of the body, certainly.

Soc. And you would admit that what you perceive through one faculty you cannot perceive through another; the objects of hearing, for example, cannot be perceived through sight, or the objects of sight through hearing?

Theaet. Of course not.

Soc. If you have any thought about both of them, this common perception cannot come to you, either through the one or the other organ?

Theaet. It cannot.

Soc. How about sounds and colours: in the first place you would admit that they both exist?

Theaet. Yes.

Soc. And that either of them is different from the other, and the same with itself?

Theaet. Certainly.

Soc. And that both are two and each of them one?

Theaet. Yes.

Soc. You can further observe whether they are like or unlike one another?

Theaet. I dare say.

Soc. But through what do you perceive all this about them? for neither through hearing nor yet through seeing can you apprehend that which they have in common. Let me give you an illustration of the point at issue:—If there were any meaning in asking whether sounds and colours are saline or not, you would be able to tell me what faculty would consider the question. It would not be sight or hearing, but some other.

Theaet. Certainly; the faculty of taste.

Soc. Very good; and now tell me what is the power which discerns, not only in sensible objects, but in all things, universal notions, such as those which are called being and not-being, and those others about which we were just asking —what organs will you assign for the perception of these notions?

Theaet. You are thinking of being and not-being, likeness and unlikeness, sameness and difference, and also of unity and other numbers which are applied to objects of sense; and you mean to ask, through what bodily organ the soul perceives odd and even numbers and other arithmetical conceptions.

Soc. You follow me excellently, Theaetetus; that is precisely what I am asking.

Theaet. Indeed, Socrates, I cannot answer; my only notion is, that these, unlike objects of sense, have no separate organ, but that the mind, by a power of her own, contemplates the universals in all things.

Soc. You are a beauty, Theaetetus, and not ugly, as Theodorus was saying; for he who utters the beautiful is himself beautiful and good. And besides being beautiful, you have done me a kindness in releasing me from a very long discussion, if you are clear that the soul views some things by herself and others through the bodily organs. For that was my own opinion, and I wanted you to agree with me.

Theaet. I am quite clear.

Soc. And to which class would you refer being or essence; for this, of all our notions, is the most universal?

Theaet. I should say, to that class which the soul aspires to know of herself.

Soc. And would you say this also of like and unlike, same and other?

Theaet. Yes.

Soc. And would you say the same of the noble and base, and of good and evil?

Theaet. These I conceive to be notions which are essentially relative, and which the soul also perceives by comparing in herself things past and present with the future.

Soc. And does she not perceive the hardness of that which is hard by the touch, and the softness of that which is soft equally by the touch?

Theaet. Yes.

Soc. But their essence and what they are, and their opposition to one another, and the essential nature of this opposition, the soul herself endeavours to decide for us by the review and comparison of them?

Theaet. Certainly.

Soc. The simple sensations which reach the soul through the body are given at birth to men and animals by nature, but their reflections on the being and use of them are slowly and hardly gained, if they are ever gained, by education and long experience.

Theaet. Assuredly.

Soc. And can a man attain truth who fails of attaining being?

Theaet. Impossible.

Soc. And can he who misses the truth of anything, have a knowledge of that thing?

Theaet. He cannot.

Soc. Then knowledge does not consist in impressions of sense, but in reasoning about them; in that only, and not in the mere impression, truth and being can be attained?

Theaet. Clearly.

Soc. And would you call the two processes by the same name, when there is so great a difference between them?

Theaet. That would certainly not be right.

Soc. And what name would you give to seeing, hearing, smelling, being cold and being hot?

Theaet. I should call all of them perceiving—what other name could be given to them?

Soc. Perception would be the collective name of them?

Theaet. Certainly.

Soc. Which, as we say, has no part in the attainment of truth any more than of being?

Theaet. Certainly not.

Soc. And therefore not in science or knowledge?

Theaet. No.

Soc. Then perception, Theaetetus, can never be the same as knowledge or science?

Theaet. Clearly not, Socrates; and knowledge has now been most distinctly proved to be different from perception.

Soc. But the original aim of our discussion was to find out rather what knowledge is than what it is not; at the same time we have made some progress, for we no longer seek for knowledge in perception at all, but in that other process, however called, in which the mind is alone and engaged with being.

Theaet. You mean, Socrates, if I am not mistaken, what is called thinking or opining.

Soc. You conceive truly. And now, my friend, please to begin again at this point; and having wiped out of your memory all that has preceded, see if you have arrived at any clearer view, and once more say what is knowledge.

Theaet. I cannot say, Socrates, that all opinion is knowledge, because there may be a false opinion; but I will venture to assert, that knowledge is true opinion: let this then be my reply; and if this is hereafter disproved, I must try to find another.

Soc. That is the way in which you ought to answer, Theaetetus, and not in your former hesitating strain, for if we are bold we shall gain one of two advantages; either we shall find what we seek, or we shall be less likely to think that we know what we do not know—in either case we shall be richly rewarded. And now, what are you saying?—Are there two sorts of opinion, one true and the other false; and do you define knowledge to be the true?

Theaet. Yes, according to my present view.

Soc. Is it still worth our while to resume the discussion touching opinion?

Theaet. To what are you alluding?

Soc. There is a point which often troubles me, and is a great perplexity to me, both in regard to myself and others, I cannot make out the nature or origin of the mental experience to which I refer.

Theaet. Pray what is it?

Soc. How there can be false opinion—that difficulty still troubles the eye of my mind; and I am uncertain whether I shall leave the question, or begin over again in a new way.

Theaet. Begin again, Socrates,—at least if you think that there is the slightest necessity for doing so. Were not you and Theodorus just now remarking very truly, that in discussions of this kind we may take our own time?

Soc. You are quite right, and perhaps there will be no harm in retracing our steps and beginning again. Better a little which is well done, than a great deal imperfectly.

Theaet. Certainly.

Soc. Well, and what is the difficulty? Do we not speak of false opinion, and say that one man holds a false and another a true opinion, as though there were some natural distinction between them?

Theaet. We certainly say so.

Soc. All things and everything are either known or not known. I leave out of view the intermediate conceptions of learning and forgetting, because they have nothing to do with our present question.

Theaet. There can be no doubt, Socrates, if you exclude these, that there is no other alternative but knowing or not knowing a thing.

Soc. That point being now determined, must we not say

that he who has an opinion, must have an opinion about something which he knows or does not know?

Theaet. He must.

Soc. He who knows, cannot but know; and he who does not know, cannot know?

Theaet. Of course.

Soc. What shall we say then? When a man has a false opinion does he think that which he knows to be some other thing which he knows, and knowing both, is he at the same time ignorant of both?

Theaet. That, Socrates, is impossible.

Soc. But perhaps he thinks of something which he does not know as some other thing which he does not know; for example, he knows neither Theaetetus nor Socrates, and yet he fancies that Theaetetus is Socrates or Socrates Theaetetus?

Theaet. How can he?

Soc. But surely he cannot suppose what he knows to be what he does not know, or what he does not know to be what he knows?

Theaet. That would be monstrous.

Soc. Where, then, is false opinion? For if all things are either known or unknown, there can be no opinion which is not comprehended under this alternative, and so false opinion is excluded.

Theaet. Most true.

Soc. Suppose that we remove the question out of the sphere of knowing or not-knowing, into that of being and not-being.

Theaet. What do you mean?

Soc. May we not suspect the simple truth to be that he who thinks about anything, that which is not, will necessarily think what is false, whatever in other respects may be the state of his mind?

Theaet. That, again, is not unlikely, Socrates.

Soc. Then suppose some one to say to us, Theaetetus:— "Is it possible for any man to think that which is not, either as a self-existent substance or as a predicate of something else?" And suppose that we answer, "Yes, he can, when he thinks what is not true."—That will be our answer?

Theaet. Yes.

Soc. But is there any parallel to this?

Theaet. What do you mean?

Soc. Can a man see something and yet see nothing?

Theaet. Impossible.

Soc. But if he sees any one thing, he sees something that exists. Do you suppose that what is one is never to be found among non-existent things?

Theaet. I do not.

Soc. He then sees some one thing, sees something which is?

Theaet. Clearly.

Soc. And he who hears anything, hears some one thing, and hears that which is?

Theaet. Yes.

Soc. And he who touches anything, touches something which is one and therefore is?

Theaet. That again is true.

Soc. And does not he who thinks, think some one thing?

Theaet. Certainly.

Soc. And does not he who thinks some one thing, think something which is?

Theaet. I agree.

Soc. Then he who thinks of that which is not, thinks of nothing?

Theaet. Clearly.

Soc. And he who thinks of nothing, does not think at all?

Theaet. Obviously.

Soc. Then no one can think that which is not, either as a self-existent substance or as a predicate of something else?

Theaet. Clearly not.

Soc. Then to think falsely is different from thinking that which is not?

Theaet. It would seem so.

Soc. Then false opinion has no existence in us, either in the sphere of being or of knowledge?

Theaet. Certainly not.

Soc. But may not the following be the description of what we express by this name?

Theaet. What?

Soc. May we not suppose that false opinion or thought is a sort of heterodoxy; a person may make an exchange in his mind, and say that one real object is another real object. For thus he always thinks that which is, but he puts one thing in place of another, and missing the aim of his thoughts, he may be truly said to have false opinion.

Theaet. Now you appear to me to have spoken the exact truth: when a man puts the base in the place of the noble, or the noble in the place of the base, then he has truly false opinion.

Soc. I see, Theaetetus, that your fear has disappeared, and that you are beginning to despise me.

Theaet. What makes you say so?

Soc. You think, if I am not mistaken, that your "truly false" is safe from censure, and that I shall never ask whether there can be a swift which is slow, or a heavy which is light, or any other self-contradictory thing, which works, not according to its own nature, but according to that of its opposite. But I will not insist upon this, for I do not wish needlessly to discourage you. And so you are satisfied that false opinion is heterodoxy, or the thought of something else?

Theaet. I am.

Soc. It is possible then upon your view for the mind to conceive of one thing as another?

Theaet. True.

Soc. But must not the mind, or thinking power, which misplaces them, have a conception either of both objects or of one of them?

Theaet. Certainly.

Soc. Either together or in succession?

Theaet. Very good.

Soc. And do you mean by conceiving, the same which I mean?

Theaet. What is that?

Soc. I mean the conversation which the soul holds with herself in considering of anything. I speak of what I scarcely understand; but the soul when thinking appears to me to be just talking—asking questions of herself and answering them, affirming and denying. And when she has arrived at a decision, either gradually or by a sudden impulse, and has at last agreed, and does not doubt, this is called her opinion. I say, then, that to form an opinion is to speak, and opinion is a word spoken,—I mean, to oneself and in silence, not aloud or to another: What think you?

Theaet. I agree.

Soc. Then when any one thinks of one thing as another, he is saying to himself that one thing is another?

Theaet. Yes.

Soc. But do you ever remember saying to yourself that the noble is certainly base, or the unjust just; or, best of all—have you ever attempted to convince yourself that one thing is another? Nay, not even in sleep, did you ever venture to say to yourself that odd is even, or anything of the kind?

Theaet. Never.

Soc. And do you suppose that any other man, either in his senses or out of them, ever seriously tried to persuade himself that an ox is a horse, or that two are one?

Theaet. Certainly not.

Soc. But if thinking is talking to oneself, no one speaking and thinking of two objects, and apprehending them both in his soul, will say and think that the one is the other of them, and I must add, that even you, lover of dispute as you are, had better let the word "other" alone [i. e. not insist that "one" and "other" are the same[1]]. I mean to say, that no one thinks the noble to be base, or anything of the kind.

Theaet. I will give up the word "other," Socrates; and I agree to what you say.

Soc. If a man has both of them in his thoughts, he cannot think that the one of them is the other?

Theaet. True.

Soc. Neither, if he has one of them only in his mind and not the other, can he think that one is the other?

Theaet. True; for we should have to suppose that he apprehends that which is not in his thoughts at all.

Soc. Then no one who has either both or only one of the two objects in his mind can think that the one is the other. And therefore, he who maintains that false opinion is heterodoxy is talking nonsense; for neither in this, any more than in the previous way, can false opinion exist in us.

Theaet. No.

Soc. But if, Theaetetus, this is not admitted, we shall be driven into many absurdities?

Theaet. What are they?

Soc. I will not tell you until I have endeavoured to consider the matter from every point of view. For I should be ashamed of us if we were driven in our perplexity to admit the absurd consequences of which I speak. But if we find the solution, and get away from them, we may regard them only as the difficulties of others, and the ridicule will not attach to us. On the other hand, if we utterly fail, I suppose that we must be humble, and allow the argument to trample us under foot, as the sea-sick passenger is trampled upon by the sailor, and to do anything to us. Listen, then, while I tell you how I hope to find a way out of our difficulty.

Theaet. Let me hear.

Soc. I think that we were wrong in denying that a man

[1] Both words in Greek are called ἕτερον: cp. Parmen. 147 C; Euthyd. 301A.

could think what he knew to be what he did not know;
and that there is a way in which such a deception is possible.

Theaet. You mean to say, as I suspected at the time, that
I may know Socrates, and at a distance see some one who
is unknown to me, and whom I mistake for him—then the
deception will occur?

Soc. But has not that position been relinquished by us,
because involving the absurdity that we should know and
not know the things which we know?

Theaet. True.

Soc. Let us make the assertion in another form, which
may or may not have a favourable issue; but as we are
in a great strait, every argument should be turned over
and tested. Tell me, then, whether I am right in saying
that you may learn a thing which at one time you did not
know?

Theaet. Certainly you may.

Soc. And another and another?

Theaet. Yes.

Soc. I would have you imagine, then, that there exists in
the mind of man a block of wax, which is of different sizes
in different men; harder, moister, and having more or less
of purity in one than another, and in some of an intermediate quality.

Theaet. I see.

Soc. Let us say that this is a gift of Memory, the mother
of the Muses; and that when we wish to remember anything
which we have seen, or heard, or thought in our own minds,
we hold the wax to the perceptions and thoughts, and in
that material receive the impression of them as from the
seal of a ring; and that we remember and know what is
imprinted as long as the image lasts; but when the image
is effaced, or cannot be taken, then we forget and do not
know.

Theaet. Very good.

Soc. Now, when a person has this knowledge, and is considering something which he sees or hears, may not false opinion arise in the following manner?

Theaet. In what manner?

Soc. When he thinks what he knows, sometimes to be what he knows, and sometimes to be what he does not know. We were wrong before in denying the possibility of this.

Theaet. And how would you amend the former statement?

Soc. I should begin by making a list of the impossible cases which must be excluded. (1) No one can think one thing to be another when he does not perceive either of them, but has the memorial or seal of both of them in his mind; nor can any mistaking of one thing for another occur, when he only knows one, and does not know, and has no impression of the other; nor can he think that one thing which he does not know is another thing which he does not know, or that what he does not know is what he knows; nor (2) that one thing which he perceives is another thing which he perceives, or that something which he perceives is something which he does not perceive; or that something which he does not perceive is something else which he does not perceive; or that something which he does not perceive is something which he perceives; nor again (3) can he think that something which he knows and perceives, and of which he has the impression coinciding with sense, is something else which he knows and perceives, and of which he has the impression coinciding with sense; —this last case, if possible, is still more inconceivable than the others; nor (4) can he think that something which he knows and perceives, and of which he has the memorial coinciding with sense, is something else which he knows; nor so long as these agree, can he think that a thing which he knows and perceives is another thing which he perceives; or that a thing which he does not know and does not perceive, is the same as another thing which he does not know and does not perceive;—nor again, can he suppose that a thing which he does not know and does not perceive is the same as another thing which he does not know; or that a thing which he does not know and does not perceive is another thing which he does not perceive:—All these utterly and absolutely exclude the possibility of false opinion. The only cases, if any, which remain, are the following.

Theaet. What are they? If you tell me, I may perhaps understand you better; but at present I am unable to follow you.

Soc. A person may think that some things which he knows, or which he perceives and does not know, are some other things which he knows and perceives; or that some things which he knows and perceives, are other things which he knows and perceives.

Theaet. I understand you less than ever now.

Soc. Hear me once more, then:—I, knowing Theodorus, and remembering in my own mind what sort of person he is, and also what sort of person Theaetetus is, at one time see them, and at another time do not see them, and sometimes I touch them, and at another time not, or at one time I may hear them or perceive them in some other way, and at another time not perceive them, but still I remember them, and know them in my own mind.

Theaet. Very true.

Soc. Then, first of all, I want you to understand that a man may or may not perceive sensibly that which he knows.

Theaet. True.

Soc. And that which he does not know will sometimes not be perceived by him and sometimes will be perceived and only perceived?

Theaet. That is also true.

Soc. See whether you can follow me better now: Socrates can recognize Theodorus and Theaetetus, but he sees neither of them, nor does he perceive them in any other way; he cannot then by any possibility imagine in his own mind that Theaetetus is Theodorus. Am I not right?

Theaet. You are quite right.

Soc. Then that was the first case of which I spoke.

Theaet. Yes.

Soc. The second case was, that I, knowing one of you and not knowing the other, and perceiving neither, can never think him whom I know to be him whom I do not know.

Theaet. True.

Soc. In the third case, not knowing and not perceiving either of you, I cannot think that one of you whom I do not know is the other whom I do not know. I need not again go over the catalogue of excluded cases, in which I cannot form a false opinion about you and Theodorus, either when I know both or when I am in ignorance of both, or when I know one and not the other. And the same of perceiving: do you understand me?

Theaet. I do.

Soc. The only possibility of erroneous opinion is, when knowing you and Theodorus, and having on the waxen block the impression of both of you given as by a seal, but seeing you imperfectly and at a distance, I try to assign the right impression of memory to the right visual impression, and to fit this into its own print: if I succeed, recognition will take place; but if I fail and transpose them, putting the foot into the wrong shoe—that is to say, putting the vision of either of you on to the wrong impression, or if my mind, like the sight in a mirror, which is transferred from right to left, err by reason of some similar affection, then "heterodoxy" and false opinion ensues.

Theaet. Yes, Socrates, you have described the nature of opinion with wonderful exactness.

Soc. Or again, when I know both of you, and perceive as well as know one of you, but not the other, and my knowledge of him does not accord with perception—that was the case put by me just now which you did not understand.

Theaet. No, I did not.

Soc. I mean to say, that when a person knows and perceives one of you, and his knowledge coincides with his perception, he will never think him to be some other person, whom he knows and perceives, and the knowledge of whom coincides with his perception—for that also was a case supposed.

Theaet. True.

Soc. But there was an omission of the further case, in which, as we now say, false opinion may arise, when knowing both, and seeing, or having some other sensible perception of both, I fail in holding the seal over against the corresponding sensation; like a bad archer, I miss and fall wide of the mark—and this is called falsehood.

Theaet. Yes; it is rightly so called.

Soc. When, therefore, perception is present to one of the seals or impressions but not to the other, and the mind fits the seal of the absent perception on the one which is present, in any case of this sort the mind is deceived; in a word, if our view is sound, there can be no error or deception about things which a man does not know and has never perceived, but only in things which are known and perceived; in these alone opinion turns and twists about, and becomes alternately true and false;—true when the seals and impressions of sense meet straight and opposite—false when they go awry and are crooked.

Theaet. And is not that, Socrates, nobly said?

Soc. Nobly! yes; but wait a little and hear the explanation, and then you will say so with more reason; for to think truly is noble and to be deceived is base.

Theaet. Undoubtedly.

Soc. And the origin of truth and error is as follows:— When the wax in the soul of any one is deep and abundant, and smooth and perfectly tempered, then the impressions which pass through the senses and sink into the heart of the soul, as Homer says in a parable, meaning to indicate the likeness of the soul to wax (κῆρ κηρὸς); these, I say, being pure and clear, and having a sufficient depth of wax, are also lasting, and minds, such as these, easily learn and easily retain, and are not liable to confusion, but have true thoughts, for they have plenty of room, and having clear impressions of things, as we term them, quickly distribute them into their proper places on the block. And such men are called wise. Do you agree?

Theaet. Entirely.

Soc. But when the heart of any one is shaggy—a quality which the all-wise poet commends, or muddy and of impure wax, or very soft, or very hard, then there is a corresponding defect in the mind—the soft are good at learning, but apt to forget; and the hard are the reverse; the shaggy and rugged and gritty, or those who have an admixture of earth or dung in their composition, have the impressions indistinct, as also the hard, for there is no depth in them; and the soft too are indistinct, for their impressions are easily confused and effaced. Yet greater is the indistinctness when they are all jostled together in a little soul, which has no room. These are the natures which have false opinion; for when they see or hear or think of anything, they are slow in assigning the right objects to the right impressions—in their stupidity they confuse them, and are apt to see and hear and think amiss—and such men are said to be deceived in their knowledge of objects, and ignorant.

Theaet. No man, Socrates, can say anything truer than that.

Soc. Then now we may admit the existence of false opinion in us?

Theaet. Certainly.

Soc. And of true opinion also?

Theaet. Yes.

Soc. We have at length satisfactorily proven that beyond doubt there are these two sorts of opinion?

Theaet. Undoubtedly.

Soc. Alas, Theaetetus, what a tiresome creature is a man who is fond of talking!

Theaet. What makes you say so?

Soc. Because I am disheartened at my own stupidity and tiresome garrulity; for what other term will describe the habit of a man who is always arguing on all sides of a question; whose dullness cannot be convinced, and who will never leave off?

Theaet. But what puts you out of heart?

Soc. I am not only out of heart, but in positive despair; for I do not know what to answer if any one were to ask me:—O Socrates, have you indeed discovered that false opinion arises neither in the comparison of perceptions with one another nor yet in thought, but in the union of thought and perception? Yes, I shall say, with the complacence of one who thinks that he has made a noble discovery.

Theaet. I see no reason why we should be ashamed of our demonstration, Socrates.

Soc. He will say: You mean to argue that the man whom we only think of and do not see, cannot be confused with the horse which we do not see or touch, but only think of and do not perceive? That I believe to be my meaning, I shall reply.

Theaet. Quite right.

Soc. Well, then, he will say, according to that argument, the number eleven, which is only thought, can never be mistaken for twelve, which is only thought: How would you answer him?

Theaet. I should say that a mistake may very likely arise between the eleven or twelve which are seen or handled, but that no similar mistake can arise between the eleven and twelve which are in the mind.

Soc. Well, but do you think that no one ever put before his own mind five and seven,—I do not mean five or seven men or horses, but five or seven in the abstract, which, as we say, are recorded on the waxen block, and in which false opinion is held to be impossible;—did no man ever ask himself how many these numbers make when added together, and answer that they are eleven, while another thinks that they are twelve, or would all agree in thinking and saying that they are twelve?

Theaet. Certainly not; many would think that they are eleven, and in the higher numbers the chance of error is greater still; for I assume you to be speaking of numbers in general.

Soc. Exactly; and I want you to consider whether this does not imply that the twelve in the waxen block are supposed to be eleven?

Theaet. Yes, that seems to be the case.

Soc. Then do we not come back to the old difficulty? For he who makes such a mistake does think one thing which he knows to be another thing which he knows; but this, as we said, was impossible, and afforded an irresistible proof of the non-existence of false opinion, because otherwise the same person would inevitably know and not know the same thing at the same time.

Theaet. Most true.

Soc. Then false opinion cannot be explained as a confusion of thought and sense, for in that case we could not have been mistaken about pure conceptions of thought; and thus we are obliged to say, either that false opinion does not exist, or that a man may not know that which he knows;—which alternative do you prefer?

Theaet. It is hard to determine, Socrates.

Soc. And yet the argument will scarcely admit of both. But, as we are at our wits' end, suppose that we do a shameless thing?

Theaet. What is it?

Soc. Let us attempt to explain the verb "to know."

Theaet. And why should that be shameless?

Soc. You seem not to be aware that the whole of our

discussion from the very beginning has been a search after knowledge, of which we are assumed not to know the nature.

Theaet. Nay, but I am well aware.

Soc. And is it not shameless when we do not know what knowledge is, to be explaining the verb "to know"? The truth is, Theaetetus, that we have long been infected with logical impurity. Thousands of times have we repeated the words "we know," and "do not know," and "we have or have not science or knowledge," as if we could understand what we are saying to one another, so long as we remain ignorant about knowledge; and at this moment we are using the words "we understand," "we are ignorant," as though we could still employ them when deprived of knowledge or science.

Theaet. But if you avoid these expressions, Socrates, how will you ever argue at all?

Soc. I could not, being the man I am. The case would be different if I were a true hero of dialectic: and O that such an one were present! for he would have told us to avoid the use of these terms; at the same time he would not have spared in you and me the faults which I have noted. But, seeing that we are no great wits, shall I venture to say what knowing is? for I think that the attempt may be worth making.

Theaet. Then by all means venture, and no one shall find fault with you for using the forbidden terms.

Soc. You have heard the common explanation of the verb "to know"?

Theaet. I think so, but I do not remember it at the moment.

Soc. They explain the word "to know" as meaning "to have knowledge."

Theaet. True.

Soc. I should like to make a slight change, and say "to possess" knowledge.

Theaet. How do the two expressions differ?

Soc. Perhaps there may be no difference; but still I should like you to hear my view, that you may help me to test it.

Theaet. I will, if I can.

Soc. I should distinguish "having" from "possessing": for example, a man may buy and keep under his control a garment which he does not wear; and then we should say, not that he has, but that he possesses the garment.

Theaet. It would be the correct expression.

Soc. Well, may not a man "possess" and yet not "have" knowledge in the sense of which I am speaking? As you may suppose a man to have caught wild birds—doves or any other birds—and to be keeping them in an aviary which he has constructed at home; we might say of him in one sense, that he always has them because he possesses them, might we not?

Theaet. Yes.

Soc. And yet, in another sense, he has none of them; but they are in his power, and he has got them under his hand in an enclosure of his own, and can take and have them whenever he likes;—he can catch any which he likes, and let the bird go again, and he may do so as often as he pleases.

Theaet. True.

Soc. Once more, then, as in what preceded we made a sort of waxen figment in the mind, so let us now suppose that in the mind of each man there is an aviary of all sorts of birds—some flocking together apart from the rest, others in small groups, others solitary, flying anywhere and everywhere.

Theaet. Let us imagine such an aviary—and what is to follow?

Soc. We may suppose that the birds are kinds of knowledge, and that when we were children, this receptacle was empty; whenever a man has gotten and detained in the enclosure a kind of knowledge, he may be said to have learned or discovered the thing which is the subject of the knowledge: and this is to know.

Theaet. Granted.

Soc. And further, when any one wishes to catch any of these knowledges or sciences, and having taken, to hold it, and again to let them go, how will he express himself?—will he describe the "catching" of them and the original "possession" in the same words? I will make my meaning clearer by an example:—You admit that there is an art of arithmetic?

Theaet. To be sure.

Soc. Conceive this under the form of a hunt after the science of odd and even in general.

Theaet. I follow.

Soc. Having the use of the art, the arithmetician, if I am not mistaken, has the conceptions of number under his hand, and can transmit them to another.

Theaet. Yes.

Soc. And when transmitting them he may be said to teach them, and when receiving to learn them, and when having them in possession in the aforesaid aviary he may be said to know them.

Theaet. Exactly.

Soc. Attend to what follows: must not the perfect arithmetician know all numbers, for he has the science of all numbers in his mind?

Theaet. True.

Soc. And he can reckon abstract numbers in his head, or things about him which are numerable?

Theaet. Of course he can.

Soc. And to reckon is simply to consider how much such and such a number amounts to?

Theaet. Very true.

Soc. And so he appears to be searching into something which he knows, as if he did not know it, for we have already admitted that he knows all numbers;—you have heard these perplexing questions raised?

Theaet. I have.

Soc. May we not pursue the image of the doves, and say that the chase after knowledge is of two kinds? One kind is prior to possession and for the sake of possession, and the other for the sake of taking and holding in the hands that which is possessed already. And thus, when a man has learned and known something long ago, he may resume and get hold of the knowledge which he has long possessed, but has not at hand in his mind.

Theaet. True.

Soc. That was my reason for asking how we ought to speak when an arithmetician sets about numbering, or a grammarian about reading? Shall we say, that although he knows, he comes back to himself to learn what he already knows?

Theaet. It would be too absurd, Socrates.

Soc. Shall we say then that he is going to read or number what he does not know, although we have admitted that he knows all letters and all numbers?

Theaet. That, again, would be an absurdity.

Soc. Then shall we say that about names we care nothing?—any one may twist and turn the words "knowing" and "learning" in any way which he likes, but since we have determined that the possession of knowledge is not the having or using it, we do assert that a man cannot not possess that which he possesses; and, therefore, in no case can a man not know that which he knows, but he may get a false opinion about it; for he may have the knowledge, not of this particular thing, but of some other;—when the various numbers and forms of knowledge are flying about in the aviary, and wishing to capture a certain sort of knowledge out of the general store, he takes the wrong one by mistake, that is to say, when he thought eleven to be twelve, he got hold of the ring-dove which he had in his mind, when he wanted the pigeon.

Theaet. A very rational explanation.

Soc. But when he catches the one which he wants, then he is not deceived, and has an opinion of what is, and thus false and true opinion may exist, and the difficulties which were previously raised disappear. I dare say that you agree with me, do you not?

Theaet. Yes.

Soc. And so we are rid of the difficulty of a man's not knowing what he knows, for we are not driven to the inference that he does not possess what he possesses, whether he be or be not deceived. And yet I fear that a greater difficulty is looking in at the window.

Theaet. What is it?

Soc. How can the exchange of one knowledge for another ever become false opinion?

Theaet. What do you mean?

Soc. In the first place, how can a man who has the knowledge of anything be ignorant of that which he knows, not by reason of ignorance, but by reason of his own knowledge? And, again, is it not an extreme absurdity that he should suppose another thing to be this, and this to be another thing;—that, having knowledge present with him in his mind, he should still know nothing and be ignorant of all things? You might as well argue that ignorance may make a man know, and blindness make him see, as that knowledge can make him ignorant.

Theaet. Perhaps, Socrates, we may have been wrong in making only forms of knowledge our birds: whereas there ought to have been forms of ignorance as well, flying about together in the mind, and then he who sought to take one of them might sometimes catch a form of knowledge, and sometimes a form of ignorance; and thus he would have a false opinion from ignorance, but a true one from knowledge, about the same thing.

Soc. I cannot help praising you, Theaetetus, and yet I must beg you to reconsider your words. Let us grant what you say—then, according to you, he who takes ignorance will have a false opinion—am I right?

Theaet. Yes.

Soc. He will certainly not think he has a false opinion?

Theaet. Of course not.

Soc. He will think that his opinion is true, and he will fancy that he knows the things about which he has been deceived?

Theaet. Certainly.

Soc. Then he will think that he has captured knowledge and not ignorance?

Theaet. Clearly.

Soc. And thus, after going a long way round, we are once more face to face with our original difficulty. The hero of dialectic will retort upon us:—"O my excellent friends," he will say, laughing, "if a man knows the form of ignorance and the form of knowledge, can he think that one of them which he knows is the other which he knows? or, if he knows neither of them, can he think that the one which he knows not is another which he knows not? or, if he knows one and not the other, can he think the one which he knows to be the one which he does not know? or the one which he does not know to be the one which he knows? or will you tell me that there are other forms of knowledge which distinguish the right and wrong birds, and which the owner keeps in some other aviaries or graven on waxen blocks according to your foolish images, and which he may be said to know while he possesses them, even though he have them not at hand in his mind? And thus, in a perpetual circle, you will be compelled to go round and round, and you will make no progress." What are we to say in reply, Theaetetus?

Theaet. Indeed, Socrates, I do not know what we are to say.

Soc. Are not his reproaches just, and does not the argument truly show that we are wrong in seeking for false opinion until we know what knowledge is? That must be first ascertained; then, the nature of false opinion?

Theaet. I cannot but agree with you, Socrates, so far as we have yet gone.

Soc. Then, once more, what shall we say that knowledge is?—for we are not going to lose heart as yet.

Theaet. Certainly, I shall not lose heart, if you do not.

Soc. What definition will be most consistent with our former views?

Theaet. I cannot think of any but our old one, Socrates.

Soc. What is it?

Theaet. Knowledge was said by us to be true opinion; and true opinion is surely unerring, and the results which follow from it are all noble and good.

Soc. He who led the way into the river, Theaetetus, said "The experiment will show"; and perhaps if we go forward in the search, we may stumble upon the thing which we are looking for; but if we stay where we are, nothing will come to light.

Theaet. Very true; let us go forward and try.

Soc. The trail soon comes to an end, for a whole profession is against us.

Theaet. How is that, and what profession do you mean?

Soc. The profession of the great wise ones who are called orators and lawyers; for these persuade men by their art and make them think whatever they like, but they do not teach them. Do you imagine that there are any teachers in the world so clever as to be able to convince others of the truth about acts of robbery or violence, of which they were not eye-witnesses, while a little water is flowing in the clepsydra?

Theaet. Certainly not, they can only persuade them.

Soc. And would you not say that persuading them is making them have an opinion?

Theaet. To be sure.

Soc. When, therefore, judges are justly persuaded about matters which you can know only by seeing them, and not in any other way, and when thus judging of them from report they attain a true opinion about them, they judge without knowledge, and yet are rightly persuaded, if they have judged well.

Theaet. Certainly.

Soc. And yet, O my friend, if true opinion in law courts [1] and knowledge are the same, the perfect judge could not have judged rightly without knowledge; and therefore I must infer that they are not the same.

Theaet. That is a distinction, Socrates, which I have heard made by some one else, but I had forgotten it. He said that true opinion, combined with reason, was knowledge, but that the opinion which had no reason was out of the sphere of knowledge; and that things of which there is no rational account are not knowable—such was the singular expression which he used—and that things which have a reason or explanation are knowable.

Soc. Excellent; but then, how did he distinguish between things which are and are not "knowable"? I wish that you would repeat to me what he said, and then I shall know whether you and I have heard the same tale.

Theaet. I do not know whether I can recall it; but if another person would tell me, I think that I could follow him.

Soc. Let me give you, then, a dream in return for a dream:
—Methought that I too had a dream, and I heard in my dream that the primeval letters or elements out of which you and I and all other things are compounded, have no reason or explanation; you can only name them, but no predicate can be either affirmed or denied of them, for in the one case existence, in the other non-existence is already implied, neither of which must be added, if you mean

[1] Reading κατὰ δικαστήρια: an emendation suggested by Professor Campbell.

to speak of this or that thing by itself alone. It should not be called itself, or that, or each, or alone, or this, or the like; for these go about everywhere and are applied to all things, but are distinct from them; whereas, if the first elements could be described, and had a definition of their own, they would be spoken of apart from all else. But none of these primeval elements can be defined, they can only be named, for they have nothing but a name, and the things which are compounded of them, as they are complex, are expressed by a combination of names, for the combination of names is the essence of a definition. Thus, then, the elements or letters are only objects of perception, and cannot be defined or known; but the syllables or combinations of them are known and expressed, and are apprehended by true opinion. When, therefore, any one forms the true opinion of anything without rational explanation, you may say that his mind is truly exercised, but has no knowledge; for he who cannot give and receive a reason for a thing, has no knowledge of that thing; but when he adds rational explanation, then, he is perfected in knowledge and may be all that I have been denying of him. Was that the form in which the dream appeared to you?

Theaet. Precisely.

Soc. And you allow and maintain that true opinion, combined with definition or rational explanation, is knowledge?

Theaet. Exactly.

Soc. Then may we assume, Theaetetus, that to-day, and in this casual manner, we have found a truth which in former times many wise men have grown old and have not found?

Theaet. At any rate, Socrates, I am satisfied with the present statement.

Soc. Which is probably correct—for how can there be knowledge apart from definition and true opinion? And yet there is one point in what has been said which does not quite satisfy me.

Theaet. What was it?

Soc. What might seem to be the most ingenious notion of all:—That the elements or letters are unknown, but the combination or syllables known.

Theaet. And was that wrong?

Soc. We shall soon know; for we have as hostages the instances which the author of the argument himself used.

Theaet. What hostages?

Soc. The letters, which are the elements; and the syllables, which are the combinations;—he reasoned, did he not, from the letters of the alphabet?

Theaet. Yes; he did.

Soc. Let us take them and put them to the test, or rather, test ourselves:—What was the way in which we learned letters? and, first of all, are we right in saying that syllables have a definition, but that letters have no definition?

Theaet. I think so.

Soc. I think so too; for, suppose that some one asks you to spell the first syllable of my name:—Theaetetus, he says, what is SO?

Theaet. I should reply S and O.

Soc. That is the definition which you would give of the syllable?

Theaet. I should.

Soc. I wish that you would give me a similar definition of the S.

Theaet. But how can any one, Socrates, tell the elements of an element? I can only reply, that S is a consonant, a mere noise, as of the tongue hissing; B, and most other letters, again, are neither vowel-sounds nor noises. Thus letters may be most truly said to be undefined; for even the most distinct of them, which are the seven vowels, have a sound only, but no definition at all.

Soc. Then, I suppose, my friend, that we have been so far right in our idea about knowledge?

Theaet. Yes; I think that we have.

Soc. Well, but have we been right in maintaining that the syllables can be known, but not the letters?

Theaet. I think so.

Soc. And do we mean by a syllable two letters, or if there are more, all of them, or a single idea which arises out of the combination of them?

Theaet. I should say that we mean all the letters.

Soc. Take the case of the two letters S and O, which form the first syllable of my own name; must not he who knows the syllable, know both of them?

Theaet. Certainly.

Soc. He knows, that is, the S and O?

Theaet. Yes.

Soc. But can he be ignorant of either singly and yet know both together?

Theaet. Such a supposition, Socrates, is monstrous and unmeaning.

Soc. But if he cannot know both without knowing each, then if he is ever to know the syllable, he must know the letters first; and thus the fine theory has again taken wings and departed.

Theaet. Yes, with wonderful celerity.

Soc. Yes, we did not keep watch properly. Perhaps we ought to have maintained that a syllable is not the letters, but rather one single idea framed out of them, having a separate form distinct from them.

Theaet. Very true; and a more likely notion than the other.

Soc. Take care; let us not be cowards and betray a great and imposing theory.

Theaet. No, indeed.

Soc. Let us assume then, as we now say, that the syllable is a simple form arising out of the several combinations of harmonious elements—of letters or of any other elements.

Theaet. Very good.

Soc. And it must have no parts.

Theaet. Why?

Soc. Because that which has parts must be a whole of all the parts. Or would you say that a whole, although formed out of the parts, is a single notion different from all the parts?

Theaet. I should.

Soc. And would you say that all and the whole are the same, or different?

Theaet. I am not certain; but, as you like me to answer at once, I shall hazard the reply, that they are different.

Soc. I approve of your readiness, Theaetetus, but I must take time to think whether I equally approve of your answer.

Theaet. Yes; the answer is the point.

Soc. According to this new view, the whole is supposed to differ from all?

Theaet. Yes.

Soc. Well, but is there any difference between all [in the plural] and all [in the singular]? Take the case of number:—When we say one, two, three, four, five, six; or when we say twice three, or three times two, or four and two, or three and two and one, are we speaking of the same or of different numbers?

Theaet. Of the same.

Soc. That is of six?

Theaet. Yes.

Soc. And in each form of expression we spoke of all the six?

Theaet. True.

Soc. Again, in speaking of all [in the plural], is there not one thing which we express? [1]

Theaet. Of course there is.

Soc. And that is six?

Theaet. Yes.

Soc. Then in predicating the word "all" of things measured by number, we predicate at the same time a singular and a plural?

[1] Reading οὐδ' ἕν.

Theaet. Clearly we do.

Soc. Again, the number of the acre and the acre are the same? are they not?

Theaet. Yes.

Soc. And the number of the stadium in like manner is the stadium?

Theaet. Yes.

Soc. And the army is the number of the army; and in all similar cases, the entire number of anything is the entire thing?

Theaet. True.

Soc. And the number of each is the parts of each?

Theaet. Exactly.

Soc. Then as many things as have parts are made up of parts?

Theaet. Clearly.

Soc. But all the parts are admitted to be the all, if the entire number is the all?

Theat. True.

Soc. Then 'the whole is not made of parts, for it would be the all, if consisting of all the parts?

Theaet. That is the inference.

Soc. But is a part a part of anything but the whole?

Theaet. Yes, of the all.

Soc. You make a valiant defence, Theaetetus. And yet is not the all that of which nothing is wanting?

Theaet. Certainly.

Soc. And is not a whole likewise that from which nothing is absent? But that from which anything is absent is neither a whole nor all;—if wanting in anything, both equally lose their entirety of nature.

Theaet. I now think that there is no difference between a whole and all.

Soc. But were we not saying that when a thing has parts, all the parts will be a whole and all?

Theaet. Certainly.

Soc. Then, as I was saying before, must not the alternative be that either the syllable is not the letters, and then the letters are not parts of the syllable, or that the syllable will be the same with the letters, and will therefore be equally known with them?

Theaet. You are right.

Soc. And, in order to avoid this, we suppose it to be different from them?

Theaet. Yes.

Soc. But if letters are not parts of syllables, can you tell me of any other parts of syllables, which are not letters?

Theaet. No, indeed, Socrates; for if I admit the existence of parts in a syllable, it would be ridiculous in me to give up letters and seek for other parts.

Soc. Quite true, Theaetetus, and therefore, according to our present view, a syllable must surely be some indivisible form?

Theaet. True.

Soc. But do you remember, my friend, that only a little while ago we admitted and approved the statement, that of the first elements out of which all other things are compounded there could be no definition, because each of them when taken by itself is uncompounded; nor can one rightly attribute to them the words "being" or "this," because they are alien and inappropriate words, and for this reason the letters or elements were indefinable and unknown?

Theaet. I remember.

Soc. And is not this also the reason why they are simple and indivisible? I can see no other.

Theaet. No other reason can be given.

Soc. Then is not the syllable in the same case as the elements or letters, if it has no parts and is one form?

Theaet. To be sure.

Soc. If, then, a syllable is a whole, and has many parts or letters, the letters as well as the syllable must be intelligible and expressible, since all the parts are acknowledged to be the same as the whole?

Theaet. True.

Soc. But if it be one and indivisible, then the syllables and the letters are alike and undefined and unknown, and for the same reason?

Theaet. I cannot deny that.

Soc. We cannot, therefore, agree in the opinion of him who says that the syllable can be known and expressed, but not the letters.

Theaet. Certainly not; if we may trust the argument.

Soc. Well, but will you not be equally inclined to disagree with him, when you remember your own experience in learning to read?

Theaet. What experience?

Soc. Why, that in learning you were kept trying to distinguish the separate letters both by the eye and by the ear, in order that, when you heard them spoken or saw them written, you might not be confused by their position.

Theae. Very true.

Soc. And is the education of the harp-player complete unless he can tell what string answers to a particular note; the notes, as every one would allow, are the elements or letters of music?

Theaet. Exactly.

Soc. Then, if we argue from the letters and syllables which we know to other simples and compounds, we shall say that the letters or simple elements as a class are much more certainly known than the syllables, and much more indispensable to a perfect knowledge of any subject; and if some one says that the syllable is known and the letter unknown, we should consider that either intentionally or unintentionally he is talking nonsense?

Theaet. Exactly.

Soc. And there might be given other proofs of this belief, if I am not mistaken. But do not let us in looking for them lose sight of the question before us, which is the meaning of the statement, that right opinion with rational definition or explanation is the most perfect form of knowledge.

Theaet. We must not.

Soc. Well, and what is the meaning of the term "explanation"? I think that we have a choice of three meanings.

Theaet. What are they?

Soc. In the first place, the meaning may be, manifesting one's thought by the voice with verbs and nouns, imaging an opinion in the stream which flows from the lips, as in a mirror or water. Does not explanation appear to be of this nature?

Theaet. Certainly; he who so manifests his thought, is said to explain himself.

Soc. And every one who is not born deaf or dumb is able sooner or later to manifest what he thinks of anything; and if so, all those who have a right opinion about anything will also have right explanation; nor will right opinion be anywhere found to exist apart from knowledge.

Theaet. True.

Soc. Let us not, therefore, hastily charge him who gave this account of knowledge with uttering an unmeaning word; for perhaps he only intended to say, that when a person was asked what was the nature of anything, he should be able to answer his questioner by giving the elements of the thing.

Theaet. As for example, Socrates . . . ?

Soc. As, for example, when Hesiod says that a waggon is made up of a hundred planks. Now, neither you nor I could describe all of them individually; but if any one asked what is a waggon, we should be content to answer, that a waggon consists of wheels, axle, body, rims, yoke.

Theaet. Certainly.

Soc. And our opponent will probably laugh at us, just as he would if we professed to be grammarians and to give a grammatical account of the name of Theaetetus, and yet could only tell the syllables and not the letters of your name—that would be true opinion, and not knowledge; for knowledge, as has been already remarked, is not attained until, combined with true opinion, there is an enumeration of the elements out of which anything is composed.

Theaet. Yes.

Soc. In the same general way, we might also have true opinion about a waggon; but he who can describe its essence by an enumeration of the hundred planks, adds rational explanation to true opinion, and instead of opinion has art and knowledge of the nature of a waggon, in that he attains to the whole through the elements.

Theaet. And do you not agree in that view, Socrates?

Soc. If you do, my friend; but I want to know first, whether you admit the resolution of all things into their elements to be a rational explanation of them, and the consideration of them in syllables or larger combinations of them to be irrational—is that your view?

Theaet. Precisely.

Soc. Well, and do you conceive that a man has knowledge of any element who at one time affirms and at another time denies that element of something, or thinks that the same thing is composed of different elements at different times?

Theaet. Assuredly not.

Soc. And do you not remember that in your case and in that of others this often occurred in the process of learning to read?

Theaet. You mean that I mistook the letters and misspell the syllables?

Soc. Yes.

Theaet. To be sure; I perfectly remember, and I am very far from supposing that they who are in this condition have knowledge.

Soc. When a person at the time of learning writes the name of Theaetetus, and thinks that he ought to write and does write *Th* and *e*; but, again, meaning to write the name of Theodorus, thinks that he ought to write and does write *T* and *e*—can we suppose that he knows the first syllables of your two names?

Theaet. We have already admitted that such an one has not yet attained knowledge.

Soc. And in like manner he may enumerate without knowing them the second and third and fourth syllables of your name?

Theaet. He may.

Soc. And in that case, when he knows the order of the letters and can write them out correctly, he has right opinion?

Theaet. Clearly.

Soc. But although we admit that he has right opinion, he will still be without knowledge?

Theaet. Yes.

Soc. And yet he will have explanation, as well as right opinion, for he knew the order of the letters when he wrote; and this we admit to be explanation.

Theaet. True.

Soc. Then, my friend, there is such a thing as right opinion united with definition or explanation, which does not as yet attain to the exactness of knowledge.

Theaet. It would seem so.

Soc. And what we fancied to be a perfect definition of knowledge is a dream only. But perhaps we had better not say so as yet, for were there not three explanations of knowledge, one of which must, as we said, be adopted by him who maintains knowledge to be true opinion combined with rational explanation? And very likely there may be found some one who will not prefer this but the third.

Theaet. You are quite right; there is still one remaining. The first was the image or expression of the mind in speech; the second, which has just been mentioned, is a way of reaching the whole by an enumeration of the elements. But what is the third definition?

Soc. There is, further, the popular notion of telling the mark or sign of difference which distinguishes the thing in question from all others.

Theaet. Can you give me any example of such a definition?

Soc. As, for example, in the case of the sun, I think that you would be contented with the statement that the sun is the brightest of the heavenly bodies which revolve about the earth.

Theaet. Certainly.

Soc. Understand why:—the reason is, as I was just now saying, that if you get at the difference and distinguishing characteristic of each thing, then, as many persons affirm, you will get at the definition or explanation of it; but while you lay hold only of the common and not of the characteristic notion, you will only have the definition of those things to which this common quality belongs.

Theaet. I understand you, and your account of definition is in my judgment correct.

Soc. But he, who having right opinion about anything, can find out the difference which distinguishes it from other things will know that of which before he had only an opinion.

Theaet. Yes; that is what we are maintaining.

Soc. Nevertheless, Theaetetus, on a nearer view, I find myself quite disappointed; the picture, which at a distance was not so bad, has now become altogether unintelligible.

Theaet. What do you mean?

Soc. I will endeavour to explain: I will suppose myself to have true opinion of you, and if to this I add your definition, then I have knowledge, but if not, opinion only.

Theaet. Yes.

Soc. The definition was assumed to be the interpretation of your difference.

Theaet. True.

Soc. But when I had only opinion, I had no conception of your distinguishing characteristics.

Theaet. I suppose not.

Soc. Then I must have conceived of some general or common nature which no more belonged to you than to another.

Theaet. True.

Soc. Tell me, now—How in that case could I have formed a judgment of you any more than of any one else? Suppose that I imagine Theaetetus to be a man who has nose, eyes, and mouth, and every other member complete; how would that enable me to distinguish Theaetetus from Theodorus, or from some outer barbarian?

Theaet. How could it?

Soc. Or if I had further conceived of you, not only as having nose and eyes, but as having a snub nose and prominent eyes, should I have any more notion of you than of myself and others who resemble me?

Theaet. Certainly not.

Soc. Surely I can have no conception of Theaetetus until your snub-nosedness has left an impression on my mind different from the snub-nosedness of all others whom I have ever seen, and until your other peculiarities have a like distinctness; and so when I meet you to-morrow the right opinion will be re-called?

Theaet. Most true.

Soc. Then right opinion implies the perception of differences?

Theaet. Clearly.

Soc. What, then, shall we say of adding reason or explanation to right opinion? If the meaning is, that we should form an opinion of the way in which something differs from another thing, the proposal is ridiculous.

Theaet. How so?

Soc. We are supposed to acquire a right opinion of the differences which distinguish one thing from another when

we have already a right opinion of them, and so we go
round and round; the revolution of the scytal, or pestle,
or any other rotary machine, in the same circles, is as
nothing compared with such a requirement; and we may be
truly described as the blind directing the blind; for to add
those things which we already have, in order that we may
learn what we already think, is like a soul utterly benighted.

Theaet. Tell me; what were you going to say just now,
when you asked the question?

Soc. If, my boy, the argument, in speaking of adding the
definition, had used the word to "know," and not merely
"have an opinion" of the difference, this which is the most
promising of all the definitions of knowledge would have
come to a pretty end, for to know is surely to acquire
knowledge.

Theaet. True.

Soc. And so, when the question is asked, What is knowledge? this fair argument will answer "Right opinion with
knowledge,"—knowledge, that is, of difference, for this, as
the said argument maintains, is adding the definition.

Theaet. That seems to be true.

Soc. But how utterly foolish, when we are asking what
is knowledge, that the reply should only be, right opinion with
knowledge of difference or of anything! And so, Theaetetus, knowledge is neither sensation nor true opinion, nor
yet definition and explanation accompanying and added to
true opinion?

Theaet. I suppose not.

Soc. And are you still in labour and travail, my dear
friend, or have you brought all that you have to say about
knowledge to the birth?

Theaet. I am sure, Socrates, that you have elicited from
me a good deal more than ever was in me.

Soc. And does not my art show that you have brought
forth wind, and that the offspring of your brain are not
worth bringing up?

Theaet. Very true.

Soc. But if, Theaetetus, you should ever conceive afresh, you will be all the better for the present investigation, and if not, you will be soberer and humbler and gentler to other men, and will be too modest to fancy that you know what you do not know. These are the limits of my art; I can no further go, nor do I know aught of the things which great and famous men know or have known in this or former ages. The office of a midwife I, like my mother, have received from God; she delivered women, and I deliver men; but they must be young and noble and fair.

And now I have to go to the porch of the King Archon, where I am to meet Meletus and his indictment. To-morrow morning, Theodorus, I shall hope to see you again at this place.

BIBLIOGRAPHY

BIBLIOGRAPHY

Plato, The Dialogues, translated by Benjamin Jowett, 3rd Edition, 1892; reprinted, Clarendon Press, Oxford, 1924.

Post, L. A. Thirteen Epistles of Plato, translated, Oxford, 1925.

Taylor, A. E. Plato: The Man and His Work; New York, 1927.

Nettleship, R. L. Lectures on the "Republic" of Plato; London, 1897.

Pater, W. Plato and Platonism; London and New York, 1894.

Barker, E. Greek Political Theory; Plato and His Predecessors; London, 1918.

Stewart, J. A. The Myths of Plato; London and New York, 1905.